ORACLE

OF LOST CAUSES

John Newman Edwards and His Never-Ending Civil War

Matthew Christopher Hulbert

University of Nebraska Press   Lincoln

All maps created by Andrew Fialka using ArcGIS. Geopolitical boundaries and city coordinates come courtesy of the National Historical Geographic Information System (https://www.nhgis.org/). The national 1861 railroad system comes courtesy of the University of Nebraska-Lincoln's "Railroads and the Making of Modern America" project (http://railroads.unl.edu/). Nineteenth-century navigable river systems come courtesy of Vanderbilt University's Jeremy Atack (https://my.vanderbilt.edu/jeremyatack/data-downloads/). Raid routes come courtesy of Mark Swanson and Jacqueline D. Langley, *Atlas of the Civil War, Month by Month: Major Battles and Troop Movements* (Athens: University of Georgia Press, 2004). All site links accessed on November 9, 2020.

The University of Nebraska Press is part of a land-grant institution with campuses and programs on the past, present, and future homelands of the Pawnee, Ponca, Otoe-Missouria, Omaha, Dakota, Lakota, Kaw, Cheyenne, and Arapaho Peoples, as well as those of the relocated Ho-Chunk, Sac and Fox, and Iowa Peoples.

Library of Congress Cataloging-in-Publication Data
Names: Hulbert, Matthew C., author.
Title: Oracle of lost causes: John Newman Edwards and his never-ending Civil War / Matthew Christopher Hulbert.
Other titles: John Newman Edwards and his never-ending Civil War
Description: Lincoln: University of Nebraska Press, [2023]
| Includes bibliographical references and index.
Identifiers: LCCN 2022056858
ISBN 9781496211873 (hardcover)
ISBN 9781496237231 (epub)
ISBN 9781496237248 (pdf)
Subjects: LCSH: Edwards, John N. (John Newman), 1839–1889. | Veterans—Confederate States of America—Biography. | United States—History—Civil War, 1861–1865—Veterans—Biography. | Journalists—Missouri—Biography. Missouri—Biography. | BISAC: HISTORY / United States / Civil War Period (1850–1877) | BIOGRAPHY & AUTOBIOGRAPHY / Editors, Journalists, Publishers
Classification: LCC F466.E26 H85 2023 | DDC
977.8/03092 [B]—dc23/eng/20230329
LC record available at https://lccn.loc.gov/2022056858

Set in New Baskerville ITC Pro by K. Andresen.
Designed by L. Welch.

For my children

Contents

Illustrations

MAPS

Preface

Coming of Age in an Age of Crisis

Kentuckians and Ohioans born in the nineteenth century couldn't remember a harsher winter. Temperatures up and down the Ohio River—the boundary that separated the two states—fell well below zero. By late January 1856, these plunges of the mercury were routine enough that long stretches of the river had frozen over from shore to shore.[1]

Before the golden age of rail in America, rivers constituted the highways and interstates of their day. The Ohio was no exception. Under normal climatological circumstances it teemed with boats of all shapes and sizes—clippers, barges, keelboats, packets, paddle steamers, and sidewheelers. Laden with coal, beef, hemp, cotton, beer, and myriad other cargoes from docks as far north as Pittsburgh, these vessels cruised to where the Ohio joins the Mississippi and then often southward all the way to the bustling markets of New Orleans. Other craft carried people—would-be pioneers, adventure-seekers, homesteaders, casualties of gold fever—from the Ohio to the Mississippi and then onto the eastward-flowing Missouri River. In every port along the way, hucksters specialized in parting these travelers from the contents of their pocketbooks. Thus it was in 1856 for livelihoods that were dependent on the flow of the Ohio River, as such a great many were in places like Louisville, Owensboro, Carrollton, Portsmouth, Ironton, Covington, and Cincinnati, that no current meant no commerce.

For others, the freeze had little to do with hawking goods or taming the frontier; rather, it was something Biblical—a godsend of the Exo-

dus variety. It had transformed the last and most formidable imped-
iment between runaway slaves and deliverance into a new kind of
thoroughfare: a pathway to freedom paved with sheets of glimmering
ice. In spite of the bitter cold—in spite of the potential hazards—this
was an opportunity a young slave woman named Margaret Garner
refused to squander. Margaret and her husband Robert (who was
also enslaved), along with her four young children, together joined
a convoy of Kentucky runaways. They set out in a stolen, horse-drawn
sleigh long before the sun rose on January 28. Hours later, just west
of Covington, they found the river. On the other side was the stuff
slaves dreamed about but dared not put into words. Free soil. Abolitionist operatives. The Underground Railroad. A chance to reclaim
stolen humanity.[2]

Once safely across the Ohio, the group began to dissolve, sepa-
rating into smaller, less-conspicuous units. Being noticed wasn't just
a problem, it was *the* problem. Merely placing one's heels on free
ground wasn't enough to ensure that they would remain there in
perpetuity. That feat required many more miles trekked, many more
borders crossed—it meant not getting pinched in Ohio before the
real expedition to New England or Canada even began.

According to the terms of the Fugitive Slave Law, recently bolstered
in 1850, a master had every right not just to recapture an absconded
slave from within the jurisdiction of a free state but also to compel
that state's white citizenry—regardless of their moral objections—to
assist in the recovering of lost chattel. It is impossible to exaggerate
the importance to Margaret and her family of avoiding detection
while still in their master's easy reach. After splitting off from the
larger group, the Garners intended to lie low in the home of Joe Kite,
a former slave with connections to the Underground Railroad. But
they had trouble finding him and asked several strangers along the
way for directions. When the Garners finally arrived at Kite's place, he
showed them in and abruptly left; Kite went looking for Levi Coffin,
a white shopkeeper and noted abolitionist, to discuss how he might
smuggle everyone out of town.[3]

Back at Maplewood Plantation, around the time Margaret and the
other runaways were taking their first tentative steps onto the ice of the

Ohio River, Archibald K. Gaines noticed things missing: a rifle, horses, a sleigh, *a complete family of slaves*. Robert. The children. Margaret. All gone. He must have put the pieces together almost immediately. And as the masters of neighboring plantations awoke to similarly less-occupied slave quarters, a heavily armed convoy formed and set out. Unlike their fleeing slaves, however, Gaines and company needed not to concern themselves with invisibility. Assisted by Federal marshals who were bound to enforce the Fugitive Slave Law, they would make a very public demonstration of force for the abolitionists of Ohio.[4]

As they wandered through the streets of Cincinnati, the Garners had also assisted their pursuers, albeit unwittingly. By virtue of being an entire Black family lost together, they made themselves memorable. In asking for directions—an exercise that, by design, requires disclosing one's destination—they betrayed their business with Kite and broadcast the location of their safe house to-be. It was a proverbial trail of breadcrumbs that even a moderately inept band of slave catchers probably could have followed. Gaines and his associates were many things, but incompetent slave hunters they were not. They soon arrived at Kite's residence.[5]

The Garners had already determined not to go quietly. Robert fired several shots from his rifle; he even managed to wound one of the slavecatchers, but it wasn't nearly enough. Before long, the posse improvised a battering ram and laid siege to the front door of the house. Robert couldn't stop them. Sensing the imminence of recapture, Margaret Garner did what could only be unthinkable to someone who had not lived her life—that is, to someone who was not the mixed-race daughter of a raped slave; to someone who had not herself been repeatedly raped and forced to bare the offspring of her owner (and half brother); to someone who wasn't absolutely certain the same form of incestuous perversion awaited her own daughters, and their daughters, and their daughters' daughters.[6]

The cycle had to end. Margaret picked up a large butcher's knife. The Garner's time as free people had run out, but a return to slavery wasn't the only option. She slid the blade quickly across her two-year-old daughter's throat. Before she could kill the other children, the door finally gave way.[7]

FROM THE INSTANT Illinois senator Stephen Douglas guided the Kansas-Nebraska Act (1854) through Congress and threw open the Kansas Territory for white settlement, two things became apparent: first, whichever faction controlled the new territory's government would count the votes that determined its slave status upon achieving statehood; and second, as that contest unfolded, neither side had any intention of subscribing to rules. Partisan lines were drawn from the very beginning. Well provisioned with whiskey and lead, proslavery Missourians paid visits from across the border to stuff ballot boxes and intimidate settlers. Undeterred, wagon train after wagon train brought antislavery homesteaders into the territory. Their guns made the pilgrimage, too. Laws were selectively enforced and extralegal reprisals, frequent. Men from each side wielded violence with the sort of self-righteousness most commonly engendered by political fanaticism.[8]

Both part and parcel of this partisan maelstrom, Lawrence, Kansas, was founded in 1854 as an outpost of the New England Emigrant Aid Company. The company, and by extension the town, had a very specific mission: to help make Kansas a free state by filling it to the brim with Yankees. Many of the Territory's most vehement "Free Soilers," men like James Lane and Charles Robinson, proudly called Lawrence home. Other, more radical opponents of slavery, such as the Connecticut-born abolitionist John Brown and his sons, also resided there from time to time. And while the Browns tended to clash with the likes of Lane and Robinson—the former urging an immediate, ultimate showdown, regardless of Pyrrhic consequence, the latter attempting to win without sacrificing Lawrence in the process—their collective presence made this upstart settlement on the banks of the Kaw an unlikely but resilient epicenter for antislavery struggles west of the Mississippi River.[9]

Such a distinction did not endear the townspeople of Lawrence to their proslavery neighbors in nearby Lecompton, Kansas. Nor did it reap them any goodwill among the slavers of Western Missouri, particularly those in and around the vicinity of Kansas City. To these men, Lawrence was more than a hindrance to the westward creep of coerced African labor. Because of what it stood for, the town's very existence represented a bone-deep affront to slavery's rightful place in American society which, in turn, reminded each man who justified and maintained the institution just how much his moral unease had been repressed. For this the Missourians and their allies not only despised Lawrence but continually plotted to wipe it from the map. Only one obstacle stood in their way.[10]

In the spring of 1856, the way in which one described the structure known as the Free State Hotel—a three-story building situated prominently on Massachusetts Street in Lawrence—really depended on one's politics. Its proprietor claimed, perhaps with a wink and a nod, that the formidable stone abode was nothing more than what its name alleged: a hotel. One with accommodations deluxe enough to rival the finest guesthouses of St. Louis. The hotel's detractors took a very different stance. To them, the Free State Hotel, with its numerous rifle ports, its impenetrable walls, and rumors of a vast arsenal within, wasn't any mere hostel. It was a fortress occupied by northeastern invaders, the anchor point of an antislavery vanguard in Kansas.[11]

Eliminating that vanguard is what brought Sam Jones, the decidedly proslavery sheriff of Douglas County, Kansas, to Lawrence on the morning of May 21. He didn't come alone. Several hundred like-minded Missourians filled the ranks of his "posse." Under normal circumstances, the townspeople of Lawrence could have more than held their own in a fight. They possessed a cache of brand-new Sharp's rifles, the most technologically advanced longarm of its day, and even found a military-grade cannon at their disposal. Better still, the Free State Hotel had been designed to withstand just such an assault. Well aware of this and having no interest whatsoever in charging into the teeth of Lawrence's defenses, Jones and his men schemed another way in—a bait and switch, Border Ruffian style.

Rather than disarming the town by force himself, Jones first had a United States marshal—yet another proslavery man—enter Lawrence to serve writs. Everyone in town knew that violently resisting a Federal agent was tantamount to treason and that charges of treason, no matter the context, would spread like wildfire. The Free Soilers' political and legal credibility would vanish. Any remaining hope of support from the territory's diffident governor, Wilson Shannon, would go up in the smoke of their rifles. They understood too the risks of surrendering but couldn't see much choice in the matter. So they voluntarily submitted themselves to the marshal and awaited the worst.[12]

At first, not much of anything happened. Maybe acquiescence *had* been the wisest play. Maybe law and order, or what passed for it on the western frontier, would prevail. There were lines, after all, that even a crooked Federal officer ought not cross. With the nation's eyes on Kansas, Jones couldn't simply ride in with warrants and let his posse burn a complying town to the ground. Such hopefulness didn't last long, though. Sam Jones came to town with something sinister up his sleeve. And as the people of Lawrence began to realize precisely what it was—and how badly they'd been duped—it was too late.[13]

After concluding his business in Lawrence, the U.S. marshal transferred all his legal authority over the Missourians to Jones and left. The restraints of Federal statute went with him. Residents of Lawrence now found themselves in an utterly helpless position. The oath-bound Federal officer in whom they'd placed their trust had intentionally abandoned them. Worse still, because the horde of Missourians had been allowed into town without a fight, a change of heart now wouldn't just be logistically impossible, it would be suicidal. They knew it. And Jones knew it too. He strutted through town at the head of his army of Border Ruffians like a Roman general on triumph. They immediately surrounded the Free State Hotel and confiscated its arsenal.[14]

Tenants received time enough to evacuate with their valuables. Then the Missourians opened fire with an artillery piece. The first shot sailed comically over its target. The people of Lawrence cheered the miscue. Subsequent rounds found their mark but had no effect on the thick stone walls. More insolent cheers rang out. This was certainly not how Jones imagined his moment of martial glory. Embarrassment gave way to distress. To be rid of the Free State Hotel once and for all, the sheriff needed a new plan, and he needed it fast.[15]

Elsewhere in town, ruffians located the headquarters of two anti-slavery newspapers, the *Herald of Freedom* and the *Kansas Free State*. The Missourians stormed the offices, ransacked presses, and for good measure, pitched typesets into the river. Both buildings were set on fire. Meanwhile, the home of Charles Robinson—the man

Free Soilers had chosen as governor of the territory in elections not recognized by the Federal government—was looted and set similarly ablaze. Back at the hotel, Jones abandoned his dramatic artillery barrage for more primitive means of destruction. Torches were gathered and lit. As flames engulfed floors, stray furniture, curtains, and roofbeams, the Free State's stone exterior could no longer protect it. Soon those walls, the charred shell of a once-imposing citadel, were all that remained.[16]

With their mission accomplished, Jones and company turned spur and rode away from Lawrence. It was as though nothing unusual had just occurred—as though they had not just sacked an *American* town.

> The senator from South Carolina [Andrew Butler] has read many books of chivalry and believes himself a chivalrous knight with sentiments of honor and courage. Of course he has chosen a mistress to whom he has made his vows, and who, though ugly to others, is always lovely to him; though polluted in the sight of the world, is chaste in his sight—I mean the harlot, slavery. For her his tongue is always profuse in words. Let her be impeached in character, or any proposition made to shut her out from the extension of her wantonness, and no extravagance of manner or hardihood of assertion is then too great for this senator.

These were the words of Charles Sumner, delivered before the United States Senate on May 19 and 20, 1856. Preston Brooks could not abide them. Or he would not. As a native of South Carolina's Edgefield District—a place renowned for the frequency with which its residents took to dueling—he had more or less been hardwired to meet verbal challenges with violent force. Because in the minds of antebellum Southerners, if an able-bodied man refused to defend his honor, he'd never really had any honor worth defending.[17]

Andrew Butler, though, was an old man, and he'd recently suffered a stroke. He was also Preston Brooks's cousin. In short, as Butler could not attend to his own honor, or to the family's, the task fell to Brooks.[18]

While determining how exactly to deal with Sumner, Brooks considered three main issues. First, he was a Democratic Congressman and Sumner was a Republican Senator—so whatever happened between them was bound to have explosive political consequences. Second, Sumner hailed from Massachusetts; he harbored little interest in Southern "affairs of honor" and would undoubtedly ignore any formal invitation to gunplay. This was of course assuming Brooks considered Sumner a gentleman worthy of challenging in the first place, which he did not. So there could be no proper duel. Third, because Southern honor culture deemed it unmanly for Brooks to shoot at an unwilling or unqualified opponent, he would have to confront the senator some other way, most likely with his fists. And therein lay the problem: Charles Sumner was much, *much* larger than Preston Brooks. The solution? Ambush.[19]

On May 22, Brooks staked out the Senate chamber. Sumner could be found there most days, and this day was no exception. Fancying himself a man of true cavalier principles, Brooks waited until early evening to make his move. Their "business," whatever it would entail, was not for the eyes of ladies. When the galleries had finally cleared to his satisfaction, Brooks entered the chamber. He spied his target and began a slow but direct approach. Sumner sat alone, writing. He was oblivious to the man with the gutta-percha cane limping in his direction. Brooks announced his intention to settle their score and brought his cane swooping down all at once. Sumner never saw it coming. He never had a chance.[20]

Though initially stunned by the sudden attack, Sumner attempted to stand. Now, however, the hulking frame that had so worried Brooks actually worked to Sumner's disadvantage. Like all the other desks on the senate floor, his was bolted to the ground. In times of spirited disagreement, the measure prevented senators from hurling furniture at each other. Now it meant that Sumner's legs were jammed beneath the desk. This made fighting back, or even effectively shielding his head from Brooks's cane, all but impossible. Blow after blow after blow came down. Sumner felt his strength failing. In a final, Herculean effort, he managed to lurch upward, tearing his desk free, hardware and all—but to no avail. His body could take no more. He fell to the floor. Blood pooled around him as the grotesque thwack of gutta-percha striking his limp figure echoed throughout the chamber.[21]

For caning Charles Sumner, Brooks was arrested, tried, and convicted of assault. Following a series of heated debates, the House of Representatives resolved not to remove him from office. In a calculated display of defiance, he resigned. And in an even greater show of impudence, the people of Edgefield—who now revered him more than ever—held a special election and sent Preston Brooks, new cane in hand, right back to Washington, DC.[22]

THE UNITED STATES in 1856 was a hotbed of irreconcilable worldviews. A woman felt compelled to kill her own innocent child rather than see the girl returned to a life of perpetual bondage. The man who legally owned them both decried not the murder but the loss of his property. The people of a frontier town found themselves at war, not with displaced Native Americans but against other white Americans who could not tolerate their stance against the spread of Southern slavery. These assaults signaled to easterners that violence went hand in hand with the debate over slavery's expansion—and would continue to do so. A congressman beat a senator nearly to death *inside the capitol building itself* and was hailed by his constituents as a hero. The fact that other South Carolinians coveted the splintered remains of Brooks's cane similarly announced to those same easterners that such lapses of peace would not be confined to the faraway, western margins of civilization.[23]

JOHN NEWMAN EDWARDS turned eighteen years old in 1856. It was an important milestone, then as now. He became unconditionally eligible for military service—the mark of a fully grown, American man. Born in Virginia, the sectional crisis had been his cradle, and it followed him to Missouri in 1855. Owing to the failed escape of Margaret Garner, the ruination of the Free State Hotel, and the caning of Charles Sumner, that cradle came crashing down just as Edwards emerged from it. Or in still more colloquial terms, John Newman Edwards came of age just as the Republic seemed to be losing its mind.

Introduction

A Man at War with the World

John Newman Edwards is customarily associated with Civil War guerrillas and postbellum outlaws. In reality he was neither. But as one of the American West's iconic newspaper editorialists, he *was* the man who made them famous. Over the course of his life, he fraternized with bandit and general alike: Frank and Jesse James, the Younger brothers, John Sappington Marmaduke, Sterling Price, Edmund Kirby-Smith. From the Northern Virginia of his boyhood, wanderlust led him to Missouri. Confederate defeat took him to Mexico. Before a revolution there brought him home, Emperor Maximilian and Empress Charlotte numbered among his friends. Quarrelsome, hotheaded, and violent, he was also hopelessly romantic, a fiercely loyal friend, and an affectionate father. Above all else, he was a wordsmith. He wrote three major books—*Shelby and His Men* (1867), *Shelby's Expedition to Mexico* (1872), and *Noted Guerrillas, or, The Warfare of the Border* (1877)—along with hundreds of columns, criticisms, and reviews. Through them all, he was a fanciful chronicler of what *might* have been, even as his literary endeavors sought to shape the memory of what had *actually* been.

To call Edwards the scion of an extended family with aristocratic bearing would be to sell the truth of the matter several measures short. Replete with Newmans, Wroes, Foxes, Monroes, and Wyatts, he descended from an intermarried who's who of the Old Dominion's first families. And owing to their specific placement in Virginia soil, these ancestral roots reached back to not one but two momentous beginnings in North America: first to the early days at British James-town and then to the founding struggles of the American republic.

By the mid-1850s, the Edwardses' bloodline still carried social clout but lacked the grandeur or affluence of generations past. To Edwards personally, the money had never really mattered; for him everything hinged on glory. Hence, his life became a quest. Not just to match the feats of storied ancestors but to make real the sort of storybook universe they occupied in his imagination. From Edwards's youth, this mission colored virtually everything—the good, the bad, the ugly, the very ugly—of his politics, his relationships, how he expressed himself with pen and press, and how he perceived the world changing, often for the worse, around him.

It is impossible, however, to begin comprehending the man, let alone his mission, without first understanding the particulars of his immediate family, his boyhood, and the 1843 event that knocked each out of orbit.

ON NOVEMBER 16, 1831, John Monroe looked on as bondsman while his cousin Mary Ann Brown (b. 1806) wed John Edwards (b. 1799) in Frederick County, Virginia. For the groom, life appeared to be on the upswing. The eldest son of Thomas and Frances Ann Edwards (née Murray) of Leesburg, Virginia, he was still relatively young at thirty-two years old and was in the process of launching a successful tanning operation. Now he had a youthful wife, and heirs would presumably follow. For Mary Ann, the daughter of John and Catherine Newman (née Monroe), the marriage constituted a second—and for all she knew, final—chance at happiness and stability.[1]

Her first husband, Francis Brown, whom she'd married in July 1822 at the age of sixteen, died in November 1823. The abruptness of his death and his seeming lack of preparation for it, left Mary Ann particularly vulnerable. At best, Francis had not had an opportunity to update his will post-nuptials. At worst he'd had the opportunity and declined. Either way, the arrangement failed utterly to provide his teenaged widow with material support.[2]

The whole of the Brown estate was liquidated at public sale by William Brown, its executor, the brother of the deceased and the man who doubtless profited most from the auction. Many desirable items, ranging from silverware to saddles to candlesticks, fell into the possession of Mary Ann's better-off Wyatt and Monroe cousins. Her own well-being amounted to an afterthought: an already aggrieved Mary Ann was forced to pay twenty-five dollars to keep a mahogany bureau that had almost certainly belonged to her in all but name prior to her marriage and her husband's demise.[3]

But that was a distant memory by 1836, when John and Mary Ann Edwards welcomed their first child, Thomas Samuel. A second boy, John Newman, followed soon after in 1838. Three years later the family added a baby girl, Susan Edmonia. By 1842, with the tanyard thriving, the Edwardses leased a sizeable home and a $1,000.00 parcel of cultivated land in Front Royal, a quaint town on the northern end of Virginia's Shenandoah Valley. They owned an ever-expanding stable of horseflesh and stock: bays, duns, and sorrels, several cows, hogs, a bull. And in addition to his business dealings, John Sr.'s involvement with the Methodist Episcopal Church had established him as a man of real standing in Warren County. All signs pointed to continued prosperity and growth for the family.[4]

Then, in January 1843, with two boys approaching peak rambunctiousness, a toddling daughter to chase, and a fourth child on the way, the thrust of that upward trajectory rudely changed direction. Following an eight-week struggle, John Edwards succumbed—at home, surrounded by his family—to a "painful illness." Lacking more specific records, we can only guess at the ailment, but cancer (perhaps brought on by exposure to leather dust and formaldehyde), "brain fever" (inflammation of the brain due to a viral infection), or dropsy (edema commonly related to heart failure) would have all been likely culprits in the mid-nineteenth century. Whatever the cause, Mary Ann Edwards was not yet forty years old, and she'd now lost her second husband. She was a widow. Again. This time, at least, there would be no scrounging up twenty-five dollars to reclaim her own bedroom furniture.[5]

Back in 1823, when Francis Brown died, one could make the argument that Mary Ann had been more child than adult. With a marriage that took her away from her people, lasted little more than a year, and yielded no dependent children, she'd lacked the standing to assert herself among relative strangers. This was not the case when she buried John Sr. In the place of an overwhelmed teenager away from home for the first time now stood an experienced woman. And with Thomas, John Jr., and Susan to support, as well as another baby on the way, Mary Ann somehow found the strength to steady herself and hold the reeling family together. Fortunately for her, and for the children, John Sr. had readied his affairs. His will—whether by her insistence, his own thoughtfulness, or some combination of the two—would keep Mary Ann from having to start over completely.

The specific terms of John Sr.'s last will and testament dictated that his estate, valued at a more-than-substantial $3,233.87 half, would be partially liquidated and then converted into a trust for the longer-term benefit of Mary Ann and the children. After the harvest of 1843, the farm lease wasn't renewed, and most of the animals were sold. Odds are better than good that the estate kept an owner's share in the tannery, while someone else—potentially John Sr.'s older brother Samuel M. Edwards—managed daily operations. After 1843 the tannery would provide the bulk of the estate's revenue and thereby the majority of the family's income.[6]

Mary Ann gave birth to Mary Catherine Francis, known fondly as "Fannie," later in 1843. Even with periodic payments from the estate, the female-headed Edwards family no longer had the prospect of earning more money and were far from affluent. Raising four children would not have been an inexpensive venture with an enterprising husband in the picture. Without John Sr. around, Mary Ann could not afford to maintain anything like their previous lifestyle. These leaner times notwithstanding, every indication is that she simply refused to skimp on her son John Jr.'s education; only now, with his father below ground, he was no longer John Jr. or John Newman. Henceforth, to his mother, his siblings, his teachers, his classmates—that is, to more or less everyone—he would just be John.[7]

In an era when it wouldn't have been unusual for a Southern boy his age—and especially for one with a single mother and younger children requiring support—to find full-time work, John received a complete common school education in Front Royal. Generally speaking, common school curricula employed rote learning and revolved around the three R's—reading, writing, and arithmetic—along with healthy doses of Protestant morality.[8]

From Alfred Lord Tennyson and Walter Scott to Victor Hugo, from *Ivanhoe* to *The Bible*, John was a voracious reader. He learned the fundamentals of history and geography; he found his earliest authorial style; and through end-of-term recitations got his first taste of performing for an audience. Given what would become a penchant for grandiloquence later in life, it isn't very difficult to imagine a twelve-year-old John dramatizing a passage from *McGuffey's Reader*. Nor is it difficult to imagine a bewildered instructor looking on as John's classmates tried—with varying degrees of success—to suppress their giggles.

Normally, the end of common schooling would have meant the end of the educational road for a child of John's limited financial circumstances. But as she was wont to do, Mary Ann ignored convention. She packed John off to an academy in Washington City, a tiny township despite its urbane name, in neighboring Rappahannock County. There at the heel of the Blue Ridge, he took on classical training in Greek and Latin. In the company of epic storytellers like Homer, Ovid, Livy, Sophocles, and Virgil, John surely found artistic inspiration. Perhaps more importantly, through their descriptions of Achilles, Hector, Jason, Caesar, and Augustus, these storytellers also provided larger-than-life images of manhood to go along with Arthur, Lancelot, and Cromwell. For a boy who'd been robbed of his father, this comprised a vital coping mechanism. Because no matter the intensity of his nostalgia, a teenaged John could never return to a time when John Sr. lived. Yet through books he could go back even further to when everything always seemed to be in proper order. Not unwittingly, John would spend his entire adult life trying to will that fantastical world into existence.[9]

In 1852 John began an apprenticeship at the *Front Royal Gazette*. He was fourteen years old. According to a retrospective profile by the Reverend George Plattenburg—who was himself an old friend of John's—the precocious intern's prose laid bare his "extraordinary powers" and won him "wide celebrity."[10]

It's a tricky undertaking to gauge what passed for literary fame within the confines of a sleepy mountain town like Front Royal, with a population of roughly five hundred. But whatever adoration John achieved with his pen, he wanted more of it. This experience, in the gossip-fueled, smoke-filled newsroom of his hometown paper, ultimately set him on that course. In one capacity or another, he would be a writer—and frequently a newspaperman—until the day he died.

The vocation made perfect sense for John in that it melded his family history and personal demeanor as well as his inherent talents and training. Losing his father at such a young age only encouraged the backward-looking elements of his personality. Such longings had led him back centuries, to realms of order and absolute authority, both real and imagined. And like all legendary kingdoms, from Arthur's Camelot to the *Domus Augusti*, that place required defending. The printed page afforded John that opportunity. With quill and typeset, he could—and would—declaim against all forms of political newness and cultural change: prohibition, tariffs, paper currency, organized labor, expanded civil and voting rights. For these were the gravest threats to the ways of the Old World he so cherished. John's classical education outfitted him with a virtually bottomless stockpile of heroes, villains, damsels, metaphors, anecdotes, scriptural references, and florid quotations to wield in his future harangues. Indeed, in the coming years, John's trademark baroque and the deep purple of his prose would become legendary.

But trademarks and legends were a long way off in 1855. John was seventeen years old and craving a larger arena. He wasn't interested in the cities of the Northeast. Instead, with his apprenticeship complete, he believed himself fully equipped to make his future in the West. Or as he probably saw it, to play some crucial role in making the future *of* the West. So when his cousin Thomas J. Yerby pitched a move to the political tempest that was Western Missouri, John simply could not resist the change of scenery or the allure of real-life adventure. Nor was he alone in trading Virginia, the de facto capital of a centuries-old plantation society that prided itself on white civility and gentility, for the rough-hewn crossroads of South and West. The Missouri-Kansas borderlands of the 1830s, '40s, and '50s were full of relocated southerners, born too late to reap the full economic benefits of their patrician heritage but determined to be among the first families of a newer, fast-developing society.[11]

People he met there appealed to John. This was especially true of Joseph Orville Shelby. In many ways, he was an expatriate unto himself. Nobody called him *Joseph*—nobody who knew him, anyway. To close friends and family he was *Jo*. To the rest, *Jo Shelby*. Later, *Colonel* or *General Shelby*. A native of Lexington, Kentucky, he came to Missouri in 1852. What's more, he belonged to one of the wealthiest, best-connected, most-storied bloodlines the Bluegrass had to offer.[12]

No account has survived of John's and Jo's first meeting, but it turned out to be one of the most consequential encounters of both their lives. Despite Jo being eight years older, not to mention his hailing from an entirely different social caste, the pair found they had much in common. Both could trace their ancestors back to Wales. They were both the descendants of Revolutionary heroes. Each had lost his father at the age of five. And both immigrated to Western Missouri in the 1850s. But given John's proclivity for heroes of the Old World variety, it should come as no surprise that he gravitated to Jo. By all accounts, the Kentuckian cut a dashing figure. He was rich. He was well educated. He'd led daring forays on horseback across the Kansas border. He was the epitome—at least from John's perspective—of cavalier sophistication. In short, he was the closest thing John had ever seen to one of his Round Table idols in the flesh.[13]

The duo hunted, fished, and imbibed together. Over many hours and many bottles, their bond solidified. Gradually the friendship became a brotherhood. It was only natural then, when secession winter gave way to bellicosity, that they went to war together. Jo of course led the way. While John, his faithful bard and squire, was always close behind—a pen in one hand, a gun in the other.

THE SAGA OF John Newman Edwards places its star in numerous roles, some of which garnered him significant fame and notoriety in late nineteenth-century America. Nevertheless, he is not nearly so well remembered today as Civil War era A-listers like Abraham

Lincoln, Robert E. Lee, Ulysses S. Grant, Jefferson Davis, George Armstrong Custer, or even John Brown. Far from a drawback, however, his achieving B-list celebrity *in so many different capacities* means his personal odyssey furnishes the scaffolding of a tale far larger, and more geographically expansive, than a treatment of any *single* contemporary might yield.

To appreciate the vastness of Edwards's story, we need only to look to its supporting cast. The list is as diverse as it is far reaching: the infamous guerrilla chieftains, William Clarke Quantrill and Bloody Bill Anderson; the James-Younger Gang; Generals like Jubal Early and Edmund Kirby Smith; famed newspapermen Stilson Hutchins and Horace Greeley; the politician Thomas T. Crittenden; deposed Mexican president Benito Juarez; the author Victor Hugo; even the imperial rulers of Mexico, Maximilian and Charlotte. All these take their turns on stage with Edwards. Thus, while framed by the lifespan of a single man, the epic whole of its parts comprises the ideas and beliefs, the wants, needs, and insecurities, the motivations (and ultimately the actions) of myriad men, women, and children—Black, white, and brown, free and enslaved, rich and poor, Unionist and Confederate, American, Mexican, French, Austrian, and even Belgian. Ultimately, then, this biography enlists not only its subject but also the worlds he inhabited (and created) to change the way we conceptualize the boundaries of the Civil War and Reconstruction.

It's quite stunning that Edwards's life, which many today would consider "made for the movies," has not been fully chronicled. Bits and pieces of his work—mostly his texts on Civil War guerrillas and postbellum outlaws—have been used to buttress the narratives explaining the fame of others. With such works, his credibility as an editor and historian varies wildly. And while virtually all recognize Edwards's personal eccentricities and belletristic tendencies, none comes close to mapping their origins or ramifications. For instance, one 1909 writer took Edwards to task, ultimately declaring that many of his conclusions were "wholly and completely refuted by the record." Nearly a century later, another categorized him as a "power broker" in Missouri, adding that without his influence, one of the world's most celebrated bandits "would probably have passed into obscurity with hundreds of other criminals." Most recently, one of Jo Shelby's biographers noted that Edwards "was born a writer lusting for an epic subject" and that for him, "the Civil War was a contest between chivalric knights of old against an ignoble, uncultured, materialistic invader." Supporting roles and passing references no longer suffice. It is time for John Newman Edwards and his *full story* to command top billing.[14]

We are beginning to understand that the Civil War unfolded much farther west and over an elongated stretch of time. Guerrillas, Indians, Mexicans, and even camels all took part in this heretofore neglected theater of war. Though they represent a marked departure from the familiar—massive armies commanded by West Pointers at places like Antietam and Gettysburg—these characters unquestionably played crucial roles in determining the new face of the nation as it spanned from sea to shining sea.[15]

We are also starting to view the coming of the war, and its execution, in more global terms. Generally speaking, new histories explore how international relations—be they diplomatic, economic, or even military—influenced the trajectory of the war in America. Most frequently, they chronicle European and Latin American actions on the respective governments of the Union and the Confederacy. Yet some also pay attention to how North Americans helped to shape foreign outcomes. Nowhere was this truer than in Mexico, where class revolution, European intervention, and civil war unraveled multiple governments.[16]

The result of all this boundary stretching is that we are finally nearing a more accurate measurement of the Civil War's scope. In an American context, this has meant reimagining the conflict as the sum of two, interconnected and overlapping parts: one fight for abolition in the East, one fight for American empire in the Far West. From an international perspective, it's involved rethinking the war as just one struggle in a series of uprisings and revolutions that shook the western world in the nineteenth century.

Bearing this in mind, the life and literature of John Newman Edwards comprises an impeccable lens to this broadening of horizons. He took part in the American Civil War. He rubbed elbows with

Maximilian's imperial court in Mexico City. He witnessed firsthand the victory of Benito Juarez over the Second French Empire. As a member of the postwar press, he made Jesse James into *Jesse James*. And in between resisting Republican Reconstruction policies, he swayed how the war itself would be remembered. Most significant, however, is that through his writing, we can see that Edwards recognized this "bigger picture" in something like real time.

On one level Edwards had a fairly conventional opinion of secession. He justified the Confederate Experiment as an exercise in safeguarding slavery within the South. Like the overwhelming majority of his fellow Confederates, he didn't possess a sprawling plantation. Similarly, he never owned a single slave. Yet he gladly took up arms and repeatedly risked his life to preserve the institution of slavery. True to his aristocratic ancestral roots, Edwards believed in maintaining order and the supremacy of select peoples over others. In slavery, he saw an effective means to that end, albeit one that accustomed all members of the society to both inflict and accept vicious brutality as part of everyday life.

On another level, though, Edwards viewed the war as being exponentially broader and of greater consequence than most men of his day. Given the importance placed on saving the Republic by Unionists and on protecting slavery by Confederates, this is really saying something. To him, and select others, the rebel states had not simply shattered the Union to defend slavery at home. They belonged to a greater movement; a collective operation of sorts, conducted by supposedly "superior" people. Their goal amounted to holding back a much larger tide of reform and egalitarianism that had been rising steadily since the 1830s. From his mid-century vantage point, the royals, nobles, and aristocrats of the Old World and the American South's elite planters and intellectuals shared timeworn traits that affirmed their right to rule. They were also similarly under siege from political radicals, boorish abolitionists, and the working poor run amok. Now they had to stick together to survive. Not in a coordinated sense. To be sure, there were no specific, unified plans for resistance. No international ententes spanned the Atlantic. But a general feeling proliferated among landed elites that times were changing—and not for the better. By the 1870s, when Edwards hit his prime as an author, it threatened to drown everything he held dear.

John Newman Edwards wasn't landed. Nor was he elite. Yet precisely because of this, he felt a magnetic pull toward absolute power and rigid hierarchy throughout his life.

His desire was for a binary world of master and subject, courageous and cowardly. It was a realm in which great men could win glory and be remembered forever. It did not matter that such a world had never really existed—at least outside of mythology and folklore. Edwards created it in the sensational tales that spilled from his pen. It guided his actions: reckless tactics on the battlefield, duels with rival authors, odes for Empress Charlotte, playing the part of crony squire to Shelby's cavalier knight routine. These things were all symptoms of Edwards trying to live out the content of his imagination. They also help explain, by personal example, his belief that elite men had to stand firm against social upheaval or risk losing everything.

The notion itself is strikingly similar to another belief shared by many Southerners of the Civil War era: that the root system of slavery would wither and die if the institution stopped actively "growing" westward. In this case, Edwards championed preservation rather than growth, but the consequence of failure would be the same. Through his own behavior, and most of all through his writing, he portended that the decline of traditional leaders with power bases abroad would weaken the footholds of their American counterparts. This meant the right people—extremely conservative white men, generally wealthy, though not always—could lose their grip on Southern society.

Fears such as these lend further context to understanding Edwards's quest. To avoid losing the social, cultural, and economic mechanisms that he assumed led to political power and personal glory, Edwards embraced a "use them or lose them" mentality. And use them he did: first on behalf of the Confederacy in the Trans-Mississippi Theater, then in French-controlled Mexico, and finally in postbellum Missouri. When considered along these lines, the Civil War and Reconstruction don't lose even a shred of their long-held importance to American history. But they do gain tremendous new value as crucial pieces of a larger puzzle.

The importance of particular spaces within this story cannot be overemphasized. In many ways, they *are* the story—none more so than "the West." Oft-amorphous and always evolving, it wasn't simply a place where "important things" happened that historians ought to chronicle. Edwards's concept of the West, whether it included Missouri, the Pacific Coast, or even Mexico, went hand in hand with the possibility of a better future for ultraconservative, white nationalist Southerners. By his logic, the West was the canvas on which the winners of the war would get to paint society as they deemed fit. The actual presence of American Indians, Mexicanos, or other nonwhites, and their longer history in the region, hardly mattered. They could all be entirely erased, or depicted as subordinates, in the final portrait. Better still, even as definitions of the West changed over time, as a concept, it always represented the last best hope as a venue wherein Edwards's fantasies might still become reality.

In this light, Edwards's devotion to simultaneously sustaining a war for restoration and a rebellion, albeit a conservative one, set him apart. He strove to restore a version of the antebellum South that appeared more a throwback to Camelot or Ivanhoe society than reality. This distinguished him from other Confederates who fought to uphold an idealized version of paternalistic slavery or even the Dixieland of moonlight and magnolia. Such a paradigm of the Old South had never truly existed either, but Edwards was hearkening back to something even older—to something more elemental. He drilled down to the cultural bedrock on which mythologies of the Old South had been anchored in the first place. While other Southerners viewed the worlds of Sir Walter Scott and Sir Thomas Malory as a cultural embellishment, Edwards saw something with genuine power. Moreover, he saw something with attainability.

This made victory imperative. And for more than just slavery. Winning the Civil War meant determining the fate of the institution, without question. As that same war went, though, so too could the imperial fortunes of the new Confederate nation be judged in the West. Certainly not all rank-and-file Confederates tethered the implications of losing the war and the West as Edwards did. Their daily thoughts centered more on finding the next meal, a dry place to sleep, and staying alive. That doesn't mean any of them were interested in being part of the generation that lost the all-deciding war, either. But in April 1865 that is precisely what they became.

On April 9, Robert E. Lee dashed Confederate hopes for a miracle when he surrendered his crumbling Army of Northern Virginia at Appomattox Court House. A few weeks later, on April 26, Joseph E. Johnston conceded his Army of Tennessee to William Tecumseh Sherman at Bennett Place in Durham, North Carolina. Other Confederate commanders held out longer. One of these stalling generals was Edmund Kirby-Smith, who didn't capitulate with his Army of the Trans-Mississippi until May 26. For all intents and purposes, he had only managed to delay the inevitable. With Lee and Johnston withdrawn from the field, the war was over. Kirby-Smith knew it. So did John Newman Edwards.

When the Confederacy perished, Edwards lost what he believed had been an opportunity to build a new society—or at least to refurbish the old, pulling it more into line with his views on social hierarchy and cultural tradition. In Mexico, he glimpsed a second chance. Maybe even a better one. After all, Mexico already had a European monarch; an Emperor descended from no less than the House of Habsburg. True, Maximilian I wasn't a commanding figure in the mold of historical autocrats like Frederick II of Prussia or Peter the Great of Russia, nor even in the mold of his own brother, Franz Josef of Austria-Hungary. But whatever Maximilian's authoritarian shortcomings, and they were myriad, his installation as emperor of the Second Mexican Empire did mean that the protocols and mechanisms for enforcing a rigid, Old World–style society appeared to be in place.

A rough outline of the caricatured European society Edwards dreamed of living in sat ready for polishing. He firmly believed that he and his Anglo companions could establish a better version of an already fanciful Old South, south of the border. Because with a patron like Maximilian—an absolute ruler, at least on paper— the ex-Confederates had discovered for themselves a new canvas to replace what they'd lost in 1865. Indubitably, such high expectations also meant that when Benito Juarez—the rightfully elected president of Mexico whom Maximilian had officially deposed in

1864—reclaimed power, Edwards had to experience the agony of defeat all over again.

Back in Missouri by 1867, a twice-defeated Edwards took solace in his writing. Soon, both his editorial and historical output hit prodigious levels. He published major books in 1867, 1872, and 1877, along with an innumerable quantity of column inches. This writing wasn't merely a way to pass the time. He was still willing to fight for America's "aristocracy." And in the western borderlands of the 1870s and '80s, Edwards saw a place to make his final stand against northern-style progress—against the reforms of the common masses. Yet there were no more set-piece, military campaigns left to wage and no more nascent empires to shape. Aside from a trip or two to the dueling grounds, the pen became Edwards's primary means of crusading. With it, he made political war, or war by other means, against those forces of modernism that he believed the North had unleashed upon the rest of the nation by way of the Civil War.

In the context of this struggle for the cultural soul of America, a true Southerner was inherently antimodern and antiauthority. Thereby, as a culture warrior devoted to resisting growth and change in a western-style democracy, Edwards was *the* quintessential Southerner of his day—much more so than Davis or Lee or any of the men his writing made famous. Over time, though, as his writing failed to shape his environment to the extent he desired, it doubled as an escape mechanism. The more unwinnable the culture wars appeared to be, the more that mechanism bordered on alternative reality.

Years passed. Elections came and went. Old friends and comrades died. Whether Edwards liked it or not, the world grew increasingly unrecognizable. He never entirely gave up on his mission. But as his goals seemed to evade him with greater frequency, Edwards also lived more and more vicariously through the characters he put down on paper. It was a natural retrogression to his boyhood days in Front Royal and then Washington City—only now he had the ability to tell the stories as well as consume them. When fantasy could no longer assuage the disappointment, Edwards mined hope in bottles. He extracted only addiction. His alcoholism steadily intensified. In 1889 it killed him.

FOR MOST OF his life, John Newman Edwards had been a man at war with the world. Which is actually to say that he'd been a man at war with himself. His was an existential strife; one that emanated from some dark, unfathomed place within the mind. More than just a romantic or even deeply nostalgic form of conservatism, the animating spirit of his political body was a total unwillingness to accept modernity in any form. He was a diehard reactionary who held, predictably, that his attempts to reverse time would yield the opposite of regression. As such, his war could never really be won, only waged without end. It is there, in the waging, that we find our story.

Oracle of Lost Causes

Into the Forge

As winter 1860 gave way to spring 1861, each and every moment that an American flag soared over Fort Sumter was one too many for its secessionist onlookers. South Carolina had bolted from the Union months before, in December 1860. Mississippi, Florida, Alabama, Georgia, Louisiana, and Texas had all quickly followed suit. Eventually they joined with South Carolina to establish the Confederate States of America. After declaring their independence, officials of the newly formed Confederacy had called frequently upon the garrison's commander, Major Robert Anderson, to withdraw. By extension, they wanted him to relinquish the authority of his government over South Carolina. With orders from Union brass to sit tight, Anderson had promptly refused every demand for surrender. Hence, the stars and stripes still flew and the fire-eaters gnashed their teeth in disgust.

Under these circumstances, the brick stronghold, isolated and alone atop its granite pilings in Charleston Harbor, had become a fulcrum of national intent: if the Union truly determined to tear itself asunder, here is where the seams—already frayed by years of western violence—would be ripped open. For their part, Charlestonians seemed to welcome just such an untethering of republican bonds. Beginning on April 8, as residents of the city anticipated the start of hostilities, socialite Mary Boykin Chesnut described "an undercurrent of intense excitement." "The streets were alive with soldiers, men shouting, marching and singing," she recorded in her diary. Chesnut's own husband happened to be the very Confederate colonel then attempting to procure Anderson's surrender—but even she didn't appear to know that, by the evening of April 11, the city's anxious wait for action was nearly over.

Before the sun rose on April 12, 1861, Confederate shore batteries burst forth with an immense barrage of shot and shell. Perched atop the roofs of their mansions, Chesnut and her friends made an occasion of it. They observed the assault, cocktails in hand, almost as if watching a boat race in the sound. For more than thirty hours, the guttural booms of cannon fire drowned out the harbor's familiar track of rotating tides, chattering birds, and cursing stevedores. When the bombardment finally broke off, Fort Sumter—the once-formidable citadel that had so rankled secessionist feathers—sat in ruin, smoke billowing from its pocked walls.[1]

Running short on both food and ammunition, Sumter's defenders had periodically returned fire but held no real hope of maintaining their position through force. After stalling for as long as he deemed both practicable and honorable, Major Anderson capitulated on April 13. For all the ordnance expended in the direction of his garrison, Anderson lost but one man, by accident. A minor miracle, no doubt. But not one that could obscure reality for long: the seams had indeed come apart in Charleston. And despite a beginning noteworthy for its bloodlessness, the coming war to determine if or how the Union could be re-stitched would upend more lives and spill more blood than anything Chesnut's posh coterie, the stubborn Anderson, or even his exultant Confederate attackers ever could have imagined.

Part 1: From the Newsroom to the Bloody Hill

Nine hundred miles northwest of Fort Sumter, Lafayette County resided in the cluster of Western Missouri counties later known as "Little Dixie"—a region within a region, renowned for a high concentration of slaves. For its free white population of roughly fourteen thousand, Lafayette County in 1860–61 teemed with economic prosperity. More than five hundred farms in the county operated on at least one hundred acres. More than thirty landowners held deed to no less than five hundred acres, while better than nine hundred slaveholders laid claim to nearly 6,400 slaves. By their involuntary labors, crops of tobacco, hemp, corn, wheat, and oats flourished. In

1860 alone, for example, Lafayette County farmers turned out nearly 160,000 pounds of tobacco and almost two million bushels of corn.[2]

The city of Lexington fronted a long, relatively straight stretch of the Missouri on Lafayette County's northern border. As a river hub of four thousand, the city's docks, warehouses, mills, markets, ferry slips, and boarding houses bustled with activity. Lexingtonians shipped crops and other local wares—wool, rope, furniture, and coal most prominent among them—off to western markets via the steam trade, a lucrative local industry unto itself. So too did the slavers of Lexington deal in commodities of the equine type, often making fortunes on the backs of their human chattel which allowed them to spend extravagantly on horseflesh. As the site of an 1855 slaveholders' convention, the commercial epicenter of the county, and as the seat of its government, Lexington provided the beau monde-types—men like Thomas Shelby and John Catron, neighbors whose respective net values hovered around the enormous figure of $100,000 in 1860—with a place to mingle in relative luxury. In addition to these commercial and social plaudits, on the eve of the Civil War the city was gaining a reputation for something quite different: a very young, very brash newspaperman out of Virginia.[3]

Almost immediately after arriving on the scene in Lexington, John Newman Edwards found work at the *Lexington Expositor*, the burgeoning city's weekly paper. He began his tenure in the newsroom as a printer, a position that tasked him with duties other than writing. But as his talent with the pen became evident, John took on more and more creative responsibility. In the beginning of his editorial career, he covered a wide range of local interests, perhaps the most interesting of all having been the marriage of Jo Shelby. By late July 1858, when the wedding took place, John and Jo had spent countless hours together. They stalked the fields and brushwood around Lexington for game. They fished along the banks of the Missouri. And they wiled away more than a few evenings in the company of a whiskey bottle, or two, or three—Jo recounting his exploits as a border ruffian and John likely equating them with tales of mythical heroes long past.[4]

John helped plan the wedding and was on hand to chronicle the entire, champagne-drenched affair. Well-heeled and politically connected Missourians turned up in force to see Jo Shelby marry Elizabeth Nancy "Betty" Shelby, his neighbor and first cousin (once removed). As the bride told it years later, Jo first encountered her in 1852, when she was eleven years old and he was twenty-two—quite an age gap even for mid-nineteenth-century notions of courtship. "He told my father that he was going to wait for me," Betty recalled, and six years later, they were at the altar. Awash in his inheritance and the spoils of lucrative rope and freight operations, Jo pulled out all the proverbial stops. A carpet of red velvet ran from the riverside mansion of William Shelby, his cousin and now father-in-law, all the way down to the water's edge. Following a Presbyterian service conducted by the Reverend B. M. Hobson, Jo's steamer, the *A. B. Chambers*, waited at the end of the red carpet to transport the newlywed couple and an entourage—John included—on a honeymoon trip to St. Louis that lasted well over a week.[5]

Lexingtonians had never seen a wedding quite like this before. Not surprisingly, to glorify his best friend, John marshalled all his literary powers to make sure they would never forget it. For *Expositor* subscribers capable of reading between the lines, John's coverage of the wedding also served a second function: it announced *his own* arrival in Western Missouri society. He had been front and center among the elite carousers. And he'd been one of the select few to accompany Jo and Betty on their lavish honeymoon. It was not in his nature to come right out and declare it, but in his own oblique way, John would not allow readers to forget him, either.[6]

Sectional animosity intensified in the leadup to Sumter and events like the Shelby wedding more frequently took a backseat to national politics. The *Expositor*, which was owned by William Anderson—a prominent lawyer and slaveholder—already packed a heavy pro-Southern punch. When John, still considered precocious in his early twenties, took the editorial reins, the paper's anti-Northern, anti-Republican, anti-Lawrence, anti-anything-vaguely-resembling-abolitionism vitriol ascended to new heights. The men of the Emigrant Aid Society, John thundered, were nothing but mercenary trouble-makers; interlopers from New England come West to mind business that was not at all their own. William Anderson's father, Colonel

1. Tintype of Joseph Orville Shelby on his wedding day in July 1858. State Historical Society of Missouri, John G. Rodgers Photograph Collection.

2. Betty Shelby (née Gratz). John covered her wedding to Jo Shelby extensively in the *Lexington Expositor*. State Historical Society of Missouri, John G. Rodgers Photograph Collection.

Oliver Anderson, put his thoughts on meddling abolitionists more succinctly: "they . . . are infidels."[7]

Yet for all of John's bombast, like most Americans in 1859 he had no reason to believe that a compromise could not—and would not—be struck with regard to slavery's expansion into the western territories. To be sure, outbursts of violence like the burning of the Free State Hotel and the near murder of Charles Sumner weren't exactly business as usual, but the republic had weathered fierce debates over the future of slavery before. In 1820, in the early 1830s, and again in 1850, sectional leaders had found the slivers of common ground necessary to avoid national catastrophe. Then, in October 1859, a seismic event shook the nation.

On the 16th of that month, John Brown led a botched raid against the Federal arsenal at Harper's Ferry, Virginia. He'd intended to plunder the facility and, with its contents, to equip slaves from the surrounding countryside for battle. In short, Brown planned to help slaves rise up and assassinate their white owners en masse. The uprising never materialized. Colonel Robert Edward Lee, then a relatively unknown officer in the regular army, arrived with a squadron of United States Marines and, together with local militia forces, retook the armory. Two of Brown's sons received mortal wounds in the melee. Not long after, Brown himself was hanged. But the damage—to whatever traces of sectional goodwill had *almost* survived the tumultuous 1850s—was already done.

Less than a week after his arrest, the proslavery *Topeka Tribune* blasted Brown, labeling him an "Abolitionist fanatic." It also crystallized in print what many Southerners were already thinking about Brown's attack against the institution of slavery and the imminent threat his brand of activism posed to white slaveowners. Brown had been willing to destroy white civilization to liberate Black slaves—and the only just result of such maniacal logic could be death. "We trust this will be a lesson to others of the Abolition stripe," the *Tribune* concluded with a healthy dose of self-righteousness. As it turned out, the paper erred in its assumption. Brown's situation would teach abolitionists a hard lesson, but not the one Southerners intended.[8]

As a case in point, on October 30, 1859, Henry David Thoreau delivered his "Plea for Captain John Brown." "I plead not for his life, but for his character, his immortal life," Thoreau prefaced. Then the well-known transcendentalist launched into the analogy that set Southern blood to boiling: "Some eighteen hundred years ago Christ was crucified; this morning, perchance, Captain Brown was hung. These are the two ends of a chain which is not without its links." Having dropped that bombshell on the incredulous South—which considered itself the victim, not the Pontius Pilate, of Brown's gory gospel—Thoreau ended his eulogy-to-be on an ominous note. He declared that he foresaw a time when "slavery shall be no more here" and when "we shall then be at liberty to weep for Captain Brown." "Then," he concluded, "and not till then, we will take our revenge."[9]

If the words of a New England radical stung Southern ears, the pain was at least not wholly unexpected. Indeed, Thoreau made no secret of his hatred for slavery long before the shots fired at Harper's

Ferry. But New York, with its numerous and strong ties to Southern business—which is generally to say, to slavery—was another matter. On November 3, 1859, the usually conservative *New York Times* wrote about Brown with unexpected reverence. "It can hardly be possible," the article stated, "that any man, whether at the North or at the South . . . should read these words by the brave old fanatic without a glow of half-compassionate admiration for the strong and sterling qualities of the nature which loads their every syllable with honest force."[10]

Calm, earnest, brave, strong, sterling, honest. *Christ-like.* Here was a renowned northern intellectual and a major northern newspaper heaping praise on the character of a man marked for death by the state of Virginia for treason and murder. Brown had surely trod an illegal path at Harper's Ferry. Not even his admirers contested that fact. But within the increasingly violent debate over slavery, there could be no higher *moral* ground than the trap door of the old man's gallows on December 2, 1859.

It undoubtedly pleased John Newman Edwards when Northern Virginia—the land of his Revolutionary forebears and the state of his birth—put an end to "Old Man Brown" the "abolitionist fanatic." In that moment, sitting behind his desk in the *Expositor* office, death must have seemed both distant and just. Then it dealt him a much more personal blow. John's mother, Mary Ann, succumbed to cancer in 1860. She was only fifty-four years old. Not long before, in 1856, already a year of meteors, cancer had also claimed the life of Mary Ann's own mother, Catherine Newman.[11]

As a single mother and widow, Mary Ann had anchored a young family in its hour of greatest crisis. She had shepherded John and his three siblings through social and financial uncertainty to adulthood. She'd seen to John's education. She'd supported his love of books. Above all else, she had encouraged John to take up the pen himself and then took immense pride in his early achievements. By way of that maternal guidance, she had done more to set the underlying trajectory of his life than any other living person. So John threw himself into his work, precisely as Mary Ann would have wanted. The "impending crisis" seemed to impend more and more with each passing day. John had lost his mother—but suffered no shortage of material to editorialize in 1860.

Proslavery men felt the national political tide reversing as John Brown underwent his posthumous transformation from madman to martyr. They also understood the potential socioeconomic dangers carried by such a sea change. Accordingly, they approached the presidential election of 1860 as a do-or-die moment for the survival of their peculiar institution. In just the way that many Northerners had imagined the South since 1856 as a backwater stocked with hotheads like Preston Brooks, now an equal share of Southerners pictured the North as a hive of murderous race-traitors like John Brown. Both caricatures were clearly divorced from the complex realities of geography and regional political identity, but such was the partisan mood of the nation when Abraham Lincoln captured the White House. A relatively unknown lawyer and former congressman, Lincoln ran on a Free Soil platform as the nominee of a new party: the Republicans. He had no interest in seeing slavery take permanent root in the West. And truth be told, he had even less interest in tampering with the institution where it already existed legally. Regardless, intentional misrepresentations of his position by Southern extremists helped trigger the first wave of seceded states in the winter of 1860–61.

Before long, the situation in Charleston forced Lincoln's next move. The new commander in chief requested that each loyal state provide manpower and arms to suppress the budding rebellion. Missouri's recently elected governor, Claiborne Fox Jackson, had other ideas. Despite having run for office as a Unionist, Jackson tried, and failed, to spearhead a secession movement in Missouri in February 1861. An overwhelmingly Unionist state convention, presided over by former Missouri governor Sterling Price, thwarted the scheme. But the attempt laid the governor's hole cards face up on the table for anyone who cared to look—and quite a few people did. Enough of them, at least, that mistrust of their double-dealing chief executive spurred Missouri's Unionists, sometimes known as "Wide Awakes," to launch a preemptive operation. In March 1861, on the orders of Captain Nathaniel Lyon, Federal forces evacuated the arsenal at St. Louis to prevent it from falling into pro-Confederate hands. The move initially caught

Jackson off balance; though he eventually responded by creating his own, state-run military organization: the Missouri State Guard.[12]

By April 1861, Jackson still fancied himself Missouri's deliverer to the Southern Confederacy. When Lincoln issued his post-Sumter call to arms, Jackson blatantly refused. Taking his rebuff even a step further, he labeled the president's effort to preserve the Union by force an "unholy crusade." To avoid accusations of outright treason, Jackson openly pledged—albeit somewhat farcically given his recent actions—to keep Missouri out of the war for either side, while advising constituents to continue following Federal laws. But secretly, he and his lieutenant governor, Thomas C. Reynolds, conspired with Confederate officials, including President Jefferson Davis himself, in Richmond. They planned to pluck Missouri from the Union, whether the majority of its residents wanted to go or not.[13]

In May Union soldiers arrested members of the governor's pro-secession militia at a training camp dubbed "Camp Jackson." A riot flared up in response to the arrests and the Federals extinguished it by gunning down multiple protestors. Sensing that street violence might necessitate more concerted military action, Jackson handed command of the Missouri State Guard over to Major General Sterling Price. Price had considered himself a unionist as late as February 1861, but the bloodletting over Camp Jackson quickly converted him to the governor's cause. Even with an experienced commander in charge of Missouri's now openly pro-Confederate militia, on June 13 Lyon—himself now a brigadier general and chief of the Union army's Department of the West—swiftly occupied Jefferson City. It was a bloodless maneuver; in fact, his men didn't discharge a single shot. Regardless, the arrival of Federal troops in the capital sent Jackson and his administration scurrying into exile. Four days later, Lyon led a larger, combined force of state and Federal infantry, with support from one regiment of Federal artillery, against pro-Confederate militias gathered at Boonville. His Union troopers manhandled the secessionists, driving them from the field in a matter of minutes. Yet however brief and one-sided the skirmish might have been, it signaled that Missouri was then truly at war. Ten men lay dead. Myriad more would share their fate before conflict's end.[14]

Like many of his contemporaries in the Southern press, John had spent the months before the war filling column inch after column inch with bold talk about the mettle of Southern men and the masculine shortcomings of their would-be Yankee foes. It's not at all difficult to imagine him boasting about the results of hypothetical battles; of southern knights fending off northern conquistadors and their hordes of Bavarian mercenaries. But for all the times he shook the metaphorical hourglass to hasten a reckoning on the question of slavery, John never imagined that the result of such bravado might be an all-out war between the states. Failure to foresee this development did not mean he regretted it, however. Not for an instant.

John had grown up idolizing the immortal warriors of history and mythology. His own kinsmen had fought against overwhelming odds to win their independence in the Revolution of '76. And now, thanks in large part to the not-so-stealthy intrigues of Claiborne Jackson and Sterling Price, he was being presented with a chance to test himself by the metric of his heroes. If he compared favorably, glory awaited. For most men, the call of war was a bittersweet, if not altogether somber occasion. Any time a man marched into battle—no matter how skilled or brave a fighter he might be—there was a decent chance he would not march out again. That reality weighed heavily on most soldiers. But John wasn't most soldiers. For him, this was the *opportunity* of a lifetime. Squandering it was simply out of the question. Therefore, when the tendrils of war took hold of Missouri in June 1861, John stood ready to wield something much deadlier than ink against the Federals.

Joseph O. Shelby had no intention of remaining a bystander either. Following the Confederate debacle at Boonville, he recruited a company of cavalrymen from Lafayette County. To most observers, this seemed like the natural thing for Shelby to do. While he carried no formal military experience into the war, he *had* led raiders across the Missouri-Kansas border on numerous occasions in the 1850s. As one of Lexington's first citizens (though he technically resided in neighboring Waverly), he was far from an unknown entity to the men now entrusting life and limb to his leadership. Moreover, Shelby wasn't content in the lone capacity of captain in command. He also took on the double role of patron-quartermaster. Putting his own fortune on the line, Shelby personally covered the tab for the outfitting of his unit.

John could hardly join fast enough. Editing the *Expositor* had brought him recognition as an editorialist, but it had not overburdened his bank account with disposable cash at a time when provisioning oneself for the cavalry was anything but cheap. Nor were finances John's only obstacle to martial glory. Aside from enthusiasm and a ranging knowledge of historic battles, John brought nothing to the table in terms of training or combat experience. So he began military life as a private, but one lucky enough to have enlisted in a company subsidized and commanded by his closest friend and mentor. John reveled in the role of loyal companion. For him, going to war alongside Jo—in the mold of Lancelot and Arthur or Antony and Caesar—amounted to a dream come true.[15]

Once fully formed, Shelby's band of horsemen fell in with the pro-Confederate Missouri State Guard. Officially, they constituted Company A of Colonel John P. Bowman's regiment. Less formally, the unit was known as the Lafayette County Mounted Rifles. For various reasons, a clear rendering of John's enlistment has eluded historians—many of whom mistakenly believe he didn't join the war until after the Battle of Pea Ridge in 1862. Others avoid a date and ambiguously offer that he joined Shelby at some point during the conflict. Most of this confusion stems from the fact that John's Compiled Service Record precluded his stint in the state-level Guard and only picked up in 1862, around the time he became Shelby's flamboyant adjutant. That the biographical section of a tribute volume honoring John after his death got the dates wrong seems only to have exacerbated the misunderstanding.[16]

To Major General Sterling Price's credit, he had not been in charge at Boonville. In at least one version of the story, he came down with a conveniently timed case of dysentery that allowed him to beg off from the battle. Now, in July 1861, Price was back. He gathered new forces daily for a battle that might help the Confederacy claim Missouri once and for all. Following a short stint of garrison duty at Independence, Missouri, the Lafayette County Mounted Rifles linked up with Price's army, which by that time had swelled to several thousand. Very soon, John would "see the elephant"—in the parlance of the nineteenth century—on the outskirts of Carthage. Located in the middle of Jasper County, Missouri, it was a far cry from the site of the Punic Wars. Nonetheless, for a young man who'd grown up on the classics of ancient Rome, it would be a fitting place, at least in name, to experience battle for the first time.[17]

THE BATTLE OF Carthage only lasted for the better part of a single day. It involved diminutive armies, at least compared to the ones soon to collide along a creek called Bull Run in faraway Virginia. Yet somehow the battle managed to spawn more dispute over its outcome than an engagement many times its size, duration, or frankly, importance. On July 4, 1861, a Union force under the command of Colonel Franz Sigel completed a twenty-mile march and bivouacked southeast of Carthage. Placing the Spring River between themselves and the supposed position of the enemy, the worn-out troopers stole what little sleep they could. With the Missouri State Guard in such close proximity—Sigel and his scouts estimated that only nine miles or so separated the two armies—they would need all the energy and strength they could muster come daylight.[18]

Just after sunrise on July 5, a portion of the Missouri State Guard marched five miles into a commanding position that overlooked the point from which Sigel's men would likely emerge for battle. With Price busy overseeing a different part of the army several miles away, the now-exiled Governor Jackson was nominally in charge. "The ground upon which our army was drawn up was a high ridge of prairie, gently sloping southward, with undulations to a creek about one mile and a quarter distant," wrote General James Rains. As the odds of a fight taking place became increasingly good, General H. H. Parsons handled preparations for the infantry, and Rains took control of cavalry operations.[19]

Parsons and Rains arrayed their army of roughly four thousand effectives in a strong defensive formation. Intending to make full use of the high ground, Parsons massed infantry at the center, with support from two batteries of four guns each. Rains split his horsemen evenly between the two ends, winging the infantry's flanks with mobile cover. A sizeable force—albeit one composed of unarmed men—remained in the rear as an emergency reserve. Supervision of these troops was entrusted to Jackson. After Boonville, no one placed much stock in the governor's Napoleonic acumen; in a telling jab to that affect, John labeled Jackson's assigned position "the line of spectators."[20]

Approximately two hours after Parsons and Rains began setting up their ranks, Sigel's army crossed Coon Creek and broke from the tree line. Through his spyglass, the Union commander surveyed a large force glaring down at him from roughly a mile up the ridge. Rains immediately dispatched Joseph Shelby and his company of Lafayette Mounted Rifles to stall Sigel's advance up the hill. Riding in the equivalent of No Man's Land, John and his fellow cavalrymen dashed forward with the eyes of two armies on them. In short order they attracted the undivided attention of Sigel's guns. Rains could ill afford to lose the unit before the real fighting even began and signaled it back to the main line. Even so, the men from Lexington had accomplished their objective—buying Parsons and Rains time to finish setting the line—and won the day's first laurels in the process. As Rains put it in his after-action report, "the movement . . . was executed with a precision worthy of the parade ground."[21]

Having dealt with Shelby's horsemen, Sigel's army of about 950 well-armed men marched quickly forward. They were outnumbered four to one by an enemy that had beaten them to the high ground. But Sigel kept his wits. As a veteran of the German wars for unification—or a "Forty-Eighter," as they were known—this wasn't his first fight in the face of long odds. Nor was it the first hairy engagement for many of the German-born men in his ranks. Sigel also fully understood the value of training and experience, which his army had much of and Jackson's had very little, if any at all. He urged his men ahead. They formed a line seven hundred yards down the hill from the center of the state guard's position. At 10:00 a.m., the Union artillery—one battery of three guns and a second of four guns, each loaded with spherical case or canister—opened fire.[22]

The first thirty or forty minutes of the battle, with the exception of Shelby's sprint forward, amounted to an artillery contest. John described it as "hot and bloody," though the Union guns did significantly more damage than their counterparts. Without proper antipersonnel rounds, the state guard's artillery lobbed solid shot at Sigel's men and, for the most part, missed badly. The more accurate Union batteries concentrated their fire and managed to silence some of Parsons's guns. Then the two sides lurched forward and exchanged musket fire for nearly two hours. At one point it appeared as though the center of state guard's line had cracked under pressure, and a repeat of the embarrassment at Boonville might be unfolding. After letting loose a great, line-wide volley, "the infantry moved in double-quick time towards the enemy, and routed him completely," Sigel observed. He also testified, "[the enemy's flight] was accompanied by tremendous hurrahs of our little army."[23]

The triumph did not last long. For want of ammunition, Sigel's artillery could not support his infantry's breakthrough, and Parsons's troops launched counter-attacks against both flanks. More problematic, Rains sent Shelby and several other cavalry companies into the woods around the extreme right of Sigel's line. Their intent was not simply to flank the Union position but to scout Coon Creek for a crossing point that would allow them to envelope Sigel's army if and when it attempted to pull back toward Carthage. In real time Sigel did not know this—and believed that the horsemen were targeting his supply train, which was located three miles back from the main line. For fear of losing his baggage wagons, and without much ability to maintain his position anyway, Sigel ordered a retreat into the cover of the woods and across Coon Creek.[24]

Long-term investment in discipline paid major dividends for the Union army as it withdrew from the battlefield: Sigel's army pulled back calmly and made the tree line with minimal losses. The Confederates followed hot on their heels, even dismounting to give more effective chase through the dense timber. But their efforts ran them straight into artillery, cleverly deployed to sweep choke points along the narrow road with devastating canister fire. Under the cover of heavy guns, the fleeing Union troops crossed back over to the southern side of Coon Creek and then over to the southern side of Dry Fork Creek. At Dry Fork, they turned on the pursuing state guardsmen and made a short stand. Then, again under the aegis of a few expertly placed cannon, Sigel's men continued their orderly retreat over Ordnuff Hill, across the Spring River, through Carthage, and into the forest beyond. With darkness falling over the countryside, the Confederates called off the chase. Now able to catch its collective breath, the Missouri State Guard could pause and take stock of what it had achieved.[25]

According to Hampton L. Boon, one of the state guardsmen who saw action at Carthage, the battle was a major victory. He believed that Sigel had been in command of some three thousand men, and while he could not provide specific casualty counts for the Union army, he recalled that many of their dead had been abandoned on the field and that many wagons and prisoners had been captured. "I have felt all the mortification of a defeat and retreat at Boonville, and I have also felt all the joy and pride of seeing the enemy driven with precipitation before us," Boon described in a letter to his father with an air of redemption. "We fought from 10 o'clock A. M. until after dark, driving the enemy from every position they took," he declared. By comparison to the intense fighting at Carthage, he categorized the guard's previous loss at Boonville as "child's play" and estimated that a mere fifteen of his comrades had been killed over the course of the entire day. General James Rains, who tallied the guard's total casualties slightly higher but still miniscule at forty-four, concurred with Private Boon's assessment. With marked pride, he diagnosed the battle as a "complete rout."[26]

Unionist newspapers agreed that Carthage had been a one-sided contest; though not unexpectedly, they heralded Sigel as its great champion. Headlines from Kansas to Washington DC to New York almost uniformly proclaimed a great triumph for the Union. On July 13 the *Weekly Atchison Champion* ran the headline: "GLORIOUS VICTORY! Col. Sigel Blows 500 of the Traitors to Hell! Sigel's Loss only 8 Killed and 40 Wounded!" The next morning, the *New York Times* touted "Sigel's Brilliant Defense" and advertised full details on the "Heavy Loss of the Rebels." That same week, the *Evening Star* of Washington DC reported that Sigel's only casualties were five men killed and two wounded in the battle, while "the loss on Jackson's side was very great" and "cannot be less than from three to five hundred." "The real victory was with Colonel Sigel," the paper concluded.[27]

The bombast of northern editors didn't faze John. He'd penned too many such stories himself to let overstated headlines spoil the moment, and he declared the engagement at Carthage an unquestionable victory for pro-Confederate Missourians. Moreover, the repulse of Sigel's army came with an additional prize. According to John, it secured a crucial "outlet southward" through which Price's troops might link up with armies of the western Confederacy, particularly from Arkansas. In his version of events, the Lafayette Mounted Rifles (which included himself) rode at the front of the state guard on the morning of July 5 and singlehandedly discovered Sigel's invasion force. John made a special point of noting that once the battle commenced, "Captain Shelby sustained himself well and had the honor of receiving the first fire from Sigel's outlying dragoons."[28]

As a man frequently celebrated for his verbosity, John's thoughts on the fight at Carthage, later published in *Shelby and His Men*—his 1867 history of the war—were curiously subdued. Yet for however much they lacked in direct coverage of himself as a soldier (this was his first real brush with combat, after all), his observations revealed as much, if not more, about his convergent approaches to winning personal glory and making his worldview reality. On the one hand, preserving the social customs and hierarchy of the Old World required heroes of legendary status to lead the defense—and John genuinely believed that Jo Shelby fit the bill. On the other hand, although he desperately wanted to win glory for himself, John would never boast directly of his own exploits. Instead, he delivered epic tales of combat from the perspective of a witness-participant; in effect, he was always presumed to have been the next man over from Shelby on the skirmish line or the next horseman over from Shelby on the charge. In this way, John's hero worship of his friend turned commander served a dual purpose. In addition to gradually transforming Shelby into a knight defender of the aristocratic order, it allowed him to accrue glory for himself through osmosis. Thus, Shelby's "honor of receiving the first fire" became, at least in part, John's honor too.

For pro-Confederates in Missouri, here was a victory to balance the ledger after Boonville. More importantly, here was a victory that might help formalize relations between the state's rebel minority and the Confederate government in Richmond. Indeed, in the immediate wake of Carthage, the future seemed bright for a Confederate Missouri. Intending to capitalize on these good feelings, Shelby rushed the mounted rifles back to Lafayette County. With eyes on a colonel's insignia, Jo planned to expand his little company. If he took command of a full regiment, it would undoubtedly open new avenues of advancement for John too. However, two major impediments blocked their potential promotions: a large Federal garrison occupying Lexington and droves of Unionist home guard prowling the pikes, trails, and taverns of Lafayette County. At least for the moment, these obstacles proved insurmountable. After several days of riding around in the brush—and raising a fair share of hell with the Lexington garrison in the process—any hope of recruiting a regiment had to be temporarily abandoned.[29]

It was a missed opportunity to be sure but one beyond the realistic control of the Lafayette County Mounted Rifles. If a promotion actually waited in the wings for John, he'd have to hold out a little longer. Though as it turned out, rapidly unfolding events afforded him very little time to pine for what might have been. Shelby's company rejoined Price's army as it geared up for another collision with the Federals—and by the look of things, one far larger than Carthage. At Wilson's Creek, a dozen miles southwest of Springfield, the state guard would again clash with Franz Sigel and his Germans. Only this time when the shooting commenced, Nathaniel Lyon himself would be in personal command of the Union's Army of the West.

Under cover of darkness on the morning of August 10, 1861, a detachment of roughly nine hundred Union infantrymen, a cavalry escort of two companies, and a single battery of six guns under Sigel's command moved into position. There, behind one of the main Confederate camps along Wilson's Creek, they waited for a signal from Lyon to attack. With a separate force of 4,200 men, Lyon confronted the combined forces of Sterling Price (with 7,000 Missouri

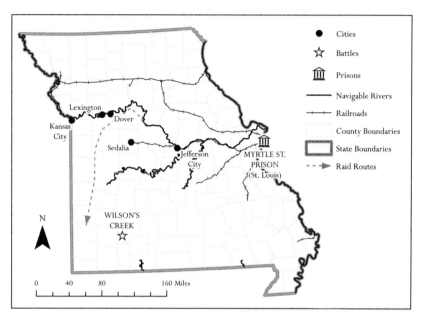

Map 1. Universal Map Key

State Guardsmen) and Brigadier General Benjamin McCulloch (with another 5,000 regular Confederate and state troops combined from Arkansas, Texas, and Louisiana) just after sunrise. Owing to a storm the previous evening, Price's subordinates had arranged no pickets. This lapse in defensive protocol allowed Lyon's army to march unde-tected and unimpeded into artillery range. His batteries, managed by Captain James Totten, quickly unlimbered and began hurling a deadly mixture of canister and solid shot at approximately nine o'clock. Caught almost entirely off guard, Price's and McCulloch's men scrambled to line up for the impending assault.[30]

The echo of Lyon's artillery also served as the signal for Sigel to begin his own attack. With the element of surprise in their favor, he and Lyon had schemed to catch the much larger but less experienced Confederate army between the crushing blades of a pincer. In splitting his army before a numerically superior force, Lyon took a momentous risk, but Sigel was all for it. The plan went brilliantly in its opening moments. Lyon's men took up an imposing position along the upper-most ridgeline of Oak Hill. Sigel's men surged forward. They swept

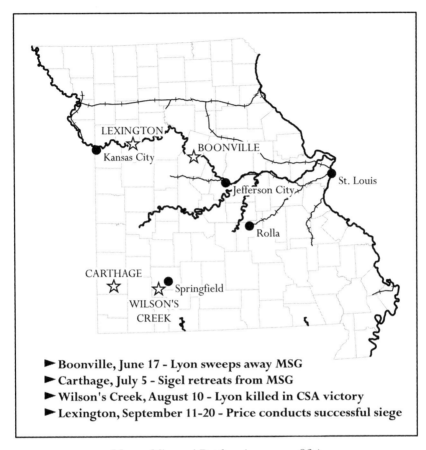

▶ **Boonville, June 17 - Lyon sweeps away MSG**
▶ **Carthage, July 5 - Sigel retreats from MSG**
▶ **Wilson's Creek, August 10 - Lyon killed in CSA victory**
▶ **Lexington, September 11-20 - Price conducts successful siege**

Map 2. Missouri Battles, (summer 1861)

into and through the camp of the First Arkansas and Third Texas. Then, by not readying for a counterattack or better preparing to cut off Confederates retreating from Lyon, they wasted precious time. As Major Samuel Sturgis later reported, "instead of standing to their guns or pursuing the enemy, [Sigel's men] turned their attention to plunder." Before long, a mass of gray-uniformed men bore down on Sigel's command. His infantrymen held fire, though, believing that the First Iowa—a Union regiment known for wearing gray—had come to reinforce them. They were wrong. The Third Louisiana spearheaded a ferocious Confederate counterassault, and what Sigel called the "unfortunate event" amounted to nothing short of catastrophe. Overrun by the Confederates, the Union line broke and ran, artillery abandoned, and all semblance of order lost. According to Sigel, his terrified troops resorted to "throwing themselves into the bushes and by-roads." Not to be outdone by his men, Sigel hightailed it more than twelve miles, all the way back to Springfield. Not once did he think to send word of his drubbing to Lyon.[31]

Meanwhile, Lyon's force remained atop the hill. Price had managed to rally his scattered command and ordered two successive frontal assaults against the Union position. As part of the initial counterattack, Price sent Rains's cavalry along with Cawthorn's mounted brigade against the left-center of the Union line while another mass of horsemen, the Kansas-Texas Mounted Regiment, charged Lyon's right flank. Some later observers of the battle have conflated these two cavalry operations, placing Shelby on the larger and seemingly more important flanking maneuver. In reality, they were part of the same overall counterattack but prosecuted by separate units against separate objectives along the Federal line. In both cases, however, concentrated downhill infantry fire and a barrage of close-range canister from Union field guns sent the horsemen thundering back from whence they'd come.[32]

After each headlong attack, Lyon's army held. But it was running dangerously low on lead, and Lyon himself had twice been wounded, once in the leg and once in the head. Following the abysmal maneuvers of his own cavalry forces, Price dismounted the rest of Weightman's mixed brigade (which included Shelby's mounted rifles) and sent them with the infantry on a third—and as it turned out, final—push against the ridgeline. Still heavily outnumbered, the Union men from Missouri, Kansas, and Iowa maintained their grip on the high ground. But they paid a heavy price: amidst the final Confederate attack, Lyon fell to the earth—dead—a ball through his heart.[33]

Overall command of the Army of the West passed to Samuel D. Sturgis. Lacking a proper report but assuming that Sigel's front had collapsed and unsure that his men could hold the hill against another infantry charge without Lyon to direct them and with cartridge boxes almost empty, Sturgis ordered a general withdrawal from Wilson's Creek. Despite repelling several major assaults and having doggedly defended their ground, under constant fire, for more than six hours, Union troops conceded the field to Price. They hastened first to Springfield and then on to the relative safety of Rolla, Missouri. The Confederates chose not to give chase as they had at Carthage.[34]

Given the circumstances of the fighting at Wilson's Creek, it isn't altogether unusual that both sides claimed victory. The dual Confederate and state guard force, which suffered greater counts of dead and wounded, had withstood the surprise of Lyon's and Sigel's initial pincer attack. Better still, they owned the field itself as the last echoes of cannon and musketry faded to silence. In the nineteenth century, final possession of the contested ground constituted a key—albeit simplistic—indicator of victory. Basic or not, it was more than good enough for a relieved Sterling Price. He proclaimed that "the brilliant victory thus achieved upon this hard-fought field was won only by the most determined bravery and distinguished gallantry of the combined armies."[35]

For its part, the Union army had only abandoned its position after withstanding several assaults executed by a much larger force. Even taking Sigel's epic blunder into account, that fact could not be changed. According to Major General John C. Fremont, Lyon's immediate superior, Lyon's men had been "opposed by overwhelming masses of the enemy, [but] the successes of our troops were nevertheless sufficiently marked to give to their exploits the moral effect of a victory."[36]

As we might expect, John took immediate issue with the Union's attempt to concoct a moral victory from technical defeat on the battlefield. "Perhaps no battle ever gained by the Confederates," he complained, "has been so universally distorted and claimed as a Federal victory." Then he set about explaining why the day really belonged to the armies of Price and McCulloch. True, John confessed, Lyon's men *had* been greatly outnumbered. "Yet half of Price's men were without guns," he countered. And due to the unforeseen attack unleashed on his unwitting men, McCulloch's numerical advantage had been "more than neutralized by the confusion and terror such maneuvers almost always inspire." In John's mind, Sigel's disgraceful performance—reminiscent of the Union's mortifying exodus from

Bull Run a month earlier—tainted Lyon's entire army and cancelled out his heroic stand. "The 3d Louisiana swept him [Sigel] away from the rear almost without a struggle, took his battery, and scattered his German mercenaries" John wrote in *Shelby and His Men*. With Sigel's command devastated and Lyon dead, "retreat was the only salvation" for the Federals. In other words, it might not have been a knockout, or even technically sound, but as Sturgis had yielded in defeat, it was a clear win nonetheless.[37]

Far more striking than his defense of Confederate credentials was the utter shock to John's system wrought by an engagement significantly larger and exponentially deadlier than Carthage. "For six hours the battle raged furiously, and though the slaughter was great, neither army had gained sufficient advantage to confide in victory," he recorded. So much destruction—and still the issue had remained in doubt until the very last moment. All told, nearly three-hundred Confederates perished and almost another thousand fell wounded. But the numbers alone didn't account for the trauma of Wilson's Creek. Just as important as how many was the manner in which they died. "The carnage on this bloody hill was dreadful," John recalled. "Regiments and brigades, without seemingly having any leaders or organization, yet marched up to it to be cut down, to be repulsed, yet straight and determined they returned again and again to its assault."[38]

Repeatedly, John's comrades had launched charges up that hill, straight into the teeth of Lyon's army. Canister maimed and decapitated victims at brutally close range. Infantry volleys proved just as deadly. Generally ranging from .54 to .69 caliber, Civil War musket and minié balls were very large, relatively slow-moving projectiles. Rather than clipping or punching through cleanly, they tended to mangle flesh and splinter bone. These globs of hot lead also tended to shatter inside men, making extraction impossible. Other times, they ricocheted internally, from bone to bone, destroying guts, organs, and innards with each bounce. Artillery explosions threw men down in contorted heaps, eyes burned and ears ringing, some dead, others wishing to be. And there was blood. Everywhere. One simply could not escape from it on a nineteenth-century battlefield. On clothes, on grass, on rocks, on guns, on animals, pooling in the dirt, clotted in hair and beards, sprayed in eyes, oozing from mouths, caked and crusted in makeshift bandages, pumping from mashed-in skulls, severed arteries, and dismembered limbs.

And if the man-made carnage had not been sufficiently brutal, the sun seemed to be waging its own war against *both* armies on that August day. "Extreme heat," John lamented, turned "many slight wounds unavoidably fatal." This combination of sanguine scenes and soaring temperatures made Wilson's Creek a hellscape for the untested masses of the Missouri State Guard.[39]

For the first time in his life, John saw the true cost of war—not on the printed page but with his own eyes. Everything he thought he knew about being a warrior—about winning glory, about being a man, about dying a hero's death—went up in the smoke of ten thousand muskets. He'd learned things about the limits of the human body that could not come from books. Nor could he ever look at his books the same way again. The Greek siege of Troy, the corpses and carcasses stacked high at Thermopylae, Alexander's defeat of the Persians at Gaugamela, Roman soldiers crushing the Jewish Revolt at Jerusalem, even the fictional fall of Camelot: all these stories, and countless others from John's boyhood, became more real in an instant. Yet they didn't discourage his soldierly will or prompt disillusion in the usefulness of war for achieving his goals. No, this deeper connection to his idols and their warrior guild only bolstered John's resolve to keep fighting.

It was a testament to the destructiveness of the battle that even a combatant so zealous as John struggled to make complete sense of the traumas he experienced. His words betrayed simultaneous feelings of horror, awe, and admiration. He saw the apex of masculine glory in a good, combat-related death. John meant it as a compliment when he said that his brigade commander, Colonel Richard Weightman, fell while personally leading his unit on a charge "with a recklessness which cost him his life." Likewise, he appreciated the bravery of his enemy.[40]

Nonetheless, in spite of the rank and file's valor, all was not well in John's assessment of his own army. The Missouri State Guard lacked food. It lacked uniforms and basic supplies. It never seemed to possess adequate quantities of lead or powder. And after months of conflict, many of its men still lacked the most basic mark of a citizen soldier: a government issued longarm. "Entire companies without one single gun of any kind among them, marched boldly to the front," John reported. There, these unarmed men "stood to be shot at until the Federal lines were driven back, that they might, in this manner, obtain muskets." Outwardly, John praised the "heroic fortitude" of the enlisted men. Yet internally, if we read deeper into his account, his words evinced serious frustration with the commanders who had first allowed the army to be ambushed and then had employed it as a blunt object throughout the day.[41]

These failures help to explain why John, usually willing to stretch every possible millimeter out of the truth on Shelby's behalf, declined to single out the activities of his commander—or even their specific unit's resume at Wilson's Creek in *Shelby and His Men*. The Mounted Rifles took part in the cavalry's calamitous charge against Bloody Hill, while the Kansas-Texas mounted regiment struck simultaneously on the other end of the line. Captain James Totten, the chief Union artillerist in Lyon's army, was not impressed. "Their cavalry," Totten sneered, "is utterly worthless on the battle-field." Given the result of the maneuver, John had little choice but to swallow such criticism and move on.[42]

That reality did not stop Ben McCulloch from using the battle as a springboard for Confederate propaganda and recruitment. On August 15, less than a week after the fight, he unveiled a proclamation addressed to the people of Missouri. "You have been overrun and trampled upon by the mercenary hordes of the North," he began, before claiming a "great and signal victory" against those "hordes" at Wilson's Creek. Now he expected action: "Missouri must now take her position, be it North or South." McCulloch would live just long enough for the Union army to deliver him an answer.[43]

In the meantime, Price and his army had free rein over southwestern Missouri. Once his men finished tending the dead, scavenging much needed weapons, and recuperating both mentally and physically, the next order of business involved wresting the most significant river port between Kansas City and St. Louis out of Union hands. That mission suited John just fine. The next time he, Jo, and the mounted rifles risked their last full measure for "home and hearth," it would not be in a figurative sense. The Confederate victory at Wilson's Creek had thrown open the path northward for Price's army, and the fight to liberate Lexington from Federal occupation was on.

Part 2: The Siege of Lexington and Van Dorn's Defeat

As it turned out, the Battle of Lexington wasn't actually a battle—or at least not one waged on the terms familiar to most casual observers of the war. Unlike a set-piece affair, in which two armies maneuvered around a tract of ground and then locked horns to capture it, Lexington had more in common with the sieges of Yorktown or Sevastopol. The first units of Price's army reached the outskirts of the city after nightfall on September 11. Their arrival did not take anyone in the Union army by surprise, least of all Colonel James Mulligan, the man tasked with leading a federal garrison of roughly three thousand effectives against Price's eventual mass of fifteen thousand men. Almost since the moment fighting at Wilson's Creek halted, intelligence reports had warned that the State Guard would move to retake the vital port and commercial center.[44]

What Mulligan lacked in manpower, he partially mitigated with a complex system of defensive works. Though they couldn't hope to hold the majority of Lexington, his men occupied a fortress built around the Masonic College on the north end of the city. And as Price's vanguard approached, Mulligan dispatched skirmishers to stall for time: the garrison was nearly done with the construction of additional earthworks on the west and north sides of the fortress and along the marble college building itself. Price took steps to ensure that Union reinforcements would not reach Mulligan in time to break a siege—and he knew that the garrison, however snug in its works, had increasingly limited access to fresh water. So he waited. He allowed his force to concentrate. As each new wave of men arrived, he gradually enveloped the city.[45]

Over the next few days, sporadic fighting broke out, the hottest at the Oliver Anderson House—the home of the father of John's former employer at the *Expositor*—which was then being used as a

Union hospital. The Confederates seized the three-story mansion and used its vantage to snipe at men inside the Federal defenses. Yet even as the situation grew bleaker for Mulligan's men—they (and their mounts) were desperately thirsty, they had conceded all of the city save for their stronghold at the college, and a relief expedition clearly wasn't going to reach them in time—he refused to wave the white flag. His determination to fight it out, to the last man if need be, forced Price to consider the same sort of deadly frontal assault that Sturgis had rescued him from at Wilson's Creek. Then, on September 19, a tactical epiphany—brilliant for its sheer simplicity—changed everything about the siege.[46]

On September 19, with Price's approval, the Missouri State Guard rolled dozens of hemp bales into position near the Anderson House and then doused them with river water. The next day, as Confederate shell and grape rained down on Mulligan's men, the bales started forward. The dense bundles of fiber were impervious to musketry. Even direct hits with heated shot from Union cannons had no discernible effect; they were simply too wet to burn. Price's men essentially became invulnerable behind their rolling fortifications. Moreover, because Price had taken the time to completely surround their position before investing in the attack, the Federals had no avenue of retreat. The formidable trenches and breastworks Mulligan's men had rushed to finish were rendered more or less useless by the hemp bales.[47]

It is little wonder then that Price later took credit for the idea, though his claim was unquestionably false, and no one appears to have taken it seriously at the time. Anyhow, in the moment, it wasn't the inventor but the *invention* that concerned Mulligan's depleted command. Because regardless of who'd devised it, the bulletproof wall of foliage snaked closer and closer, making the Union situation more and more desperate. Eventually, it rolled so near to the Union works that Price could leverage his overwhelming numerical advantage, storm the college grounds, and wipe out what remained of its defenders. Mulligan grasped his predicament fully—and fortunately for his men, did not waste their lives with any doomed heroics.[48]

The Union garrison at Lexington surrendered on September 20. Frank Wilkie, an embedded correspondent for the *New York Times* whom Price had briefly captured, described the results of the siege on the city:

> The first thing perceptible is the horrid odor of rotting flesh, whose origin became apparent as I pushed through the crowd and reached the seminary. In this building were some sixty or seventy wounded, dirty, bleeding wretched, groaning in agony, covered with flies, dirt and filthiness, and disgusting in every respect to the last degree.

Before this grotesque backdrop, and many similar others, the stunned Federals forfeited their rifles—three thousand of them—and whatever horses hadn't been mangled by shell or died of thirst. Then they signed paroles. All save for the colonel himself, that is. As a Federal officer, Mulligan flatly refused to recognize that Price, as commander of the Missouri State Guard, had any authority whatsoever to legally take prisoners or issue paroles. Already known for his affability, Price apparently enjoyed Mulligan's defiant performance; he eventually sent the Union colonel and his wife safely back to Federal lines.[49]

On September 23, Fremont wired the War Department in Washington: "Lexington has fallen into Price's hand, . . . I am taking the field myself and hope to destroy the enemy either before or after the junction of forces under McCulloch." It was too little, too late from the Pathfinder; responsibility for failing to reinforce Mulligan ultimately rested with him. That same day, General Winfield Scott cabled back, "The President is glad you are hastening to the scene of action. His words are, 'He expects you to repair the disaster at Lexington without loss of time.'" The *disaster*. Unlike after Carthage and Wilson's Creek, there would be no spinning of moral victories, no orderly retreats dressed up with silver lining, no congratulatory orders read throughout the army.[50]

Lexington constituted Price's greatest victory as commander of the Missouri State Guard—and arguably his greatest victory as commander of anything. "The visible fruits of this almost bloodless victory are very great," he assessed. By his reckoning, the haul included "about 3,500 prisoners . . . 5 pieces of artillery and 2 mortars, over 3,000 stands of infantry arms, a large number of sabers, about 750 horses, many sets of cavalry equipments [sic], wagons, teams, and ammunition, more than $100,000 worth of commissary stores, and a large amount of other property." If Price's report reads with a hint of giddiness, it wasn't without reason: his men had just pillaged more supplies from Mulligan's garrison than it had received from its own government in months.[51]

While the hemp bales rolled toward Mulligan's befuddled troopers, Shelby and his mounted rifles had remained on the periphery of the city. But in the case of Lexington, the periphery had actually been one of the most important sectors of the operation. Given his numerical advantage, Price would eventually break Mulligan's defenses in an uninterrupted siege. So everything about the campaign hinged on the ability of Federal forces to break the Confederate's stranglehold on Lexington. Shelby's company detached from the main body of Price's army and crossed the Missouri River. There, with other cavalry units, John and the rest helped screen against relief expeditions and policed the water for any signs of a riverine rescue operation.[52]

John lacked a formal military education, but even he understood from the outset that the grounds of a siege were no place for mounted men or headlong charges. "Indeed, it was a battle for sharpshooters—a regular Donnybrook fair of a thing," he wrote. Then John made what would seem to be a puzzling remark considering the importance of victory at Lexington to the Confederate cause in Missouri—and especially puzzling coming from a man as renowned for hyperbole as John: "No brilliant fighting was necessary, and none was, therefore, attempted." It's difficult to decode precisely what message John intended these words to freight. Was he simply being realistic—and showing uncharacteristic restraint—in his coverage of the siege? Was he self-conscious of the fact this his unit had taken no part in devising or implementing the famous hemp wall and therefore sought to minimize its ingenuity? Or was he taking yet another veiled shot at the abilities of his commanding general? We'll never know for sure, but a mixture of all three seems most probable.[53]

Of greatest note is how John took the opportunity to lay the foundation for a comparative framework that informed his entire coverage of the war: Jo Shelby's men vs. the rest of the western armies. As the size of Shelby's command grew, so would the division between the two subjects. At Lexington, John pronounced Shelby "distinguished for his untiring energy and intelligence during the investment." Likewise, he reported that the Lafayette Mounted Rifles had, under Shelby's leadership, "furnished General Price with valuable information in regard to the movements of various detachments marching to the relief of Lexington." These were carefully chosen words. Shelby, a mere captain of volunteers, came off as indispensable to the overall mission. He took initiative. He wasn't afraid to make decisions and stand by the outcomes. He was bold, but not free with the lives of his men. Meanwhile, the horsemen under his command performed with skill and efficiency seemingly beyond their limited terms of service. They rode and scouted and fought as if they'd been *born* to defend traditional Southern society from the saddle. Which, of course, was precisely what John believed.[54]

Then came the second half of the comparison. John described the majority of Price's command at Lexington as "a mob." For this undersupplied, ill-equipped mishmash of men, he wrote, "the war was too young" and "the personal consequences too remote" for total investiture in the cause. Put another way, they meant well, and they were brave enough, but they lacked the innate qualities that made Shelby and his company elite. This was not merely hindsight at work, either; a mechanism for displacing blame for defeat to other men. John genuinely held that men of certain, superior stock were fit to ascend the ladders of society. Only *they* could preserve the old order of things. And Shelby's company brimmed with such characters. Indeed, even at this early stage in the war, his writing hinted that the "royals" of Lafayette County—and their faithful warrior-bard (himself)—had far greater glories awaiting them in the future than victories led by Price and made possible by rolling barriers of vegetation.[55]

This explains, at least in part, John's dismissiveness of the origins of the hemp-bale idea and his increasingly passive-aggressive coverage of Price as a commander. Concerning the former, he wrote that "Colonel Thomas Hinkle, of Wellington, claimed the hemp-bale idea, and whoever originated it certainly had a clear, mathematical head." In other words, the tactic had been a means to an end, but not particularly dignified, and John simply didn't care enough to make a final determination. Concerning the latter, after Lexington it becomes somewhat clearer that John did not begrudge Price because he favored the enlisted man—just the opposite, in fact. John simply did not consider Price to be part of the group—the "royals" of the South—that he believed should reign in the new, aristocrat-ruled kingdom established by overall Confederate victory. Before any of those visions of grandeur might become reality, however, they had to escape with the rest of Price's army to Arkansas.[56]

General John C. Fremont attempted to make good on his promise to the president. A massive Union army under his command lurched out of St. Louis with the objective of cutting Price off from McCulloch. In effect, the two armies would race to the Arkansas border. If Price didn't get there first, his army ran the risk of being isolated, enveloped, and destroyed. Now, as John put it, "the non co-operative policy under which McCulloch acted" in refusing to join Price at Lexington "was now plainly seen in all of its unfortunate bearings." According to John's account of the rapid retreat, Shelby "led the van of the army, and, by his activity and energy, kept General Price duly informed of all movements of the enemy necessary to be known." Eventually, Fremont gave up the chase. He pulled his force back to St. Louis to wait out the cold. In turn, he allowed Price to set up winter quarters at Springfield, from whence he reorganized his army, issued a call for fifty thousand volunteers, and sent recruiting officers to every corner of the state possible.[57]

Meanwhile, while Price regrouped, Claiborne Jackson called together a rump legislature at Neosho, Missouri. Under the exiled governor's watchful eye, the group passed an ordinance of secession on behalf of the entire state. On its face, the proclamation seemed to be a futile gesture. Federal forces occupied much of Missouri and weren't likely to abandon their positions simply because a disgraced executive and a handful of secessionist legislators claimed the state had exited the Union. Just below the surface, though, the proclamation raised the stakes of future fighting in Missouri: the Confederacy now had an official reason to invest military resources in defense of territory it believed itself to own and now any major Union blunder might appear to affirm the voting at Neosho.[58]

For this reason, when the first blooms of spring appeared in 1862, both armies felt heightened pressure to win. In March, Fremont's army, under the direction of Major General Samuel Curtis (not to be confused with Samuel Sturgis) and Sigel, drove straight toward Price's headquarters at Springfield. The move sent Price hurtling toward McCulloch in Arkansas. It also set up a momentous showdown in the extreme northwestern corner of the state at a place called Pea Ridge.[59]

THE FIGHTING AT Pea Ridge unfolded over the course of two, snow-filled days, early in the spring of 1862. As with nearly all multiday battles, a cause-and-effect relationship between the first and second days is not difficult to establish after the fact. Indeed, when observed through the powerful optics of hindsight, the opening bouts of March 7 unquestionably set the stage for the engagement's seemingly inevitable conclusion on March 8. Yet for the Confederate rank and file at Pea Ridge—nearly sixteen thousand of them—the emotions and expectations engendered partway through the first day told a radically, if not entirely, different story than those of the second. As it were, by battle's end the events of those two days might as well have been separated by a century.[60]

As another major clash of men and steel loomed, General Samuel Curtis kept the War Department apprised of his movements but came off as less than assertive on the eve of battle. In fairness, he had much to worry about. Tracking Price to the Arkansas border had significantly stretched the Union supply line. Moreover, the coming fight would mark his—and his army's—first venture in truly Confederate territory. These items in mind, Curtis's last prebattle cable to Washington predicted little and guaranteed nothing; it read simply, "We will give them the best show we can."[61]

Confederate general Earl Van Dorn felt quite differently on March 6. As a graduate of West Point, a seasoned Indian fighter, and a combat veteran of the Mexican War, he exuded confidence in his own abilities. Given his new assignment, the Confederate War Department appeared to share that aplomb. Richmond had dispatched Van Dorn to oversee Price's and McCulloch's joint defense of Arkansas. Thereby, his arrival on the scene pulled both generals under the umbrella of a newly created Confederate Army of the West. Van Dorn could hardly wait to throw this creation into action.[62]

In spite of a late-season blizzard and food shortages, he launched an aggressive, complicated, dual-flanking operation against Curtis's smaller—yet well-entrenched, more amply provisioned, and better rested—Army of the Southwest, then numbering some ten thousand men. Price and his division of Missourians would march to a position north of the Elkhorn Tavern and hit Curtis's left, while Van Dorn tasked a hodgepodge of Texans, Louisianans, Arkansans, and Indians under McCulloch's command with approaching from the South. From there they would strike the Union right. Though starting miles apart, the two wings would ideally reconnect in the process of enveloping and annihilating the enemy.[63]

Good as the plan might have sounded at a staff meeting, with maps laid out and cigars in hand, Van Dorn was rolling the dice and he knew it; for if Price and McCulloch failed to link up, the Confederates' numerical advantage over Curtis would be squandered. Despite the risks, much as Lyon's had at Wilson's Creek, the operation *appeared* to be running smoothly in its opening hours. But as John, Shelby, and the rest of the Missourians under Price soon learned, first appearances could be especially deceiving when shrouded in the fog of war.

On the morning of March 7, Price's troops put Colonel Eugene Carr and his division of Midwesterners back on their heels. Much to Curtis's dismay, the Confederates captured—severe casualties notwithstanding—significant ground on the northern front of Pea Ridge. As the sun set and the guns went temporarily silent, John must have been elated by the day's events. This must have seemed like the battle that could—and would—turn the tide of war in the Border West in favor of the Confederacy. So he, Shelby, and the rest of the Missourians reveled in their success. And perhaps more importantly, they assumed more of the same come morning. Little did they know, however, just how poorly McCulloch's division had fared a few miles to the south.[64]

With Texans leading Louisianans, Arkansans, and Indians, McCulloch's assault did not fail for lack of resolve; the Confederates south of Elkhorn Tavern mounted a formidable attack against the Union divisions of Peter Osterhaus and Colonel Jefferson C. Davis. Osterhaus technically answered to Sigel, but minus the general's immediate presence on the field, Osterhaus operated more or less independently. For his part, Davis headed an independent division from the start, his orders coming straight from Curtis. Regardless of who ranked whom, together their men from Missouri, Illinois, and Indiana held the line. More problematic still for the Confederates, amidst the hail of afternoon volleys a round cut McCulloch down. He died instantly on the field. In his place thirty-three-year-old James McIntosh, a brigadier, took command and attempted to rally the division. In the process of doing so, he too found himself on the wrong end of a Union sharpshooter's rifle-musket. He fell roughly fifteen minutes after McCulloch. Now with two commanders slain in what seemed like a moment's time, the southern jaw of Van Dorn's would-be vise fell first into disillusion and then into disarray. It never made contact with Price.

March 8 began with a massive artillery barrage led by the recently disgraced Brigadier General Franz Sigel. Curtis had managed to consolidate his forces under Carr, Davis, and Osterhaus, and then bolstered them with Sigel's relatively fresh troops. Together they pushed Price and his Missourians back across all the territory they'd fought so hard to seize the day before. Sigel led the infantry charge himself, calling it a "delightful moment" when "the enemy was routed and fled in terror and confusion in all directions." His gallantry prompted a commendation from Curtis and, in the eyes of many, restored a measure of the honor he'd lost at Wilson's Creek.[65]

For the Confederates, or at least their commanders, the morning's reversal was not entirely unexpected. Overnight Van Dorn had learned of McCulloch and McIntosh. Even he, in spite of his prebattle bluster, understood that the only remaining course of action involved *escaping from* the Battle of Pea Ridge, not winning it. He informed Price of the change in plans; also of the crucial role Price's men would play in the army's survival. Thus, the Missourians awoke to news that they *would* fight. However, instead of driving Curtis from the field, they would attack to buy time for McCulloch's division to limp away safely. General James Rains, John's divisional commander, recalled, "The movement was reluctantly obeyed by the whole of the command . . . [and] for the first time I realized the fact—the fight was over." "The victory within our grasp," he lamented, "was lost."[66]

Much as they'd done in the retreat from Wilson's Creek, Shelby and his company of Lafayette County cavalrymen distinguished themselves. According to Rains, "Captain Shelby acted with his well-drilled company during the day with Colonel Gates, on the extreme left, where he was much exposed and did efficient service." Late on the second day of the battle, to ensure that the army might escape, John and the rest of the unit tied their mounts and charged along with the infantry of Lieutenant Colonel John Bowman. Their efforts were successful: Van Dorn's army managed to evacuate itself from Pea Ridge, relatively intact.[67]

As we might expect, the newspaperman in John couldn't resist wading into the maelstrom generated by the defeat. He'd come to the service with no prior martial experience—but this was *precisely* what he knew how to do best. As Sterling Price knew all too well, John wasn't one to spare the high command from criticism; it would be no different for Earl Van Dorn.

John charged the defeated Major General with enacting a plan ill matched to the size and operational capabilities of his army. "General Van Dorn divided his army into two divisions," John wrote, "and embracing an extensive field of operations, lost much of that unity and compactness so essentially necessary in the operations of small armies." Or in other words, Van Dorn had been so excited to throw his new army into combat using the most complicated maneuverings possible, he hadn't truly considered what would happen if things went awry. And when things did go awry—as they were liable to do in the nineteenth century when commanders got too "fancy" with their tactics—John suggested that Van Dorn "had deprived the division separated from the commander of much of his personal supervision and direction" and "left much to chance which could have been overcome by his personal attention." In short, Van Dorn failed twice.

First with the initial plan and second to adapt when the plan went haywire. And in both instances, the Missourians had absorbed many of the consequences. [68]

In direct contrast to the inept Van Dorn, John continued to construct the base layers of an Arthurian narrative centered on his own unit; Jo Shelby the natural warrior-leader, riding before a unit of modern-day knights. By John's reckoning, the men of Lafayette County had, once again, dashed forward to save the army from complete ruination during the retreat. And in leading them under such trying circumstances, Shelby's star shined brighter than ever. "Here Captain Shelby particularly distinguished himself," John opined. "Exposed to heavy fire, he maneuvered with admirable precision, and by a rapid attack upon the head of a cavalry regiment, succeeded in preventing the cutting off and capture of one of Price's infantry battalions which had remained, without orders, long after the army withdrew."[69]

In John's account of the ordeal, Shelby didn't just physically protect the army by maintaining the extreme rear and repulsing "frequent dashes of the Federal cavalry"; he also set a lofty example for the bedraggled men. "Throughout all the dreary march," John concluded, "Captain Shelby maintained the high discipline of his company, and from the rear brought up every straggler and broken artillery conveyance."[70]

As much as John took the opportunity of a loss at Pea Ridge to heap praise upon Shelby and the Mounted Rifles, in the matter of battlefield atrocities, he came down decidedly *against* his own army. He offered nothing on the subject of German troops under Sigel's command who were accused of gunning down Confederate soldiers as they attempted to surrender. Synchronously, he had much to say about the Indians who marched into battle under Van Dorn's command. According to John, the Indian troops—who technically belonged to brigadier general and Confederate Indian agent Albert Pike— "scattered beyond all concentration" after a number of well-placed shots from Sigel's field artillery. For this he deemed them "a great source of weakness" to the Confederate army. Then John betrayed his own racist proclivities.[71]

More than just inept soldiers, he deemed them deficient as men. "The Indians," he derided, "were wholly unfit for any warfare on earth, except massacre and plunder." Put another way, they were savages. Given the extent to which John would later sympathize with and even mythologize Missouri bushwhackers—men not unfamiliar with the mutilation of felled foes—it becomes apparent that when defining an atrocity, the color of one's skin mattered a great deal. And the Germans, foreign as they might have sounded, were still white. By virtue of their race, John appears to have afforded them the benefit of the doubt and assumed they fought like real (white) men.[72]

FOLLOWING THE DEBACLE at Pea Ridge, a significant portion of Sterling Price's army gave way to the wind, while a small but devoted following returned to Missouri with the general to regroup. Shelby had plans of his own. He too journeyed back to Missouri, with John and the men of Lafayette County at this side. But it wasn't to help reorganize Price's broken command—it was to build one of his own. The time was right, or at least so Shelby believed, to revisit the colonel's insignia that had eluded him after Carthage. To John, three stars on Jo's epaulets might mean a promotion to adjutant and regular opportunities to wield his pen in a more official capacity. As they rode home from Pea Ridge, it must have occurred to John that the mounted rifles had entered the forge of western war in 1861 and emerged in 1862 as iron.

A Brigade of Iron

An air of hardness hung over Jo Shelby's company as it rode into Dover. The unit's demeanor was a combination of weariness and determination, shot through with the stark realization that after seeing what they'd seen and after doing what they'd done at Wilson's Creek, a man could come home, but he could never really *come home.* They were pleased, no doubt, to be back in Lafayette County, among kin and creature comforts. Nevertheless, with Federal troops prowling the area, this was by no means a social call.

The column halted alongside the gardens of a large, two-story brick mansion. Completed by slave labor in the 1850s, it was the residence of the Virginia-born Judge James Shelby Plattenburg Sr.; his wife, Laura; and their children, ages ranging from five to nineteen.[1]

In addition to his seat on the bench, Judge Plattenburg was a major landholder in and around Dover. He owned many slaves and oversaw a prosperous mercantile operation. Occasionally, he even ran the post office. He was just the kind of local dignitary Shelby wanted to bless his mission to transform the company into a regiment and, in turn, his captaincy into a colonelcy. As Shelby's star rose, John's status within the Confederate army would also rise, minus the length of a coattail. But perhaps more striking to him in the moment, the Plattenburg home is probably where John laid eyes on the Judge's fourteen-year-old daughter Mary Virginia for the first time.[2]

It's impossible to know if John fell in love instantly, as did so many of his literary heroes, or if Mary—called Jennie by friends and family—would have been in any position to recognize, let alone return, the affections of a combat soldier ten years her senior. In fact, we can't even confirm that the duo exchanged a single word. What can be said with absolute certainty, however, is that Jennie's devotion to John eventually became so great that she would defy her father's objection to their incestuous marriage. (As it turned out, John's paternal aunt, Mary Murray Edwards, was also Jennie's maternal grandmother; the arrangement made John and Jennie first cousins, once removed.)[3]

That was all very far in the future, though, on August 18, 1862, when two of Jennie's brothers—Harvey and John Quincy—joined the new regiment. Their mother, sister, and other local girls made a grand, swooning show of the occasion. They cheered Shelby's men and showered them in acclamations in the form of handsewn flags, lavish bouquets, even flower petals strewn about their boots. Not uncharacteristically, John basked in the high theater of the scene. He took special pleasure in noting that weeping mothers "held up their children to see the goodly sight," while "fathers presented their half grown sons and bade them join the ranks of one who had marched so far and dared so much." So for a moment—a single, fleeting, illusive moment—the men forgot about forlorn charges and mangled limbs or dying in macabre, lonely ways. Then reality retightened its grip. Much work remained. The regiment would not recruit itself.[4]

AS JOHN TOLD it, onlookers were overcome by the historic magnitude of Shelby's purpose. Yet to imply as John did that the *real* Confederate careers of Shelby, himself, or the rest of the men were launched amid celebration in the Plattenburg Garden is only half correct. Technically, or at least as far as recordkeepers in Richmond might be concerned, the Lafayette County Mounted Rifles had transferred into Confederate service at Duvall's Bluff, Arkansas, on July 1, 1862. After that, with orders in hand to secure the remainder of a regiment numbering roughly one thousand men from the counties of Western Missouri, it took Shelby's company weeks to complete the trek back to Dover.[5]

Under the weight of more scrupulous examination, the festivities that awaited them in Dover also lose a measure or two of spontaneity. Because in addition to Harvey and John Quincy, a third Plattenburg brother, James, had already enlisted in Arkansas almost two months earlier. It was no coincidence, then, that Shelby called a halt at the judge's home. And when John portrayed "three manly, fair-haired boys . . . waiting for a mother's kiss and a father's farewell" as if war had snuck up on the unsuspecting family, he tipped one of his signature traits as a narrator. He wasn't being intentionally dishonest, not in a malicious sense, anyway. He just wouldn't allow a seemingly insignificant kernel of truth—otherwise known as context—to spoil the story.[6]

That same week in August 1862, John's method of storytelling became particularly important. Undoubtedly owing to their personal relationship, Shelby promoted John to First Lieutenant (Company A) and, more significantly, appointed him adjutant of the regiment. In this role of official scribe, his inclination toward melodrama and purple prose mattered a great deal. He wasn't simply another man in the line anymore. Now when John chronicled command decisions, the outcomes of bloody assaults, or deeds of individual heroism while penning Shelby's official reports, he was laying a foundation for how his service—and Shelby's and the regiment's—might be remembered for generations.[7]

Before the regiment could be immortalized in ink, though, it had to be built—a feat more easily bragged about than accomplished given the circumstances. Recruiting any army unit in wartime brought a litany of logistical headaches. Establishing a Confederate regiment, in broad daylight, in a state that saw two-thirds of its regular military enlistments break for the Union, generated much additional risk. Even in the familiar, mostly sympathetic confines of Lafayette and neighboring Little Dixie counties, the danger of large muster groups being discovered and set upon in camp by Federal patrols loomed constantly. Untrained and often unarmed, these men looked to Shelby, their new leader, for protection. Shelby decided to concentrate new recruits on the ground he knew best: at Waverly, his hometown. According to John, once the call for men went out, even in spite of the danger, "troops came pouring in for enlistment." "Ten companies were organized in a day," he boasted (in reality it was more like four or five days) and "Captain Shelby had one thousand men of the best blood in Missouri."[8]

While it was obviously not his intention, Union Brigadier General John M. Schofield helped send some of that "best blood" scampering in Shelby's direction. On July 22, 1862, Schofield issued General Order No. 19. The edict demanded that all able-bodied Missourians "repair without delay to the nearest military post" and report for duty with the Enrolled Missouri Militia (EMM), a new auxiliary force tasked with antibushwhacker and garrison duties on the home front. By simple process of elimination, any man who failed to register with the EMM was disloyal to the Union. In this way, Schofield made it very difficult for closeted Confederates to remain closeted. And the Fifth Missouri Cavalry, the official designation of the new regiment, gave them a way out apart from joining a guerrilla band or feigning loyalty. Or at least a way out if they were game for a fight. The men of the Fifth would see action almost immediately—and they would remain habitually engaged for the rest of the war.[9]

Part 1: Missourians on the Attack

Once Shelby's Fifth Cavalry rosters reached capacity, he moved the entire regiment into Arkansas. There, on supposedly safer ground, a detachment of the Sixth Kansas Cavalry (USA) promptly attacked the Fifth along the banks of Coon Creek. In John's words, the Missourians met the August 24 ambush "with such a sudden, deadly fire, that they [the Kansans] withdrew altogether from the contest, leaving in Shelby's hands eleven killed and five wounded." Following the skirmish, he alleged—perhaps too coolly, given the afternoon's action—that "supper was cooked and eaten in peace."[10]

After the fray at Coon Creek, the Fifth pitched camp near Newtonia and rendezvoused with a mounted regiment commanded by guerrilla turned colonel Upton Hays and another led by the hard-fighting—and hard-drinking—Colonel John Trousdale Coffee. A regimental election formalized for Richmond what the Lafayette County men had known all along: Shelby was their colonel. But then Major General Thomas Hindman, who'd given Shelby permission to recruit a regiment in

► Pea Ridge, March 7-8 - Heartbreaking defeat for pro-CSA Missourians
► Newtonia, September 30 - Confederates temporarily hold Newtonia
► Cane Hill, November 28 - Marmaduke retreats under white flag
► Prairie Grove, December 7 - Blunt and Herron defeat Hindman

Map 3. Western Battles (1862)

the first place, did him one better: in September 1862, Hindman joined the three regiments, and as reported by John, "Colonel Shelby assumed command of that immortal brigade which afterward carried its flag triumphantly in a hundred desperate conflicts, and poured out its blood like water from Kansas to the Rio Grande."[11]

Not unpredictably, John conferred the command its nom de guerre: "The Iron Brigade." This passage from his 1867 history of the war in the West codified his logic in print. To John, this was more than a flashy moniker; it captured the unit's essence:

> Many times naked, destitute, worn by incessant fighting, freezing, starving—it never abandoned the stern discipline so often inculcated, nor put off for an instant the indomitable pride and chivalry of its organization. Surrounded, it never surrendered; surprised, it never scattered; overwhelmed, it never wavered; decimated, it bled in silence; and victorious, it was always merciful and just.[12]

Melodrama and purple prose indeed. Yet John was only getting started. He also lauded Shelby's credentials as the Iron Brigade's noble, near-supernatural, commander. "It happens now and then, in the ages, that a soul is born which has no weakness of self. . . . Such souls are the apparition of gods among men." "Colonel Shelby," John declared, "was one of these men." A far greater compliment, however, was the Arthurian analogy that he deployed in asserting that Shelby had gathered the Missourians around him "as Arthur did his knights." Here he presented Shelby as a living personification of the *new* Old World—replete with virtuous and selfless leaders, fearless knights, and storybook endings—that he'd dreamed military success might yield in a *new* Old South. In this manner, while further entrenching himself as Shelby's troubadour, John made clear that he harbored far greater, and far more complicated, expectations for Confederate victory than the average Johnny Reb.[13]

On September 15, 1862, a Federal brigade commanded by the Prussian-born Brigadier General Frederick Salomon occupied Newtonia, a community of a few hundred people, mostly farmers. From the vantage of grand strategy, Newtonia didn't comprise a vital target. For pro-Confederates on the march in Southwest Missouri, wanting for foodstuffs but lacking consistent support from any government, the town's flour mill seemed more than grand enough. As it happened, Newtonia also was located a stone's throw from the Iron Brigade's current base of operations. Shelby dispatched Colonel Upton Hays and his regiment, the Twelfth Missouri Cavalry, to dislodge Salomon's troops. Though two years younger than Shelby, the thirty-year-old Hays sported a resume that belied his age. He'd spearheaded violent raids across the Kansas border in the 1850s and continued orchestrating guerrilla operations in 1861 and 1862. Hays was also renowned for his fearlessness. On this particular mission it would initiate his undoing.[14]

In John's rendition, Hays personally spotted Union sentries and charged off to capture them, well in advance of his regiment. Upon reaching Salomon's men, Hays—still in the saddle—leveled his revolver at one of the Federals and squeezed the trigger. The gun's hammer fell with a snap, but no explosion followed. Wet powder instantly turned the proverbial tables on Hays. Without any hesitation, the fortunate dragoon "fired his carbine full in Colonel Hays' face, the bullet crashing through the brain, and destroying life as suddenly as the flashing of an eyelid." Hays toppled over, stone dead, in full view of the regiment. Enraged by the loss of their beloved commander, they stampeded the Union garrison at Newtonia just as recklessly as Hays had charged its pickets. In the course of a running fight, Salomon's troops abandoned the town. Having accomplished their objective, the Twelfth brought Colonel Upton Hays back to camp "pale, and quiet, and sleeping his last sleep."[15]

Sensing how the brigade was shaken by Hays's death, Shelby tried—literally—to get them back in the saddle quickly. Roughly a week later, an opportunity for action and vengeance presented itself. As John put it, "News came at length by one of Colonel Shelby's innumerable scouts that a large body of Pin Indians and runaway negroes were camped in a skirt of timber near Carthage, levying black-mail indiscriminately upon the inhabitants, and murdering right and left with habitual brutality." Carrying orders from Shelby, Captain Ben Elliott, a Virginia Military Institute (vmi) graduate in command of Company I, set out with his own men and detachments from several other companies. In the predawn hours of September 24, his raiding force surrounded the camp of Indians and runaways. With daylight came a charge from all sides, and shortly thereafter, a massacre. "Surprised, ridden over and trampled down, the Indians and their negro allies made but feeble resistance," John reported. "Everywhere amid the heavy brushwood," he declared, without even a hint of regret, "a silent scene of killing was enacted." Per John's version of events, the Indians didn't pray for mercy, "well knowing that their own previous atrocities had forfeited it." "In two hours," he concluded matter-of-factly, "this band of two hundred and fifty savages was exterminated almost completely."[16]

Habitual brutality. Savages. Justified extermination. Just as in the aftermath of Pea Ridge, John displayed an utter disregard for the humanity of Indians. He preempted those observers who might frown on a small-scale genocide with news that dozens of white scalps were found among the Indians' possessions, taking special care to highlight that one belonged to a white woman. His only "praise" for the slaughtered Indians amounted to a white supremacist stereotype relayed by way of a highly dubious anecdote: with the fight lost, John alleged that the Indians displayed "the stoical hardiness of their race" by tearing open their shirts and, unafraid of death, allowing themselves to be shot in their exposed chests.

At first glance, it's easy to read John's commentary on purely racial terms. That is, the Indians were not white, so they had it coming anyway. But in light of his hopes for a Confederate West, John's specific racism toward Indians should be distinguished, at least in part, from how many Southerners viewed Black slaves and should be considered as a symptom of his broader imperial ambitions. Hence, John not only foreshadowed what would become a familiar narrative in the postbellum West—white cavalrymen tasked with extermination, riding roughshod over Indian villages—but he also previewed *how* a West stocked with nonwhite "impediments" might still have become a blank canvas for victorious Southerners.[17]

In the days after the Pin Indian massacre, the Confederates made full, undisturbed use of the flour mill. Needed reinforcements arrived in the form of Colonel Douglas Cooper's division, which consisted of Texans and Indians. The latter, of Major Joel M. Bryan's Cherokee Battalion, along with two other regiments of Choctaw and Chickasaw, enjoyed a less-than-enthusiastic welcome from the Missourians, who were not inclined to differentiate "savage" from "savage." Regardless, the Indians took their orders from Cooper, and as Cooper ranked Shelby, now the Missourians did too. On September 29, two days after Cooper assumed full command, Confederate pickets reported a significant force of Union infantry lumbering in his direction. Just after sunrise the next morning, September 30, an artillery barrage rocked the surrounding countryside. By way of this opening salvo, Brigadier General Frederick Salomon signaled his willingness to serve as the day's aggressor. He commenced the battle for Newtonia—and as it turned out, for military control of southwestern Missouri.[18]

Behind Salomon marched a hodgepodge of volunteer Kansans and Wisconsin men. John made a point of noting how well the Germans marched, quipping that they were "as pretty Dutch as ever bolted a bologna or swallowed the foaming lager." Unfortunately for Newtonia's Confederate defenders, the mountain howitzers brought up by Salomon's men weren't firing bolts of cured meat or casks of beer. For nearly two hours, and at nearly point-blank range, Union gunners from two batteries of six guns each rained down shot on their outnumbered Confederate counterparts. Around 9:00 a.m., Cooper's batteries ceased firing, their munitions totally spent.[19]

Like Franz Sigel, Salomon was a veteran of the failed 1848 March Revolution in Germany. Also like Sigel, Salomon wasn't afraid to order a head-on assault and lead it from the front. When Cooper's field guns went cold, Salomon determined to take Newtonia by brute force. He sent forward the Ninth Wisconsin, a predominantly German-American regiment—only now, their advance wasn't so amusing to John. As he put it, "the finely-drilled regiment, one-thousand strong, spread out like a fan, and when the fan closed it had Newtonia encircled."[20]

In the opening phase of the assault, the Ninth Wisconsin pushed Cooper's Texans, about two hundred to three hundred strong, back on their heels—but before Salomon could strike a final, decisive blow, help arrived. Upon Cooper's call for a regiment of cavalry, Shelby sent his own Fifth Missouri, which included John.[21] Led by Lieutenant

Colonel Benjamin F. Gordon, the Missourians charged headlong into the Ninth Wisconsin, stunning its men, and stalling the advance. Then a second wave of reinforcements crashed against the Union position: this time, it was the Choctaws. Unable to resist a jab at the Indians—even those on *his* side—John reported that the Missourians were forced to protect their dazed "Dutch" prisoners from whooping, frenzied savages "rushing up for the scalp scene."[22]

After losing its initial momentum, Salomon's attack never righted itself. Cooper's replenished batteries provided cover for a counterassault along the entire Union line. John and the rest of the regiment, along with Lieutenant Colonel Beal Green Jeans—who had succeeded to command of Upton Hays's Twelfth Missouri—struck the left and center of the Federal line. The Choctaws simultaneously launched their own attack against Salomon's right. Per his official report, Salomon decided to "fall back on [his] defenses [at Sarcoxie]" after learning that General Rains and other Confederate reinforcements were arriving on the field. John, naturally, suggested a different version: "The whole line gave way almost immediately . . . the victory won by the Confederates was decisive."[23]

Cooper was magnanimous in victory; he noted after the battle that Shelby deserved "great credit for his promptness in sending re-enforcements." Great credit or not, the men of the Fifth Missouri paid for their plaudits in blood; indeed, they sustained more killed and wounded than any of the other Confederate units engaged at Newtonia. John's own cousin, Private William "Henry" Yerby, was among the severely wounded—his arm mangled by lead. Then just four days later, the Fifth found itself under still heavier fire, as Brigadier General John Schofield returned to Newtonia with a significantly larger army to finish what Salomon had started. Given his numerical advantage, Schofield wanted a fight; for the opposite reason, Cooper couldn't oblige. Instead, Shelby's horsemen covered the total evacuation of Newtonia.[24]

Union commanders labeled Confederate resistance "feeble" and their own casualties "trifling" in the wake of this second, virtually bloodless, contest for Newtonia. As Shelby's command slipped away from Schofield's divisions and into Arkansas, the futility of men dying for ground, only to see it squandered without a fight days later, wasn't lost on John. He might have been a mere lieutenant, but his access to Shelby afforded him a more intricate—and perhaps more cynical— look behind the curtain of high command in the Department of the Trans-Mississippi and even Richmond. In the coming weeks, his frustration with the "higher-ups" would grow exponentially.[25]

The issues rankling John were nothing new in the Trans-Mississippi. The "trans" in this case meant "across the" and "Mississippi" referred to the river. Thus, as a theater of war, it was gargantuan. Missouri, Kansas, Arkansas, most of Louisiana, the Indian Territory (present-day Oklahoma), all of Texas, and depending on who one asked, sometimes even the territories of Arizona and New Mexico were included. As a department of the Confederate military, its size, its diversity of inhabitants, and the fact that it contained two *Union* states all combined to make overall command a nightmare.

At any given moment in 1862 or 1863, the logistical needs and operational goals of Missouri didn't align much with those of Texas— nor Texas with Kansas nor Kansas with the Indian Territory nor the Indian Territory with Western Louisiana nor Western Louisiana with Arizona. For instance, as Curtis and Van Dorn were slugging it out at Pea Ridge to decide the political fate of Missouri, Henry Sibley was off leading an ill-fated expedition to conquer the New Mexico Territory. Surely, that Van Dorn and Sibley were leading armies and expeditions in the first place only underscored that the Trans-Mississippi was not where the Confederacy sent top-tier talent. To be fair, it wasn't that Jefferson Davis and his advisors didn't care. They, and particularly Davis, just weren't capable of efficiently directing such a vast conflict. The farther a department from Richmond, the more likely it was to be mismanaged.[26]

For John, the mismanagement was mindboggling. To him, the Trans-Mississippi—and the West writ large—was the great *prize* awaiting the war's victor. It was a territory to prioritize, not to omit strategically and then use as a backwater purgatory for misfit commanders. Years later he would blast away at the Confederate brass for not understanding "the great importance of the Trans-Mississippi Department." He even accused of Davis of appointing departmental commanders who'd been "relieved from duty in Virginia because of their ignorance and unfitness for any position whatever." In the fall of 1862, however, John was in no position to share those opinions out loud. And he certainly couldn't put them in print.[27]

Before their next fight, John and the rest of the brigade dealt with command shakeups at both the regimental and divisional levels. General James Rains, the Missourians' original divisional commander—who had bestowed them their first written praise at Carthage—was sacked for drunkenness and incompetence by another of Shelby's patrons, General Thomas Hindman. Hindman also ordered Colonel John Trousdale Coffee arrested and stripped of command. Coffee had commanded the Sixth Missouri since the inception of the Iron Brigade. The charge against him, drunkenness, floored no one, including John. He made no effort to defend Coffee—or Rains—from Hindman's hatchet but heartily endorsed the arrival of the "young," "gallant," and newly promoted Brigadier General John Sappington Marmaduke. Following the debacle at Boonville—the fault for which, it should be remembered, really lay with Marmaduke's uncle, Claiborne Fox Jackson—Marmaduke remade his reputation with a serious wound at Shiloh. Now he returned to the Trans-Mississippi just as battle clouds began to form over Cane Hill.[28]

October rolled into November. Hindman's Army of the Trans-Mississippi milled about Arkansas as the weather grew colder—and as the supply situation, for both man and horse, became increasingly problematic. A foraging party sent to Cane Hill brought temporary supplies of meat and grain, but in the middle of the month, Hindman sent another scout, under Marmaduke's command, to hold Cane Hill and gather winter foodstuffs. This second Confederate provocation in as many weeks prompted Brigadier General James Blunt, one of Schofield's divisional commanders, to take offensive action. He brought his entire division—numbering some five thousand men along with thirty pieces of artillery—to bear against Marmaduke's two thousand men and their half-starved horses.[29]

Much to John's satisfaction, Marmaduke positioned Shelby's brigade directly in the *assumed* path of Blunt's marching columns. He saw it as a sign of the Missourians' growing reputation for combat. From the start, however, things did not go as planned for the Confederates. Blunt moved against Cane Hill by an alternate route, which caught Shelby wrongfooted. Just how wrongfooted depends on which version of the story one chooses to believe. John penned both; one in the days immediately following the action and the other a few years later in *Shelby and His Men*. The report of December 1, 1862, likely John's first official write-up of a battle as Shelby's adjutant, explained as follows:

> The enemy, by his skillful management, fell upon me sooner than I would have desired considering that a portion of our division was encamped some distance in my rear and I had but little time to give them the notice required.

By 1867, the story had evolved to include a beautiful young maiden rushing to warn Shelby of Blunt's approach—but Shelby already knows of Blunt's deception and unleashes a brutal ambush on the vanguard of his force. In that version of the opening moments at Cane Hill,

> the Federals entered the cornfield in fine style and advanced in line of battle upon the crouching Confederates . . . When within point-blank range, the snaky fence, lit up by the flash of three thousand muskets, revealed a line of sullen men pouring death into the shattered ranks. The well-dressed line melted away like snow in a thaw, and shivering to the pitiless shock every living man turned and fled in one rushing, frenzied mass—order, command, discipline, all gone, and the yelling Confederates following on foot until distanced in the face.

Shelby might've had time to reposition his men for an ambush before the shooting began, and Blunt's skirmishers might, indeed, have been momentarily taken aback by a Confederate ambush. But Blunt's vanguard hardly melted. In truth, his vastly superior artillery—rifled guns and many more of them than Marmaduke could muster—made Shelby's position, and by extension that of Marmaduke's entire division, untenable in about an hour.[30]

In serving as the rear guard for a general retreat to new defensive works, Shelby engineered a system in which small units of his brigade lined up at intervals along the path of Blunt's men, almost like the rungs of a ladder. One unit would fire on the pursuing Federals and then fall out and around to the back end of the ladder, forming a new last rung. None of the individual rungs were large enough to completely halt Blunt's advance, but the constant stream of fire created by their leapfrogging slowed the Federals down long enough for Marmaduke to establish a secondary line. John called it Shelby's "own peculiar system of fighting on a retreat"—and even Blunt confessed to its effectiveness in his official report, stating that during the retreat, "every foot of the ground was fought over and hotly contested."[31]

In spite of their new defensive position, the Confederates simply could not cope with the onslaught of the Union artillery; they were pushed back again. Then, just when it seemed the running battle might turn into a complete rout of the Rebels, Marmaduke appears to have pulled one over on Blunt. With the sun hanging low and wounded men from both sides strewn across the miles-long field, Marmaduke sent Shelby and another officer to meet with the Union commander. They requested a ceasefire to collect the dead and wounded, to which Blunt agreed, partly because of fading light and partly because laying somewhere on the field was a badly wounded Lieutenant Colonel Lewis Jewell. At that moment, however, Blunt didn't know that Marmaduke had already ordered a general retreat, which—thanks to the agreed on ceasefire—his exhausted men and batteries could now execute without further fear of pursuit or capture.[32]

Whether or not Blunt could have finished off Marmaduke's division is debatable. Odds were probably better for than against. At the very least, Blunt believed he was on the verge of capturing Marmaduke's field guns. Regardless, Marmaduke escaped with his division *and* with the supplies foraged from Cane Hill. That notwithstanding, Blunt's departmental boss, Major General Samuel Curtis, was happy enough with possession of the field. "The victory was complete," he reported. "Our loss is not great. The enemy much more. Our forces camp on the battle-field."[33]

John, as he was wont to do, spun a different interpretation of the battle. It was so different, in fact, that an unwitting reader might actually have assumed that the Confederates won the battle. Amidst a trove of poetic verses and clichés John managed to conclude his (Shelby's) report "with the proud satisfaction of knowing that we did our duty, and are anxious once more to meet the enemy in a fair field and an open fight." This was hardly reflective of a day that involved Shelby caught off guard, multiple retreats, and an escape from superior numbers by way of a white flag. Even less representative of the rough time the Confederates endured at Cane Hill was the rendition John concocted for *Shelby and His Men*—which includes a version of the parlay meeting so fantastical that he dared not include it the official 1862 report:

> "Whose troops fought me to-day?" asked General Blunt. Colonel Shelby's brigade," replied the generous Marmaduke. "How did they behave, General?" "Behave," answered Blunt, "why, sir, they fought like devils. Two hundred and fifty of my best men have fallen in this day's fight, and more heroic young officers than I can scarcely hope to get again." "I don't understand your fighting," he continued, "when I broke one line, another met me, another, another, and still another, until the woods seemed filled with soldiers, and the very air dark with bullets."

This account of the encounter between Shelby and Blunt is clearly fabricated and overdramatized—the dialogue painfully so. But it provides an opportunity, the first of many involving John's pen, to examine two reports from the same man about the same battle, written under wildly different circumstances. In December 1862, John was having the time of his life as adjutant for a fast-rising cavalry commander. The thought of losing the war never crossed his mind. By contrast, the bulk of *Shelby and His Men* was penned in Mexico after 1865, whence John and others sought to establish a new network of Confederate colonies. The comparison illustrates how John evolved as a propagandist between 1862 and 1867—but also, and perhaps of more consequence—illustrates that the cultural mission underlying his writing did not change with the downfall of the Confederacy proper.[34]

In December 1862, John, Shelby, and the rest of Hindman's troops still itched for that "open fight" with Blunt. Hindman's collective force, which included Shelby's brigade (still under Marmaduke's division), now outnumbered Blunt. But Blunt's men were better armed, better fed, better clothed, better shod, and better mounted. Moreover, they still possessed a significant artillery advantage. Knowing this, Hindman understood that he couldn't afford to lose numerical superiority for any reason. Consequently, when Blunt called for reinforcements from Brigadier General Francis J. Herron—who began a forced march from Western Missouri with two full divisions—Hindman was forced to alter his original plan. Instead of slamming into Blunt with the full weight of his army, he would feint against Cane Hill, while actually attacking Herron's still-marching troops. Hindman needed to keep the two Union commands apart, to destroy them "in detail," which simply meant one piece at a time.[35]

Blunt's men awoke on the morning of December 7, 1862, looking less like formidable invaders and more like very cold, very anxious farmers, clerks, and shopkeepers from Kansas. All around them, the signs from Hindman's Confederate front indicated a major assault would be launched against them at any moment. The signs, as it so happened, were intentionally misleading. Herron's advance cavalry had begun arriving in Cane Hill on December 5, but his infantry—what really worried Hindman—was still a few hours' march from Blunt's position—and Hindman decided to hit Herron first, before turning his wrath on Blunt. Fires burned up and down the Rebel encampment; a show of strength that indicated an early morning attack. In reality, the bulk of Hindman's army—John, Shelby, and the Iron Brigade included—had slipped away in the middle of the night and was moving to pounce on Herron's sleep-deprived divisions eight miles to the east at Prairie Grove.[36]

In the simplest terms, the plan didn't work. Hindman managed to startle Herron—and he got to strike from high ground of his own choosing. Early in the battle, a flanking force of Shelby's men and Quantrill's bushwhackers—the latter disguised in stolen Union uniforms—captured several wagonloads of food and supplies meant for Blunt at Cane Hill. In spite of these advantages, the Confederates again struggled to match-up with Union batteries and Hindman could not budge Herron's force. To be fair, Herron couldn't budge Hindman's army either. Multiple failed assaults proved that point. The upside for Herron, however, was that he didn't *have* to defeat Hindman by himself; he simply needed to hold out long enough for Blunt to arrive. Together, they could close the vise on Hindman and crush his army. Darkness saved the Confederates from physical destruction, but Hindman needed a way out of the mess he'd created—so he borrowed an old trick from his cavalry commander, Marmaduke.[37]

With fighting halted for the evening, Blunt sent a medical emissary through the Confederate line and proposed that both sides be allowed to provide supplies for their men wounded behind enemy lines. Hindman agreed. Then, through a series of communications with Blunt, including one face-to-face meeting on the morning of December 8, Hindman convinced the Union commander to accept a six-hour truce that would allow each force to gather up its dead and wounded from the field. Unbeknownst to Blunt, or Herron for that matter, Hindman's men had been retreating all night—they even used blankets to silence the wheels of limbers and caissons. In essence, it was Cane Hill all over again: Blunt had agreed to another truce that made it impossible for him to pursue and attack a Confederate army as it limped away.[38]

Blunt let Hindman know exactly what he thought of such sneaky tactics with a tongue-lashing that began on December 9 when Hindman dared write to Blunt about confiscated rifle-muskets. A Confederate burial detail had used the truce to scavenge badly needed firearms from the field. Such practice demonstrated a direct violation of the ceasefire, and Herron's staff stopped it immediately. This prompted Hindman to claim—somewhat incredibly considering his army *had fled from Prairie Grove in the middle of the night*—that the Confederates actually won the battle and, as rightful possessors of the field itself, were allowed to scavenge arms. He wanted the weapons returned. It is impossible to know what sort of reply Hindman expected. Yet we can say with near certainty that Blunt's response—a barrage of sarcastic jabs the likes of which are seldom found in correspondence between enemy officers—was not the variety Hindman had hoped for.[39]

Undaunted by the absurdity of his own position, Hindman wrote back on December 10. He iterated that his men had indeed won the field because Union attacks had not forced them from their original lines in daylight. The withdrawal, he contended, only became necessary due to an "utter lack of subsistence"—the implication being that the logistical shortcomings of the Confederate army were somehow the Union's problem. "Your remarks about the 'battle-field won by your men," Blunt shot back, "is considered here as a very good joke."[40]

The situation laid bare by Blunt's commentary could not be avoided—so it had to be explained. Doing so on favorable terms was a tall task, even for John. On one hand, he needed to convince Southerners, including men who actually fought at, bled on, and fled from Prairie Grove, not to trust their own eyes. Because even a fanatical Confederate, were he being semi-honest with himself, knew deepdown that Hindman's army had abandoned the field under serious duress. And if that same Johnny Reb happened to be in the mood for total honesty, he would likewise admit that the divisions commanded by Blunt and Herron formed the source of said serious duress. On the other hand, Blunt had launched a broadside against the honor of Southern warriors which, to John, meant the Iron Brigade first and foremost. He couldn't let that attack on Shelby, the men of the brigade, or himself, go unanswered—regardless of how thin it meant stretching the truth about Hindman's exit from Prairie Grove.

Shelby's official report on the battle, penned almost entirely by John save for a few remarks on individuals' conduct near the end, read like a pro-Confederate fairy tale. Indeed, if not for a buried reference to Hindman's order to secretly withdraw, that same unaware reader duped by John's coverage of Cane Hill might again walk away thinking that Confederates had prevailed.

As Herron's divisions repeatedly assaulted Confederate positions on the high ground at Prairie Grove, Shelby's men fought on horseback and then dismounted alongside the infantry. John described the gunfire roaring "like a storm at sea" while "death, with its black banner on the breeze, nerv[ed] each heart and cheer[ed] them on to the rough, red fray." "Night," he concluded, "had closed the march of death, and the idle breeze now gave no murmur back to tell of what had been passing but a few brief moments before, when—

Our bugles sang truce and the night cloud had lowered,
And the sentinel stars kept their watch in the sky;
When thousands had sunk to the earth overpowered,
The weary to sleep and the wounded to die."

What the higher-ups in Richmond—or even Hindman—thought of the sudden effusion of "poetic license" within Shelby's official reports isn't recorded. Someone in the Confederate War Department must have at least found them an entertaining change of pace from bland orders of battle and casualty figures. Whatever attention John garnered with his pen, he also distinguished himself enough on the field itself to warrant a mention from Shelby: "I will here also state that I noticed with much pleasure the adjutant of the First Regiment, John [N.] Edwards, who was actively engaged in watching the movements of the enemy upon every corner, and with his regiment aiding and cheering them on to victory or death." However others felt about John's cavalier attitude toward men fighting and dying, none could say he didn't practice what he propagandized when the lead was flying.[41]

Unionist newspapers in late 1862 and early 1863 saw things quite differently. By the time word of Prairie Grove reached the Eastern Theater, Union Major General Ambrose Burnside had suffered a staggering, and in many ways senseless, defeat at Fredericksburg. So with the Federal military's flagship army in want of a competent commander and Robert E. Lee's victorious Army of Northern Virginia looming ever larger in the minds of panicked Americans, the win in Arkansas took on additional symbolic, as well as logistical, importance. For grand strategists, Hindman's loss in Northern Arkansas mattered because it forced the Confederacy to contract from territory in the Trans-Mississippi that it would never again control. For the vast majority of victory-starved Unionists in the East, it provided a clear-cut victory to help ring in the new year.

For John, playing up the fighting prowess of Shelby's men and underscoring their on-field exploits enhanced their reputation. But it did very little to distract from the ultimate result of the battle. John waited nearly five years to start rearranging those facts. Not coincidentally, before the fighting at Prairie Grove even began in *Shelby and His Men*, he laid the foundation for justifying Hindman's retreat: he was simply being a loyal officer and following orders. The real culprits were General Theophilus Holmes and Jefferson Davis.

In this alternate version of events, "Night alone closed the battle, leaving the Confederates in possession of the field and believing in victory, though somewhat scattered and demoralized." John conceded that Hindman's army absorbed a heavy blow and that ammunition was low and provisions lacking—but those were only "strong and additional reasons for abandoning the field *after it was won*." "The retreat," he reiterated, "had been a foregone conclusion from the first."[42]

With Hindman's departure from the field explained, John went to work on the charges of trickery and unmanliness against the fleeing Confederates. In his rendition of the ceasefire talks between Blunt and Hindman, it is the former, not the latter, who requests a halt to fighting—just as it is the troops of the former, not of the latter, who violate the sanctity of the white flag by interfering with burial details. According to John, these men were "unarmed and wearing across their shoulders the badges of mercy and protection," but still found themselves under arrest and "sent North to languish in lonesome prisons." Moreover, as we saw in John's version of parlay talks at Cane Hill, Blunt makes a point of lavishing praise on the toughness of Shelby's men. In fact, Blunt didn't imprison any of Hindman's men after the truce began. But John was especially touchy about the subject of tarnished chivalry and poor "white flag etiquette" for a reason. As it turned out, the men reprimanded by Union officers for dishonestly collecting weapons from the field belonged to Shelby's brigade. With the unit besmirched, it had become a matter of "family" honor.[43]

Once the Confederates, and Shelby's horsemen in particular, were cleared of ill deeds at Prairie Grove, John related two new anecdotes not included in his original 1862 report. Akin to the dialogue he'd concocted at Cane Hill, these tales were simply too far fetched for submission to department headquarters. The first was an elaborate retelling of Shelby capturing supply wagons as the battle began. Dashing off ahead of his men, Shelby encounters a Union major and a company of infantry who demand his surrender. Shelby doesn't respond. "Surrender, do you hear!" the major bellows again, adding "surrender or I fire," while holding a cocked revolver to Shelby's head. Then, with all the cool and calmness of a mythological protagonist, Shelby replies: "You are mistaken . . . it is you who are my prisoner. Call off your men, and listen behind you." Sure enough, scores of Missourians come thundering down and surround the Federals. After refusing to take the major's sword, the chivalric Shelby proclaims, "It was never stained, as I have learned, in the blood of the helpless around Newtonia. I respect an honorable foe."[44]

The second anecdote starred Colonel Alonzo Slayback. And if Shelby's "gotcha" moment couldn't be included in the official report, Slayback's supposed exploits represented a whole new level of off-limits. As John told it in *Shelby and His Men*, "amidst cannons booming and men falling, mortally wounded, all over the field," Slayback attempts "an adventure thought of many centuries ago by thousands, no doubt, when knights wore greaves and vizors, and when that war-cry rang over the won field of Bannockburn—'St. James for Argentine.'" In far simpler terms, Slayback mounts his horse, charges toward a nearby unit of Federal cavalry, and challenges "any one to single combat." A wily captain from Arkansas accepts the invitation to "joust" and Slayback manages to defeat his inferior foe—without killing him, it's worth noting—before returning to the Confederate line entirely unscathed.[45]

It isn't difficult to dissect the motive underlying John's "addendums" to the narrative of Prairie Grove: An Odysseus-like Shelby outwitting and ensnaring Union troops before stoically claiming the moral high ground. Slayback, in the form of a Colt-toting Galahad, besting his challenger and then exhibiting his true manliness by sparing the vanquished enemy's life. They served another purpose, too; one far more important to John than bragging rights at Prairie Grove. By design, both accounts accentuated the idea that even among Southerners, only a select few men exhibited the qualities of true valor and leadership found in the scenes crucial to John's worldview, which is really to say, the scenes crucial to the bedrock of Southern culture as

John imagined it. Ergo, in the grander scheme of a rebellion intended to preserve, not upheave, John fashioned Shelby and Slayback as the kind of Old World heroes who could hold the line not only against Union invasion but also against the gradual disappearance of the old ideas and customs that such a war for abolition signaled.

After Prairie Grove, the brigade marched to Little Rock, and then established winter quarters at Lewisburg, forty miles northwest of the city. There, the logistical and material shortcomings of Hindman's army began to catch up with the men. Boots worn down to nothing. Starvation rations. Animals dying by the dozen. Disease felling men just as quickly as their horses. And bone-chilling weather—which only served to exacerbate their other problems. Still, at least as John told it, Shelby "yet rose sterner and greater as the darkness thickened around him" and his men "took their punishment like Spartans." For John personally, it was a bittersweet period; his unit was clearly suffering badly, but his older brother, Thomas Edwards, joined the brigade on December 31, 1862.[46]

For days before his reunion with Thomas, John heard rumors of a dash into Missouri—a hit and run operation, just the Iron Brigade's style. Then the rumors became plans, and the plans became orders. Marmaduke's raiding party would cut the tether between Blunt's divisions in Arkansas to their supply base at Springfield, Missouri, and then generate havoc on the roads between Springfield and the railhead at Rolla. Without supplies, Blunt would be forced to retreat from Arkansas, yielding the control recently consolidated at Cane Hill and Prairie Grove. On the same day that Thomas Edwards became a private in Company B of the Fifth Missouri, the brigade set out with the rest of Marmaduke's division and rang in the New Year as they'd spent much of the last—in the saddle.[47]

Marmaduke's Expedition, as observers dubbed it, offered secondary benefits. In addition to removing Blunt from his supply train, a series of winter raids would simultaneously push Federal soldiers out of winter quarters while also making it unnecessary for the Confederates to ever *enter* winter quarters—something they lacked the supplies to do properly anyway. Of course, this all depended on successful assaults against various Union garrisons, particularly the one at Springfield. And heavily fortified as Springfield was, this latter feat would come at a grisly price.[48]

Marmaduke divided his invasion force into three columns, commanded by Shelby, Colonel Emmett McDonald, and Colonel Joseph Porter, respectively. Shelby and McDonald set a course for Springfield, while Porter rode in the direction of Hartville, thirty-five miles east of Springfield. As with so many Confederate plans lately hatched in the Trans-Mississippi, the operation initially showed great promise. En route to Springfield, various columns hit small fortresses and encampments, even temporarily clearing out the Federal garrison at Ozark, roughly twenty miles due south of Springfield. However, the attack in Ozark alerted Union forces in the area of Marmaduke's advance. When the Confederates arrived on the outskirts of Springfield, late in the morning on January 8, whatever element of surprise they'd hauled across the Arkansas-Missouri border had vanished.[49]

This was a problem—though Marmaduke would not grasp it in full until *after* he'd thrown two of his columns into an all-day fight against the heavily fortified Union garrison. Because Springfield served as a nerve center for Federal supply operations in Western Missouri and Eastern Arkansas, its defenses were impressive: multiple stone stockades and permanent rifle pits. And before even reaching those obstacles, the Confederates would need to slug their way through the city. Potentially fighting street to street, or even door to door, created yet another set of difficulties for cavalrymen. They would have to proceed on foot. All of this considered, when Shelby's and McDonald's columns converged on the city around 10:00 a.m., Marmaduke ordered shelling. It would be the prelude to a mass assault, albeit at two-thirds strength. (Marmaduke attempted to recall Porter's column to assist before attacking, but the message did not arrive in time, and so neither did Porter.)[50]

General Egbert B. Brown, the Union commander at Springfield, got a wire out just before the fighting began. His tone could not have struck General Samuel Curtis, commander of the Union Army of the Frontier, as overly confident. "I shall fight as long as I can," Brown

► **Springfield, January 8 - Confederate attackers thrown back**

► **Hartville, January 11 - Marmaduke retreats back to Arkansas**

Map 4. Marmaduke Expedition (1863)

reported, "in hopes re-enforcements will reach me in time to save the stores. I give you all my plans, as I have no doubt the enemy is in force, and will attack me." Moments later, Marmaduke's batteries did just that.[51]

After the artillerists plied their trade, Shelby led his men forward. The Confederates sustained heavier losses than Marmaduke originally expected, but they gained ground. What dawned on them, however, is that while they were steadily taking control of the residential sectors of Springfield, that wasn't what actually mattered. Defeating Springfield's garrison—and commandeering the city's rich trove of supplies—required seizing the stone stockades and rifle pits. And Brown's Federals, understanding what was at stake, put up one hell of a fight to keep them. Roughly midway through the battle, which lasted for more than eight hours, Shelby's column charged stout Union defenses to rescue McDonald's men from their own stalled surge. By then Brown knew he held the Confederates in a tight spot. "I am holding the strong positions," he relayed to Curtis, "and as night is closing, the enemy must fight as I want to, or not to-night." Brown closed his report with a telling statement, one that likely said as much about the collective gauntness of Marmaduke's command as it did their motivation for repeatedly slamming into Brown's defensive works. "They are fighting for bread," the Union general noted. Thankfully for Marmaduke's men, as daylight waned, so did their commander's stomach for frontal assaults.[52]

Throughout the night, Brown remained convinced that the Confederates would attack again at first light. But when the sun rose, it revealed no besiegers. "At dark the fighting ceased," Marmaduke later wrote in his official report of the battle. "The greater part of the town, the fort, and many of the dead and wounded Federals in my possession . . . I did not deem it best to renew the attack, and the next day marched toward Rolla." Earlier in the same report, Marmaduke seemed pleased with himself for "driving the Yankees before me, and into their strongholds." But then, in a subsequent report, confessed that he had badly misjudged Springfield's defenses, believing that the city was "strongly fortified" but "weakly garrisoned." Thus, not unlike Hindman claiming his men retreated from Prairie Grove due to starvation and that fleeing from an enemy on those grounds didn't count as a loss, Marmaduke suggested that his men had won the battle—up until the Union defenders of Springfield actually decided to use their defenses, after which having to retreat by moonlight wasn't his fault.[53]

Whatever Marmaduke's reasoning, for the second time in as many battles, a victorious Union commander made a written complaint about the unchivalrous nature of the Confederates' conduct. "He moved right up and immediately commenced the fight by cannonading the town, without having given a moment's time to move the sick and the helpless women and children," a severely wounded Brown snarled in a statement to Curtis. Curtis assessed the outcome more bluntly: "The enemy got nothing but a good thrashing and one gun."[54]

In Shelby's official report, John treated the single-day siege as a "mission accomplished" within the broader scope of Marmaduke's raid. And owing to the scaled-down arena of battle—which allowed for a tighter focus on the Iron Brigade—and the unusually prolonged engagement of Shelby's men fighting as infantry, John didn't think twice about spinning the battle into something like a medieval folktale.

> The sun came up on the morning of the 8th like a ball of fire, and the day was gloomy and chill, but Springfield loomed up before us in the distance like a beautiful panorama, and the men, catching the inspiration of the scene, forgot all their trials and hardships, and were eager for the rough, red fray.

John took especial delight in the charge to support McDonald's column. "Gallantly it was done, and as gallantly sustained . . . a thousand warriors sprang for their feet, and, with one wild Missouri yell, burst upon the foe." Then, apparently unable to contain himself, he began to narrate the battle as if it were unfolding for the reader in real-time: "Bravely my fighting brigade meets the onset, and stubbornly they resist; blow falls upon blow, shot follows shot . . . and the contest rages, and the wild death-dance goes merrily on." Toward the end of the report, John reverts to the past tense, as if suddenly reminded that the Confederates lost. The Iron Brigade "suffered seriously in the attack upon Springfield," he touted, "but it covered itself all over with glory, and won imperishable laurels."[55]

This wouldn't be John's last report in which it's nearly impossible to discern what mattered more: glory or victory. Far from it, actually. Yet it does reveal that a sort of "thinking glitch" existed within John's own worldview. When combined with his extraordinarily skewed coverage of the fight for Springfield in *Shelby and His Men*, the revelatory effect is even more pronounced. In that later version of the engagement, Shelby and the Iron Brigade win the *fight* single-handedly, against harrowing odds, while Marmaduke mismanages the situation and technically loses the *battle*. The distinction—"fight" from "battle"— truly mattered. Gallantry in combat. Unyielding loyalty to one's noble commander. A willingness to lay down one's life for king, country, and perhaps even a fair maiden. According to John's code—his animating force, as it were—these components of personal honor held the power to remake a select breed of men into living folk heroes, or better still into living legends.

Then again, the burden of becoming memorable rested far more on the means than the end. Courage, loyalty, and giving the final measure did not require victory. And therein lay the problem. Losses, no matter how draped in glory, could not hold territory, fend off occupying armies, or avert the social and political upheaval made possible by Confederate defeat. That is, losses could not preserve the world as John imagined it—the cultural place in which a warrior-troubadour's honor and chivalry counted for nearly everything. That realm, or at least the possibility of it, could only survive through victories.

Any such victories, however, would have to wait until the spring. After breaking off the siege, Marmaduke's bedraggled army burned a few Federal outposts between Springfield and Rolla, and then fought another, even bloodier, battle at Hartville. His expedition's concluding fight cost Marmaduke two regimental commanders—McDonald and Porter both died from wounds sustained at Hartville—and took a gruesome toll on the ranks of the Iron Brigade. Its lackluster finale also confirmed the overall pointlessness of the raid. True, Curtis recalled Blunt's army back into southeast Missouri. Also true, the move did very little—if anything at all—to change the broader military situation along the Arkansas-Missouri border. Curtis and Blunt still held the high cards while Missouri, despite Hindman's and Marmaduke's and Shelby's best efforts, appeared no closer to truly joining the Confederacy in early 1863 than it had in 1862 or even 1861.[56]

Knowing this, the men of the Iron Brigade weren't just downtrodden about Hartville or the harsh winter awaiting them in Northern

Arkansas; worse than a lost battle, cold, or even hunger, was homelessness. They were exiles—again. In late January, they finished limping back to their snow-laden camps around Batesville. From nearly the instant of their arrival, the Missourians longed for a second expedition. Next time, they dreamed, it would reap glory *and* victory.[57]

The Costs of Valor

The emergence of spring in 1863 in Northern Arkansas revealed a mostly intact Confederate Army of the Trans-Mississippi. Marmaduke's and Shelby's men had endured the winter—but with very little to show for their months of martial hibernation. Harsh weather, stacked on top of material deficiencies, fostered suffering, not recuperation. And while the rising temperatures and blooming foliage of April certainly represented a welcome change for John and the rest of the Iron Brigade, the shifting seasons could not allay paucities of food, clothing, and footwear. Local sympathizers helped as best they could, but a quartermaster's department they were not. Beyond the condition of the men, the thaw exposed other command obstacles. Fresh horses—the lifeblood of effective cavalry—were a rarity. Ample fodder for the few that remained was similarly scarce. Perhaps worst of all, as the war entered its third year, myriad Confederates in the Trans-Mississippi *still* lacked a government-issued longarm. As Marmaduke himself later alluded, against Federal troops armed with cutting edge rifle-muskets and artillery pieces, even zealous Rebels could only make do with scatterguns and squirrel rifles for so long.[1]

For Shelby's Missourians, and especially for veterans of the original Lafayette County Mounted Rifles, none of those privations mattered when word arrived from Little Rock to spearhead another invasion. For four months—four agonizingly cold, gloomy, lonely months— they'd dreamed of marching back across the border, liberating their homes, and seizing Missouri for the Confederacy once and for all. Therefore, according to John, when news of the operation reached their encampment, "the old brigade shook itself into a compact mass of defiant soldiers again," and "*St. Louis* became the watchword." In reality, the goals of departmental chieftains paled in comparison to the soaring anticipations of the rank and file. Reading between the lines of *Shelby and His Men,* John seemed to grasp this, despite putting on such optimistic airs.[2]

In short, with winter over, Holmes and Marmaduke needed something for the army to do, lest it disintegrate. Planning a worthwhile campaign with such a worn-out force proved challenging. Ultimately, they settled on harassing Union outposts in southern Missouri. At the very least, the mission would get homesick men out of camp and onto their native soil for a few weeks—an easily accomplished morale boost. Between four thousand and five thousand men set off in two columns under Marmaduke's command. However, as a result of the same hardships that had complicated planning for the expedition in the first place, nearly half the invasion force lacked a proper weapon and nearly one-quarter of its cavalrymen departed without a mount. Marmaduke begrudgingly brought these troops along. He really didn't have a choice. Any man left behind, or so it was widely believed, would simply desert and return to Missouri on his own.[3]

MARMADUKE'S DIVISION SPLIT up and staged minor raids against Union garrisons at Patterson, Bloomfield, and Fredericktown. The Confederates confiscated some supplies, but overall, their plundering fell well short of expectations. Then Marmaduke dispatched one of his columns, led by Colonel George W. Carter, in pursuit of John McNeil and his nearly two thousand men. The Canadian-born McNeil wasn't just any brigadier in the Union army; pro-Confederate Missourians held him in particular contempt because of his involvement in a pair of shootings that many Southerners considered atrocities. In May 1861 McNeil commanded some of the Union troops that fired on and killed rioters during the protests over Camp Jackson. Then in October 1862, while conducting antiguerrilla operations in northeastern Missouri, he oversaw the execution of ten Confederate POWs. Critics coined it the "Palmyra Massacre." Perhaps it was the thought of finally bagging the "Butcher of Palmyra" as he fled to Cape Girardeau that lured

Carter too close to the river hub's network of four, heavily armed fortresses. Regardless, his command found itself trapped. Their rescue brought Shelby and the Iron Brigade to Cape Girardeau and, as a result, drastically altered the trajectory of John's wartime experience.[4]

Late in the morning on April 26, Shelby's column, along with Shanks's Battalion and the regiment of Colonel John Q. Burbridge, laid into Union pickets and skirmishers around Cape Girardeau. As it had done in many fights before, the Iron Brigade made the attack on foot. John recollected that "the battle became stubborn and severe directly, but the Federals were finally driven back on all points from the timber and into the first line of fortifications." For an instant, the Union retreat might have seemed like a positive development. Then what John described as "a terrible artillery fire" burst forth from the stone citadels. A hail of shot and shell rained down on Marmaduke's entire division. Confederate artillerists found themselves even more overpowered than usual; gunners died so quickly under the barrage that batteries struggled to even return fire. Volunteers to work the guns "came in dozens," John observed, "and melted away almost as fast as they came."[5]

After only a few hours, Marmaduke decided to cut his losses which, by then, were quite heavy. Shelby called a charge. Marmaduke countermanded the order. The entire division pulled back to Jackson, ten miles northwest of Cape Girardeau. There, cloaked by darkness, a brigade of Federals under William Vandever ambushed elements of Marmaduke's bloodied force. The Missourians suffered more casualties—and lost many horses in the confusion of the night assault. This second defeat effectively ended the expedition. With all hope for a triumphal homecoming dashed, the Iron Brigade spent the better part of a week fending off Federal pursuers before crossing safely back into Arkansas on May 1. The brigade, that is, minus John.[6]

John's own ambiguity on the matter makes it difficult to pinpoint when a ball crashed through his upper leg and left him disabled at Cape Girardeau. In keeping with his tendency not to focus directly on himself in print—à la his coverage of Shelby's wedding party— John completely omitted his personal ordeal from *Shelby and His Men*. None of his other writings shed light on the wound, nor does any of his surviving correspondence. Likewise, Colonel G. W. Thompson's vague after-action report from Cape Girardeau listed John among those who "fell, severely wounded, while gallantly leading and encouraging their men upon the field" but provided no additional details. What we do know is that when a stretcher finally evacuated John from the field, the men bearing it wore blue uniforms. On May 26, 1863, Lieutenant John Newman Edwards added a new distinction to his military resume: prisoner of war.[7]

Part 1: From Cape Girardeau to Johnson's Island

If any unpleasant words passed between Marmaduke and Shelby after the debacles at Cape Girardeau and Jackson, John obviously wasn't present to witness them firsthand. For his part, Shelby failed to file a report of the battle; hardly coincidental, given the sudden unavailability of his adjutant. Years later, though, John took Shelby's side in *Shelby and His Men*. He conceded outright that capturing the town "had never been intended," before countering—rather absurdly, given the situation—that Shelby believed "a united attack by Marmaduke on the forts, with his entire force, might probably have resulted in their capture." Yet in May 1863, after the supposedly omnipotent Shelby's aggression had landed John in prison, he was hundreds of miles away. Inmate J. N. Edwards would have to fend for himself.[8]

Though technically a prisoner, John spent the first seven weeks of his captivity at the Union Post Hospital in Cape Girardeau. In this regard, he was luckier than most. The proximity of the battlefield to the hospital spared him the agony of a long, overland journey with an open wound. And at this point in the war, especially in the Trans-Mississippi, a brick-and-mortar Union facility was almost certainly better accoutred than a Confederate field hospital. That said, just getting oneself before a physician hardly ensured survival. Hospitals oftentimes claimed just as many victims as combat—and they could do so in equally frightening ways.[9]

For surgeons, speed mattered a great deal in the wake of battle. This was partly due to volume: pitched fights created large, overlapping waves of trauma patients. Men needed to be assessed and dealt with quickly to make room for those with better odds of survival. Performing a procedure swiftly, especially if it involved removing a limb or probing vital innards with sharp objects, could also spare a patient bleeding to death or dying of shock. Men shot in the extremities were better off than their gut shot comrades, but that wasn't always a high bar to reach. When large, relatively soft chunks of lead collided with even softer assemblages of bone, muscle tissue, and tendon, it frequently left an arm or leg damaged beyond repair. Assuming the owner of the mangled limb lived long enough to reach medical care, this meant a trip to the amputation room—which often amounted to nothing more than planks or an old door thrown across barrels, a "handwashing" basin of blood-tinged water, and perhaps a flimsy curtain.

Wherever they took place, mid-nineteenth-century amputations weren't a sight for the squeamish or weak hearted. A man was strapped down or held down depending on the nature of his wound and his level of hysteria. He might be given an anesthetic or a swig of liquor or nothing at all to calm nerves and to dull excruciating pain. Then a surgeon, sporting a bloody, sweat-soaked apron, would take various blades into his grimy hands and slice away tissue and tendon. A saw would be enlisted to cut cleanly through bone. Afterward, assuming the patient was still breathing, flaps of skin and stitches created the stumps borne by untold Civil War veterans into the twentieth century.

While John failed to dodge the literal bullet at Cape Girardeau, he at least sidestepped its metaphorical cousin. Simply put, the projectile missed his femur; it produced a nasty flesh wound, but a flesh wound, nonetheless. So John got to keep his leg. He also avoided an infection and was restored to active status on June 14, 1863. Then he departed immediately for St. Louis, one hundred miles northwest of Cape Girardeau. There, on June 16, 1863, John was officially received as a ward of Myrtle Street Prison.[10]

Named for its location at the junction of Myrtle and Fifth, Myrtle Street Prison opened in September 1861 on St. Louis's east end. The two-story, brick warehouse, confiscated by Union authorities from a Confederate sympathizer named Bernard Lynch, housed a mix of captured Confederates, disloyal civilians, and Federal deserters. While not typically remembered as one of the Civil War's largest or most notorious prisons—certainly not on par with the likes of Andersonville in Georgia or Elmira Prison in New York—Myrtle Street claimed its fair share of unpleasantries.[11]

Like virtually all military penitentiaries, big or small, it habitually lacked the necessary space for proper sleeping arrangements and hygiene. Originally assessed as capable of housing one hundred prisoners, Myrtle Street sometimes exceeded that figure by 50 percent. Guards routinely packed prisoners into poorly lit, ill-ventilated rooms, where they slept shoulder to shoulder, huddled beneath rotting blankets on filthy floors. This overcrowding, combined with poor nutrition and insufficient heat when temperatures dropped, triggered outbreaks of disease. The natural human byproducts of disease only worsened the already unsanitary conditions. In May 1862, authorities deemed Myrtle Street too noxious to operate in good conscience—which was really saying something given the standards of Civil War prisons—and shuttered the facility. However, six months later, in November 1862, Myrtle Street reopened due to overcrowding in other nearby prisons.[12]

On June 18 Lieutenant John Newman Edwards sat for an interview with an assistant adjutant general. The purpose of the meeting was simple. The adjutant would discern John's suitability for prisoner exchange. That such an interview took place at all speaks to the irregular nature of John's POW experience. Technically, on May 5—more than a month before the interview—John had *already* received a parole. Union authorities didn't need his consent to issue a parole. It may even have been finalized without his knowledge. Still, the parole's validity only held if John promised to honor its provisions. In basic terms, here's how parole worked for a "normal" Confederate POW: the captured soldier swore off future military service in exchange for freedom and safe passage through Union-occupied territory. Owing to logistics, paroles were self-enforced. Both sides issued them on an honor system. Theoretically, John could have left the hospital at Cape Girardeau with parole in hand and gone home to Western Missouri. But he wasn't a normal Confederate POW. He refused to quit the war, even temporarily.[13]

In choosing prison over parole, John preserved his ability to honestly, and thereby honorably, serve in the Confederate army. He also took an enormous risk. Maintaining his active military status in no way guaranteed that John would ever get to exercise it again. Just as likely, he might remain in prison for the duration of the war. And that was assuming he survived. Civil War prisons, like battlefields and hospitals, broke men. All told, they claimed some fifty-six thousand lives. Thereby much depended—which is to say, everything depended—on John's interview. And the interview itself depended on a litany of factors well beyond his control, right down to the mood of his interrogator.[14]

Lieutenant Clemens, first name unknown, listed John as "truthful," "candid," "firm," and "healthy." In his own statement, John made clear his refusal to take any oaths of loyalty to the United States. Additionally, he still considered himself a member of Shelby's Confederate cavalry. While brash at first glance, this declaration gave John value as a unit of exchange. That in mind, the adjutant's office rendered a verdict "that he [John N. Edwards] be exchanged as a prisoner of war." On July 6, 1863, he departed St. Louis to await exchange at Johnson's Island Prisoner of War Depot, situated at the mouth of Lake Erie's Sandusky Bay, near Sandusky, Ohio.[15]

The prison on Johnson's Island opened and began receiving inmates in early spring 1862; for the duration of the war, its imprisoned population hovered between 2,500 and 3,000 Confederates, guarded by some one hundred Federal soldiers. With a dozen two-story barracks, a hospital, stables, and a cemetery, all neatly organized and enclosed by a fifteen-foot perimeter wall, Johnson's Island resembled a small village. There was even a sutler's station, where inmates with spending money could purchase additional food, clothing, and supplies. This wasn't a coincidence. Unlike many makeshift Civil War prisons and jails, Colonel William Hoffman designed the facilities at Johnson's Island specifically for the purpose of housing enemy POWs under more humane conditions.[16]

Even as an officer, John could not avoid the breaking in that confronted all new arrivals to the barracks—also known as "the pen."

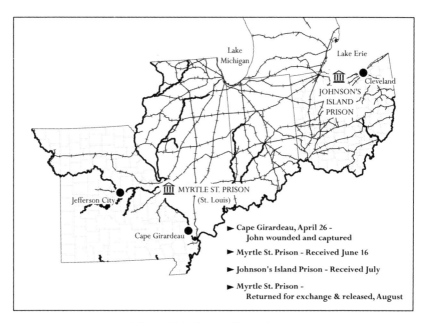

Map 5. John's POW Experience

Once John got settled, Johnson's Island wasn't a terrible place to queue for exchange. Without question, the setting—the sights and sounds of Sandusky Bay and Lake Erie—and the provisions of Johnson's Island represented a drastic improvement over Myrtle Street. As did the fact that Johnson's Island wasn't a repurposed slave pen. One prisoner, writing not long before John's arrival, insisted, "I enjoy this prison especially; we have good faire—molasses, sugar, ice, beans beef, bakers bread, tomatoes, cucumbers, and apples and peaches; we have as good society as we can afford." Another boasted, "We had a Thespian Society and Band of Negro Minstrels, among the prisoners, and many of the plays, and nearly all the songs were written by the prisoners. . . . Our Songs could be sung with impunity." It's difficult to imagine John not enjoying these performances. The men were also permitted to write two letter per week.[17]

At first sight, and especially for men who could afford to bolster their diets and wardrobes with goods from the sutler, a few sunny months at Johnson's Island could almost pass for a "destination furlough." Upon closer inspection, the life of a POW wasn't all bountiful feasts and ribald shows. Prison was a dangerous place, and Johnson's Island was no exception. The guards, as one captive contended, were "generally made up of raw recruits" or "of scoundrels who were too cowardly or too corrupt to be trusted"—men who either didn't know how to wield their power responsibly or who did but consciously chose not to. Still another prisoner noted, "We were not allowed to approach neared the fence than a certain marked line—if any one died so, he was immediately shot."[18]

Surviving until his exchange also required John to navigate internal, patriotic divisions among the Confederates themselves. In addition to the usual enforcement of hierarchy found in a prison, wartime politics and charges of disloyalty heightened the stakes. Whether intentionally started by guards or not, rumors circulated constantly that certain inmate cohorts planned to take the Oath of Allegiance. This generated suspicion and even violence between prisoners, and sometimes between entire rival mess groups. For men without friends—and protection afforded by numbers—this could prove especially dangerous.[19]

John was lucky not to experience the effects of an Ohio winter at Johnson's Island. In another sense, though, time was distinctly *not* on his side. Whether he knew it or not, the longer John waited for an exchange, the more potential for complications—or outright cancellation—grew. The Dix-Hill Cartel, the body formed in 1862 to manage prisoner exchange, was breaking down by summer 1863. The admission of Black troops to the Union army rankled the slaveholding brass in Richmond; incensed by Abraham Lincoln's decision to recruit Black men and then recognize them as legitimate soldiers, the Confederate government responded with threats to enslave them if captured, their free status before the war notwithstanding. Jefferson Davis and company further taunted that the white officers who led Black troops in battle could be executed as criminals if captured. Union responses to such provocations, in tandem with Ulysses S. Grant's belief that prisoner exchange aided the Confederate Army far more than his own, placed John's return to the Iron Brigade in serious peril.[20]

Then, on August 14, 1863, the same Colonel William Hoffman who'd designed Johnson's Island, now the Union commissary general of prisoners, ordered John back to St. Louis. Just when it appeared proslavery blowhards in Richmond might sink his chance of an exchange, John caught one final break. For months, Hoffman worried that Confederate soldiers who refused to take the Oath of Loyalty while waiting for exchange at Johnson's Island—that is, unrepentant Rebels like John—would harass Confederate POWs who *had* pledged loyalty to the United States and were also waiting to leave. Ironically, then, disloyalty almost certainly expedited John's exchange, bumping him ahead of other, newly loyal men, for the sake of their own protection. Hazy records make it impossible to discern the precise day John returned to St. Louis, which happened to be the major Union rail hub closest to his point of capture. Nor can we know how long it took John to reunite with the Iron Brigade after departing St. Louis. At the latest, he reached Shelby and company by September 12, 1863. On that date, he became Captain John Newman Edwards—as well as inspector general of the Iron Brigade.[21]

Part 2: The Raids of '63 and '64

The war took little notice of John's captivity. It raged on without him. On most fronts, the fighting did not go well for the Confederacy. In the eastern theater, one of Robert E. Lee's corps commanders, Lieutenant General Thomas "Stonewall" Jackson, died on May 10, marring an otherwise successful effort at Chancellorsville. Then on July 3, 1863, the Pickett-Pettigrew assault against Cemetery Ridge failed at Gettysburg. Lee managed to guide his devastated Army of Northern Virginia back across the Potomac—but neither he nor it would ever again invade Union territory. On July 4, from a point roughly one thousand miles southwest of Gettysburg, Major General Ulysses S. Grant wired President Abraham Lincoln the ultimate Independence Day gift: word of Lieutenant General John C. Pemberton's formal surrender at Vicksburg. After nearly two months of continuous siege operations, Grant shelled and starved the last Confederate stronghold on the Mississippi River into submission. Union control of the "Father of Waters" effectively cut Richmond off from already isolated and underserved Confederate commands in the Trans-Mississippi.

Though not present at Vicksburg, the Iron Brigade saw action on July 4 too. As part of a plan concocted by Lieutenant General Holmes, Shelby's men helped launch an ill-fated attack on Helena, Arkansas, in the hope that it would divert attention from Grant's siege downriver. It didn't. The engagement at Helena ended in disaster for the Confederates. It also left Shelby with a partially crippled right arm. Two months later, on September 10, General Sterling Price conceded Little Rock to Union forces.[22]

Shaken by these setbacks—and in spite of the victory notched by General Braxton Bragg's Army of Tennessee at the Battle of Chickamauga—the Confederacy in fall 1863 was a nation teetering on the edge of destruction. Adding insult to injury, John and the rest of the Iron Brigade faced another harsh winter in Arkansas without ample food or equipment. Assistance from Richmond appeared unlikely *before* the catastrophe at Vicksburg. Now it was virtually impossible. John recalled that Shelby had no intention of sitting cold and idle while Missouri remained in Union hands. After Helena, his troops needed another morale boost. Better still, they needed something— *anything*—to do other than waiting around for more bad news from the East. Shelby proposed a raid into Missouri.[23]

Yet by late September 1863 the Missouri that Shelby intended to invade was a changed place—its military politics permanently altered a month prior by William Clarke Quantrill's sunrise assault on Lawrence, Kansas. On August 21, as if out of thin air, approximately three hundred pro-Confederate bushwhackers descended on the abolitionist stronghold. Much like in 1856, the townspeople stood little chance. After overwhelming a small Federal encampment, Quantrill's men broke into bands and swept through Lawrence. They moved methodically from house to house, store to store, killing, burning, and pillaging as they went. Owing to their experiences in the Missouri-Kansas guerrilla war, the bushwhackers chose targets liberally. They were accustomed to a conflict of household against household—a struggle in which the traditional line between soldier and civilian largely vanished. Teenaged boys, old men, and even preachers were cut down along with the Union recruits stationed in the city.[24]

The "Lawrence Massacre," with its nearly two hundred dead and $2 million in property destruction, shocked Unionists from coast to coast. Easterners in particular were not accustomed to the domestic nature of irregular war in the western borderlands. They didn't like what they saw. It seemed uncivilized—conduct unbecoming a war of Christian gentleman. They wanted it stopped. And four days after the massacre, the commander of the District of the Border, Brigadier General Thomas Ewing Jr., thought he was doing just that with General Order No. 11. By way of Ewing's decree, all rural residents of Jackson, Cass, and Bates counties, along with part of Vernon county, had to either prove their loyalty to the Union or evacuate the district within fifteen days. The vast majority couldn't, or wouldn't, demonstrate loyalty, and Ewing knew it. That was the point. If his garrisons couldn't catch up with bushwhackers in the field—particularly those of Lawrence infamy—Ewing would simply exile the family networks that supported and supplied them. As the guerrillas followed their "quartermasters," they would become someone else's problem.[25]

At first, Shelby's proposal fell on unsympathetic ears. His military superiors weren't interested in another Missouri raid. They had ample problems to solve in Arkansas—a state that actually belonged to the Confederacy proper. But the exiled governor of Confederate Missouri, Thomas C. Reynolds, was more than interested. He liked the idea, and he liked Shelby. What's more, he did *not* like General Sterling Price, one of the raid's chief naysayers. So Reynolds—who also happened to be an intimate friend of Jefferson Davis—threw his weight behind the expedition and secured its approval. Shelby's men were to scrounge needed supplies, utilize outrage over Order No. 11 to replenish rosters, and raise all manner of hell among Union garrisons in the process. If Shelby's blitz across the border could delay Union troop movements and alleviate pressure points elsewhere for the Confederate military, so much the better. Detachments from the Iron Brigade numbering roughly six hundred set out on September 22.[26]

John had waited most of his life for just such a moment. The Confederacy appeared to be in jeopardy. His adopted homeland, Missouri, remained under the heel of Federal intruders and their foreign mercenaries. The men of the Iron Brigade were tired and outgunned. Yet here they rode, straight into the proverbial lion's den, one step behind their larger-than-life commander. Their mission had all the trappings of a mythological epic. It just required an ending. For John this wasn't just an opportunity to gather fresh recruits or winter supplies—it was a chance to do something that might be remembered forever, irrespective of how the war turned out.

The expedition rode northwest toward the Missouri border, skirmishing occasionally with bands of what John labeled "Confederate deserters and Union jayhawkers" but without major incident until September 27. Early that afternoon, a few miles south of the Arkansas River, the vanguard of Shelby's force collided with—and quickly scattered—two companies from the First Arkansas Infantry. However one-sided, the engagement risked alerting Union observers to Shelby's presence. In response, he pushed the men to cross the Arkansas River as rapidly as possible. In John's words, following the successful river fording, "the last beams of the golden sun went down upon 600 veterans with bright eyes looking far away northward, and the stern purpose in their hearts to conquer or die." Soon Shelby had them across the Boston Mountains. On September 31, Colonel Dewitt C. Hunter and two hundred new recruits joined the expedition. Then on October 2, the same day the Iron Brigade trod back onto Missouri soil, Colonel John Coffee—the officer once exiled by Marmaduke for drunkenness—brought another four hundred horsemen under Shelby's command.[27]

The whole invasion force now numbered in excess of one thousand mounted troopers. At first light on October 4, they arrived on the outskirts of Neosho. The Union garrison there was well known to the Iron Brigade. As John put it in Shelby's after-action report, the Federals at Neosho weren't just an occupying power; they were "a terror to the country, the insulters of unprotected women, and the murderers of old and infirm men." Despite his numerical advantage—roughly 1,200 against 300—Shelby opted not to storm the town. He took time to encircle it—then pushed in the Federal pickets like a rabbit driven toward the snare. The garrison immediately fell back to a fortified position that John described as "a strong brick court-house, pierced and loop-holed for musketry." From there, the Federals laid down a heavy fire on Shelby's skirmishers. Though almost certainly caught unawares by Shelby's sudden appearance north of the border, the Union militiamen felt confident in their ability to stop a frontal assault. That is, until the Confederates rolled up rifled field guns which, in John's words, "tore through the brick walls like pasteboard." Even if the garrison managed to shoot its way out of the crumbling courthouse, it had no avenue of escape from the surrounded town.[28]

The Union commander at Neosho begrudgingly accepted Shelby's demand for unconditional surrender. Horses, tack, blankets, jackets, pants, underwear, socks, boots, spurs, foodstuffs, medical kits, Sharps rifles, Colt revolvers, ammunition. "This capture," John stated matter-of-factly, "proved a godsend." Instantly, the men of the Iron Brigade came into more and better supplies than they'd seen in many months, or in some cases, ever. After distributing immediate necessities and packing the rest of the windfall into wagons, Shelby set his command back on the road that very afternoon. It was a propitious beginning to the expedition, but with the men's collective appetite for raiding now whetted, it was just that—the beginning.[29]

Next the Confederates rode through Sarcoxie, once a small bastion of pro-Confederate sympathizers. As reported by John, when Shelby and his troopers arrived, all that remained were "bare and fire-scarred chimneys point[ing] with skeleton fingers to heaven." Shortly there-after, they returned the favor in Bower's Mill. Years later in *Shelby and His Men*, John termed Bower's Mill "a militia harbor, covered with the blood of murdered southerners, crammed with prostitutes and stolen goods." He made no secret of how the Iron Brigade dealt with Missourians that allegedly turned on their "Southern" neighbors: "Fire is more powerful than water, and purified and drank up many ghastly stains not then dry in the valley. Not a house stood when the rear guard passed, and not one vestige of life remained except the terrified women clinging to one another in counterfeit dread."[30]

From the smoldering ruins of Bower's Mill, they continued toward Greenfield. On October 5, Shelby's men sacked the town, captured its garrison, and put its brick courthouse to the torch. Anything and everything useful went into Confederate saddlebags or supply wag-ons. A similar story unfolded in Stockton, where "all along the road old men and women had brought from their houses every article of furniture and piled them in great heaps, expecting Colonel Shelby to kill, burn, and destroy as he advanced." Yet unlike at Bower's Mill, per John's rendition of events, Shelby refused permission to burn Stockton and "not an article was touched nor a single private dwelling entered." The next day the Federal garrison at Humansville fell. The Confederates commandeered more horses. And perhaps for the first time, the Iron Brigade looked like a real army—albeit one wearing blue overcoats and belt buckles stamped with the wrong nation's acronym. Undeterred by these details, John wrote, "Every man, now superbly mounted, clothed, and armed, felt long of wind and fierce of mood as a blood hound."[31]

October 7 brought a skirmish outside of Warsaw, in Benton County. The Iron Brigade made quick work of a hopelessly outnumbered Union garrison and gathered "vast quantities of stores of every kind and description." It was another small victory—but it came at greater cost than Neosho, Greenfield, or Stockton. The raids prior to Warsaw had been sprung on unsuspecting towns and garrisons. Now, however, Shelby's men were entering the northern half of Missouri, within striking distance of Jefferson City, even. For Union authorities, a roaming group of Confederate horsemen—whoever led them, a guerrilla chieftain or a Confederate colonel—immediately raised fears of another Lawrence Massacre. As John indicated in Shelby's report, after Warsaw "the telegraph flashed out its view-halloo, and the railroads groaned under the dire preparations to meet me, and the thunderer of Saint Louis threatened vengeance as dark as death and terrible as the grave."[32]

Unfortunately for the residents of Cole Camp, a predominantly German neighborhood lying between Warsaw and Sedalia, the "thunderer of Saint Louis"—General Schofield—couldn't catch up to the Iron Brigade in time to stop it from plundering their cellars and stables. After Cole Camp, a now perfected sequence of events unfolded at Tipton on October 10: the Confederates enveloped the town, seized the garrison, and added all available supplies to the rolling stockpile. Following another brief encounter with Union skirmishers, Shelby's horsemen moved into position near Boonville. Neither Shelby, nor

John, nor the men, had any way of knowing, but their approach to Boonville marked the beginning of the end of the expedition. The Confederates momentarily captured and pillaged the town, without firing a single shot. Within hours, multiple bands of pursuing Federals prompted Shelby to move on or risk capture. Owing to this new pressure, Shelby abandoned plans to assault Jefferson City. Instead, the men would ride through Marshall en route to Waverly.[33]

In the early morning hours of October 12, the walls seemed to be closing in on the Iron Brigade—and fast. Union troops caught them off guard at Salt Fork Creek. More used to playing predator than prey thus far on the expedition, the Confederates nonetheless executed a hasty but orderly retreat toward Marshall. Part of the brigade even paused to ambush and slow down two companies of pursuing Federal militiamen along the banks of the Lamine River. The Confederates made camp outside Marshall. There, for a change, it would be Shelby and his men lured into the trap.[34]

For the Iron Brigade, the October 13, 1863, Battle of Marshall quickly became an exercise in survival. In his front, Shelby faced the cavalry command of Lieutenant Colonel Bazel F. Lazear. Acting on orders from Brigadier General E. B. Brown—who'd overseen Marmaduke's defeat at Springfield in 1862—Lazear broke off his direct pursuit of Shelby and moved his men onto the best defensive ground Marshall had to offer. When the Iron Brigade moved on the town, Lazear was waiting; so were his men, a force roughly equal to Shelby's, and better rested to boot. More problematic still, Brown had moved in directly behind Shelby with his own command of approximately eight hundred militia troops. After encircling so many outnumbered garrisons in the past few weeks, a startled Shelby found his own command outnumbered and on the verge of being surrounded.[35]

In order to hold off Brown, which would allow him to fight through Lazear's line and out of the closing circle, Shelby detached Major David Shanks and his battalion at a bridge along Salt Fork Creek. The orders given to Shanks were blunt and simple: delay Brown's crossing at virtually any cost or risk destruction of the entire brigade. The rest of the Confederates at Marshall engaged Lazear on foot. They made initial gains against the Union left but fell back in

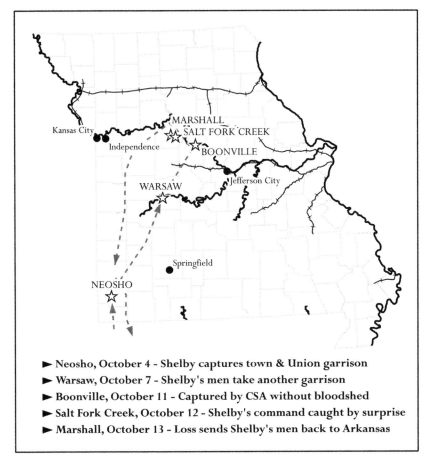

- ▶ Neosho, October 4 - Shelby captures town & Union garrison
- ▶ Warsaw, October 7 - Shelby's men take another garrison
- ▶ Boonville, October 11 - Captured by CSA without bloodshed
- ▶ Salt Fork Creek, October 12 - Shelby's command caught by surprise
- ▶ Marshall, October 13 - Loss sends Shelby's men back to Arkansas

Map 6. Shelby's Raid (1863)

the face of reinforcements and counterattacks. Then cannon fire announced Brown's crossing of Salt Fork Creek. For hours, Shanks's men had offered a borderline suicidal defense of the crossing; eventually, though, Brown's attackers flanked the Confederate position and crossed Salt Fork Creek anyway.[36]

Shelby remounted the men and rushed them into column by regiment. He ordered the supply wagons, laden with plunder from all over the state, into the middle of the column. Time had run out for the Iron Brigade. They would either punch through Lazear's line before it could link up with Brown or they would be enveloped and cut to pieces. The survivors would be captured and sent to a Union prison camp. In point of fact, considering the number of Confederates clad in stolen blue uniforms, they might be *lucky* to end up at Johnson's Island. The entire command, minus Shanks's men, again surged against the left end of Lazear's line. It broke. Shelby and approximately 1,200 horsemen galloped north to the relative safety of Waverly, and then turned south. Shanks's detachment also escaped but fled east from Marshall, before eventually bending southward as well. The two pieces of Shelby's expeditionary force reunited on October 20 near Berryville, Arkansas, and returned safely to the Confederate capital of the state at Washington on November 3.[37]

Despite sinking numerous supply wagons in the Missouri River to increase travel speed, Shelby's official report lauded the raid as a great success. Submitted to General Price's adjutant, Major L. A. MacLean, on November 16, it claimed that the Iron Brigade confiscated or destroyed nearly $2 million worth of Union property over the course of a forty-one-day, 1,500-mile-long trek—everything from wagons, boots, animals, and weapons to iron rails and telegraph wire. This rendition of the expedition runs several pages, includes minute details throughout, and even supplements pivotal moments with melodramatic dialogue—one of John's specialties. Given these particulars, it isn't difficult to read the final line as a tongue-in-cheek jab at the senior officials who'd doubted the expedition: "Hoping this report may prove satisfactory, I remain, major, very respectfully, your obedient servant."[38]

Satisfying as a dig at Price may have been, military decorum prevented John from penning a full-throated, fantastical account of the campaign. Conveniently enough, a letter to the editor of Washington, Arkansas's local paper, the *Telegraph*, offered just such a narrative on November 18. Signed only by "Missourian," the identity of the author—who just happened to have firsthand knowledge of the entire raid and thought the world of Jo Shelby—cannot be proved with absolute certainty. But as circumstantial cases go, it's as sure as they come. The prose is vintage John from start to finish. He labels the raid "the most extraordinary, perhaps, the world ever saw." Just two days after the submission of Shelby's official report, he'd already added millions to the ledger, claiming the brigade destroyed $3 million in railroad property alone. The account ends with a sentence of more than one hundred words, all dripping the deepest shade of purple John could muster:

> When history lifts the veil from the terrible drama of this war; when the white pinions of peace float over our distracted country, soft as angel footfalls on some velvet floor; when the red banners of strife and carnage have gleamed o'er the last foughten field, and the universal anthem of a land redeemed comes swelling up from valley and glen, whose eternal chorus was born in heaven, this raid of gray jackets over the border into the valley and shadow of death, with no light but opposing cannon, and no friends but ruddy steel and trusty rides, this raid will stand out grand, glorious, sublime—a monument of daring—an example of dash and recklessness never surpassed.[39]

Years later, in *Shelby and His Men*, John could *openly* lavish attention on the expedition. The count of captured garrisons grew, as did the tallies of forts destroyed and arms seized. Ignoring their desperate flight from Marshall, John offered that Shelby made it "in his own good time—unharmed, unwhipped." Even for a troubadour with John's chutzpah, these assertions stretched the tale to new heights. At first glance, the explanation seems obvious. With the war over and lost, exaggerating the military importance of the Iron Brigade's signature campaign shielded the unit from blame for Confederate defeat. In reality, perceptions of the *raiders themselves* mattered more to him than any material or logistical metric. It was imperative to John that people saw Shelby and the men the way he did—as heroes cut from different cultural cloth than standard fare Rebels.[40]

With that agenda at the fore, he laid out the comparison, at the expense of other high-ranking officers—and sometimes even friends. "Believing the expedition would be a failure necessarily," John wrote, these authorities, "contended from the first that Shelby's ambition was unreasonable and foolhardy; that his discretion was weak and his temerity a passion." Having set up his targets sufficiently for rhetorical shelling, John fired the heavy guns: "They did not know or care to inquire about his genius, his dash, his valor, his iron endurance, the idolatry of the men who followed him, and their resolution to triumph or die." In other words, not only were the men of Shelby's command fundamentally different from other Confederate units—and not only was Shelby fundamentally different from other Confederate commanders—but the "other" Confederates and their commanders weren't even fully capable of understanding what set them apart. As far as John was concerned, Shelby and his men were already the stuff of legend.[41]

It almost goes without saying that John tailored his treatment of the raid to suit a personal agenda. After all, what could bolster his case for Arthurian-style supermen more than a bona fide deed of folk heroism? In portraying the expedition as a miracle, he wasn't entirely wrong, either—at least not as other borderlanders, and especially other pro-Confederate Missourians, understood things. What was once a common refrain among veterans of the war in the Trans-Mississippi illustrates the point well: "You've heard of Jeb Stuart's ride around McClellan? Hell, brother, Jo Shelby rode around *Missouri.*"[42]

Yet for all the dash and daring, for all the supplies plundered, enemies harassed, and new enlistments secured, not much had really changed in those forty-one days. Circumstances in Confederate Arkansas remained bleak at best. Prospects for a Confederate Missouri bordered on hopeless. And Richmond seemed to have neither the will nor the way to improve either situation. The gloomy political forecast notwithstanding, local dignitaries in Washington wanted to celebrate the expedition's success with a party.

John set the scene vividly in *Shelby and His Men.* Not coincidentally, his coverage called to mind a victorious king and his knights at an imaginary medieval banquet. "Wine hid away in dusty cellars" came out just for the occasion and "blushed rosy in the goblets pledged by women's lips." "Music swelled out in delicious strains upon the perfumed air" and "toasts were drunk in joyousness and glee." "For in the festive hour," John rhapsodized, "war's red terrors were laid away and only love and mirth held high carnival."[43]

Not long after the feast, a bit of good news further cheered the brigade, and John in particular. Governor Reynolds followed through on a promise made to Shelby back in September—orchestrate a successful raid and find the sash of a brigadier general waiting upon your return. The promotion wasn't literally waiting for Shelby, but close enough; Reynolds tapped connections in Richmond and, about a month later, secured the promotion in December 1863. For John, Shelby's jump into the ranks of the generals was a win twice over. First, it played directly into the narrative of Shelby as a "chosen one" leading his select band of cavaliers in defense of home, hearth, and tradition. And second, as the chosen one's pen hand, it meant advancement. Only two months after becoming a captain, John ascended again, this time to major and adjutant of the brigade.[44]

MORE SO THAN ever after Shelby's raid, veterans of the Iron Brigade pined to go back to Missouri. Due to more pressing military concerns, though, their wait dragged on for nearly a year. And by August 1864, when Edmund Kirby Smith finally got around to vying for Missouri, the sands of war in all three major theaters had shifted drastically.

In the West, General Braxton Bragg attempted to follow up his victory at Chickamauga by laying siege to Chattanooga, a Union-occupied rail hub in southern Tennessee. In the November 1863 showdown for Chattanooga, Bragg squared off against Ulysses S. Grant. Federal efforts to break the siege involved heavy, uphill assaults against Missionary Ridge and Lookout Mountain. These attacks succeeded in dislodging and driving off Bragg's run-down Army of Tennessee. Meanwhile Lieutenant General James Longstreet's corps, temporarily detached from Lee's Army of Northern Virginia, had kept Union troops pinned down in Knoxville and away from the fighting at Chattanooga. When Bragg retreated, Grant dispatched Major General William Tecumseh Sherman to relieve Knoxville. With Sherman's victory over Longstreet, the Union consolidated control of Tennessee and established a perfect launchpad for an invasion of the Confederate heartland. In February 1864 Sherman captured Meridian, Mississippi. Eight months later, on September 2, he took Atlanta.

Confederate operations didn't fare much better in the East. In March 1864 Abraham Lincoln promoted Grant to Lieutenant General—the first since Winfield Scott—and made him commander of all Union armies. Then beginning in May 1864, Grant and Robert E. Lee clashed in a series of engagements north of Richmond. At the Wilderness, Spotsylvania Courthouse, and Cold Harbor, the Army of Northern Virginia and the Army of the Potomac slammed into each other with gruesome effect. Even in defeat, and very much unlike his predecessors, Grant refused to disengage. He hounded Lee's exhausted, ill-equipped army—baying it within the gates of Petersburg.

West of the Mississippi River, far from the losses at Chattanooga and Atlanta, and even farther from Petersburg, the Confederacy still managed a significant trade in cotton. In Texas, especially, slavery and plantation agriculture went on largely unimpeded. Union forces had tried and failed to make inroads against this important source of Confederate income: they lost control of Galveston in January 1863, and several months after that, a Federal raid into Texas by way of Sabine Pass ended in humiliation. Major General Nathaniel P. Banks hoped to make up for those losses—and then some—with a sweeping invasion of the Red River Valley. He failed. In April 1864 Banks lost battles at Mansfield and Pleasant Hill in Louisiana; his invading force turned tail for New Orleans without ever setting foot in Texas.

Following the Union's failed Red River Campaign, General Edmund Kirby Smith saw an opportunity and authorized another Confederate attempt to conquer Missouri. As things turned out, it would be the *last* such invasion—not that knowing would have mattered to John or the rest of the Iron Brigade. As the legend of Shelby's raid swelled, one more chance for success was all they thought necessary. To head up the incursion, Kirby Smith tabbed Major General Sterling Price. Once upon a time, the pick made perfect sense. Price had been a man on the rise. After studying law at Hampden-Sydney College and joining the Virginia Bar, he relocated to Missouri. Price represented the state in Congress, recruited a regiment, and commanded it with distinction in Mexico, all before turning forty years old. After the Mexican-American War, Missourians elected him as their eleventh governor. Naturally, then, many looked to Price for calm and steady as the secession debate gave way to gunplay.[45]

Those days were long past. Years of eating and drinking well in camp, even on active campaign, took their toll. He'd grown portly in stature and ungainly in the saddle. These qualities left him inclined to softer paces and frequent rests; they made the Sterling Price of August 1864, with his distinguished tuft of silver hair, habitually late—an awkward quality indeed for the leader of an all-out cavalry blitz deep into enemy territory. For whatever it was worth, the rank and file still liked him. They knew Price as "Old Pap," a moniker that stemmed from his grandfatherly demeanor. It was an endearment, to be sure, but one that reflected very little in the way of *martial* confidence.[46]

Price set out from Princeton, Arkansas, on August 29. While en route to Missouri, he collected a strike force of three cavalry divisions, commanded by Major General John Marmaduke, Major General James Fagan, and Brigadier General Joseph Shelby. Shelby's division—the smallest of the trio—linked up with the expedition last. John and the rest of the Iron Brigade joined the march on September 13 at Powhatan, roughly forty-five miles south of the border. Six days later, they crossed into Missouri. At twelve thousand men, Price's "Army of Missouri" represented an imposing force on paper. In truth, it was hampered by severe logistical shortcomings from the start. Roughly one-third of the Confederate invaders trod onto Missouri soil without a firearm. Food stores and ammunition were also in short supply. Kirby Smith and Price hoped plunder from Union garrisons and supply depots would solve these problems as the operation progressed. In plainer words, they were outright depending on it.[47]

Despite these issues, the campaign started well enough. After entering Missouri, the Confederates spent the rest of September capturing small garrisons, pillaging supply depots, and razing rail lines. Shelby's men were particularly busy, overtaking a Union garrison at Patterson on September 22 and then destroying four bridges in the lead up to a battle at Ironton. Brigadier General Thomas Ewing—of Order No. 11 infamy—arrived with troops from St. Louis and engaged Price at Ironton on September 27. The Confederates overwhelmed Ewing's line and forced a Federal retreat to Fort Davidson, just north of Ironton. Though earthen, the hexagonal fort boasted ten-foot-thick walls, rifle pits, a dry moat, and even a drawbridge. Apparently unaware of these features, Price ignored the role patience had played in his successful siege at Lexington in 1861. Instead, he reverted to the commander who'd sent wave after wave into the meatgrinder at Wilson's Creek. Ewing's men threw back multiple headlong assaults against Fort Davidson and then snuck away under cover of darkness. The next day, Price triumphantly claimed the abandoned fort and its remaining supplies; the stores and arms undoubtedly helped, but powder and shot remained scarce. In the process of evacuating the fort, Ewing's men detonated the powder magazine.[48]

John and the rest of Shelby's division didn't suffer the headlong charges against Fort Davidson. In fact, they completely missed the fighting at Ironton. While Price bloodied Fagan's and Marmaduke's commands, Shelby overran the garrison at Potosi and gathered additional supplies. With or without Shelby's men, Fort Davidson served Price a harsh dose of reality. His divisions struggled to seize a tiny fortress manned by two regiments. They could never breech the defenses being amassed around St. Louis, let alone occupy the city. To try would be utter madness. Even Price could see that now. He turned his attention west, along the line of the Missouri River. The invasion took on a new chief objective: capture the state capital at Jefferson City.[49]

Over the course of the next week, Price's army moved in that direction. They fanned out to strike small garrisons and vandalize the railroad along the way. The Iron Brigade exceled at these lightning strikes. Occasionally, though, they incurred heavy losses. While destroying a Pacific Railroad bridge over the Osage River, multiple balls struck Colonel David Shanks in the chest. The impact dehorsed him. He died before hitting the riverbank. For the core of Shelby's command, it was a devastating blow. Not only did Shanks lead Shelby's old regiment, the Fifth Missouri, he was also one of the original Lafayette County Mounted Rifles. The next day, during a skirmish just miles from the capital city, Price grasped that it too was defended beyond the capabilities of his men. For Shelby's inner circle, this sudden realization was salt in an open wound: Shanks died facilitating an attack that would never be made against a position that could never have been taken. They would have to move on. Again.

This time, Price chose to swing farther west along the Missouri River, toward what he hoped were softer targets at Boonville, Lexington, and Independence.[50]

The decision changed the entire complexion of the campaign. In his official report, Price heralded Shelby's capture of the supply-rich garrisons at Boonville and Glasgow on October 9 and October 15, respectively. But even Old Pap knew by the middle of October that the mission was a failure. If his little army couldn't capture Missouri's most important city (St. Louis) or the seat of its government (Jefferson City), it wasn't capable of dragging the state into the Confederacy by force. Furthermore, even if Confederate-sympathizing Missourians ballooned the size of his divisions, without rifles seized from St. Louis and Jefferson City, Price couldn't arm them anyway.[51]

The latter problem did not require a solution, at least. No throngs of Missourians flocked to Price's lines. And Union commanders weren't allowing Price to stay still for long. Rightly sensing weakness from the Confederates, Federal pursuers closed in from multiple angles. Even in the friendly confines of Western Missouri, operating room disappeared rapidly for Fagan, Marmaduke, and Shelby. On October 19, at Lexington, Price's army plowed through a much smaller Union force led by Major General James Blunt and occupied the town. The next morning, along the banks of the Little Blue, Price's men again collided with two regiments of well-entrenched Federal troopers. Over a two-day fight, the Confederates drove Blunt's army into and then out of Independence.[52]

The Confederates fared well in these battles, thanks largely to numerical superiority. When a full-strength division of Union cavalry, under Major General Alfred Pleasanton, entered the equation, Price found himself between enemy forces that now outnumbered him in total. On October 22, thanks to a flanking maneuver from Shelby's men, all three Confederate divisions fought their way across the Big Blue River. On the other side, they found Price's nemesis from Pea Ridge, Major General Samuel Curtis, with *another* Union army. It blocked the trail west. If Curtis, Blunt, and Pleasanton managed to combine forces, Price's eight thousand armed effectives would face a better-fed, better-clothed, better-armed enemy, twenty thousand

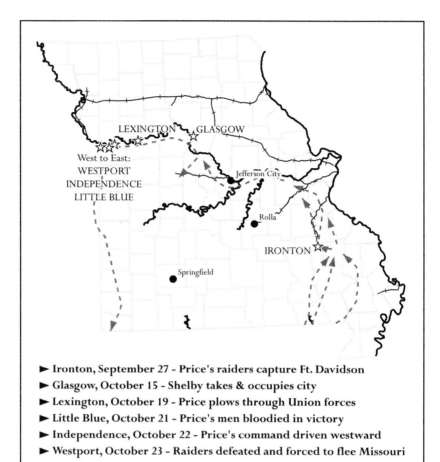

► **Ironton, September 27 - Price's raiders capture Ft. Davidson**
► **Glasgow, October 15 - Shelby takes & occupies city**
► **Lexington, October 19 - Price plows through Union forces**
► **Little Blue, October 21 - Price's men bloodied in victory**
► **Independence, October 22 - Price's command driven westward**
► **Westport, October 23 - Raiders defeated and forced to flee Missouri**

Map 7. Price's Raid (1864)

strong. One choice remained: engage and destroy Curtis's army before Pleasanton could cross the Big Blue.[53]

On October 23, the Battle of Westport kicked off at dawn. A combination of Curtis's and Blunt's men struck first; they crossed Brush Creek, just south of the city, and slammed into Shelby's and Fagan's divisions. Colonel Charles "Doc" Jennison led one of the Union cavalry brigades. The presence of a jayhawker so notorious as Jennison on the field no doubt motivated the Confederates to hold firm. They did—and then countered aggressively up the Fort Scott Road. Brigadier General M. Jeff Thompson, known as the "Swamp Fox" in some circles, led the Iron Brigade's charge. Thompson rose to command the brigade when Shelby rose to command the division. Together, for an instant, it looked like they might crush Curtis's army in Westport and notch a colossal, campaign-defining victory for the Confederacy. Then, all at once, the problems that had hindered Price's army since the day it left Arkansas came calling. Ammunition ran dangerously low. Too few to sustain the counterattack's momentum for long, the men spread themselves dangerously thin. Timely Federal reinforcements and a flanking maneuver reversed the Confederate gains.[54]

As the Iron Brigade's fortune changed, Marmaduke's line faltered. Before giving way, his division held Pleasanton and thousands of Union cavalrymen out of the fight at Westport. Now those Federals stormed across the Big Blue and threatened to roll over Shelby's and Fagan's former right flank. Price instantly found his men in a fast-closing vise; Curtis saw too and ordered an all-out push to close it before the invaders could slip through. Serving as a rear guard, the Iron Brigade stalled the Union advance just long enough for Price's drubbed army to escape. As they galloped over the prairie south of Westport, the Confederates set fires to screen their retreat. Walls of thick, black smoke billowing over the scorched landscape spawned an apocalyptic scene, one altogether symbolic of the moment. For John and the other Missourians, the war wasn't technically over. But any hope for a Confederate Missouri perished in the flames.[55]

THE NARROW ESCAPE from Westport signaled the end of one crisis and the beginning of another. However worn down, Price's army risked total annihilation if it stopped moving. Pleasanton refused to give up the chase. Nor was Pleasanton's the only Union command hunting the Confederates. Federal cavalry caught up with Price's train at a river crossing on October 25. Most of the Army of Missouri escaped. Major General John Marmaduke and several hundred men did not. They became POWs. Three days later, at Newtonia, Price called an afternoon halt and promptly found his army ambushed. At first, the Confederates offered token resistance. Exhausted, starving, and poorly armed, many broke ranks and ran for their lives. Regiments of Colorado and Kansas cavalry under Blunt sheered through them and threatened to wipe out Price's entire command.[56]

Into this breech rode Shelby's division, led by what remained of the Iron Brigade. "Dismounting every man of my division," Shelby explained in his official report, "I formed my line of battle just in time to meet the onset." After days of bloody charges and hair-raising retreats, the Missourians thundered back from the front of the column to the shooting. They dismounted and threw themselves against both ends of Blunt's smaller line. To avoid being encircled, Blunt's men had no choice but to fall back and wait for additional numbers. As a result, Shelby's report triumphantly noted that "night closed the contest, and another beautiful victory had crowned the Confederate arms." Labeling the fight at Newtonia a "beautiful victory" was certainly a stretch. As late-arriving Union reinforcements bolstered Blunt's regiments, sunset probably saved Shelby's division from an overwhelming counterattack. In any event, the engagement allowed the rest of Price's army to slip away from Newtonia, whence it made a break for the Indian Territory.[57]

Part 3: The End of the Beginning

After zigging and zagging through Missouri, Kansas, and the Indian Territory, Major General Sterling Price crossed back into Confederate Arkansas on November 1, 1864. He set up headquarters at Laynesport on December 2 and filed his official report on December 28. Despite failing to capture St. Louis or Jefferson City, Price's account painted a rosy picture of the invasion: his men seized or destroyed $10 million in Federal property, gathered five thousand new recruits, and invigorated anti-Union feelings all across Missouri. The report hints that yet another invasion might finally claim the state for the Confederacy. To that end, in a statement verging on alternate reality or insanity or both, Price wrote, "I am satisfied that could I have remained in Missouri this winter the army would have increased 50,000 men." What he might have done with forty thousand additional men that he could neither mount nor arm—or even feed—remains a great mystery.[58]

About Shelby, to whom Price owed the escape of his army from Missouri, the major general gushed: "Brig. Gen. J. O. Shelby, commanding division, added new luster to his past fame as a brilliant and heroic officer, and without disparagement to the officers I must be permitted to say that I consider him the best cavalry officer I ever saw. The services rendered by him and his division in this expedition are all beyond praise." This amounted to high acclaim even in an era known for "lush" martial prose. Even so, Shelby's division did execute nearly all the campaign's few highlights. Price understood that. And with his reputation hanging in the balance, it isn't astonishing to see Price cloak himself with the success of his subordinate.[59]

What *is* surprising, at least initially, is how Shelby's own account didn't refuse any of Price's semidelusional observations. "The expedition was full of hardships and suffering in some respects," the report suggested, "yet General Price accomplished much, and stamped his expedition as one of the most brilliant of the war." "History," the report further opined, "will crown it with the laurel wreath of fame." Looking closely at the document, the language is John's, per usual. But its tone and brevity indicate that Shelby took the fallout of the botched invasion very seriously. Heads higher up the chain of command than his might roll—especially if Thomas Reynolds had any say in the matter. In December the exiled governor supposedly published a letter in the *Marshall Texas Republican* that landed on Price like a bombshell: "His regular course was to sit in his ambulance at the head of his train on the march, rarely mounting his horse; to sip his copious toddy immediately after going into camp, and in view of the soldiers passing by, and soon generally after to take a nap." "The disorder in his army was terrific," Reynolds further charged, "and the main cause of it palpable; he could not enforce laws, regulations or orders, because he conspicuously violated them himself."[60]

Based on the vernacular and style of Reynolds's account, he either discussed the expedition at length with John prior to publication or John helped ghostwrite the letter. The references to Baron Munchausen and Marshal Marmont, or to "merry madcaps" and Shelby in the form of a cornered lion, are simply too John-esque to constitute a coincidence. Either way, until Shelby knew precisely where things stood, it was a dangerous time to play the part of a know-it-all subordinate. Accordingly, in the report that *he* had to sign, Shelby went the diplomatic route and kept his normally verbose adjutant on a tight leash. No sardonic jabs at superior officers this go-round; they would let the division's exploits and Price's failures speak for themselves. And they would let Reynolds lead the public attack.[61]

Even as part of a clever political maneuver, this constituted a new experience in John's military career. It wasn't often that Shelby muzzled him. After the war, we can only presume how John gloried in narrating the invasion without fear of bureaucratic reprisals. It's worth recalling, too, that he composed nearly all of *Shelby and His Men* in Mexico, living and working in relative proximity to Price. Personally, he harbored no ill will toward Price. Just the opposite: like most of the men, John saw the general as a nice old man. But the legacies of Shelby and the Iron Brigade came first. He brought the hammer down on "Old Pap" with full force.

John bemoaned the decision not to assault Jefferson City. He stopped short of openly blaming the change in plans on cowardice but implied it by arguing that Price greatly exaggerated the capital's defenses. Generally speaking, John condemned the whole expedition for its "slowness of movement" and "fickleness of purpose"—which was simply his way of saying that Price couldn't maintain the discipline or inspire the energy necessary to get the job done.[62]

In the pages leading up to Westport, John not only criticized the pace of Price's march but also the commanding general's carelessness with human life. John complained that Price moved "too slowly, not seeming to think that all the brave fellows falling around Shelby were so many useless human sacrifices." He followed that stinging accusation with open indictments of Price's military acumen: "Never did nature form a grander battle-field, and never were the principles of military science so sadly abused and ignored as by General Price."[63]

Even years after the fact, the expedition remained a raw spot for John. His trenchant observations made that much clear. The question is why. John certainly lamented the loss of David Shanks and other fallen comrades. Yet he knew fully and well that combat involved killing and dying. He knew that the immense pressure of leading a campaign caused even the best officers to make mistakes. And deep down, he surely understood that a man who heralded war as the ultimate path to glory, and glory as the primary stuff of immortality, had no business holding the natural byproducts of war against an army commander. John's hero, Shelby, generated a wealth of casualties himself.[64]

No, this grudge almost certainly transcended the dead—and even the realization that Missouri would not be wrested from the Union. The failed invasion exposed something about the world as John wanted to see it, so he lashed out at the man in charge. Without saying so directly, he blamed Sterling Price for not being Joseph Shelby. He blamed Price for not recruiting the class and caliber of men who followed Shelby; for not riding as Shelby rode; for not leading as Shelby led; for not fighting as Shelby fought; and for rendering pointless the pinnacle of soldierly glory—dying in combat—with an unachievable objective. The Iron Brigade didn't resemble other Confederate volunteers because they *weren't like* other Confederate volunteers. Instead, John portrayed them as adherents to an older, nobler lifestyle and as devoted practitioners of its violent customs. "The code was recognized, dueling tolerated, insults were to be avenged, and an insulted officer must either fight or resign," he testified proudly.[65]

Confederate mismanagement in the Trans-Mississippi tested that model of the universe. No matter how gallant or ingenious Shelby and his men might prove, they were always a Theophilus Holmes or a Sterling Price or an Edmund Kirby Smith away from ruin. Then again, in 1868, when *Shelby and His Men* went to press—and definitely as he wrote the book in 1866–67—John still believed that the old ways could be preserved. On one level, John revealed what the war really meant intellectually and ideologically and who actually understood it:

> It was a war of races and he [Shelby] knew it. He knew that constitutions were paper and political parties mere wills-of-the-wisp before the blood of rival parties struggling for an idea and heated seven fold by gunpowder and civil feuds.[66]

To John these grander stakes had always been obvious. This wasn't just a civil strife over slavery in the territories or the legality of secession.

As he saw it, the war tapped directly into an ancient, ongoing conflict that raged in Western Europe for generations before jumping the Atlantic. It pitted the culture and sophistication of the Old World, the ways of the "Cavaliers" and "Patricians," against "Puritans" and the "Proletarians," the reformists and paper pushers who sought to overturn tradition and upend the social hierarchy. In John's logic, the two sides could not coexist. The fight must eventually end in death for one or the other.[67]

On another level, John could finally recount the story of October 28, 1864—of Shelby's Thermopylae-like stand at Newtonia—minus restraint. And through it, he could add to the mythic foundation laid by his coverage of Shelby's own incursion into Missouri. Reveling in the melodrama, John set the scene with precise intent:

> He immediately assumed command of the rear by the inherent right of genius and of superior skill and courage. He at once brought into requisition all his eloquence, activity, and aroused energy, and labored to reduce the chaotic mass into some kind of order and to take advantage of the timid pause the enemy had made in their attack, and in the meantime, the rest of the army, forming two thirds or three fourths of the whole, drove recklessly and confusedly before the storm.[68]

In this version of the battle, distinctions between the select few and everyone else are glaring. Price lost control of his army. The bummers and pretenders quit and showed the enemy their backs; they abandoned arms and plundered what little remained of their own stores. In their hysteria, these men lacked even the good sense of animals to flee properly. All was lost. Then Shelby arrived and "barred the triumphant pursuit of the Federals with those iron ranks they could never break." He brought order to the chaos. He commanded Price to regroup and form whatever men possible for a grand, decisive fight. And as John told it, following a final, ferocious charge, "the indomitable courage of the men, the electricity coming out from his [Shelby's] actions like balm, the heroic devotion of his officers, and the unconquerable chivalry and discipline of his division triumphed." A contest to the death, indeed.[69]

SHELBY'S MEN WINTERED in northern Texas. It was there, in April 1865, that they learned of Lee's surrender to Grant at Appomattox Courthouse. In days gone by, the Army of Northern Virginia seemed invincible. During the Seven Days and at Second Manassas, Fredericksburg, and Chancellorsville. But no longer. After holding on for months around Petersburg, Lee's men finally cracked under the pressure of constant bombardment. The army went into flight. Grant caught it once and for all at Appomattox. The story really shouldn't have stunned observers in the Trans-Mississippi; news from back East had not been good for some time. Actually, news from *anywhere* in the Confederacy hadn't been good for some time. Regardless, John reported that it "burst like a thunderbolt" on the department.[70]

At Marshall, Texas, Edmund Kirby Smith conferred with the Confederate governors of Louisiana, Arkansas, and Texas. Unbeknownst to him, field commanders from the department held a war council of their own. Based on the fear that Kirby Smith would surrender the department without a fight, the officers agreed to demand his resignation. For the sake of letting an old man save face, they would give Kirby Smith an opportunity to voluntarily turn over command to his chief of staff, Major General Simon Bolivar Buckner. Shelby informed Kirby Smith that the army no longer believed in his leadership and that the men overwhelmingly wanted Buckner. First shocked, then humiliated, Kirby Smith consented through tears. Shelby, Buckner, and the others left the meeting jubilant. Everything was in order. They would fight for every last inch of Texas. They would support the other Confederate commands east of the Mississippi however possible.[71]

Unexpected news of Abraham Lincoln's murder bolstered optimism in the Trans-Mississippi. About the assassination, John later wrote that "it would be useless to deny that the soldiers rejoiced over it," confessing that the men "fired salvos and shouted glory to God." The good times didn't last long, though. Hot on the heels of the Lincoln story came another titanic development: on April 17, at Bennett Place in North Carolina, General Joseph E. Johnston surrendered the Army of Tennessee to Major General William Tecumseh Sherman. As part of the agreement, Johnston also gave up all the remaining Confederate troops in Florida, Georgia, and the Carolinas. He did so against the wishes of Confederate president Jefferson Davis, then in exile due to Grant's seizure of Richmond.[72]

For Buckner, standing alongside other Confederate armies, even from a great distance, was one thing. Standing alone against the full might of the Federal military machine was another. As John told it, Kirby Smith came to his former Chief of Staff's rescue. Kirby Smith had given up control of the army to Buckner, but not control of the Trans-Mississippi Department itself. Thereby, with no objections from Buckner, who had already submitted the army, Kirby Smith went back on his promise to Shelby's conspirators and surrendered everything—the entire department—at Galveston on June 2, 1865.[73]

John conceded that Kirby Smith and Buckner genuinely believed they were doing the best thing for the men. Still, he could not help feeling disgusted. Not so much by losing—but by the manner through which the war's outcome was sealed. "In the conference held at Marshall," John complained, "Shelby had plead, begged, and entreated for a prolongation of hostilities—if for no other purpose, *just to save the honor of the Trans-Mississippi Department.*" Put another way, he believed that Kirby Smith robbed the Iron Brigade of its chance to end the contest like true warriors.[74]

For this perceived betrayal, in *Shelby and His Men*, John treated Kirby Smith with a full-on jeremiad. John accused Kirby Smith of squandering men and resources, of being "totally destitute of enterprise"—a man "without the faint whisperings even of ambition." In John's estimation, Kirby Smith "demoralized the entire department, mildewed the army, disgusted his subordinates, and when the time for action came he [Kirby Smith] was left almost alone—powerless for good or for evil."[75]

Having thoroughly denounced Kirby Smith's record as a commander, John closed the books on his own Confederate career with another over-the-top declaration: "History must damn to all eternity these last days of the Trans-Mississippi army, when it tells how sixty-thousand well-armed, well-appointed, well-fed, healthy and well-officered men, with not an enemy nearer than two hundred miles, spontaneously gave way to a universal desire for desertion, and disgracefully surrendered everything, without the exhibition of a single heroic impulse or the exercise of one manly virtue with which to crown their previous honorable endurance and well-earned reputation." On that disaffected note, the same day Kirby Smith surrendered, Shelby formally disbanded his division. Men who had fought and bled together since 1861 embraced, sobbed, and said their farewells. Most went home to rebuild their old lives in Missouri. Others would take their chances south of the border with Shelby. With dreams of imperial grandeur, John spurred his horse for the Rio Grande.[76]

In Quest of Camelot

The Rio Bravo del Norte, which translates to "Fierce River of the North" in English, originates in the snowmelts of southern Colorado. Better known to Anglos as the Rio Grande (Spanish for "Big River"), it descends from high up in the Rocky Mountains before cutting a southerly path through New Mexico. As a result of the 1848 Treaty of Guadalupe-Hidalgo—signed by Mexico's government under extreme duress following the Mexican-American War—the Rio Grande becomes the southern border of the United States when and where it arrives in Texas, just north of present-day El Paso. From there, it absorbs the Pecos River near Del Rio, flows by Eagle Pass, Laredo, and McAllen, and then spills into the Gulf of Mexico at Brownsville.

For the caravan of grim riders that refused to accept Kirby Smith's capitulation, the Rio Grande represented more than the end of Yankee jurisdiction. Because of what waited on the other side—or at least because of what some *imagined* was waiting—their crossing into the land of people who knew the river as Rio Bravo del Norte signified new life. For John, arguably the most imaginative exile of all, the border crossing called to mind a second sort of new life: a royal ending for the Confederate epic.

NEARLY A MONTH after the surrender at Galveston, the remnants of Major General Joseph Orville Shelby's cavalry command rode into Eagle Pass, Texas. Numbering only a few hundred men, they arrived not as a division, but a regiment. As part of this reorganization, they had elected Shelby as their colonel, just like in the glory days of the

Fifth Missouri. Unlike those halcyon times, however, the unit lacked any attachment to a national or even a state government. It was more than a little ironic—having no immediate cause to fight for save their own survival—that the Missourians found themselves better armed now than ever during the war. Each man claimed a new Sharp's carbine, a new Enfield rifle, multiple new Colt Navy revolvers, and as many sabers and bowie knives as he could carry. Their new weaponry came courtesy of apathetic teamsters who didn't know what else to do with the stuff after Confederate dissolution.[1]

The Missourians' trek to Eagle Pass had been eventful to say the least—so these upgrades to their "iron" couldn't have come at a better time. They encountered bandits, bank robbers, deserters, cattle rustlers, and cutthroats of every denomination. Throughout Texas, especially, they took in scenes of pandemonium, despair, and ruination. When the Confederacy collapsed, so too did the state government, followed by city and town governments. With these administrations went the last shreds of confidence people had in Confederate currency. Conditions were primed for law and order to disintegrate at the local level. And it did—with alarming swiftness. Gangs of men, often ex-Confederates with empty wallets, grumbling stomachs, and nothing better to do, exploited the chaos created by their own defeat. They drank everything in sight; and once amply fortified by liquid courage, they swarmed depots, commissaries, and storehouses. With surplus guns easy to come by, they cut down anyone who got in the way. Some enterprising freebooters even set up protection rackets to extort terrorized citizens for all they were worth, which generally wasn't much. In a peculiar way, this landscape of heartless marauders and forlorn townspeople—verging as it did on the postapocalyptic—appealed to John's love of binaries: good vs. evil, hero vs. villain, strong vs. weak. It was a tailor-made backdrop for contrasting Shelby's "gallant knights" with what he considered the lesser rungs of Southern society.

John fully leveraged the opportunity. In his telling of the tale, first published as *Shelby's Expedition to Mexico* in 1872, the journey to Eagle Pass is marked by frequent acts of selfless heroism and feats of immense courage—a record consisting of equal parts Robin Hood and King Arthur, but noble through and through. All along the road, the Missourians stopped to protect supply depots and arsenals from looters, ensuring that downtrodden Southerners would receive their fair share of the goods and sustenance. Historically speaking, these confrontations all really occurred *in some form or another*. Yet in John's hands, they instantly became the stuff of gunslinging folklore: steely eyed glances and stare downs, pithy retorts, veiled threats of supernatural shooting prowess, and "clamorous ruffians" cowed into rightful submission by chronically outnumbered heroes.

"We are Missourians, we are leaving Texas, we have no homes, but we have our orders and our honor," Shelby's men announced to an armed mob in Houston. The would-be bandits took the hint and dispersed. Raiders in Tyler were more tenacious. They ordered Shelby's men to yield a depot or be forced aside. "Come and do it," one of the Missourians replied coldly, a pistol in each hand. "These are Shelby's soldiers, and they don't know what being taken means. Pray teach it to us." Though momentarily frozen by fear, the plunderers couldn't retreat fast enough when the Missourians emptied kegs of powder in the street then threatened to blow up the depot and everyone around it. At Austin, the state capital, Shelby's men interrupted a heist from the Confederate treasury building. According to John, when offered a reward from the former governor of Confederate Texas himself, a stoic Shelby demurred, instead declaring, "We are the last of the race, let us be the best as well."[2]

By the time the regiment reached San Antonio, criminal debauchery there had festered beyond the control of local authorities. As John recounted it, "Men sententious of speech and quick of pistol practice" had "taken immediate possession of the city" and were "rioting in the old royal fashion." At the behest of what passed for city fathers, the Missourians put their new arsenal into use. They marched in, occupied the city, and restored order by the barrel of a gun. Resisters among the "desperadoes" were shot down on the spot. After clearing the city of renegades, Shelby's men made quite a discovery: several elite Confederate officers and politicians, all in flight from a U.S. government they assumed would imprison or execute them for treason, had congregated in San Antonio to mull the future. In fact, it was a veritable who's who of the Trans-Mississippi Department that included former major generals Sterling Price, John Bankhead Magruder, and Thomas C. Hindman; the exiled governor of Missouri Thomas C. Reynolds; and even Edmund Kirby Smith himself. Traveling under an assumed name, Kirby Smith was holed up in a room at Menger's Hotel, just a stone's throw from the Alamo. Many of these one-time dignitaries were Mexico-bound anyway; so when Shelby's column resumed the journey to Eagle Pass, they fell in and marched along.[3]

Part 1: El Camino a La Mexico Imperial

Built along the eastern bank of the Rio Grande, Eagle Pass was as close to Mexico as one could get while still standing on American soil. On the opposite shore was Piedras Negras, an occupied city controlled by supporters of Benito Juarez. In the common parlance of Anglo-Americans, these devotees of the deposed president of Mexico were known as "Juaristas" or "Liberals." Juarez had taken office in 1858, the second elected president of the Second Federal Republic of Mexico, and guided the nation through a vicious, yearslong civil strife. Largely seen as an effort to reform the very powerful, very conservative Catholic Church, the war fomented much social and political instability. The empires of the Old World took notice. France in particular eyed Mexico wantonly during this hour of great vulnerability—but ultimately decided against an incursion. Any intrigues that might violate the Monroe Doctrine could necessitate a head-to-head fight with the newly industrialized United States. The French government harbored no interest in such a conflict.[4]

Enter a cadre of secessionist zealots, better-known as "fire-eaters," in Charleston, South Carolina. When the Confederacy launched its own head-to-head war against the Union in April 1861, France took full advantage of the diversion. Under orders from Emperor Napoleon III—the nephew of France's original emperor, Napoleon Bonaparte—the French Foreign Legion landed in Mexico in winter 1861. By summer 1863, just a few weeks before Robert E. Lee ordered Pickett's fateful charge at Gettysburg, an alliance of French and conservative Mexican troops seized Mexico City. Forced to abandon the Palacio National, Juarez took his government into exile. The following spring, an interim, pro-French government extended a royal invitation—literally—to a Habsburg archduke named Ferdinand Maximilian. Not to be confused with his nephew, Franz Ferdinand, whose assassination helped ignite the First World War, Ferdinand Maximilian was the younger brother of Austro-Hungarian emperor Franz Josef.[5]

By accepting Mexico's imperial throne, the thirty-two-year-old Maximilian transformed himself; formerly the overlooked younger brother of one of Europe's leading rulers, he instantly became a monarch of international significance. Maximilian's wife, Princess Charlotte, accompanied him from Vienna to Mexico. In addition to marrying an Austrian archduke, Charlotte was a scion of the House of Orléans—meaning she boasted a pedigree that could easily rival Maximilian's and was anything but a stranger to regal life. Her father, King Leopold I, had ruled Belgium for better than three decades. Her brother, Leopold II, now sat on the same throne. Charlotte's maternal grandparents were the late Louis-Philippe I, last of the French kings, and his queen consort, Maria Amalia. With these lofty credentials, the newly coronated imperial couple established their court at Mexico City in June 1864. They initially tried to win over native Mexicans with a surprisingly reformist agenda. For their trouble, Maximilian and Charlotte only alienated the elite conservatives and Catholic officials whose support their regime truly needed.[6]

Around the time Shelby and his men were establishing camp at Eagle Pass, the United States government returned its gaze south of the border. Lincoln was dead; his mistrusted and soon-to-be immensely unpopular vice president, Andrew Johnson, occupied the Oval Office. As congressional Republicans and cabinet officials sparred with Johnson over Reconstruction policy, it was General-in-Chief Ulysses S. Grant and one of his trusted wartime subordinates, Major General Philip Henry Sheridan, who closely monitored the French "buccaneering expedition." Neither man thought any good could come of Maximilian usurping power in Mexico at the behest of a financially strapped, land-hungry French emperor. To that end, in an 1866 letter to Grant, Sheridan opined that, "The sympathy of the whole South is with Maximilian, they know that there never can be a rebellion again against the Government except in connection with France and other European nations, and it still gives them a hope, which they hold hidden."[7]

On the point of Southern hope for European intervention in the war, John proved the Union general correct. Back in the summer of 1865 he genuinely believed the French government was only weeks away from formally recognizing and militarily assisting the Confederacy before Lee, Johnston, and Kirby Smith all waved the white flag. For his part, Sheridan camped near the border with troops at the ready, waiting to assist the Juaristas on Grant's command. Having just concluded one war with 750,000 dead—and with American soldiers still actively engaged in brutal Indian wars on the Great Plains—Grant was justifiably hesitant to initiate another conflict. But American passivity with regard to French intervention in Mexico would only stretch so far. What is more, Napoleon III and Maximilian both knew it.[8]

By opening negotiations with an envoy of the Mexican government, the Missourians willingly stepped into this geopolitical spider's web. Their first foray into international diplomacy as exiles involved Republicans, not Imperialists. John labeled Andres S. Viesca Bagües, the governor of Coahuila, "a most polished and elegant man, who quoted his smiles and italicised [sic] his gestures." He and hundreds of armed soldiers in Piedras Negras observed the arrival of Shelby's regiment, complete with artillery, and assumed that more pro-Republican gringos had arrived to fight for Juarez. In a face-to-face conference with "Governor Biesca"—John never could bring himself to properly spell Viesca's name in *Shelby's Expedition to Mexico*—Shelby did very little to dispel the notion. In John's description of the meeting, Viesca offered Shelby permission to recruit and then command an entire division of American mercenaries and bragged about generous land rewards and political titles that would follow a successful overthrow of the French. Shelby undoubtedly liked what he heard.[9]

The rest of the men had other ideas. This included John, in one of the rare instances that he openly disagreed with Shelby's proposed course of action. John's rendition of the decision-making council went like this:

SHELBY: "If you are all of my mind, boys, and will take your chances along with me, it is Juarez and the Republic from this on until we die here, one by one, or win a kingdom."

COL. BEN ELLIOTT: "General, if you order it, we will follow you into the Pacific Ocean; but we are all Imperialists, and would prefer service under Maximilian."

SHELBY: "Is this your answer, men?" And Shelby's voice had come back to its old cheery tones.

MEN: "It is."

SHELBY: "Final?"

MEN: "As the grave."

SHELBY: "Then it is mine, too. Henceforth, we will fight under Maximilian."

Then, as the meeting was breaking up and men ambled back to their campfires, Shelby allegedly muttered to John, "Poor, proud fellows—it is principle with them, and they had rather starve under the Empire than feast in a Republic. Lucky, indeed, for many of them if to famine there is not added a fusillade." Some later historians and biographers of Shelby took this complaint as a lament for pragmatism and economic opportunity lost; or put another way, as the placeholder for a future "I told you so" if and when the United States government finally ran Maximilian off the continent. However, that Shelby's men would follow him through the entire war and into foreign exile, only then to spurn perhaps the most important guidance he would ever give them, is a strikingly odd proposition. And odder still is the notion that Shelby, supposedly renowned for prioritizing the survival of his men, would not command them to do something that he ardently believed was in their best mortal interest. Other observers have even cited the quote as evidence of Shelby's higher racial tolerance and his genuine desire to fight alongside the Mexican Juaristas—though dialogue attributed to him in subsequent pages of John's book would seem to undermine that idea in short order.[10]

What to make then of the possible rift between colonel and regiment as penned by John? Taken in the context of his role as loyal PR man, it appears that John's intent was not to present Shelby as out of touch with the regiment but as their father figure. Hence, why else would the "old cheery tones" return to Shelby's voice when the men rejected Viesca's offer unless he too was drawn to Maximilian's side? But as the man responsible for all the rest—for their weapons, their food, their shelter, their survival—John paints Shelby as a paternalist obligated to present his wards with the safer, more sensible option first. This conflicted rendering cleverly equipped Shelby with an out on both ends. He got to be a romantic imperialist *and* a political realist, irrespective of how things turned out between Maximilian and Juarez. In truth, odds are good that Shelby wanted to have his proverbial cake and eat it too; anyone could see that Juarez was a better long-term political bet, but by Shelby's racial metric, Juarez and his men weren't white, and they weren't civilized. Thus, while admittedly confusing for posterity, John's treatment of the Liberal vs. Empire debate is probably best read as a reflection of the Missourians' *own* confusion and their *own* indecisiveness in a critical diplomatic moment.[11]

Precisely none of that mattered to Viesca. "Governor Biesca's bland face blankly fell when Shelby announced to him the next morning the decision of the conference," John wrote with just a touch of satisfaction. Even fully aware of their intention to side with Maximilian, it wasn't really in Viesca's interest to deter the Missourians. For one thing, they were battle-honed to an edge the Mexican troops in Piedras Negras could not match. The Juaristas might overwhelm them, certainly. But at great cost in lives and at the greater political hazard of crossing onto American soil to do it, where Shelby had very thoughtfully perched his field guns. For another, while Shelby's regiment was armed to the teeth, his expedition lacked sorely in food and provisions. Avoiding bloodshed, then, was a material opportunity for both sides. Seeing this, Viesca and Shelby came to an arrangement: the government of Coahuila purchased the cannon, musketry, wagons, and mule teams from the Missourians for approximately $16,000 in gold. The men kept their sidearms and blades and received a partial share of the overall commission. The remainder would be used to purchase foodstuffs—though some men didn't stick around long to see what was on the menu. With precious metal in hand, many galloped off to start their lives anew in Texas. For the Missourians that remained, there was one thing left to do before crossing the river.[12]

John claimed it was the 4th of July 1865. The exact day of the ceremony remains disputed. Whatever day it happened to be, Shelby's regiment stood arrayed along the eastern bank of the Rio Grande. An air of pomp and circumstance hung over the Missourians' parade line—an atmosphere very much at odds with their recent defeat and subsequent descent into homelessness. Some men stood silent, hats in hand. Others openly wept. They all watched as the old division's colonels—Blackwell, Elliott, Gordon, Slayback, and Williams—wrapped the stars and bars around a large stone. Shelby offered remarks, and while his words are lost to time, it is universally agreed that after speaking he pulled the black plume from his hat and added it to the folds of the tattered emblem. Together, flag and feather were then interred on the river bottom.[13]

A natural-born troubadour, this was the kind of moment John lived to mark with prose. Notably, then, it also seems to be one of the few times in his long career as a writer of books, editorials, and private correspondence that he wasn't sure what to say. Unable to decide on a single trope or train of commemorative thought, John instead produced a jumbled mess of mixed metaphors and Victorian grandiloquence. He condensed four years of killing, dying, raiding, retreating, winning, and losing into a single, over-burdened sentence. Despite the genuine emotional weight of the moment on John, his words rang strangely hollow, a eulogy that somehow seemed to say everything and nothing at the same time:

> Rent and bruised, and crimson with the blood of heroes—it had never been dishonored. Missouri breezes had felt the flapping of its silken folds; woman's imperial hand had decorated it with battle-mottos; sweet, coy victory—her locks heavy with the dust of conflicts and red with the blood of martyrs—had caressed it often and tenderly; ambition had plumed it with the royal crest

of rough stormy waves of battle waters; shining like the face of a struggling king; it had gleamed grandly through the smoke and the sorrow of two hundred desperate fields; and broad barred now, and worn, and old—it was displayed once more to its followers before the swift waves of the Rio Grande closed over it forever.

The morning after symbolically drowning their Confederate past, the Missourians next hoped to drown their sorrows. They caroused in the cantinas of Piedras Negras. Before long, shooting broke out between some of their own men and men from Viesca's garrison. Like a reporter who serendipitously finds himself at the scene of a story as it breaks, John giddily narrated the would-be showdown. One of the Missourians hacked off another man's arm with a saber. The Juaristas responded and lead soon filled the air. Shelby's bugler sounded a call to arms. Amidst this chaotic spectacle, John wrote that "women went wailing through the streets; the church bells rang furiously; windows were darkened and barricaded." Then John claimed that as the Mexicans formed a line of battle and the Missourians mounted for a charge, "Governor Biesca rushed down into the square, pale, his hat off pleading in impassioned Spanish, apologizing in all the soft vowels known to that soft and sounding language." Eventually cooler heads prevailed, and a full-on battle was averted. But now on high alert for midnight treachery, Shelby's men allegedly refused to return a captured Juarista cannon until the following morning.[14]

Another of Shelby's men, Thomas Westlake, left a slightly different account of what he dubbed the "little Scrap with the Mexicans." Whereas John pinned blame for the dustup on scheming horse thieves and piratical Mexican soldiers, Westlake's explanation seems more sensible: a volatile combination of hard liquor, flirtatious foreigners with money to spend on female company, and resentful Mexican soldiers. "They [the Mexican soldiers] were intruding on our Rights or We on theirs There seemed to be a littl [sic] difference of opinion of the matter," Westlake reported. That difference of opinion erupted into gunfire—and per Westlake, it was Shelby, not Viesca, who used anything but "soft vowels" to halt the skirmish. Westlake recalled with amusement how Shelby "ordered the Greasers to disperse Using some Languag that would not be very appropriate in a Prayr meeting." His diary mentioned nothing of the confiscated cannon, and almost immediately after the aborted battle, the Missourians departed for the Pacific Coast by way of Monterrey.[15]

The road out of Piedras Negras was significantly harder—and bloodier—than the one leading into it. Shelby's men dealt with Apaches who were understandably hostile because the Missourians were trespassing. Upon reaching Monterrey, the Missourians conferred with Colonel Pierre Jeanningros of the French Foreign Legion. He approved their course for Mazatlán, a coastal city just opposite the southern tip of the Baja Peninsula. En route to another stopover at Parras, Shelby's men survived a midnight raid by Juarista guerrillas; once there, they watched Shelby nearly duel an obstinate and inebriated French colonel. Jeanningros arrived in time to stop the affair of honor, but he also carried bad news for the Missourians: Marshal François Bazaine, Jeanningros's superior officer, was ordering them south to Mexico City.[16]

Some of the high-ranking former Confederates who'd linked up with Shelby and the regiment at San Antonio were already in Mexico City. The Missourians especially trusted Reynolds and Magruder, so Shelby sent John ahead to confer with them about how best to pitch their military services to the emperor. The rest of the regiment arrived at the imperial capital on September 3, 1865, bedraggled and exhausted. Two days later, on September 5, Shelby received an audience with Maximilian. Also present at the meeting were John, acting as Shelby's personal advisor; ex-Confederate diplomat Matthew Fontaine Maury; Magruder; Bazaine; and Bazaine's chief of staff, the Count De Noue. In John's version of the negotiation between Shelby and Maximilian, the bluntness of Shelby's proposal raised more than one set of European eyebrows.[17]

American political pressure, Shelby argued, would soon force Napoleon III to withdraw the Foreign Legion from Mexico. In its place, the battle-hardened Missourians were willing to serve as the nucleus of a replacement army—in exchange for certain social and economic considerations. Essentially, Shelby asked Maximilian for the same offer the Missourians had already received and turned down from Vicsca. This time, however, it was the Missourians who found themselves spurned. Maximilian listened politely to Shelby's application for a military command. And then, just as politely, the emperor rejected it. Maximilian planned to establish a friendly relationship with the American government. In turn, he feared that employment of unsurrendered Rebels would hinder that diplomatic mission. John also alleged that after Maximilian left the conference room, the emperor's own military advisors confessed folly in his course of action, including Bazaine. But they were unable to convince Maximilian that Secretary of State William Seward was not—and never would be—his political friend.[18]

Shelby and John immediately broke the news to the regiment. "We are not wanted," Shelby blurted to the men, "and perhaps it is best so." Understandably aggrieved—they'd come a long, hard way from home to be rebuffed, after all—the Missourians soon learned that everything was not lost. Some of the same friends in high places they'd trusted to arrange the sit-down with Maximilian now came to their assistance. Thomas Reynolds convinced Bazaine that, were it not for his order redirecting Shelby's regiment to Mexico City, the Missourians would have reached the Pacific Coast and easy access to California. Instead, they were penniless, deep in the Mexican interior. Bazaine accepted his part in their failed proposal to Maximilian and offered each of the Missourians fifty dollars in gold. They could either use it to fund passage home or put it toward permanent settlement in the Empire.[19]

For the men who wished to remain in Mexico indefinitely, Magruder and Maury came through in a big way. The former served as imperial commissioner of the land office while the latter worked closely with Maximilian as imperial commissioner of emigration. Consequently, if a mercenary turned colonist desired land to homestead in Maximilian's domain, these were the right men to know. As it so happened, a large expanse of fertile territory was available near Cordoba, or "Cordova," as John habitually misspelled it. (He never did manage to discern the *b*'s and *v*'s of Spanish.) John reported that the tract had once belonged to the Catholic Church before it was "rudely and unscrupulously confiscated by Juarez." Rather than giving it back to the same Catholic elites who only offered him tepid support, Maximilian appropriated the land for incoming Anglo-colonists. With the American Civil War over, he expected a great many disgruntled Southerners might be interested in a change of scenery.[20]

For a while, it looked like the emperor was really onto something. Thanks in part to Maury's recruitment efforts back in Dixie, a colonial settlement sprang up, then swiftly matured into a city. Located roughly 175 miles southeast of the capital and 125 miles west of Veracruz, it was accessible to emigrants from the coast but also situated within the orbit of protection that emanated from the French troops posted at Mexico City. Best of all, the land wasn't just cheap; it was an absolute steal. Men with families could obtain 640 acres of arable ground, and men without families 320 acres at approximately $1.00 to $1.25 per acre—all payable later when crops became profitable.[21]

It almost seemed too good to be true. And yet for John, the opportunity to build a new society, under the aegis of an Old World emperor and alongside men he believed had constituted the cultural nobility of the antebellum South, was more tempting than he could resist. That the colony was named Carlota, an homage to Empress Charlotte, whom he declared "the most perfect woman of the Nineteenth Century"—and with whom he was clearly smitten—only made it feel like destiny. He claimed his 320 acres without delay.[22]

Part 2: The Life and Times of a Confederado

Among historians, the term *Confederados* is applied loosely to groups of former Confederates that fled to Latin America in the aftermath of defeat. Mexico, Cuba, Brazil, and present-day Belize, then known as British Honduras, were their primary destinations. The list of reasons an ex-Confederate might have chosen Mexico is lengthy. Moreover, its entries were not mutually exclusive, and each came with the built-in bonus of not requiring overseas travel like Cuba or Brazil. Some men fled for fear of arrest and imprisonment by the Union military. More than a few hoped to dodge political persecution in a divided community, especially in the wake of Abraham Lincoln's assassination. Many defeated Rebels sought to safeguard personal wealth and moveable property, including those they held in slavery, at a time when the Southern economy had imploded. And virtually all Confederados desired to escape from a social and racial hierarchy supposedly turned upside-down by the Thirteenth Amendment.[23]

Which is all to say, John hardly experienced the transition from soldier to private citizen of the empire alone. Soon the colony brimmed with former Confederates, many of them generals at that. According to John, Sterling Price "built himself a bamboo house in the town of Carlota, and commenced in good earnest the life of a farmer"—though it was later revealed that he spent most of his time in the shade, telling stories, nursing cocktails, and putting on airs. Most of the other colonists were far more industrious than "Old Pap." Indeed, the Confederados in and around Carlota established sawmills and mining operations; they cultivated cotton, corn, and coffee; and they found employment as land surveyors, engineers, and railroad controllers.[24]

Some of the men excelled above the rest in this entrepreneur-friendly environment. Thomas Hindman, fluent in Spanish, set up a law practice in Cordoba. On top of overseeing a new coffee plantation, Shelby jumped back into the freight business. Though a far cry from the steamships he'd contracted before the war, his men ran wagons back and forth between Paso del Macho and Mexico City. And perhaps most intriguing to John, Maximilian earmarked money for Henry W. Allen, the former governor of Confederate Louisiana, to launch a newspaper in the colony; an English weekly, they christened it the *Mexican Times*. In retrospect, John wrote fondly of this "honeymoon phase" at Carlota. He contended that everything "grew apace and was prosperous . . . and from a jungle the plantations soon boomed and blossomed like another paradise."[25]

However, while John waxed lyrical about "long sunshiny days . . . in which the trade winds blew and the orange blossoms scented all the air," all was not well in Maximilian's kingdom. Upon learning of the recruitment efforts spearheaded by Maury back in the American

3. General Sterling Price in Confederate uniform. John strongly criticized Price's leadership late in the war but welcomed his presence in Mexico. Library of Congress, Prints and Photographs Division.

South, Major General Philip Sheridan simply banned sea travel from Texas or Louisiana ports to Mexico without written authorization from the Union military. As Sheridan later put it in his memoir, "This dampened the ardor of everybody in the Gulf States who had planned to go to Mexico" and "led ultimately to failure" in Carlota. Around the

4. Emperor Maximilian of Mexico in the 1860s. Maximilian never lived up to John's expectations of a Habsburg ruler. Library of Congress, Prints and Photographs Division.

5. Charlotte of Mexico in 1864. John idolized the empress as a perfect noblewoman. Library of Congress, Prints and Photographs Division.

same time Sheridan drastically curtailed the flow of new immigrants to Carlota; in October 1865 Maximilian issued what became known as the *Black Decree*. At the urging of Bazaine—or at least so Maximilian later claimed—this draconian order marked the immediate institution of a total war policy against the Juaristas. Under its terms, a mandatory death sentence awaited anyone caught taking up arms against the empire or directly enabling others to do so.[26]

For the Missourians, this must have conjured mixed emotions. They despised Thomas Ewing for enacting General Order No. 11. But that edict, following in the wake of William Quantrill's August 1863 raid on Lawrence, Kansas, wasn't nearly so draconian as to include compulsory executions. Nevertheless, they understood—perhaps better than anyone in the mid-nineteenth century—how policies designed to douse the flames of guerrilla war instead tended to stoke it. Maximilian's forces struggled to cope with the irregular tactics employed by the Juaristas. Bazaine and his lieutenants never managed to stamp out the "guerrilla problem"; so, slowly but surely it grew, as Maximilian's treasury, never overflowing to begin with, emptied with alarming haste.[27]

In light of these factors, the surviving correspondence between John and his sisters, Fannie and Edmonia, back in Virginia, reveals a man utterly unwilling to admit defeat a second time in as many years. The letters illuminated the extent to which John committed himself to building a permanent home in Maximilian's empire. But more to the point, they evidenced John's steadfast belief that the Old World of his imagination could *and would* prevail in Mexico—meaning, he refused to believe that the Old World-bloodlines of Europe would truly abandon one of their own to the likes of Juarez and Seward. His lesson to the contrary came as a long, painful lecture on global politics and ruthlessness.

John's first letter back to the States betrayed his homesickness. This was understandable considering he had not seen Fannie or Edmonia since before the war. And given the mileage John had covered between 1861 and 1865, that must have felt like a lifetime ago. "You do not know how badly I wanted to hear from you and see you," he moaned. He then asked about "the freeing of the negroes" and inquired, with some trepidation, whether Southern society was "gradually relapsing into its old state again." These were questions that would seem to be probing the safety of a return home. Yet in this same missive, John noted that, "The Empress and Emperor here are very favorably disposed to Confederates, and ere long our party of exiles hope to be well settled."[28]

In April 1866, when John again wrote to Fannie and Edmonia, traces of homesickness still lingered. "I would be willing to shorten my life by ten years to be with you to night, and be to say to you I am able to provide you a home and we will never separate again. . . . The day when I can do this is close at hand," he declared. He also assumed that much correspondence to and from his sisters had been confiscated by Union authorities before reaching Veracruz. "I cannot account for it," John complained, "unless because all letters coming to this country are subjected to the petty surveillance of military puppies, who, in their profoundest knowledge of what is right and wrong, throw everything aside." Multiple letters *are* missing from the exchange between brother and sisters—though how they came to be lost has itself been lost to time. His rant about the mail aside, the bulk of this letter, significantly longer than the first, revolved around all the reasons John would stick it out in Mexico: the long-term value of land there, the cozy relationship of the Confederados with Maximilian's government, and the conviction that European monarchs like Napoleon III, Franz Josef, and Leopold II would intercede against the United States at any moment.[29]

On the agricultural front, John liked his prospects as a planter. "I have a farm at Cordova," he proclaimed proudly, "which is to-day worth 25 dollars an acre, and I have 320 acres." He also introduced his partner in the venture, Dr. John S. Tisdale. A Missourian, Tisdale had served during the war as assistant surgeon of the Third Battalion, Missouri Cavalry, and periodically as a contract physician detached from the unit to assist hard-up civilians. Like John, he was a bachelor-colonist in Mexico.

John was quite pleased with the particulars of their arrangement. He announced that, between them, the duo owned "640 acres of as fine land as you ever saw, on the great Imperial Railroad from Vera Cruz to this city." He further explained that by the fall they would have a full coffee crop planted—but that coffee would require three years of cultivation before harvest. In the meantime, they could make ends meet by rotating fields of corn, beans, and red chili peppers, in addition to breeding hogs. "Bacon is worth 75 cents a pound, and cured hams sell readily at $1 per pound and scarce at that," he added for emphasis.[30]

Even while tempering Fannie's and Edmonia's expectations with the reminder that "everything is in its infancy yet," John couldn't help counting his future earnings. After disclosing that he'd paid $1 per acre—which meant he had five years to pay back the $320 plus six percent interest—John boasted that just fifty acres of coffee, "with even an average yield," would "pay in Spanish doubloons ten thousand dollars the third year after it is planted." Even adjusted for inflation, $10,000 amounted to more than double the value of their moderately affluent father's entire estate in 1843.

Throughout, he used the plural pronoun "we" without hesitation. What John really meant was that Dr. Tisdale oversaw the plantation at Carlota while he, having accepted a staff position with the *Mexican Times*, took up safer and more sophisticated quarters in Mexico City. "He [Tisdale] lives on the land, cultivates it, and works like a negro," John confessed. "I live in Mexico [City], send him all the money I can raise, and work like a negro too." "Between us," John continued, "we will have in a short time as fine a farm as you would wish to see." It's little wonder that he enjoyed the life of a planter, then, because within this arrangement, it never required he actually plant anything.

When, precisely, John went to work at the newspaper in unclear. We know that he began working for Henry Allen, the editor in chief and founder of the *Mexican Times*, sometime between September 1865 and early spring 1866—and that he started as a printer. This clearly constituted a step down from his prewar days as a fiery editorialist, but it was a job, and he probably didn't have to suffer it long, either. Owing to Allen's declining health, which left him unable to fill column space on his own, it appears John moved into a content-producing role quite quickly. By the time of this second surviving letter in April

1866, he'd been promoted to full partner—which also meant half-owner—of the entire operation. John claimed to "have abundant hopes of success" for the paper, which was available by subscription for one dollar per month, and touted all things immigration.[31]

Regardless of how profitable his stake in the *Mexican Times* may or may not have been—the paper remained afloat because Maximilian's government bankrolled it for the first year of publication—it kept John in the mix at Mexico City. He was naturally inclined to the formality of a royal court, with its customs and uniforms and titles, and he admittedly basked in the pretentiousness of the imperial government.[32]

It's unknown how frequently John encountered his favorite resident of Mexico City face-to-face. What *is* clear was that after laying eyes on Empress Carlota, John found his virago for all time; a living, breathing version of all the virtuous royal damsels and fair maidens he'd spent the last twenty-odd years rescuing in his imagination. It would be easy for later observers to assess John's description of Charlotte as over-the-top drivel or even as blatant objectification. But while the prose is admittedly purple, in keeping with John's worldview, he genuinely modeled his written admiration for Charlotte after the way he believed a medieval knight of centuries past would praise a queen—in a purely chivalric and agamous way. "Her dark auburn hair was heavy, long and silken . . . Her mouth was large and firm, and her teeth were of the most perfect white . . . Her nose was aquiline, the nostrils open and slightly projecting, recording, as if upon a page, the emotions of her heart, and the dauntless courage which filled her whole being."[33]

John found himself less impressed with Maximilian's physical appearance. The emperor sported what John called the "Hapsburg lip": "that thick, protruding semi-cleft under-lip, too heavy for beauty, too immobile for features that, under the iron destiny that ruled the hour, should have suggested Caesar or Napoleon." In John's estimation, anything Maximilian lacked in good looks, he made up for with refinement and sophistication. John marveled at the monarch's fluency in German, English, Hungarian, French, Italian, Spanish, and Slavonic. He noted that Maximilian was a gifted equestrian, an expert fencer, and well-versed with a broadsword. (This last talent must have especially pleased John given his love for all things Arthurian.) Not coincidentally, the qualities that most drew John to Maximilian—the emperor was an unabashed romantic who loved poetry, music, flowers, astronomy, and literature—are almost certainly the ones he believed they had in common.[34]

Ironically, though, these same features of the emperor's personality might have been red flags to John, had he not been so enamored with the royal couple: Maximilian was indeed a Habsburg, with a grade "A" pedigree, and all the gentlemanly trappings one might expect of an Old World royal. As a ruler, Maximilian had issued to the "Black Decree" and before that, he'd implemented new regulations on the sale and consumption of liquor that native Mexicans deemed oppressive. But he was never, and simply could not be, the all-powerful potentate that John yearned for—nor could Maximilian truly provide the blank canvas upon which John dreamed of recreating an idealized, fantastical version of the Old South at Carlota. And as emperor himself stated privately, even if it was within his capability, he didn't want to be that sort of ruler. Writing in 1865 to a personal friend, Maximilian declared, "Even if I no longer have the breeze of the Adriatic here, the aroma of Lokrum, I still live in a free country, among a free people, where principles prevail that one cannot even dream of at home; no limitations inhibit me anymore, and here I am allowed to openly say that I will the good." "We have healthy democratism here," the emperor continued, "without all the sickly European-style fantasies, but with that strength and conviction that would probably take only fifty years of intense struggle to develop where you are."[35]

As much as John enjoyed the gilded veneer of the imperial court, and however misguided his impression of Maximilian's authority may have been—and much as he luxuriated in the distant presence of Empress Charlotte—it was impossible for him to ignore the momentous political developments rocking Mexico City. In January 1866 Napoleon III folded under the weight of enormous political pressure. Yielding to American clamor over the Monroe Doctrine, the French government announced it would gradually evacuate regular army troops from Mexican soil. The withdrawals would proceed by division, beginning in November 1866 and concluding in November 1867. At that point, Maximilian would have to defend his throne with only native Mexican troops and the few Belgian and Austrian diehards that formed the Foreign Legion and his palace guard.[36]

Then as now, it didn't require much in the way of Machiavellian prowess to realize there's no *good* moment for an embattled monarch to lose the bulk of his or her military might—or to have such a loss publicly announced amidst an ongoing war. But the timing of Napoleon III's concession to Washington was especially bad for Maximilian. All along the peripheries of the empire, and especially on the outskirts of the Anglo-settlements, Juaristas lurked in increasingly greater numbers. As Maximilian stretched garrisons thinner and thinner to meet the expanding threat, the guerrillas became increasingly aggressive. An attack launched against Shelby's own plantation, formerly thought to be on unassailable ground in Cordoba, signaled that none of the Confederados' homes was beyond the reach of raiding Juaristas.[37]

John refused to allow these events to spoil the flush times he chronicled in Maximilian's empire. In the same letter that publicized his partnerships with Tisdale and Allen, he used as much ink defending Maximilian and the empire's alleged allies in Europe as he did in addressing his own affairs. "You say this is all very fine, but the Empire will not last—Maximilian will be forced out—anarchy and revolution will usurp the present order of stability and order," John preemptively sneered to Fannie, Edmonia, and the extended family he knew would also partake in the letter. Then he launched into a pro-Mexico, pro-imperial, anti-American tirade:

> There you are mistaken, but your mistake is that of Americans, who never know how little other people care for their country until they leave it. I know the United States government despises this Empire as badly as the South hates the United States North; I know that the Washington Cabinet don't care one straw for the so-called liberal Juarez.

After summing up the postbellum Union as "a carnival of broken heads, and rent bodies, and Sanitary Fairs, and Young Men's Christian Associations, and Sewing Societies, and Yankee lust and free-loveism," John boldly predicted, "there will be no war, and all this Yankee insolence, bullying, and bluster will turn out a humbug as great as Barnum."[38]

In other words, while many observers—on both sides of the U.S.-Mexico border, and across the Atlantic too—presumed that the Union military would make quick work of Maximilian with the American Civil War ended, John knew the truth: that Andrew Johnson or "Satan [Charles] Sumner" or "Iron Works [Thaddeus] Stevens" didn't have the guts to cross Old World empires and their armies. To the contrary, he ended the letter on a positive note, reporting that numerous former generals in Mexico are "well satisfied and doing well" and that many "Confederate ladies" had begun to join their husbands in the colony. Despite the setbacks, it was obvious in John's mind that the empire—and thereby the colony—would endure.[39]

John spent the rest of spring 1866 haranguing Radical Republicans in the United States. As was his custom, John seemed to think that if he wrote fervently enough about a given outcome, it might be willed into existence. In his editorial of May 12, entitled "The United States and Mexico," he blamed Radical Republicans for plunging the nation into an unnecessary civil war then accused them of trampling the Constitution in its aftermath. In America, which he labeled "*There*," John complained that "a rabid Directory of Jacobins in the legislature" overruns the Executive; the population is taxed "to the last degree of human endurance"; and that "orders are given by military commanders that citizens of the United States, shall not emigrate to a neighboring country."[40]

John suggested a very different story about life in Mexico, "*Here*," under the benevolent rule of Emperor Maximilian:

Here, though people differ in politics and have fought for those differences of opinion, yet there is no one class bent upon destroying another, and above all, when men here cease to contend and in good faith give in their adhesion to the Government, as the people of the South have done, they are received as friend and treated as if nothing had occurred. *Here*, the utmost freedom is allowed in the expression of political opinions, the Sovereign being the most liberal of all.

This message was directly in keeping with the founding mission of the *Mexican Times*—to recruit new Anglo-colonists—and made clear why the imperial government had agreed to subsidize it as an organ of state propaganda. However, just to drive the point home, John laid it on a little thicker for Southerners who might have been pondering an escape from Emancipation and Reconstruction. As a result of the imperial couple's benevolence, "security for life and property is becoming greater every day."[41]

For would-be immigrants fretting over the loss of French military support, another editorial published on May 19 put the matter to rest—at least as far as John was concerned. "History has taught the world," John wrote, "that France can no more be bullied than she can be beaten." Then as if speaking for the Confederados in Mexico collectively, he labeled Napoleon III's promise to evacuate the nineteenth-century equivalent of "fake news." "We do not believe, in the first place, that the French troops *will be* withdrawn," John stated matter-of-factly, noting that "Eighteen months is a long time and radical North American insolence [sic] and aggression may become insufferable." Best of all, he hedged, "If the French do go—there is still left hope." All the empire needed was a little folk-heroism: "Let the young Emperor and Empress raise here their banner of right and justice. Call around it the young and the brave of every clime, open up the vast tracts of uncultivated land, give homes to the enlisters, stimulate the exiles to exertion by justice and protection which will make them stand like Arthur's knights around the throne."[42]

At first glance, this is not a particularly well-founded analysis of the political situation in Mexico. John genuinely believed that white men of honor and high culture, the Missourians chief among them, could occupy a new Roundtable in support of Maximilian's throne. And by way of their victory over the "puritan spirit of aggression," time as a conveyor of egalitarian reforms might be halted if not reversed. At its core, then, John's version of a new Old South in Mexico wasn't just an homage to the prose of Scott and Mallory, it was an opportunity to raise Camelot from the dead. Watching closely from across the border, Philip Sheridan wasn't concerned about fabled kingdoms or Roundtables—but he did have at least one belief in common with John. "I have not much confidence in the truth or sincerity of Louis Napoleon," Sheridan wrote to Grant in May 1866. "Should the condition of our country from party strife or any other cause, during this period, give him the slightest hope, we might say good by to his protestations or present intentions."

In September 1866, another of John's letters reached Virginia, this time addressed only to Fannie. A great deal had changed since April. For one thing, with just two months left before French troop evacuations were to begin, Empress Charlotte sailed to Europe in her capacity as an imperial diplomat. She would plead with her brother, her brother-in-law, with her cousins—with conservative royals all across Western Europe and even the Pope in Rome—to rally behind Maximilian's regime; to stand fast against the bullying of a crass, upstart nation like America. In short, she would raise the banner "of right and justice." But her mission did not end like one of John's cavalier fantasies. No goodly king emerged to champion the distraught empress's cause. As it turned out, none of Europe's power players would risk war to rescue Maximilian. Consequently, and unbeknownst to her at the time, Charlotte would never again see her husband alive.[43]

In addition to the absence of the empress from Mexico City, Henry Allen had died on April 22, 1866, almost immediately after John composed his previous letter to Fannie and Edmonia. Now John informed Fannie that he was the sole proprietor of the *Mexican Times*—an imperially subsidized newspaper with subscribers on both sides of the Atlantic. She wasn't around to see it, but Mary Ann's devotion to her son's education was starting to pay dividends. John thought so, too. "If the future is as peaceful as my hopes are bright," he predicted, "I have every prospect of success."[44]

As was becoming apparent to nearly everyone but John, a peaceful future was not in the cards for Mexico. In fact, the first issue of the *Mexican Times* to carry his name on the masthead, published June 16, 1866, reported that "the colony at Cordova has suffered a serious interruption, at the hands of Liberals or robbers it is not known which." Regardless, John remained bullish on Mexico and equally bearish on a post-Appomattox recovery for the South—no doubt also influenced by his own white supremacist sentiments. While slavery de jure wasn't possible in Mexico, he implied that the Confederados were happy to get by with peonage if it meant not having to live along-side freedpeople. "I believe Mexico, with its vast mineral resources, its great agricultural wealth, and its undeveloped richness will be more favorable for my success than desolated Virginia, crammed with liberated negroes, preyed upon by Freedmen Bureau agents, and exhausted by four years of continual strife," John opined to Fannie. Along these lines, he'd enclosed pro-immigration literature with his letter and reminded her, "I have sent you my paper with the entire programme in it, and you can give it to anyone desiring to learn about the country with an intention of emigrating."[45]

Though technically a paid spokesman for the imperial colonization effort, John seems to have convinced himself, even at this late hour in Maximilian's reign, that his future in Mexico was viable. Whereas he saw cheap, abundant land and the opportunity to start life over in an empty frontier in Mexico—empty, at least if one ignored the myriad Mexicans and Indians who already lived there—John forecast further misery for the ex-Confederate states. "It is, however, only a matter of time," he wrote, "before the Radicals triumph and commence their devastating work upon the South." He bemoaned, "In the inevitable defeat of the Conservative party the Confederate states must either submit to the greatest possible degree of social and political degra-dation, or appeal again to the sword. The latter I fear will never be done no matter what provocation is offered or what insult given." With that, John signaled to Fannie that his residency in Mexico had become permanent by choice rather than necessity. He still lamented the separation of their family and hinted that he might come back to Virginia—though the context of his letter indicated he would only be visiting.[46]

The same day John wrote to Fannie, as if out of nowhere, his brother Thomas reentered the picture. After joining the Iron Brigade in 1862 and participating in Marmaduke's first raid into Missouri, Thomas was dispatched to Arkansas on army business and, as far as his record indicates, never rejoined the unit. Now, four years later, John attempted to facilitate a reunion. Given the dire situation in America, he urged Thomas to become a citizen of the empire—and even offered to pay for his immigration. "I write advising you to come as soon as you can . . . how you wish money sent and where I shall send it to, I will furnish you sufficient to come to me here." "General prospects are good," John noted.[47]

That was really saying something—because in the very same letter, he also informed Thomas that "Cordova is dead beyond resuscitation." Though it hardly looks like a sales pitch for immigration at first glance, John explained that the colony was killed "by the infernal greed and avarice of the Anglo-Saxon race. They wanted more land than they could cultivate, they wanted doubloons to grow on trees and coffee to be sacked ready for shipment, and because all these things were not found most of the emigrants went back cursing the world, the flesh, and the devil." In his own way, John told his brother that for men willing to work hard and wait patiently for profit, Mexico was still a worthwhile destination.[48]

As insinuated by John's own editorials, time to be patient was fast running out. In the weeks following his letters to Fannie and Thomas, John penned a series of anti-Republican and anti-Black screeds. On October 8, in "American Extremity is Mexican Opportunity," he predicted that Radical control of the United States would trigger a race war which, in turn, would provoke Southerners to fight again. This time, however, John argued that the nations of Western Europe—horrified by the monstrousness of the American government—would help crush the Union as they should have done in 1861.[49]

A November 5 column, simply entitled "A Word to the Mexicans," blueprinted a conspiracy by which the Radical Republicans would annex Mexico, occupy it in the manner of the ex-Confederacy, and then strip native Mexicans of all their rights. John's prescription for stopping the invasion rang eerily similar to his previous calls for men to rally behind Maximilian. This time, however, with no "young and brave" arriving from Europe, he'd downgraded his hopes to an army of conservative Mexicans: "If every Mexican who loves his country, who wishes to see it free and independent, who has no desire to have Butlers in Veracruz and Chivingtons in Guarrero, who holds the honor of his nation a priceless gem above all price and above all reproach, would come out boldly and manly to the support of the Empire, the danger of annexation would lose all its terrors, and the selfish partizans [sic] of Anglo-Saxon lust and greed would be disarmed and paralyzed."

In early November 1866 the subsidy originally awarded to Henry Allen ran out. With the imperial coffers all but empty and immigration from abroad at a standstill, no second installment was forthcoming. John managed to keep the paper going for a few weeks—either on subscription money, his own money, or a small combination of the two—but the issue of November 19 marked his last as proprietor of the *Mexican Times*. Not coincidentally, as the first division of French soldiers sailed away from Veracruz, John concluded his editorship with a final plea to native Mexicans to preserve the empire. "There is still time for the Mexicans to save Mexico," he announced, "but by them alone can it be done." "We would conjure the Mexicans to come up as one man now in support of the Emperor Maximilian, as the last barrier, the last heroic bulwark against political degradation and territorial dismemberment." It was the last time John would ask anyone—European or Mexican—to fight for Maximilian and Charlotte in print.[50]

That didn't mean he was giving up on the empire. John also used a few lines in his last issue to announce that Shelby had established a new colony at Tuxpan, on the coast near Veracruz. It seems fitting, given his role as Shelby's devoted adjutant, to chronicle one last deed—and to add just a little more to the legend he'd been writing since 1861. "With him there is no such word as fail," John claimed of Shelby, "and the man who went from Captain to Major General along a path illuminated only by the light of his sword and the blaze of his genius, will find it easier to destroy the obstacles of nature alone than to overcome the barriers of man and nature, both combined, as he always did." Tellingly, though, John did not join Shelby at Tuxpan. His days as an (absentee) gentleman planter were over.[51]

An incomplete letter to his sisters narrated the demise of John's plantation at Carlota. Though the surviving page is undated, its contents show the letter was written sometime after the pair of September 18, 1866, notes to Fannie and Thomas but before John lost the newspaper. After the French Army left, according to John, "murders, robberies, and anarchy came, and we were all forced to abandon the half-tilled land, the half matured crops, and all." Still, even after losing everything, John wrote optimistically, if not in delusion, "I have as much hope as ever. I firmly believe I will make money very soon—enough to send you and Edmonia at least a thousand dollars." And he must have believed, because John then advised his sisters not to sell land the family owned in Kentucky—land he could have returned to and worked on at any time since May 1865.[52]

Part 3: Firing Squad

Perhaps to spare them from excessive worry, the version of the Carlota raid relayed by John to his sisters sold its seriousness somewhat short. He provided a more complete, graphic—and likely hyperbolic—account in *Shelby's Expedition to Mexico*. With the French evacuation underway, John recalled that "city after city received the Liberals with many demonstrations of joy." These liberation celebrations frequently turned violent. John also reported that some of the Juaristas instituted a "Black Decree" of their own, expelling, imprisoning, and even executing "those Mexicans who had sympathized with the Empire." As Juarez's influence in the vicinity of Mexico City grew, so did the danger for Confederados. After all, they had never been favorites of the native Mexican population—and for good reason. Much of the "frontier" land "settled" by colonists was usurped from indigenous occupants, often by force. Therefore, a move against the now-vulnerable Anglo-interlopers could hardly be unexpected.[53]

As John told it, "The armies of Juarez were recruited by a levy en masse of all capable of bearing arms in the territory overrun by his ragamuffins." With bolstered ranks and with material support from the American government, the Juaristas executed a night assault against the plantations around Cordoba, including those at Carlota. "A band of freebooters from the mountains, nearly two thousand strong, poured down through the gap the French left unprotected, and the pillage was utter and complete," he wrote. The raiders torched cabins, destroyed farming equipment, slaughtered livestock, and trampled or burned crops in the field. More terrifying still, John also described how roughly one hundred men from the colony "were captured in the night and marched far into the gloomy places and recesses of the mountains." For a month, he claimed, the Anglo hostages were beaten and tortured with sabers and lances, starved, and exposed after the Juaristas stole their clothes and boots. When a band of survivors finally wandered back to French lines, the men looked more dead than alive. Even still, they were considered the lucky ones. "The blow," John pronounced, "finished the colony."[54]

Events at Carlota foreshadowed a general breakdown of the empire's ability to defend its subjects, which in turn signaled a rapid decline in Maximilian's political fortunes. Juarez gained ground all over the map. Sonora fell. Then Matamoras. And still the French army withdrew. Soon only the foreign legion remained to defend Mexico City. John claimed in *Shelby's Expedition to Mexico* that a frantic Maximilian turned to Shelby for a military solution. According to John's rendition of the terse exchange between emperor and subject, it was the commoner who spoke with authority, not the monarch. A frustrated Shelby informed Maximilian that it was far too late to raise an army of Southerners. What's more, he'd warned the emperor of just this calamity back in September 1865. Understanding Shelby's admonition but not yet resigned to losing his throne, Maximilian took to the field himself in winter 1867. He was captured by Juaristas following a prolonged siege at Queretaro on May 16, 1867. In the end, one of Maximilian's own commanders, Colonel Miguel Lopez, head of the Empress's regiment, conspired with the Republicans and sealed the emperor's fate.[55]

BY THE TIME Republican forces captured, tried, and executed Maximilian, John had returned to Missouri. In mid-spring 1867, with the settlements of Cordoba and Carlota already in ruin, Shelby's new venture at Tuxpan finally fell into Republican rifle sights. Very few French troops remained in the country, and given the emperor's dire need for soldiers around the capital, the last units protecting Tuxpan and Veracruz were siphoned away. Realizing that his neo-Confederate dreams in Mexico were dead and that overstaying his welcome would likely incite a nightmare, John agreed to escort Shelby's wife, Betty, as well as the Shelby children from Veracruz to New Orleans in March 1867.[56]

After setting foot on American soil for the first time since July 1865, John spoke to a reporter about the downfall of the Confederados in Mexico—and about Maximilian's impending plight. "There is no love for the people of the United States," he said, "and the only sympathy for them at all is because they are presumed to represent opposition to the French and to have expressed dislike for them." "The settlement at Cordoba," John concluded, "is among the things of the past. General Shelby still remains in Cordoba, and probably will remain for several months to come." At the time he spoke those words—"several months to come"—John obviously didn't know that Maximilian's capture and court-martial would expedite Shelby's return to America in June 1867.[57]

After learning of Maximilian's imprisonment, many of the same European monarchs that had spurned Charlotte's pleas for help in the summer of 1866 now tried to barter with Benito Juarez for the deposed emperor's life. Even following a visit from the Prussian minister Baron Von A. V. Magnus, the Republican president would not change his mind. "I am pained to tell you," Juarez replied to Magnus through an aide, "in answer to the telegram which you have been pleased to send to me to-night, that, as I declared to you day before yesterday, in this city, the President of the Republic does not believe it possible to grant the pardon of the Archduke Maximilian, through the gravest considerations of justice, and of the necessity of assuring peace to the Republic." Having once decreed no quarter for rebels against the government of Mexico, Maximilian would now receive none himself.[58]

Adding further anguish to his death sentence, Maximilian was informed—erroneously, it turned out—of Charlotte's death in Europe. His sole remaining wish was to be buried alongside her. On June 19, 1867, at the age of thirty-two, Maximilian faced a Juarista firing squad.

John's narration of the execution suggested that even after four bullets struck Maximilian in the chest, he remained alive, softly muttering to himself. A Republican soldier stepped forward and fired at close range into the royal's stomach—but that didn't kill him either. Finally, a point-blank shot to the heart dispatched Maximilian. The first and *only* emperor of the Second Mexican Empire was dead. As John put it, "The tragedy was ended."[59]

Only for John it really wasn't. In June 1865 he and the other Missourians had jumped right out of one internecine conflict and into another. In the technical sense, they experienced Confederate defeat. But the nature and timing of their exile—and the possibility of an imperially subsidized "do-over" in Mexico—had allowed John to compartmentalize and minimize the loss. Now, back in a Missouri occupied by Federal troops and with Freedman's Bureau agents operating in select parts of the state, the dual losses of the Confederacy and the Empire hit him all at once. John needed to process and cope with losing a new national opportunity not once, but twice.

For some of the Confederados, the fall of Maximilian's government was inconvenient but not an existential blow. John's friend and business partner Henry W. Allen had viewed the situation in Mexico through a very different lens. Writing in July 1865, almost immediately after arriving in Mexico City, Allen stated, "It is my intention to settle permanently in that place [Mexico], as I have no idea *that I will ever be permitted to return* . . . as I see by the United States newspapers that all who are excepted from the proclamation of amnesty will be brought to trial. It is a hard fate to be cut off from home and all we hold dear on earth." Allen's macabre disposition did not stop him from commenting frequently on the amenable climate of Mexico, which he dubbed the "garden-spot of the Continent." Nor did it keep him from plugging the abnormally cheap price of arable land when subsidized by Maximilian's government. Allen also confessed to liking the Imperial couple very much, especially Empress Charlotte. She had gone out of her way to make Allen and the other Confederados feel welcome. "She assured us," he reported to a friend, "that we poor Confederate exiles had her heartfelt sympathy, and that we were welcome in Mexico."[60]

Yet the stress resulting from this political turmoil and personal uncertainty led Allen to make an odd—but illuminative—confession in an 1866 letter: he often found himself repeating over and over again lines of Poe's "The Raven" that dealt with loneliness. Though it may not have dawned on him at the time, those forlorn verses more or less summed up Allen's time in Mexico. He walked *in,* but apart *from,* Mexican society, always anxious for the worst possible outcome—and all the while incapable of imagining a future for himself in Mexican space that was not entirely at odds with the past he missed so dearly. Henry Allen didn't live long enough to die on his native soil.[61]

As it so often happened, John was another story. Owing to his worldview a complicated exit was more or less inevitable. He brought deeply held, overly romantic beliefs about Old World social hierarchy and imperial authority with him to Mexico. He touted the climate and the soil of Mexico—and the coffee and sugar it might yield—as an *upgrade* from the American South. Allen made similar observations about his new environs but pined to escape from them. And while Allen saw internal instability and fiscal mismanagement in the empire, John viewed the relationship of ex-Confederates to Maximilian and Charlotte so favorably because in the authority of a Habsburg monarch he saw the power to make his dreams of a new Old South, south of the border, come true. That Maximilian generously subsidized real estate deals and treated the ex-Confederates like special dignitaries at court only added to John's impression that the emperor might enable what the Confederate state could not.

Against this backdrop, it is not difficult to see why John remained in Mexico despite a litany of financial setbacks, why he refused to go back in spite of the knowledge that President Andrew Johnson had no interest in punishing former Confederates, or why he made his home in Mexico even after it became clear that he owned arable land in Kentucky to which he could apply his labors. Nor is it particularly taxing to understand why he derided the would-be colonists who came and went quickly—scheming men, by his logic, who were scared off by the necessity of long-term investment and the prospect of placing great faith in Maximilian's government.

John iterated throughout his time in Mexico that the American war was over. In his professional opinion, the battle for Southern independence in America could not, and would not, be rekindled. Simultaneously, John steadfastly rejected that the other imperial powers of Europe would forsake one of their own. The upstart Union, he believed (in what turned out to be a momentous showing of naivete) would not cross the likes of France, Austria, Spain, and Belgium. The ultraconservative line of the Old World would hold, and the ex-Confederates would get to take up their rightful place within it.

Of course, the Union did cross the Old World, with virtually no consequences. And the ultraconservative line failed to bridge the Atlantic in any meaningful way. So now, nearly six years after John had left his home in Lexington behind—along with his job at the newspaper, his reputation as a rising journalistic star, and his American citizenship—it was time to start all over again. He needed to see about a girl at the Plattenburg farm. He knew he wanted to see his name on the masthead of a newspaper again. And while he didn't need to look over his shoulder for raiding Juaristas anymore, guerrillas of the American variety would occupy much of his time—and his writing—in the years to come.

War by Other Means 5

The Western Missouri to which John repatriated in 1867 was a different world than the one he left in 1861. Then-President Abraham Lincoln's 1863 Emancipation Proclamation had applied only to states in open rebellion against the Union. The Thirteenth Amendment, however, was ratified in December 1865, outlawing the institution of slavery throughout the entire nation. The same Radical Republicans responsible for the demise of slavery took control of state government in Missouri. That turn of political fate was almost as jarring to conservative Missourians as emancipation itself. Before the war forced Claiborne Jackson into exile, Democrats had held the governorship since 1820—an uninterrupted line of succession dating back to when Missouri first achieved statehood. Now Thomas Fletcher, an unabashed radical, pulled the strings in Jefferson City. Federal troops—a good many of them Black—stood by, rifles at the ready, to enforce the terms and policies of Reconstruction. Ex-Confederates and former slaveholders watched with a mix of contempt and dismay as freedpeople exercised the rights of citizenship formerly reserved for white Missourians. A different world, indeed.

Obviously, John had changed too. When he quit his post at the *Lexington Expositor* in 1861, he'd been more boy than man, rushing off after Shelby, determined not to miss the fight. Slightly bookish, energetic, and promising with his pen, he craved action. Yet he was also detached from real responsibility and blind to all the things he didn't know. That version of John did not survive the war. He had killed utter strangers and watched dear friends bleed to death. He had looked on, time and again, while inept Confederate generals bungled the war in the Trans-Mississippi and slaughtered their own men in the process. And he himself had been shot, captured, imprisoned, and later exiled. In short, John came back to Missouri a worldlier man in 1867, though his education had not come cheap. He still had energy, and he could still wield his pen like a battle ax, but he now bore the weight of two causes lost. As before the war, in times of distress and uncertainty John put ink to paper. The next decade would prove to be the most turbulent—and the most prolific—of his writing life.

IF JOHN INTENDED to swing his battle ax at Republican Reconstruction policies—and he most certainly did—he first needed to find a job. His prewar reputation at the *Expositor* spoke for itself among Missouri's conservative political set. Those credentials, paired with his closeness to Shelby, made the transition from Mexican exile to Missouri editor quick and easy. John soon found himself living at the Olive Street Hotel in St. Louis and working a political beat for the *St. Louis Republican.* Very little is known of his tenure at the paper, save that it was short-lived. The intercession of an old comrade would help see to that. In the meantime, though, John had other business to attend. Almost immediately after returning from Mexico in 1867, he came to terms with the Miami Printing and Publishing Company out of Cincinnati, Ohio. The firm published his first book, *Shelby and His Men: Or, The War in the West* that same year.[1]

For many fledgling authors in the nineteenth century, producing and selling a book meant much more than just writing it. John was no exception. The printing house circulated advance copies to generate published reviews. But marketing beyond that, at least in the beginning, often fell back on the author. John placed ads in various papers to hire local selling agents, who would then peddle the book to merchants, book dealers, or anyone who might potentially place a subscription. Fortunately for John, it was a good time to be selling military history. *Shelby and His Men* met with a public consumed by the history of the war it had just waged.[2]

Though Shelby and the Iron Brigade were not so well known as Lee, Jackson, or the Army of Northern Virginia, the topics of other best-selling books at the time, John did have an advantage over his literary peers, especially among readers in the Trans-Mississippi Theater: as would-be historians clamored to cash in on eastern generals and their armies, no other book told the story of the war in Missouri, Arkansas, and the rest of Kirby Smith's old dominion. For a short but critical while, John enjoyed a monopoly on the subject matter—and by the time competitors emerged, *Shelby and His Men* was already the standard against which new accounts would be judged. A September 1867 review from the *Daily Appeal* in Memphis helped explain the book's popularity and staying power. *Shelby and His Men,* the reviewer proclaimed, "is a work which will be read with interest and pleasure by all who wish to examine an authentic and attractive history of the military movements in the Trans-Mississippi Department." Judging the book "written in a style which continually challenges the reader's interest, and charms by lively anecdote, graphic sketch and graceful allusion," the review concluded that it "must necessarily meet with a ready reception from the public, and be rewarded with a liberal patronage."[3]

The author's preface to *Shelby and His Men* put John's political shrewdness on full display. As Shelby's adjutant in a military district known for backbiting and infighting, then as a front-row observer to the inner workings of an imperial court, he had learned a great many Machiavellian lessons. More simply put, he knew precisely which angles would play with disgruntled conservatives and seems to have anticipated, both in substance and vernacular, the signature traits of a brewing Lost Cause Movement. "Believing that the Confederate War was a grand panorama of heroic endurance and devoted courage," he waxed, "I bring this picture as an offering and lay it upon the altar of Southern glory and renown." Then with a calculated dose of self-deprecation, he dedicated the book to "the memory of my dead comrades of Shelby's Missouri Cavalry Division—to the youngest and the brave who fell fighting manfully for the proud, imperial South— this monument is erected by the unskilled hands of the Author." The *imperial* South. Not an accidental choice of words by any stretch of the imagination. Not for John. To be sure, the dedication was an ode to what might have been. But then, in light of John's soon-to-be-launched crusade against all things Republican, it also sent a veiled message to white Southerners; not quite a call to arms, but a reminder of who they once were and of the sort of society they might still salvage from the Confederate wreckage.[4]

It is unclear if John's new literary celebrity had much—or anything—to do with Colonel John C. Moore approaching him with a business proposition. In fact, it's not even known for certain which of the former Confederate cavalry officers first approached the other. Moore's access to start-up capital, and John's lack of access to much money of any kind, made it likely that Moore did the recruiting. Either way, sometime in 1867 they began to draw up plans for a fervently pro-Democrat newspaper. Headquartered in Kansas City, on the Missouri side of the border, they would christen their new venture the *Kansas City Times*.[5]

In more ways than not, John and Moore were made for each other. Born in Tennessee, Moore ran a newspaper and served a term as the mayor of Denver, Colorado, before joining the Confederate cavalry in Missouri. For a time he worked as Marmaduke's chief of staff, and even assisted as a second when Marmaduke famously—and very illegally— killed fellow Confederate General Lucius M. Walker in a duel. After the war, Moore threw in his lot with Shelby's Mexican caravan. Like John, Moore had a keen interest in Confederate history. Also like John, he harbored old-fashioned ideas about honor and chivalry, particularly concerning interactions with the opposite sex. Unlike John but much to John's liking, Moore's experience with the code duello was not limited to being a second. His deadly exploits were well known and greatly influenced John's conduct in the coming years.[6]

Once incorporated, John and Moore established a second-floor office at 813 Main Street. It appears that each man had an equal, half-stake in the company, though Moore became editor in chief. (This arrangement further hints that Moore was the senior member of the partnership and probably recruited John for his skills as an editorialist.) John's position was that of associate editor, and he was responsible for political commentary, which was his specialty. Important as their titles might have appeared in the bolded text of a masthead, both men hit the street to collect headlines, and at least in the earliest days of production, they pitched in with typesetting and printing duties until the staff grew larger. The first issue of the *Kansas City Times* came off the press on September 8, 1868. The precocious boy who'd won fame for his article in Washington, Virginia, now owned a newspaper.[7]

Part 1: Outlaw Politics and Political Outlawry

Given the size of their personalities—and of their ambitions—it ought not to come as a surprise that John and his partner would launch the *Times* smack dab in the middle of an era-defining presidential election. And that's precisely what they did. In less than two months, white Americans, North and South, would return to the polls as a single electorate for the first time since 1860. Freedpeople would join them in casting ballots for the first time ever. In their collective grasp was the fate of Reconstruction and the legacy of the war that had necessitated it.

The contest pitted former Union General-in-Chief Ulysses S. Grant (Republican, Ohio) and Schuyler Colfax, the sitting Republican Speaker of the House of Representatives, against Horatio G. Seymour, the former Democratic governor of New York, and former Union Major General Francis Preston Blair Jr. If elected, the Grant-Colfax ticket promised to hand the reins of Reconstruction over to the radicals in congress that John had so utterly despised in his letters home from Mexico. Better still, the commander once dubbed "Unconditional Surrender" by the Northern press planned to back radical policy with the full might of the Federal military. Southern Democrats pushing Black codes and paramilitary groups were on notice: in U. S. Grant they would not be dealing with a white supremacist do-nothing of the Andrew Johnson variety.

Seymour favored a rapid end to Federal oversight in the ex-Confederacy and hoped to sidestep any further punishment for the defeated Southern states. He also operated at a net disadvantage. In addition to ex-Confederates in readmitted states who had not yet regained suffrage, the states of Texas, Virginia, and Mississippi failed to meet the requirements for rejoining the Union, and as a result their voters could not participate in the election. Making matters even more interesting for John and the *Times* was that Seymour's running mate, Francis Blair Jr., hailed from Missouri. He'd once represented the state's First District, a densely populated territory that included St. Louis. When war broke out, Blair remained a steadfast Unionist and rapidly ascended the ranks of the Union army—a rise perhaps facilitated, at least in part, by the prominent position of his father, Francis Blair Sr., in the Lincoln White House. The younger Blair had been a Republican in those days, but no longer. Disenchanted with the GOP's vision of Reconstruction, he defected to the Democratic Party and now stood vehemently opposed to any course of legislation that might bestow freedpeople with equal rights.[8]

Whatever hope John and other Democrats had of seizing power in the first national election since Appomattox fizzled fast. While the "magic number" needed to win the election was 148, Grant seized a commanding 214 to 80 majority in the Electoral College. Likewise, the Republican ticket won the popular vote by more than 5 percent, claiming several ex-Confederate states—Florida, Alabama, Arkansas, Tennessee, and both Carolinas—in the process. Though Missouri was not technically a member of the former Confederacy, Blair failed to deliver it for the Democrats. Grant took all eleven electoral votes in the adopted home state of Jo Shelby and Sterling Price and actually ran several percentage points ahead of his national mark. On the coattails of Grant's strong showing in Missouri, Republican congressman Joseph W. McClurg won the gubernatorial election in a near landslide and fellow-Republican John H. Stover handily defeated a Democratic challenger for McClurg's vacated seat in the House of Representatives. In the senatorial election, German-born Carl Schurz joined the already-seated senator Charles D. Drake for a Republican sweep of the upper chamber.[9]

While these were clearly not the headlines the proprietors of the *Kansas City Times* had hoped to set before the election, the sting of defeat—and his loathing of all things radical—motivated John to push back in new, creative, and even criminal ways. Which does not mean that John's despair over Republican dominance drove him to a life of literal lawlessness; rather, it is to say that he believed standard fare punditry would no longer get the job done. With the *Times* as a vehicle, he needed to wage something like an editorial insurgency. But that was easier said than done—because for all the hyperbolic power of his pen, John could not create the news from whole cloth. He needed a flashy, partisan story and the right set of willing subjects to weaponize against the Republican agenda. As luck had it, a group of former Confederates with insurgent, anti-Reconstruction plans of their own were ready and waiting for an editor like John to take up their case. Even more fortuitously for him, a few were old acquaintances from the war in Western Missouri.

Though he had not fought as a guerrilla during the war, John's path had inevitably crossed with some of the men who served under guerrilla chieftains like William Clarke Quantrill, "Bloody Bill" Anderson, and George Todd. Even Upton Hays led an irregular band before raising a regiment of regular Confederate cavalry. At Independence and Lexington, guerrillas had fought alongside Confederate troops. And on the homefront, when men from the Iron Brigade, including John, socialized with civilians, it was often with the families and neighbors of guerrillas.

Actual irregulars—or *bushwhackers* as was the most common term in the 1860s—were hard men. They had waged war against the Union in a state that never managed to secede. Instead of leaving to ride with Shelby or Price, or to fight on still more distant battlefields in the eastern theaters, they stuck close to home. Supplied with food and intelligence by their own mothers, wives, daughters, and female cousins—and not technically bound by the mainstream rules of war—they utilized deception, mobility, and ruthlessness. Working in small, mounted bands, and always favoring braces of revolvers over long arms, they were masters of the ambush. They struck along lonely bends in the road, in isolated fields, and on front porches. Theirs was a war to the last knife, hyperpersonal and hyperlocal. Assassination, torture, arson, white on white rape, and even massacre were the calling cards of guerrilla war in the Missouri-Kansas borderlands. In this theater of war, waged from and upon individual households, neither age nor sex guaranteed protection from the violence. To pro-

Confederate relatives and friends, bushwhackers were a resistance front against Union invasion. To loyal Missourians, and especially to German Unionists, they were a source of perpetual terror.[10]

In the aftermath of the war, the majority of bushwhackers followed in the footsteps of their counterparts from the regular war: they simply returned to their former communities and resumed farming. It was very difficult for Union authorities to keep track of individual bushwhackers, many of whom operated in secret. Owing to this wartime anonymity, they had not achieved lasting notoriety and, generally speaking, represented fish too small for catching in Union nets after the fact. But for a select few, returning home—doing so peacefully and safely, anyway—was another matter. For men who *had* made names for themselves—that is, who had achieved infamy through terror— lingering animosity and threats of retribution afforded them far fewer options for survival. In turn, a very small minority turned to banditry. From this group, two sets of brothers, the Jameses, Frank and Jesse, and the Youngers, Cole, John, and Jim, emerged as the principal objects of John's attention.[11]

Various incarnations of what would become known as the James-Younger Gang—including some that did not actually include the group's purported ringleader, Jesse James—had been committing robberies since 1866. That February, a band of ex-bushwhackers with ties to James knocked over the Clay County Savings Bank in Liberty, Missouri. Over the next three years, the group carried out heists in Missouri, at Savannah and Richmond, and in Kentucky, where it relieved the Nimrod & Co. Bank in Russellville of some $12,000. John's involvement with the gang began a few months after another robbery at the Daviess County Savings Bank in Gallatin, Missouri. Frank and Jesse James, it was unanimously believed at the time, were in on the job. And rumors spread like wildfire that it was Jesse who personally shot down the bank's unarmed cashier, John W. Sheets, because he mistakenly believed Sheets had been involved in the killing of his old commander, Bloody Bill Anderson.[12]

That ex-Confederate bushwhackers robbed a bank and killed a man in cold blood probably didn't shock survivors of the borderland guerrilla war. After all, the wartime tactics employed by the Jameses,

Youngers, and other irregulars were perfectly suited to armed robbery. Both involved small bands of heavily armed men. Both involved quick strikes without warning. Both involved ruthless efficiency. And both involved hasty retreats in the face of larger, pursuing forces. Bushwhacker and bandit alike ran away to live and fight another day. What may have caught Missourians off guard about the crime was how John elected to cover it in the *Kansas City Times*. He didn't condemn a brazen daytime heist as an affront to civilized society or lament the murder of an innocent party. John made contact with the James brothers, befriended them, and some months later, printed an open letter from Jesse James to Missouri's governor, Joseph W. McClurg.

In his preface to the letter, published in late June 1870, John suggested that no one had heard from either of the James boys in the months since the sheriff of Clay County had attempted to apprehend them in a shootout. "Yesterday, however," John reported without a hint of incredulity, "we received the following letter from Jesse W. James, the eldest brother. It had neither post office mark nor was it dated upon any day, but had evidently been enclosed to us by someone else." John's level of editorial involvement in the letter is debated but ultimately unknown. What is quite likely, however, is that he received the missive directly from Jesse James—though his misidentification of Jesse as the "eldest brother" indicates that he was not yet totally familiar with their backstories.[13]

The letter, intended to serve as a proclamation of innocence, doubled as a list of grievances suffered by ex-Confederates since the end of the war. "I can prove, by some of the best men in Missouri, where I was the day of the robbery and the day previous to it," the message began. But James had no intention of entrusting his own safety to the state. "The past is sufficient to show that bushwhackers have been arrested in Missouri, since the war, charged with bank robbery, and they most all have been mobbed without trials," James alleged. "When I think I can get a fair trial," he pledged, "I will surrender myself to the civil authorities of Missouri. But I never will surrender to be mobbed by a set of bloodthirsty poltroons. It is true that during the war I was a Confederate soldier, and fought under the black flag, but since then I have lived a peaceable citizen, and obeyed the laws of the United States to the best of my knowledge." In other words, as Jesse James saw it, these trumped-up charges had nothing to do with evidence and everything to do with punishing him and his brother Frank for their wartime activities.[14]

For John, it was a partisan goldmine. Here were two boys from a well-established, land-owning family, still in their early twenties, who simply wanted to go home to their mother's farm. Yet in this version of the story, they couldn't because Radical Republicans like McClurg wouldn't allow the war to end. Compelling as the narrative might have been—particularly in light of James's claim to an alibi with multiple witnesses—it surfaced in a tense moment of change for Missouri Democrats. The party was moving away from its older, proslavery, pro-Confederate stances; it needed to evolve and modernize for the sake of attracting a broader portion of the electorate or risk permanent obsolescence. At first glance, glorifying homicidal bandits ran the risk of alienating law-and-order conservatives from both parties. But Democrats couldn't just abandon the perspective of the relatively small but still very powerful ex-Confederate element within Western Missouri either. So here was an opportunity for John to fashion martyrs that he might use to depict radical leadership within the Republican Party as vindictive, overreaching, and corrupt. Making sure the focus remained on the *why* and not the *what* of the robbery was John's chief task as propagandist. It was a risky move—for his own reputation and that of the paper—but the potential payoff in public sentiment was substantial.

Leading into the state elections of 1870, driving a wedge between more conservative Republicans and the Radical Republicans empowered by Grant in 1868 was critical for Missouri's Democratic establishment. The former, in many cases, believed that Reconstruction had been achieved; that it was time for the Federal government to turn control back over to the Southern states and move on to other national business. The latter, understanding what such a concession would mean for freed people in the ex-Confederacy, balked at abandoning them. In addition to protecting the civil rights of the newly emancipated, Radicals also had a pragmatic reason to delay the end of Reconstruction. They had no intention of seeing a massive new voter bloc—one that had belonged entirely to U. S. Grant and other Republicans in 1868—suddenly disenfranchised again by Democrats when Federal oversight of law *enforcement* in the ex-Confederacy waned. These fears were applicable to Missouri as well. Though the state had never formally left the Union, many Radicals considered it pseudo-Confederate territory. And for good reason: notable violence against African Americans in Missouri made it one of only two loyal states during the war that still required branches of the Freedman's Bureau.[15]

John hoped throwing a spotlight on the plight of Frank and Jesse James might widen the divide between Republican factions in Missouri; he wanted to underscore, in real human terms, the negative impact of prolonged Federal meddling on everyday citizens. The beauty of the arrangement was that whether voters believed the James's protestations of innocence or not, John had an angle prepared to woo them. If conservative Missourians—Democrats *or* Republicans—took James at his word, his persecution was a prime example of how Reconstruction had morphed into something corrupt and abusive. Then again, if observers held James responsible for the bank robbery in Gallatin, John could simply ask how Republicans could have mismanaged control of the government so badly that fine young men needed to emulate Robin Hood and his cohort of social bandits just to survive. Though perhaps not in command of the moral high ground, by wielding both sides of the banditry coin to the same end, John could crusade against Reconstruction without taking a blatantly unreconstructed stance. Put another way, it was in his best political interest to chip away at Radical Republican power, whether he believed the story he used to do it or not.

In the gubernatorial contest of 1870, Republican infighting did, in fact, yield results for Missouri Democrats. Former Republican senator Benjamin Gratz Brown, along with sitting Missouri senator Carl Schurz, broke with the Grant administration on matters of Reconstruction policy. Spearheading a new party, the Liberal Republicans, they campaigned on the notion that the goals of the war and Reconstruction were accomplished. It was time for the Federal government to leave the South be and take stock of its own house. In this case, *liberal* actually meant more conservative, in the traditional sense of the word, when it came to racial issues. Sensing an opportunity, Democrats threw their support behind Brown, despite his pro-Union, antislavery positions before and during the war. Given the circumstances, the enemy of Radical Republicans was a friend to Democrats and they helped Brown trounce McClurg at the polls. As a candidate of both the Liberal Republicans and the Democrats, Brown claimed more than 60 percent of the vote. Without question, Democrats would have greatly preferred one of their own taking office in Jefferson City—but Brown represented a step in the right direction. And thanks to Missouri's short, two-year terms of office, Democrats would not have to wait long for another shot at the governorship.[16]

It would be tempting to draw a clear line of cause and effect between John's opening salvo as the James-Younger Gang's publicist and McClurg's ouster in 1870. But even to assign partial credit would be jumping the gun by an election cycle if not two. The story simply wasn't big enough yet. The Jameses needed more time to become marquee names outside of Western Missouri. Following the Gallatin heist, the outlaws actually abstained from crime for eighteen months. By the time the gang hit another bank, this time in Corydon, Iowa, in June 1871, the election was long over and James's letter to McClurg forgotten. Even for an editorialist as creative and willing to sensationalize as John, a consistent media campaign framed around the social banditry of former Confederates was going to require an equally consistent campaign of criminal activity. But just as the strategy employed by Liberal Republicans at the state level in 1870 represented a harbinger of larger developments in 1872, so too did John's early weaponization of the James brothers against Reconstruction. As the bushwhackers turned bandits graduated from local interest to national notoriety over the course of the 1870s, John would be waiting in the wings to spin their increasingly violent holdups into acts of paramilitary resistance against the state.[17]

Part 2: Changings of the Guard

Around the time he began cultivating a relationship with Jesse James, news from Europe struck John like a lightning bolt. Maximilian's widow, the Dowager Empress Charlotte, was certain to die at any moment. For all John knew, she had already passed by the time the story reached him. On May 29, 1870, he published an emotional eulogy in the *Times*; one that betrayed the courtly feelings he'd sheltered for the patroness of the Confederados since 1865. Now, presuming Charlotte had joined her husband in death, all of John's feelings poured forth in lavish prose, growing more purple with each additional clause: "Pure as all women; stainless as an angel-guarded child; proud as Edith of the swan's neck; beautiful; a queen of hearts where honor dwelt; mistress of the realms of music; rare in the embroidery she wove; having time for literature and letters; sensuous only in the melody of her voice; never a mother—it was as though God had sent an angel of light to redeem a barbaric race and sanctify a degraded people."[18]

It's unclear who Charlotte had been sent to redeem, her husband's Mexican subjects or mankind generally speaking. Either way, despite John's outsized reaction, the comings and goings of European royals meant very little to most Americans. For the average reader of the *Times*, the dispatches from Belgium would hardly have prompted a reaction—save for perhaps wondering where Belgium was on the map. For John, however, the impending demise of "Poor Carlota" meant that part of his past, and the dream of a future that might have been, was also dying. He lamented Charlotte and the grand opportunity lost in Mexico in the Old-World cultural vernacular he knew best.[19]

The alleged passing of Charlotte—who, it is worth pointing out, did not die in 1870 and ironically outlived her distraught eulogist by decades—and the entrance of Jesse James into John's life signaled a deep-seated change in his sensibility. That Lancelots and Arthurs now resided in the afterlife wasn't coincidental. As the last link to Maximilian's Empire, Charlotte had typified everything John believed was good about the Old World: royal bloodlines, imperial power, sophistication, chivalry, rigid hierarchy, and order. The loss of Charlotte as a muse forced him to recognize that that world—of warrior kings, virtuous maidens, and devoted knights—was forever out of reach. Or at least, it forced him to recognize the fact in print for the first time. In her place, John adopted an outlaw. Whereas Charlotte had been genteel, James was rough. Whereas she had been a patron of the arts and herself a musician, James did his finest work with a .38-caliber Colt revolver. But for all that James lacked in royal blood or sophistication, he abounded with raw ferocity and the will to survive. As John's modus operandi evolved, these were the qualities he sought to further his new mission: preserving whatever remained of the old and aristocratic in Southern culture. More simply put, the dream of winning a blank canvas, either in the Confederacy or in Imperial Mexico, and establishing an Old World society upon it was over. Now it was time to play defense.

With his coverage of the James brothers at a temporary lull, and perhaps inspired by Maximilian and Charlotte, in spring 1871 John focused his attention on matters of the heart. As with seemingly everything he touched lately, controversy ensued. Mary Virginia Plattenburg was born in nearby Dover, Missouri, in 1848, the eldest daughter of James Shelby Plattenburg—the same judge who'd helped Jo Shelby, then an ambitious colonel, launch his military career almost a decade prior. Since the end of the war, Jennie—as she was called by family and her closest friends—had lived on her father's estate in Lexington. Unlike the bachelor's quarters that John occupied in Kansas City, life at the Plattenburg homestead was luxurious. Listed in the 1870 census as a "retired merchant," Jennie's father boasted $25,000 in real estate wealth and $5,000 in personal wealth. Those were both substantial sums at the time. No longer able to keep slaves, the family still employed domestic servants around the house.[20]

It's unknown for how long John courted Jennie. Nor is it known for how long the pair was engaged before their wedding. Regardless, it was a matter of public knowledge that the elder Plattenburgs objected to the union, though not for the reasons that first jump to mind. It didn't bother Jennie's family that John was ten years her senior—that age difference meant next to nothing in the nineteenth century. And while John's recent association with the James-Younger Gang had injected his public persona with an element of notoriety, he and Judge Plattenburg likely shared much common ground when it came to politics. After all, three of Jennie's brothers—John, James, and Harvey—had marched off to war with Shelby in defense of slavery. Politically and professionally, John had a steady job and at least gave the appearance of being a man on the rise. What set James and Laura Plattenburg against their daughter's union with John was the simple fact that they were first cousins. In a bizarre twist of fate for the young lovers, John's paternal aunt, Mary Murray Edwards, who died several years before he was even born, doubled as Jennie's maternal grandmother.[21]

Granted, it was not unusual for first cousins to wed in nineteenth-century America. Far from it, actually. So mild incest notwithstanding, John refused to give up on the relationship. For him, Jennie was too perfect of a match to let go. In many ways, he must have viewed her as his version of Charlotte. She was an avid reader; she adored literature and poetry. Her cousin, the Reverend George Plattenburg, once noted Jennie's "uncommon literary faculty" and hinted that she was more than an intellectual match for John, whom he considered brilliant. Given his own lack of parental support, the rejection of his in-laws-to-be must have wounded John, particularly the rebuke of Judge Plattenburg. With his thriving farm and looming stature in the community, the Judge at sixty-three was what many had assumed John's own father would become before sudden illness struck him down at forty-four. It is doubtful that the parallel was lost on a man as wrapped up in the past as John.[22]

In this moment of conflict and uncertainty, he turned to his old friend and commander Jo Shelby. Coincidentally, Shelby had been through this before. In 1858 he'd married his first cousin once removed to joyous applause from friends and family. But John wasn't a wealthy shipping magnate nor was he the scion of an aristocratic family. Shelby could not change Judge Plattenburg's mind, and so he agreed to host the nuptials on his farm near Aullville, Missouri, in Lafayette County. Surviving accounts of the ceremony are few and far between, but all indicate that the bride's parents refused to attend. Reverend George Plattenburg appeared accepting of the marriage in retrospect, though he did not officiate the ceremony, and it's unclear if he attended. In any case, on March 28, 1871, Mary Virginia Plattenburg defied her parents and became Mrs. John Newman Edwards.[23]

However disappointed John might have been by the situation with his in-laws, a major behind-the-scenes development at the *Times* helped buoy his spirits. Around the time of the wedding, Dr. Morrison Munford took over day-to-day management of the newspaper. Born in Tennessee in 1842, Munford was a tall, thin man with large, sad eyes and a face that contemporaries described as boyish. Perhaps to help look his age, he cultivated a thick mustache and, beneath it, a tuft of long, wispy chin hairs in the "imperial" style. Munford's arrival was part of a broader corporate shakeup at the *Times*. An investment group including John J. Mastin, Thomas H. Mastin, Amos Green, and Munford, bought complete control of both the paper and its printing operation. Everything was then reorganized under the corporate umbrella of The Times Publishing Company. "It is the intention of the proprietors," a notice from the new owners read on August 20, 1871, "to fill every department with capable and efficient men, to infuse new life and energy into its conduct, and to supply the public with a first class and reliable newspaper." With that goal in mind, in addition to being named secretary of the firm, Munford assumed responsibility for the day-to-day business management of the paper itself. This was wonderful news for John, both personally and professionally.[24]

He and Munford—whom he called "Morry"—knew each other well. Truly, with a few notable exceptions, Munford probably knew John better than anyone. They first met in September 1868, when the paper was putting its first issues to press. Munford, a Confederate veteran turned school teacher turned medical doctor turned real estate speculator traveled from his home in Kansas to visit a cousin in Kansas City. Somewhat serendipitously, that cousin turned out to be Colonel John C. Moore, John's partner at the *Times*. While socializing at the *Times* office one evening, Munford crossed paths with John, and the pair struck up a conversation about politics. "I had come down from intolerant Kansas," Munford recalled, "where an ex-Confederate soldier barely had the right of existence. I wanted consolation and comfort, and I got both from John Edwards that September night in 1868."[25]

When Munford moved to Kansas City in 1869, he and John became roommates. They lived together until Munford got married about a year later. "The memory of my bachelor days twenty years ago, with John Edwards as my chum, lingers as a sweet unction," Munford wrote many years later. "I was then in a business that required no night work, but nearly every night would find me seeking the *Times* office, and together, after the paper had gone to press, we would wander homeward to our bachelor quarters. The communings we then had, the confidences we mutually bestowed, the castles in the air we then built are all, all a glorious recollection." Their correspondence verified Munford's nostalgic sentiment; they trusted each other without shame or reservation.[26]

The combination of his marriage to Jennie and his new business partnership with Munford marked a pivotal moment for John. He would always be tethered to Jo Shelby by their experiences in war and exile. Shelby would always stand tall in John's mind as a paragon of cavalier manliness and martial prowess. And John would vigorously defend the legacies of Shelby and the Iron Brigade until the day he died; they shared a bond of brotherhood forged by the experiences they endured and the dreams they lost together. But Shelby's role as primary counselor and confidant was now largely at an end. In his place, Jennie and Munford became the two great stabilizing forces in John's life—Jennie his constant support and moral anchor at home, Munford his de facto therapist and career advisor.

Amidst this "changing of the guard" in his personal life, John's career continued to thrive. He was a favorite target for rival newspapers throughout the summer of 1871. This partisan sniping—and the large bull's eye now on John's back—indicated that he had become an adversary against whom political foes measured their own prowess. A case in point: his version of the war in *Shelby and His Men* and his subsequent work with former bushwhackers Jesse and Frank James clearly struck a nerve with the editors of the *Daily Kansas Tribune* of Lawrence, Kansas. With not a little disgust, the paper quoted a *Times* piece in which John opined, "The only regret we have concerning the Quantrell massacre is to be found in the fact that the editor of the

Fort Scott *Monitor* was not there to be killed with the balance of his brethren." The *Tribune* then explained to readers that "Shelby was a rebel guerrilla, and the author, we are informed by the *Monitor*, was one of his men." As the *Tribune* saw things, John didn't just write about the badmen of Missouri, in more ways than not, he was one of them.[27]

Though Republicans in the western borderlands might have viewed John as a political villain, albeit the one they loved to hate, within conservative circles his voice grew increasingly influential. With that influence came certain rewards. In December 1871, for instance, news broke of his nomination by the Democratic Caucus to the position of state printer in Missouri. John's new status as the state's foremost pro-Democratic editorialist also boded well for his next book.[28]

Published in fall 1872, *Shelby's Expedition to Mexico: An Unwritten Leaf of the War* enjoyed two key advantages over *Shelby and His Men*. The first was a ready-made audience among *Times* readers and readers of the smaller, local papers that regularly reran John's articles. In fact, not only did the *Times* run segments of *Shelby's Expedition* in serial form—a common tactic in the nineteenth century to tantalize readers—but the printing side of the *Times's* operation, the Kansas City Times Steam Book and Job Printing House, actually served as publisher. The second advantage was John's own celebrity. In 1867 John had been a relative nobody writing about Missouri's most-beloved Confederate general. Five years later, Shelby still reigned over the state's ex-Confederate set, but John's name was just as recognizable. Better still, through his fiery editorials, John found his way into the homes of untold borderlanders on a weekly basis—for many, his columns were part of daily life.[29]

John's narrative of the journey to and time spent in imperial Mexico framed Shelby and his followers as gallant knights of old—as men renowned for chivalry and fortitude, taking their rightful place among the society of an old-world royal. In the context of John's deep love for the classics, it is easy to imagine him seeing *Shelby and His Men* as a Missouri-centric Iliad, while *Shelby's Expedition to Mexico* recounted an Odyssey-like adventure, with Mexican bandits and double-dealing Juaristas in place of lotus eaters, sirens, and cyclopes. Unlike Odysseus and his men, though, the Missourians in *Shelby's Expedition* do not return to their old, rightful home after a victorious war effort. Instead, they abandon the defeated South and go in search of a different realm in which to establish a new, Old South. And while Odysseus's tale enjoys a happy ending, John's saga of Confederados concluded with a kingdom fallen and the bullet-riddled corpse of a monarch slumped in the dirt. Despite its gloomy ending, and John's propensity for indulging his love of lavish, melodramatic prose, *Shelby's Expedition to Mexico* enjoyed widespread popularity. For decades, it was considered a decisive historical account of Southern colonization efforts and the expulsion of the Second French Empire from Mexico.

The man who did more to foil John's plans in Mexico than any other—President Benito Juarez—died in 1872, just a few months before the release of the book. The task of eulogizing him for the *Times* fell to John. Generally, John highlighted character strengths and achievements even when covering the death of a former opponent. This was partly out of respect for the dead and partly because from John's perspective it made sense to measure one's own causes by the magnitude of its enemies. His oft-complimentary assessments of Federal adversaries in battle are a prime example. With that in mind, it is a testament to the grudge John held against Juarez—for allowing his men to wage unrestrained, irregular war against the colony at Carlota, for executing Maximilian like a common criminal, and for cutting short the attempt by former Confederates to build the South of their dreams in Mexico—that he opted not to spin an epic tale of political maneuvering and military campaigning, or even outright villainy, from the story of Juarez's life. In fact, it is a misnomer to even call John's sterile, twenty-line column a eulogy; it announces a sudden death by stroke, notes who would succeed Juarez, and then nothing. If John could not beat Juarez in life, it appears he sought to settle the score in death.[30]

To put the bare bones coverage of Juarez in context, it's useful to consider the way John treated former Secretary of State and ardent abolitionist William H. Seward following his death a few months later, in October. John noted bluntly that "death did not blight Mr. Seward any remaining usefulness to his country. . . . He had been as dead politically since '68 as he was now corporeally." This jab was a reminder of Seward's support for Andrew Johnson during the latter's impeachment trial and the falling out it caused with Grant's new administration.[31]

Then the tone of the obituary veers in a more positive direction. Seward, John contends, "is numbered among those, who, like Webster, Clay, and Calhoun, were too great to be President, and great enough to make Presidents tremble." So great, in fact, were Seward's powers that it was actually he and secretary of war Edwin Stanton, according to John, who had defeated the Confederacy: "Seward and Stanton, like two Roman consuls, governed the country. There was at that time a man in the White House named Abraham Lincoln, but his duties were only ministerial. His two subordinates—the one cold, weary, keen, and smooth; the other hot, impetuous, irresistible, and blunt—swayed him as they did everything and everybody else."[32]

The point was clearly being exaggerated at Lincoln's expense, and in doing so John revealed an important metric for how he judged himself via the prowess of an adversary. Yes, Seward was "beloved by his neighbors," and yes, he was "respected and feared by his political friends." Those qualities mattered—and they made for nice words on paper. But throughout his career Seward had cultivated and wielded enough influence to transcend typical postmortem niceties. Men of Seward's elite political class, few and far between as they might have been, were "hated and anathemized beyond measure" by their "political foes." This special animosity was reserved for the best of the best. And for that distinction of formidability—one which John was slowly acquiring for himself on a relatively smaller scale in the western borderlands—the obituary showed immense respect.[33]

Part 3: Political Alliances, New and Old

The power of political giants like Clay and Calhoun was already on John's mind when he sat down to lionize Seward. Better still, in recounting the great partisan operators of Seward's generation, John appeared to be wondering whether any such men remained to lead the Democratic Party to victory in elections that, by October 1872, were only a month away. Politically and economically, the contest between Republicans (led by the incumbent Grant) and a coalition of

Liberal Republicans and "New Departure" Democrats (spearheaded by famed newspaperman Horace Greeley and Missouri governor Benjamin Gratz Brown) would function as a bellwether for the fate of Reconstruction. For John, who had been running full tilt on electoral politics for more than a year leading up to the election, the race was a do-or-die moment for the Republic itself.

Generally speaking, New Departure Democrats sought to move on from the past—which is to say, from the Confederacy—and conceded certain elements of Reconstruction as an indicator of their American-ness. If they could prove their loyalty to the nation, the logic went, they might also prove prolonged Federal occupation unnecessary. Not concerned with reigniting the war, this wing of the Democratic Party eyed economic recovery and a quiet reconsolidation of white power over the ex-Confederacy and freedpeople once Republicans were out of the way. For their part, Liberal Republicans represented a departure of their own from the Republican majority; as in 1870, they too thought Reconstruction had gone far enough and, in some cases, even recoiled from the racial consequences of their own party's legislative handiwork.[34]

In Missouri, and specifically in St. Louis, where the Liberal Republican movement began, ancient enemies found themselves in common cause. Once easily delineated by their stances on slavery, antebellum Democrats and their German Republican rivals now combined their efforts to halt radical policy. This anti-Republican union also put John in a strange position. Moving on from the past went against his nature. More often than not, *returning* to the past was his ultimate goal. He'd just published a book that simultaneously glorified the exploits of Shelby's Confederates and took the Union government to task for its boorish policies toward Mexico. At the same time, he was actively using the James-Younger Gang as a bludgeon against Radical Reconstruction. That said, John did agree wholeheartedly with one tenet of the Liberal-Democratic alliance in 1872: that corruption was rampant in the Federal government from the presidency on down and that reform meant cleansing the capital of Grant's thieving Republicans. Whether the Unreconstructed Rebel in John advocated so strongly for the New Departure in his commentary for the *Times* on principle or because it was the most pragmatic way to rid the South of so-called carpetbaggers and scalawags is difficult to determine with absolute certainty. But based on his personal track record and the shrewdness he'd already displayed as a political operator, the safer bet in this case would be on pragmatism.[35]

As early as September 1871 John began preparing his readers to strive for a partial victory. That meant electing a Liberal Republican to defeat Radical Republicans because it was the best option available. The Radicals, he goaded his ex-Confederate subscribers, were already assuming that backward-looking Democrats would nominate a former Confederate leader for the presidency—which would make reelecting Grant much easier. John beseeched Missouri's Democrats to make Grant run on his tainted presidential record and not allow him to resume the role of Confederate conqueror.[36]

It was one thing for Democrats to harp on the alleged corruption within the Grant administration—the episodes they believed tainted the former general in chief's record as commander in chief. It was another thing entirely for a well-known Republican newspaper to do it. That in mind, in November 1871, John took special delight in relaying to readers in Kansas City that "Dr. Greeley declares war on the administration finally and without compromise." The reference to "Dr. Greeley" referred to Horace Greeley, the antislavery Whig turned Republican who had championed both Abraham Lincoln and the Union cause during the Civil War. As founder and editor of the nationally renowned *New-York Tribune*, Greeley's break with Grant offered Democrats a ray of hope. And while Greeley intended his call to arms against "thieves and bribe-givers and bribe-takers" in government to apply to either party, John took the opportunity to launch a broadside solely at Republicans. "The party name the majority happens to bear is the universal Shibboleth," he fulminated, "[and] all manner of abuses are perpetrated under it, and cry out as they may for reparation, the cry is smothered by the sound of the party slogan."[37]

A week later, John's anti-Republican commentary featured what he considered a smoking gun in the account of Major R. A. Calhoun, a pension agent appointed by Grant who stood accused of embezzling more than $8,000 from needy veterans. Per John's version of the story, when confronted with the charges of financial impropriety, Calhoun feebly maintained his innocence. Then, sensing real danger, he commenced with political posturing and bootlicking. Calhoun declared himself a personal friend of President Grant and boasted, "I am equally inflexible in my adherence to Radical principles and the great leader who now fills the office of President." To Liberal Republicans, this was a damning optic. To Democrats like John and his readers, it was an abomination. "Faith without works is dead," John sneered. "To be an 'earnest friend of Gen. Grant and his adminis-tration' without stealing something, is to be a hypocrite with more temerity than Calhoun possessed."[38]

In the same issue of the *Times* that excoriated corruption in Wash-ington, John also supplied coverage of what current misdealings in the capital—and the possibility of four additional years of Radical rule—meant for everyday Southerners. "Gen. [Francis P.] Blair had returned from the South, where as one of the members of the Con-gressional Committee, he has been rigidly investigating the recent Ku Klux outrages," John reported. According to John, Blair "declares them great exaggerated [sic]—in fact more of a myth than reality." Worse still, the senator from Missouri described the condition of the South as "simply deplorable." In Blair's testimony, Grant and his toadies stood by while innocent white Southerners were "crushed down by taxation, plundered at will by the carpet-baggers, preyed upon by the negroes, maligned and lied upon at the North, prose-cuted at home, and outlawed and ostracised [sic] generally." These conditions noted for the record, John commanded his readers to accept the "passive policy"; they *must* vote Liberal Republican to end Reconstruction and reform the government. Without cooperation between the two anti-Republican factions, John saw only doom for Democratic causes.[39]

The following spring, all seemed to be going according to plan. In May 1872 Horace Greeley accepted the nomination of the Lib-eral Republican Party for the presidency. Greeley was an interesting character—he'd hounded Lincoln to abolish slavery and then played a pivotal role in the postbellum liberation of Jefferson Davis—but he brought national name recognition and a built-in fanbase to the ticket. Benjamin Gratz Brown, then the sitting governor of Missouri, was tapped to be Greeley's running mate. The Democratic Party, realizing it had zero prospects of winning a national election without the support of anti-Grant Northerners who would all break for Greeley, essentially seconded the motion and adopted the Liberal Republican ticket. That suited John just fine. Through the summer of 1872 and into the fall, he would back Greeley and Brown as if they were genuine Democrats. Not even the birth of John's first child, a healthy baby boy named John Newman Edwards Jr., could pull him away from the campaign trail. Yet as his return to the saga of Jesse James in September 1872 made clear, John had no qualms about playing both ends against the middle. With his left hand, he was publicly urging Democrats to ally with former Republicans and decrying sleaze in the government, while with his right, he was touting Jesse James—a violent, unapologetic, pro-Confederate outlaw—as an anti-Reconstruction Robin Hood.[40]

AS LATE AFTERNOON became evening on September 26, a few patrons still strolled among booths showcasing Missouri's native fruits and plants. Some inspected prize livestock or took in collections of fine art. Still others explored a large, domed fountain around which an exhibit of live birds had been arranged. For the most part, though, the day's visitors to the Kansas City Industrial Exposition had already left or were in the process of leaving the fairgrounds. Those who happened to remain in the vicinity of the ticket office on 12th Street received far more excitement than the cost of entry had promised.[41]

Just before sundown, a trio of masked riders approached the office. If the face coverings had not alerted bystanders to forthcoming trouble, the Colt Navy revolvers brandished by each horseman certainly made the riders' intentions clear to all but the densest observers. One of the men dismounted and approached the cashier. He demanded the cash box. *Or else.* Believing—correctly—that he would be shot for noncompliance, the stunned cashier turned over the box. From their saddles, the other two bandits warned a growing assemblage of witnesses not to interfere. Again, *or else*. And like the cashier, onlookers judged the threat to be a serious one. No one attempted to halt the robbery in progress. Then, as the stickup man moved toward his horse with the money till in hand, the cashier saw his chance and lunged. Amidst the brief scuffle between burglar and ticket-seller, a shot rang out. Or several shots. Accounts of the holdup differed drastically when it came to the gunplay. When the smoke cleared, the cashier was unscathed. A young girl standing nearby hadn't been so lucky. The bandit's bullet struck her in the leg and, with her wounding as a diversion, the three riders thundered away from the fairgrounds with nearly $1,000. It wasn't a robbery in broad daylight, but it was close enough. The heist at the Kansas City Exposition became an instant media sensation.[42]

Of all the editors, Democratic or Republican, that propagandized the robbery for partisan ends, John made by far the most of it. His coverage of the next morning labeled the crime the "most desperate, daring and determined deed of robbery ever known in the annals of Missouri was done." After recounting the story for his readers—a narration replete with threats of "instant death" and "petrifying terror"—John assessed the episode as follows: "Taking the affair all in all it surpasses anything in the criminal history of this country, at least, if it does not overtop the exploits of Claude Duval or Jack Shepherd in the way of cold-blooded nerve and stupendously daring villainy." Perhaps finding his own giddiness a bit much for some readers, John conceded, "of course it is a crime and must be reprehended and denounced." That said, a "but" was coming—a significant one. "But one thing is certain. Men who can so coolly and calmly plan and so quietly and daringly execute a scheme of robbery like this, in the light of day, in the face of the authorities, and in the very teeth of the most immense multitude of people that was ever in our city, deserve at least admiration for their bravery and nerve."[43]

Anyone caught off guard by John's positive spin on the robbery must have been completely taken aback by his follow-up column on September 29. He seemed to realize this, too, because he began the piece—tellingly entitled "The Chivalry of Crime"—with an explanation for his previous excitement and seeming approval. "There is a dash of tiger blood in the veins of all men, a latent disposition, even in the bosom that is a stranger to nerve and daring, to admire those qualities in other men." "And this penchant," John continued, "is always keener if there be a dash of sin in the deed to spice the enjoyment of its contemplation." In other words, if one set aside the armed robbery and the shooting of an innocent child, who could blame him for admiring the pluck of men who rode into a heavily guarded space, held numerous onlookers at bay, and rode off into the night like ghosts? Asked another way, who could blame him for touting men unafraid to stick it to the establishment, no matter the odds. With an eye toward the upcoming election, this would be the crux of John's coverage moving forward—and it was only getting started.

The rest of "The Chivalry of Crime" made a novel argument. John started with a rundown of common criminals one might find in Kansas City. These villains, he suggested, were cowardly because they worked in secret and without daring. There was nothing redeeming in highwaymen who ambushed victims under moonlit skies or pickpockets who hid in plain sight or bank robbers who sneaked in and out of unguarded vaults. Especially bad were murderers who killed slumbering victims or used poison to do the work of death without physical effort. According to John these types of criminals were "execrated of men and condemned of God and His Commandments." Consequently, he concluded that "there are thieves and pickpockets and burglars and garroters in Kansas City, who, it were better for the city, should sleep some night under the still shade of a tree with no ground for the soles of their feet to touch."[44]

Then the column pivots to the Exposition bandits. "But," John offered, "there are things done for money and for revenge of which the daring of the act is the picture and the crime the frame it may be set in . . . a feat of stupendous nerve and fearlessness that makes one's hair rise to think of it, with a condiment of crime to season it, becomes chivalric; poetic, superb." After openly declaring that the means of the robbery justified it, John hinted at the identity of the thieves, who had not yet been identified by authorities, by describing them as former Confederate guerrillas from Jackson, Cass, and Clay counties. Supplied with this information, it might have occurred to readers that the *Times* had devoted significant column inches back in 1870—even going so far as to print an open letter to the governor—from outlaws who fit this exact description.[45]

"These men are bad citizens," he conceded, "but they are bad because they live out of their time." Almost anomalous in the nineteenth century, John pronounced that such bold men "might have sat with Arthur at the roundtable, ridden at tourney with Sir Launcelot or worn the colors of Guinevere." On a roll with his favorite metaphorical subject matter, John simply couldn't help himself: "It was as though three bandits had come to us from the storied Odenwald, with the halo of medieval chivalry upon their garments and shown us how the things were done that poets sing of." By the end of his column, John had not only excused the robbery but had made the case that Missourians should feel grateful for the experience of having been robbed by such paragons of cavalier manliness and bravery.[46]

Having been sufficiently lauded, the stage was now set for the Exposition bandits to respond. That came in a letter published in the *Times* on October 15, 1872. After justifying the Exposition heist along the same criteria John had already laid out—"it is true, we are robbers, but we always rob in the glare of the day and in the teeth of the multitude"—and offering to cover medical expenses for the accidentally wounded girl, the bandits got down to the sort of messaging that most interested in John: the presidential election. "Some editors call us thieves. We are not thieves—we are bold robbers," the letter argued. "It hurts me very much to be called a thief. It makes me feel like they were trying to put me on par with Grant and his party." Once on the subject of Radical corruption, the so-called bold robbers unleashed a barrage so in keeping with John's rhetoric over the previous year it's difficult to believe he didn't have a hand in composing it.

> Grant's party has no respect for anyone. They rob the poor and rich, and we rob the rich and give it to the poor . . . I will close by hoping that Horace Greeley will defeat Grant, and then I can make an honest living, and then I will not have to rob, as taxes will not be so heavy.

The public might not have known that Jesse James was the author of the letter—but John undoubtedly did. For the previous year, John had persistently attacked the Grant administration for corruption and incompetent management of Southern affairs. He'd also spent the same span of time trying to convince Democrats that a coalition with Liberal Republicans was the only way to oust Grant and liberate the South. Now James drove home the point with his endorsement of Greeley. And by echoing John's distinction between shadowy, secretive, unmanly crime and a deed of "utterly indescribable daring," the bushwhacker turned bandit sent a clear message about what needed to happen come November: real men took what they needed, in broad daylight, without concern for the numbers opposing them. Only when Southerners dared to take action—to stand up and fight back (albeit with votes)—against the men robbing them would conditions improve. To many *Times* readers, this would have sounded familiar.[47]

In late September 1872, just a few days before the Exposition holdup, John had published a column entitled "The Importance of Registration." Beginning in 1872, every Missouri voter had to reregister to vote, regardless of past participation in state electoral contests. According to John, since the Republican's hostile takeover of Missouri in 1862, Democrats had been disfranchised and shut out of state government. And owing to a decade of oppression, he confessed that many Democrats had simply become apathetic and given up trying to vote. The Democratic Party "had the numbers," John bemoaned, "but those number were powerless." "This must all be changed," he thundered. "The man who declines now to put himself on record in favor of reform and good government is responsible, as far as his influence goes, for all the evils which follow, and to that extent arrays himself on the side of military tyranny and official corruption." It was this supposed military tyranny that Jesse James claimed as a justification for banditry and this official corruption which he claimed to counter by robbing the rich to aid the poor. Simply put, for readers who chose to sympathize with James's version of events, the letter from Shepherd, Turpin, and Duval was John's same pitch for voting—but it came straight from Robin Hood's mouth.[48]

Five days later, on October 20, 1872, the *Times* published a second letter from Jesse James. He and his brother Frank were accused of the Exposition robbery in an article from the Independence *Herald.* Jesse felt compelled to reply publicly. "This charge is baseless and without foundation," he protested, "and as you have always published all articles that I have sent you for publication I will just write a few lines on this subject." At first glance, this appeared to be a boiler-plate denial of wrongdoing. However, upon closer inspection, James inadvertently outed himself as "Jack Shepherd," the previous letter's author, while also confirming his role as one of the burglars and as the gunman who accidentally shot the little girl.[49]

Prior to this letter of October 20 John had only published one letter in the *Times* on behalf of Jesse James. That was his June 1870 plea of innocence in connection with the December 1869 bank robbery at Gallatin. Yet here James slipped and referenced multiple occasions ("all article*s*" plural) in which he'd worked with John to make public announcements related to criminal accusations. The only logical conclusion to draw is that James counted the letter he'd recently signed under an alias toward the total. Furthermore, in the first mes-sage, signed facetiously by Shepherd, Turpin, and Duval, the writer posing as Shepherd stated, "I will give a few lines to the public, as I am one of the party who perpetrated the deed." In the second note, which James signed in his own name, he proceeded with, "I will just write a few lines on this subject, and here is what I have got to say to the public." For a man who received very limited formal schooling, James was quite a competent correspondent. In this instance, though, his own writing style—apparently limited to the recycling of certain phrases—betrayed his identity.[50]

Interesting as it may be in hindsight, with just a few weeks to go before Missourians took to the polls, the rhetorical slipup hardly mattered. Criminal rumors were already swirling around the Jameses. Missourians inclined to view the burglars as Robin Hood figures assumed their technical guilt but didn't care. Within the bounds of this perspective, the Jameses *had* to commit crimes to achieve their status as social bandits—but that status inherently justified the crimes. And those who viewed the former Confederate guerrillas as common thieves disliked them in the first place *because* they were former Confederate guerrillas. Whether they were truly guilty, and in this case, it seemed they were, often came off as less important than how the story could be manipulated for grander partisan purposes. In short, both sides in Missouri went into the election feeling motivated and morally righteous. Now it would come down to numbers.

On November 3, two days before voting day, John understood that minds had long been made up and turnout would rule the day. "The lines, we take it, are drawn as tight as it is possible to make them," he noted. "Nothing now remains to be done except to insist upon a stern, persistent, and resolute forward movement. Into the fight the Democrats and Liberals should make it a point to carry every man, for there are times when a squad or a company might turn the tide of the conflict, and give victory to the cause of justice and the right." Having reminded readers of their duty to come out and vote, John carried the military metaphor a step further. "Shoot all deserters," he blustered, explaining that it "will be ammunition well used and righteously distributed." Then, perhaps concerned that this martial imagery wasn't conveying his point zealously enough, John turned to the Bible for his final pitch. "Democrats," he proclaimed, "everything demanded of you is to vote your full strength. The Radical party has neither Ark, Noah, nor Ararat, and so let your ballots be a deluge. Literally sweep it away from the face of Missouri."[51]

On the morning of election day, everything hung in the balance. The governorship of Missouri. The presidency. The course of Reconstruction. The relevance of the Democratic Party. "To-day is the day of battle," John announced to readers. "The issue has been made up, the lines have been formed, the combatants are face to face, American liberty is the question at issue, the struggle will be one of giants, and we must not lose." That being the case, John did virtually everything but beg Democrats to vote that they might preserve what remained "of a blackened and mutilated constitution." He even reminded them to help their sick or crippled friends and neighbors travel to the polls. In the morning's excitement, every single ballot mattered.[52]

That hopefulness quickly gave way to disappointment. "At this writing, 3 o'clock a.m.," John reported, "enough has been received to indicate the complete success of the administration party, showing unprecedented and unexpected gains all through the Eastern States." Grant comfortably carried the northern states, the Midwest, and the Far West, as expected. But among the eleven states of the ex-Confederacy, he emerged victorious in all but three. Virginia, once home to the Confederate capital, went to Grant in a very tight race—less than one percent. In other one-time bastions of Rebeldom, such as South Carolina and Mississippi, the former Union general-in-chief won by landslide margins. All told, Grant captured the popular vote in thirty-one out of thirty-seven states and carried the national tally by more than 700,000.

In May 1872, several months before the election, Grant had signed the Amnesty Act and restored suffrage to virtually any white man in the South who'd lost it as a result of secession. That development, combined with the New Departure, is almost certainly why the pro-Republican returns from Louisiana, North Carolina, South Carolina, Alabama, Arkansas, Mississippi, Florida, and Virginia took John by such surprise. Convenient as it might have been, the blame for Democrat-Liberal losses in those states couldn't be pinned on Charles O'Connor, either. A conservative from New York, O'Connor ran as a noncoalition Democrat. Even in states where he actually received at least one vote, which was only in eighteen out of the aforementioned thirty-seven, his totals were miniscule—often less than a percentage point. Nationally, he polled less than one-half of one percent of the popular vote.[53]

What John and his Democratic allies—and for that matter, what Greeley and other Liberal Republicans—had not counted on was the resounding support Grant's ticket received from freedmen throughout the South. Despite years of Reconstruction, in spite of the 15th Amendment, and a Federal military occupation of the South notwithstanding, for a black man to vote in the ex-Confederacy it often meant risking his life. Yet in this pivotal moment for the future of Reconstruction, when the Republican Party was splintering over the issue of continued Radical oversight in the South, freedmen cast ballots by the tens of thousands and helped deliver Grant a forceful triumph.

Given the enormity of Greeley's defeat, John's update on Missouri couldn't amount to full-fledged silver-lining, but it was at least positive news. "In the West, however, it is not so bad," he reported. "Missouri is firmly Democratic by a very large majority, and probably elects an entire Democratic Congressional delegation." In fact, Greeley won the popular vote in Missouri by more than ten percent—no doubt aided by native Missourian Benjamin Gratz Brown's presence on the ticket. However doomed Greeley's broader electoral fate may have been, his success in Missouri boosted Democratic chances in down ballot races. Silas Woodson, an outright Democrat, defeated Republican John B. Henderson for the governorship. It was the first time a Democrat claimed the office since Claiborne Jackson died in exile in 1862. In the House of Representatives, John was overoptimistic about a complete sweep, but Democrats did reclaim the overwhelming majority of seats within the Missouri delegation.[54]

BY DECEMBER 1, 1872, the national popular vote was tallied. All that remained was to award Grant the corresponding electoral votes. After his inauguration, Democrats could begin another four-year countdown to the election of 1876.

Yet on that first morning in December, a headline in the *Times* probably shocked readers more than the lopsided nature of the election. "Obituary. Honors to the Memory of the Dead Journalist. His Political Opponents Testify Their Personal Esteem. General Expression of Respect from all portions of the Country. The Funeral to take Place Next Tuesday." Horace Greeley, the man who four weeks earlier had gained nearly 3 million votes, was dead. His personal physician labeled it "inflammation of the brain." Reading this news, for a fleeting moment, John's readers must have fantasized about a Missourian occupying the White House. It was admittedly a tortured sequence of hypotheticals—but had Greeley won the election and then lived long enough to claim the electoral college, his sudden demise would have elevated Benjamin Gratz Brown to the presidency.[55]

It wouldn't have taken long for reality to reassert control. Greeley didn't win the electoral vote. He hadn't even come close. And his death signaled the end of the Liberal Republican insurgency. Despite delivering Missouri a Democratic governor, the short-lived alliance between Liberals and Democrats had not come close to killing off Radical Reconstruction. If anything, in 1872, after watching a massive new voter bloc in the South break entirely in favor of Republicans, some Democrats wondered how they would ever again seize national office. John already had a plan. He would double-down on Jesse James as a battering ram against Reconstruction. But as John would find in the coming years, while other schools of Confederate commemoration deified Lee and Jackson, so closely tying Missouri's national reputation to a bushwhacker came with great political and cultural risks.

Architect

When 1873 began, John's professional prospects had never looked better. Owing to the popularity of *Shelby's Expedition to Mexico,* his literary profile soared among Democrats and ex-Confederates. The Democratic Party might have lost ground nationally in 1872, but Missouri's returns were a different story. Thanks to month after month of anti-Grant, anti-Radical crusading, combined with victories in Jefferson City, wins in state congressional races, and selective memory when it came to his support for Greeley, John boasted a new degree of partisan clout. He was now one of Missouri's preeminent conservative commentators.

It couldn't always be about an election, though. In the wake of such a momentous contest, political burnout among everyday Missourians was natural. For some editors, this posed a serious problem. A postelection malaise might lead to fewer readers, and fewer readers could mean a downturn in advertising revenue. At the end of the day, newspapers lived and died by circulation—and humdrum content didn't keep subscribers on the line or books in the black. To some extent, John was immune to this issue. Not the need for attention-grabbing headlines, but to a dependence on the political calendar to boost them. Election or no election, his signature grandiloquence constituted a draw in and of itself. And his continued affiliation with the James brothers, Frank and Jesse, as well as their various "associates," generated just the right amount of salaciousness to keep even straitlaced readers secretly coming back for more.

What the casual reader, or even subscribers to the *Times*, didn't realize was just how much Morry Munford's presence meant to John as an editorialist. With Munford to tend the business side of the house, John found himself with more latitude to experiment rhetorically. More than ever before he could focus entirely on putting ink to paper. Just as important, his home life offered similar support. Jennie was raised in the home of a successful merchant. She understood how to manage money. She also had a knack for organization. As a voracious reader herself, Jennie appreciated the time and effort and anxiety that went into creating text. With her running the Edwards household, John not only belonged to a complete family unit—but also a stable one—for the first time since the 1840s.

At first glance, at second glance, and even at third glance, the foundation of John's life in Kansas City was solid. He was only thirty-five years old. Western Missourians loved him. It looked as though he would continue to prosper at the *Times* for many, many years to come. He might have, too, had Stilson Hutchins not come calling.

IN SOME WAYS John and Hutchins were very much alike. They were dyed-in-the-wool Democrats. Each had lost his father at a young age. Both had subsequently been raised by a mother absolutely determined to see her son receive a better-than-normal education. As a result, John and Hutchins both experienced childhood as a wunderkind; John as a small-town writing prodigy in Virginia, and Hutchins as a publishing entrepreneur in Iowa. After the war both men helped establish new newspapers in Missouri.[1]

These resemblances could not mitigate that John and Hutchins hailed from different worlds—or the fact that most, if not all, of the advantage lay with Hutchins. John came from an ancient Virginia family but inherited little more than an impressive genealogy. When the war finally came, he dropped everything in a quest for personal and familial glory. After defeat and exile, John had to start his economic life all over again. Hutchins, by contrast, was the offspring of a New Hampshire clan with elite forebears *and* ample resources. Even after the death of his father, a noted politician, Hutchins never wanted for creature comforts. He moved in blue-blooded circles and attended college in Boston. He touted states' rights in 1861, in spite of his northeastern upbringing, but never swapped pen for rifle-musket. Essentially untouched by the war or Reconstruction, Hutchins accumulated a fortune by founding and then liquidating his interest in a series of western newspapers.[2]

John utterly lacked that sort—or any sort—of business acumen. Likewise, while John basked in suggestions that he run for office, he never did. John was a political wonk, plain and simple; he could communicate broad strategy and sling editorial mud with the best of them. But his personality, which is a diplomatic way of referring to his intellectual eccentricities, did not always translate into political realism. His naive read on Maximilian's long-term prospects in Mexico serves as evidence of that. Hutchins was just the opposite. He was more than a smooth political operator. He understood how to convert financial success into other forms of power, winning a seat in the Missouri state legislature in 1872 and successfully defending it in 1874.[3]

Therefore, when Stilson Hutchins approached in early fall 1873—with stern face, well-kept mustache, hair neatly parted on the left—he appeared every bit the wealthy Victorian gentleman to John; better still, in his well-tailored suite, Hutchins looked like a man who had a habit of winning and making money. The job offer itself was straightforward: come write for the *St. Louis Dispatch*. Hutchins had recently purchased the paper and now he wanted to buy John as its main attraction. The specifics of what was promised have been lost to time. In any case, the combination of riches and political influence Hutchins pitched was simply an offer John couldn't refuse.

Accepting Hutchins's proposal meant uprooting a young family. John could not edit the *Dispatch* from Kansas City; he would need to move across the state. That meant abandoning the paper he'd help build from the ground up. Much as she loved and supported her husband, this could not have been a thrilling prospect for Jennie. Relocating to St. Louis entailed leaving Western Missouri for the first time, which also pulled her away from a close-knit network of friends and family. John's best friend and business partner didn't see the wisdom in leaving, either. Always straightforward with John, Morry

Munford advised him not to trust a wheeler-dealer like Hutchins. To be sure, Munford wasn't totally without bias. He wanted to keep his star editor. But he also seemed to understand that his friend was dangerously out of his depth and likely to get hurt.[4]

Whatever the reasoning, it didn't really matter. Nothing anyone could say would dissuade John once he'd made up his mind to go. The more they tried, the more determined he became to prove them wrong. On Saturday, September 20, 1873, the *Weekly Caucasian* of Lexington, Missouri, noted that "Mrs. Jennie Edwards, the wife of our gallant friend, Major John N. Edwards, of the Kansas City Times, is visiting the family of her father, Judge Plattenburg, at Dover." This wasn't an ordinary visit. Jennie was getting in her goodbyes before the big move. She had two days left, according to the article. "Major Edwards will pass through here Monday," it announced, "on his way to assume the editorship of the St. Louis Dispatch."[5]

Part 1: The Criminal Crescendo

Early on the evening of July 21, 1873, two months before John left Kansas City for St. Louis, a gang of men waited for a train in Adair County, Iowa. Nestled right in the center of the state's southwestern quadrant, Adair County had been a Unionist stronghold during the war and was still one now. The train in question belonged to the Chicago, Rock Island, and Pacific line. Every Monday it traveled through the grain fields that blanketed the area, transporting an overnight express out of Omaha. Stands of native oak occasionally dotted the route too. They were a visual respite from the corn and wheat; more pertinent on this night than the view, the trees made it possible to hide from the oncoming train.[6]

The men were armed. That was almost a given in the postbellum borderlands. One might also have gone a step further and said they were heavily armed—though even to go "well heeled" while traveling in the country wasn't entirely out of the ordinary. After all, *there were bandits about.* The other accessories packed by the men lacked such simple explanation. Each carried a burlap hood, later described as "Ku Klux" in style. These masks would have portended serious trouble had anyone else been around to see them. But the men weren't waiting at a terminal or depot. Nor even at a mail stop or watering station. Instead, they skulked in the nearby timber. Concealed by darkness and shadow—and without a signal fire—they still knew the locomotive would stop within reach. Or at least they knew a missing piece of rail tended to have that effect on trains.

The train approached around 8:30 p.m., and as it did the engine slowed considerably to round a sharp bend in the track. It seems the men had chosen their position specifically for this reason—to catch the train at a vulnerable point on the line. Earlier in the day they used a hammer and spike to dislodge a piece of rail. After attaching it to a tether, they set it back in place. When it seemed like the train had passed the point of no return, they struck, jerking the loose rail away like hunters springing a trap. Even in the dark, engineer John Rafferty realized that something up ahead was very wrong. According to one account, "He instantly reversed his engine and applied the air brakes, and while in the act of doing it, bullets came pelting into the engine like hail." Concerned they had sprung their trap a moment early, the men opened fire on the engine. It was too late for the locomotive and its coal car; both lurched from the track and crashed. Most of the train, though—including two of the three passenger coaches and both baggage cars—remained upright. Everyone on board had Rafferty to thank for that minor miracle. Unfortunately, the heroic engineer would never know it. His bruised, lifeless body, broken at the neck, lay amid the wreckage of engine and tender. He left behind a wife and three children.[7]

The plan to immobilize the train had worked. The men donned their hoods. Emerging from the shadows, they approached and then boarded the train with revolvers in hand. They hollered at gawking passengers to get out of sight or else. It was now clear to everyone within the coaches what was happening. There *really were* bandits about. As a precaution, some of the gunmen held the terrified passengers as hostages. Logistically speaking, this was a smart thing to do. Virtually all the passengers were unarmed, yet they were numerous. One older gentleman, later described as "plucky," told the outlaws to "go to hell." He tried—and failed—to rally a mob to retake the train. "Come out and go for the villains," he pleaded, "and do not let them rob the whole train!" None of the other passengers shared his courage, but had enough men joined in, the outnumbered robbers might also have had their necks broken. Needless to say, they weren't taking any chances.[8]

Other members of the gang went straight for the baggage car that contained the weekly express shipment. That was where they expected to relieve the railroad company of a small fortune. "Give us those keys, god damn you," barked one of the bandits to the express messenger, "give us those keys, or I'll blow your brains out! Give us the money or I'll blow you to hell!" Finding no hollowness in the threat, the express agent quickly handed over the key. He then stood back and offered no resistance as the robbers dug into the contents of the safe. The take turned out to be less than expected—just a little more than $2,300 in cash. This put the leader of the robbers on edge, but he had no intention of hauling away crates of immensely heavy gold bullion that were also in the baggage car. The $2,300 would have to do. With money in hand, the thieves paused their retreat to express sorrow for the killing of Rafferty. The gesture seemed genuine, though it was also mind-boggling given that their stunt with the rail could have easily killed dozens more passengers. Having paid their respects, they made a clean getaway into the Iowa night. Behind them, the men who held up the Rock Island Express left an empty safe, a wrecked locomotive, a trove of gold and silver bullion, the corpse of an innocent man, dozens of people lucky to be alive, and one whale of a news story.[9]

IT WASN'T TECHNICALLY the first robbery of a moving train in America, but the practice was still so new in 1873 that newspapers from coast to coast ran with the story. The Chicago, Rock Island, & Pacific put up a $5,000 reward for the capture of the outlaws, which only added to the frenzy. Sometimes the facts got lost amid the excitement and the rush to press. One paper suggested that the bandits had piled timber on the track to stop the engine. One claimed that John Rafferty had been shot to death. Another report asserted that the passengers had been robbed of their personal belongings. The number of robbers supposedly involved in the heist fluctuated widely between publications. This last bit of journalistic uncertainty was at least understandable. Virtually none of the passengers had witnessed the robbery in its entirety, so it was very difficult for any single one of them to determine how many bandits were involved. As a case in point, a brakeman who escaped from the train during the robbery ran to the nearby town of Anita for help. He had initially declared to residents there that between fifty and seventy-five highwaymen were attacking the train.[10]

For the most part, commentary on the hijacking did not favor the bandits. Three days after the robbery, the *New York Times* ran an article entitled "A New Peril of the Rail." While the piece dealt harshly with a broader surge in train hold-ups across the country, it singled out the Iowa job, stating that "in boldness and in atrocity the crime has never been equaled." Chief among the goals of the article was to head off any attempts to categorize the crime as social banditry. At first sight, that wasn't necessarily a given. The bandits hadn't robbed individual passengers. The bandits hadn't shot anyone aboard the train. And the money they purloined did technically belong to a large express firm. But as the *Times* meticulously outlined, it could have been—and probably should have been—remarkably worse.[11]

"For it must be remembered," the editor pointed out, "that these Iowa robbers did not confine their plans to mere plunder. They included the probability, almost the certainty, of murder on a large scale." Highwaymen were heavily armed for a reason. If passengers *had* listened to that plucky old man and put up a fight, men would undoubtedly have been gunned down. Moreover, it was a wonder that men were alive to decline resistance in the first place. According to the *Times*, had the engineer not immediately taken steps to halt the train, "the loss of life might have been appalling." In short, any resemblance the Iowa train robbery held to a Robin Hood–style caper was a surface-level coincidence. The bandits were plain lucky, the *Times* concluded. Lucky that yanking away that piece of rail didn't end in a bloodbath and luckier still that virtually no one raised a finger to defend the wrecked train's treasure.[12]

Almost as if he were reading the mind of a certain newspaperman in Missouri, the author of the *Times* piece next launched a series of accusations against the bandits. Each charge undermined a previous claim about the conduct, dash, and daring—about the supposed exceptionalism—of Missouri's outlaws. In "The Chivalry of Crime," John had lauded the outlaws as courageous and manly for striking in the open, in a public place, and for exposing themselves to risk in the process of carrying out the stick-up. The *Times* countered the notion with a blanket declaration: "the Western thief, like most other thieves, is in the great majority of cases a coward. He will not attack where there is much chance of defense." In letters John had printed from the James boys, Jesse James stated that he and Frank would gladly surrender to the state if the governor could guarantee their safety. The Jameses boasted that a jury would clear them of all wrongdoing in a fair trial—while concurrently lamenting that they could not receive that chance for equal justice under the law. The *Times* called their bluff with another general statement, asserting that "Ruffians have a dread of the organized machinery of the law which acts the same at all times, and which punishes next year as pitilessly as this." In sum, the Jameses and their outlaw ilk wanted to see the inside of a courtroom about as badly as an editor for the *New York Times* wanted to be on a train derailed by masked highwaymen.[13]

Given the long-term investment John had in the narrative of the James brothers as Robin Hoods, readers of the *Kansas City Times* might have expected an article celebrating the spectacle of the train robbery. They didn't get one. Whether John saw the piece out of New York or not, it contained some unavoidably strong points—points that he was not in a position to immediately rebut. The threat of future, seemingly random, derailments by outlaws was a legitimate fear for train-goers. Sabotaging the track in Iowa had put the lives of innocent bystanders, including women and children, in mortal danger in a way that politics couldn't explain away. The next time a car bowled off the tracks or a tipped-over engine's boiler exploded, being a Democrat wouldn't make the difference between life and death for passengers.

Problematic from a PR standpoint, too, was that while the bandit's method of stopping the train miraculously claimed just one life, it killed the story's only true hero. Jumping aboard a train of unsuspecting, terrified civilians hardly looked courageous when examined alongside John Rafferty's quick thinking under both literal and figurative fire. Rather than risking a backlash, John chose to say nothing.

On July 23, two days after the robbery, and then again on July 25, the *Kansas City Times* simply recycled stories from the *Chicago Evening Journal* that detailed the robbery and provided a few details about the bandits. Their height, weight, and approximations of age. Injecting partisan commentary into the story at this stage wasn't an option. Even for John, it was simply too hot to touch.[14]

Several weeks later, in mid-September, an update on the pursuit of the Iowa bandits circulated in newspapers throughout the country. According to the article, the railroad had hired a dozen men, including a detective, to "ferret out the thieves and bring them to justice." Because it was believed that the Jameses were hiding out in Lafayette County, Missouri, the Lafayette County Vigilance Committee threw in with the detective's outfit and claimed to have been hot on the heels of the outlaw brothers—so hot, in fact, the posse nabbed one of the Jameses' horses. When the trail in Lafayette County went cold, the posse stormed a house in St. Clair County in search of the Youngers. They found only women and children, and after the unproductive raid the members of the vigilance committee abandoned the search.[15]

More of interest to readers—and of far more importance to John— was the "inside information" supplied to the article by one of the vigilance committee members. He was a local and claimed to be well acquainted with the bandits and their backstories. "The criminal record of the robbers dates back as far as 1861," per the source, "and, although they have done little but murder and pillage, no one of them has ever been taken." "Undoubtedly," he declared "the desperado most feared is Arthur P. McCoy. He is about thirty-five years of age, a giant in stature, and brave as a lion." The article relayed how McCoy had spent the war years as a guerrilla of "the most bloody type" and how he then transitioned to prodigious criminal after Appomattox: "He has had a hand in every bank robbery of consequence that has occurred in Missouri, and has also 'worked' in Kentucky and other Southern states. McCoy has earned the reputation of being the deadliest pistol shot in America on horseback, and is a stranger to fear."[16]

Working under McCoy, the article categorized Frank and Jesse James as "the clever members of the 'mob'," the ones who were "always assigned the responsibility of planning the robberies." The source described the James boys as expert marksmen and skilled horsemen, saying they were "as 'good grit' as ever drew trigger or handled knives." The informant contended that the Younger brothers had been "noted desperadoes since they were big enough to handle guns, and like the balance of their associates, are crack shots with either rifle or pistol." "They have been known for years as notoriously bad men," the source asserted, before suggesting that they "were outlawed by Governor Fletcher for refusing to surrender and take the requisite oath at the close of the war."[17]

The update on the Iowa bandits was clearly intended to cast the Jameses, the Youngers, and Arthur McCoy in a negative light. The people of Iowa, let alone of Massachusetts and Vermont, did not look fondly on bushwhacking aptitude or criminal prowess. All six of the outlaws were presented as defectives. They weren't men forced into lives of crime by postwar persecution. They were violent ne'er-do-wells doing what came naturally to them. While it painted a damning picture of the outlaws, more critical to John was what the article didn't say. It wasn't about the details of the robbery. It had nothing to do with Rafferty's heroism or his tragic demise. Nor did it harp on the mortal danger posed to the other passengers by the derailment. The public's shock at the robbery had waned. By focusing coverage on the bandits—on their personal histories and wartime experiences—the article provided John with just the opportunity he'd been waiting for to get back into the propaganda fight.

By November 1873, it probably seemed to many that media coverage of the train heist had finally burned itself out. There were no new details to report; no arrest or trial updates to provide. The bandits were all still at large. The money was still gone. Then John, now officially writing for the *St. Louis Dispatch*, announced himself boldly on November 22 with a long-form article entitled "A Terrible Quintette." Decades later, it would be the signature piece of his editorial career. In real-time John had no idea how future generations would remember the article—but he *did* know it was exactly the sort of work his new employer had in mind. "A Terrible Quintette" threw the editorial equivalent of kerosene on the Iowa robbery's last flickering embers. It was penned to sell, certainly, but also to rekindle a political wildfire. And did it ever.

In his typical self-deprecating way, John claimed no personal investment in the article. By his own description, he was merely a correspondent asked by his bosses at the *Dispatch* to research a story of common interest to readers. In reality John poured far more time into the "A Terrible Quintette" than he let on. Partisanship lay at the heart of his effort. Far more so than the train robbery itself, it was the *men* involved that struck John as a powerful weapon to wield against Republicans. Those men were the Jameses, Frank and Jesse; the Younger brothers, Cole and John; and Arthur McCoy, the same men recently lambasted in the national media. "Much has been said and written lately concerning these men—much that was purely sensational, fictious, and romantic," John avowed. Yet now he promised to serve up the whole truth and nothing but the truth about them. Better still, he claimed to have personally interviewed three of the accused outlaws. No other reporter had dared to attempt that feat. Thanks to his previous work with the James brothers, John was probably the only newspaperman in America with the connections to pull it off.[18]

In a piece meant to capitalize on a sensational event, John went out of his way to gloss over the details. After all, the job in Iowa wasn't like holding up a provincial savings bank or galloping off with the ticket proceeds from a fair. The bandits in Adair County derailed an occupied train. With faces hidden and pistols waving, they stormed aboard and robbed an express shipment. They killed an innocent man and had risked the lives of every other person on the train. For John's purposes, though, brevity made the most sense. It would do him no good to fixate on the facts of the crime already laid out so damningly by the *New York Times*. Instead, the "bold robbery committed in Iowa," as he called it, was merely the pretext—or the gathering bell—for an airing of political grievances. Readers expecting a moment-by-moment breakdown of the heist were probably left disappointed with only a single sentence to summarize the entire affair: "A railroad train had been thrown from the track, an engineer had been killed, a pistol fusillade had been opened upon some of its officials, an express car had been robbed, there had been terror and confusion generally about the event; and then flaming accounts in all the newspapers."[19]

Those newspapers, John contended, had been quick to print public assertions of guilt. "The robbers were known, described, located and individualized. They were from Missouri, they were from Western Missouri, they were highwaymen by practice and profession, they were guilty beyond all probability of a doubt, and they were Jesse James, Frank James, John Younger, Coleman Younger and Arthur McCoy." Worse still, John suggested that "in no single instance, so far, has a single newspaper described the men properly, and in no article so far published about them has anything like reality been told of their history." This was a direct reference to the "update" article from September. And here was the political bait and switch, set up and carried out by a master propagandist. Whether the Jameses and the Youngers had wrecked a train and made off with a few thousand dollars interested John very little. Nor did he castigate the papers for claiming the members of his terrible quintette actually committed the crime. History was what concerned him. If manipulated properly, the backstories of these Confederates-turned-(accused)-highwaymen might deliver a substantial political payload in the present.[20]

John's primary objective, then, was not to explain why the Jameses or the Youngers had chosen a life of outlawry; it was to blueprint how years of Republican abuses—dating back to the war itself—had *created* the version of the young men who derailed trains and gunned down strangers. This was the exact opposite of the perpetual ne'er-do-well portrait painted by northern newspapers. "The five men you desire a history of are eminently creatures of the war—three of whom lived upon the border and were tried in the savage crucible of border warfare," John prefaced, before describing his research process. "Your correspondent rode unarmed and alone. When one hunts for information, one does not hunt with either revolver or shot-gun. Others who are paid for it do this, but not those who seek to satisfy that great hungry devil-fish—public curiosity."[21]

The story began just outside of Kearney, Missouri. John rode through a gate and into timber so thick it blocked out the noonday sun. His horse crept silently through the shadows, when "suddenly a remarkably clear and penetrating voice called out, 'Halt,' and before its echoes died away, two men, superbly mounted and splendidly armed, rode out from a clump of bushes in the middle of the road and drew up their horses as picquets on an outpost." Before John materialized the James brothers, Jesse on the right, Frank on the left. That both carried a veritable arsenal did not escape his notice. "Each one," he reported approvingly, "had a Spencer rifle, with sixty rounds of ammunition to the gun, and each also had three breech-loading dragoon-size Smith and Wesson English pistols, the deadliest and most accurate patent in the known world."[22]

In John's rendition of the meeting the Jameses know and trust him as the former editor of the *Kansas City Times*. When he makes the long trek west from St. Louis, unarmed and in search of the truth, they oblige him with their whole sad story. While that version made for good theater, the interview was undoubtedly less spontaneous than John implied. They easily could have bushwhacked John and melted back into the countryside. But they didn't. Arrangements had obviously been made in advance, meaning John found the two most wanted men in the state because they wanted him to. Likewise, he lived to the tell the tale of their meeting, literally, for the same reason. Though John didn't mention it in the story, they had good reason to trust him. They had conferred before. He'd printed their letters in the *Kansas City Times*. These were clearly men who knew how to get in touch with one another.[23]

In the shade of the trees not far from their boyhood home, the brothers recounted to John how Unionist militiamen had terrorized their family, tortured their stepfather, and sent them into the bushwhacking ranks. Initially, they served together under William Clarke Quantrill. When Quantrill's command splintered, Jesse rode under William "Bloody Bill" Anderson and Archie "Little Arch" Clement. Frank stayed with Quantrill to the bitter end, even following him to Kentucky in 1865. The same aggressors who pushed Frank and Jesse James into the war refused to let them resume normal lives afterward. Months and even years after the official end of hostilities, attempts were made on their lives. It became impossible for either brother to maintain a normal job. Staying put long enough to work on their mother's farm was entirely out of the question. As a result, according to Jesse, much as bushwhacking kept them alive during the war, banditry facilitated their survival in its aftermath. Even so, the brothers were quite picky about what crimes they would admit to committing.[24]

The critically important point in the tale John wove for *Dispatch* subscribers was that the Jameses did not choose their nefarious path. It was foisted upon them. John went out of his way to make clear that these were not impoverished thugs looking to steal an easy dollar. Before the war, theirs was a respectable, land-owning family in Western Missouri. They were not predisposed to killing. They had no criminal record to speak of. Jesse had only been sixteen years old when he became a guerrilla in 1863. By nearly any metric, on the eve of the Civil War, Frank and Jesse James were all-American teenagers with bright futures. Yet in 1873 they had to remain on war footing. The brothers truly believed their lives depended on it, and John was happy to take them at their word.

Next John sought out the Younger brothers, Cole and Jim. He was apparently unable to secure a face-to-face audience but told their story anyway. The wartime ordeal of the Younger family wasn't a secret to Western Missourians. John could get it secondhand from any number of friends, neighbors, and extended kin. Much like the Jameses' plight, the Youngers' saga involved antebellum affluence and political harassment. Cole and Jim's father, Henry Washington Younger, was a politically connected slaveowner in Cass County. In 1862 he was ambushed and shot to death by Union home guards. Fearing a similar fate, his sons took to the bush with Quantrill. As John told it, the Youngers faced a postwar situation almost identical to that of the Jameses: Yankee abuses forced them into lives of crime. Minus a face-to-face component, John's coverage of the Youngers lacked the cloak and dagger suspense of a secret meeting, but nonetheless begged the same question of Missouri Democrats that his coverage of the Jameses did. How long would they sit by while Republicans destroyed the lives and families of men like Cole and Jim Younger?[25]

With the Youngers sufficiently martyred, that left only Arthur McCoy. Ironically, considering how he was recently cast as the all-powerful ringleader, McCoy was the odd man out of the quintette in the sense that he was the only one of the five who had not fought as a bushwhacker during the war. "McCoy was never a guerrilla," John explained, "but few of the horrors of border warfare ever passed before his eyes. What killing he did, he did in open combat, body to body and fortune the arbiter between." Indeed, John was probably able to secure a prolonged interview with McCoy—he claimed the men talked for the better part of three days—because the latter had also served under Jo Shelby's command. Even without the irregular credentials possessed by the Jameses and the Youngers, McCoy's post-bellum experience fit snugly within the partisan story John desired to tell. And to some extent, McCoy's record of regular soldiering was actually an advantage. It was one thing for guerrillas to have trouble rejoining postwar society; it was another for a veteran of the regular war. McCoy potentially appealed to a segment of Missouri's conservative population that the Jameses couldn't reach, namely those who hated Republicans but weren't keen to aggrandize bushwhackers.[26]

Not unlike the Jameses and the Youngers, McCoy contended that the war had followed him home. He alleged that "certain of his Montgomery County neighbors" harassed him and spread vicious rumors about him being an outlaw. They did this, McCoy insisted, to punish him for his Confederate politics. Before long, the St. Louis police department was hunting him. According to John, "your correspondent found him the same reckless, dashing, devil-may-care-man, that he had represented as being. He, like the balance, had the splendid horse, the Texas saddle, the Spencer rifle, and the English breech-loading Smith & Wesson pistol. Like all the balance, his eyes were never at rest—his horse never beyond his instant reach." While those attributes impressed John, they didn't seem to matter nearly as much to McCoy. "I have tried as hard as a man ever tried on earth," he complained, "to make a living for myself and family," but "I have been lied upon, persecuted, and oppressed."[27]

McCoy's closing statement exemplified the underlying moral of the editorial: Republican lies, persecution, and oppression had warped decent, hardworking, God-fearing Southern boys into second-class political criminals. On the face of it, this was not a new idea. Readers familiar with John's previous work knew it well. His first bandit expose, "The Chivalry of Crime," used social banditry as a lens to the shortcomings of Reconstruction. In the process of trying to outrage demoralized Democrats into voting, John had flirted with the notion that certain illegal activities—robbing a ticket booth in Kansas City, for instance—might be justified, or at least understood and forgiven, depending on the panache of the bandits and the political inflection of the crime. However, because John was a leading proponent of the alliance with Liberal Republicans in 1872, an alliance built on concessions from conservatives, he had to tread cleverly, if not lightly, in promoting extralegal partisanship. John needed to avoid the appearance of an unreconstructed Rebel in November 1872, even as those feelings simmered just below the surface.

A year later, political as well as personal circumstances had changed dramatically. In the fall of 1873, Greeley was dead. Grant was just beginning a second term. The coalition of Democrats and Liberal Republicans was a thing of the past. Republicans still reigned in Washington DC, and so Reconstruction continued, but conservatives (or "Claybanks") had reclaimed significant influence in Missouri. These circumstances left John much freer to deal in incendiary rhetoric, and given such autonomy, he was no longer content to highlight modern-day Robin Hoods as a way to score points on civil service reform or Republican misrule. Now he was unequivocally justifying the actions of the James-Younger Gang as an insurgency against unjust government policies; now John glorified the former guerrillas as men willing to take a violent stand on behalf of all downtrodden Southerners. In this way, "A Terrible Quintette" was actually a marked departure from "The Chivalry of Crime."[28]

The Missourian, John boasted, "is cooler, quicker, more accurate, and more in practice with the revolver than with any other weapon." By exalting the abilities of the quintette with guns, horses, and irregular tactics—by decorating them with heroic, hypermasculine qualities in return for their extralegal service—John was propagating a message that could not have been clearer to other Southern Democrats: where efforts with the ballot box failed, powder and lead might still get the job done. He obviously had a different story about *the reason* the bandits were committing crimes, but this explains why John took no issue with outlandish claims in Northern papers about their knack for violence or their feats of horsemanship and stamina. He *wanted* them to come off as supernatural. Because in a state, and in a region, already brimming with anti-Reconstruction paramilitary organizations, when it came to extralegal violence, John was preaching to a choir of disgruntled ex-Rebels and white supremacists. Moreover, he knew it. The real trick, then, was to spin what were meant to be criticisms and evidence of degeneracy as positives; to recast the outlaws from super villains to superheroes—and to swap out Arthur McCoy for Jesse James as the new mythology's chief protagonist.[29]

Jesse James clearly understood what was expected of himself and Frank in facilitating that "antihero" turn. Four days after Christmas in 1873, the *St. Louis Dispatch* printed a letter signed by Jesse but written on behalf of both brothers. It was supposedly postmarked from Montana in an attempt to prove that the Jameses had nothing to do with any recently committed or soon-to-be-perpetrated robberies in Missouri or the surrounding borderlands. As with all his letters to John at the *Times*, Jesse repeated the now familiar chorus about submitting to authorities if only safe passage and a fair trial could be arranged. This time, however, it came with a twist. James clearly worked in themes from "A Terrible Quintette" to dovetail with John's war-rooted explanations for outlawry while still denying responsibility for any specific deeds of banditry. At this point, these cries of innocence came with a wink and a nod, particularly as Jesse James had brazenly removed his mask during the Iowa train robbery and fit the description given of the bandit leader right down to his "tolerable short nose, a little turned up."[30]

Per usual, James declared that the brothers would turn themselves over if the governor of Missouri would "give us his word that we shall not be dealt with by a mob." Then he stated that "we would most certainly be [dealt with by a mob] if the militia of Daviess County could get their hands upon two of Quantrell's and Anderson's best men, or if the Iowa authorities could get us for a crime that we never committed." Here the point was implied: the Daviess County militia and other Unionists weren't really after the James boys because of bank or train heists. No, this was a continuation of the war itself. Then for good measure, James came right out and said it, explaining to readers that, "We have many enemies in Missouri because of the war—many who want to see us killed if they can get other people to do the killing." Before signing the letter, James affirmed that the brothers did "not mean to be taken alive," yet they would relish "in having this long and sleepless vigilance on our part broken up." Translated in the context of John's political maneuvering, the Jameses would love for the guerrilla war in Missouri to finally end, but that play wasn't theirs to make. A spree of robberies in 1874 and 1875 only amplified the message.[31]

THE ESCALATION FROM rhetorical exposé in "The Chivalry of Crime" to violent provocation in "A Terrible Quintette" coincided with a shift in John's own political demeanor. For the sake of uniting the electorate against Grant, he'd supported the "New Departure" within the Democratic Party. That meant getting over the war to appease younger, non-Confederate interests. Now he was done playing by other people's rules, and "A Terrible Quintette" announced to readers that when it came to matters of propaganda, the past—and the war—was precisely where John intended to dwell. In Missouri, and in the western borderlands more generally, that meant digging up black flags.

According to John in "A Terrible Quintette," as he traveled the backroads of Western Missouri in search of the Jameses and the Youngers, he conversed with several former guerrillas. As with his version of meeting the James brothers, there was more to this story than he revealed to readers. As a former resident of Lafayette County himself, John was well acquainted with the families of several prominent bushwhackers before the war began. And the Iron Brigade, itself a unit of regular Confederate cavalry, had frequently collaborated with irregular combatants—including Quantrill's raiders—while fighting in Missouri. Many of these conversations, then, were not coincidental or serendipitous; nor were they idle time-passing. Owing to his historical impulse, John began to collect and store away tales of bloody ambuscade, of hair-raising escapes, of midnight marauding and ruthless killing. He reveled in claims that Frank and Jesse James had each killed eight men during the Centralia Massacre of 1864 and painted an equally hellacious portrait of Cole Younger in battle. Apparently unable to settle on a single metaphor, John likened Younger interchangeably to a "lion," "a red Indian," and a "Centaur."[32]

The clumsily made image of a lion-headed Indian with hooved feet might have signaled otherwise, but this wasn't John's first time romanticizing the fighting prowess of bushwhackers. In a May 1872 article eponymously entitled "Quantrell," he painted the late guerrilla chieftain as "a blonde Apollo of the plains." At the time, certain Confederate irregulars from the East—most notably the "Gray Ghost," John Singleton Mosby—were rehabilitating their images at the expense of Missouri's guerrillas. John deemed that commemorative comparison unjust to the Missourians and let loose with a series of grand pronouncements and historical predictions. "If there is a race without fear," he trumpeted, "Quantrell belonged to it." "No nation equals in individuality the American. Her people possess all the elements to make the finest soldiers on earth." Having set the lofty standard in print, John resolved that as a perfect example of the American warrior breed, "Quantrell will live as a model." To be sure, these were controversial statements in the western borderlands. Unionists and Kansans certainly noticed. But the world beyond the borderlands didn't, and the article was soon buried by a flurry of election coverage.[33]

Even in hindsight it is impossible to discern when John realized William Clarke Quantrill and the Missouri bushwhacker would be the subject of his next book. In 1872 he was just recovering from *Shelby's Expedition to Mexico*. But it isn't a stretch to imagine that by the winter of 1873–74 he might have begun outlining the project in between editorials and encounters with the James brothers. Combating Reconstruction was still his primary concern, and John had no way of knowing when Reconstruction would end. At the same time, he could appreciate that the usefulness of outlaws would not last forever; in his political experience, nothing did. Then in 1874, Missouri Democrats won the governorship and flipped a senate seat. They followed that up in 1875 with ownership of every seat in Missouri's delegation to the House of Representatives. These state-level gains were, in fact, part and parcel of a much broader wave of mid-term success. Nationally, thanks in large part to a stagnant economy following the Panic of 1873, the Democratic Party gained significant ground in the Senate and had actually seized control of the House of Representatives. Owing to this resurgence, a day was coming when John would no longer need to sugarcoat the violent antics of the Jameses and the Youngers.[34]

Precisely when that day would arrive was a matter of debate. As of December 1874 the *Chicago Tribune* didn't see it coming any time soon. The paper ran an editorial blasting Missouri for its outlaw problem and suggesting that the state had earned "a most unenviable reputation as an encourager of banditti and a shelterer of murderers." When the article accused the state of misdeeds, it really meant *the* state too. Members of the Missouri state legislature, the piece alleged, were part of a conspiracy to shield politically important outlaws from justice. Believing that Missouri's criminal roots were set deep in Jefferson City, the *Tribune* implied that the chances of reform were bleak if not altogether hopeless.[35]

In predicting no end to the banditry, the *Tribune*'s editorialist erred in a revealing way: he focused more on the criminals and their sensational antics than on the political climate that made them useful and thereby tolerable. In effect, conservative Missourians in the early 1870s were like a patient undergoing a radical—even experimental—treatment to get rid of Reconstruction. At first the problem appeared to justify anything and everything, including side-effects like murder, the destruction of property, and a sinking national reputation. But as the political situation in Missouri improved for Democrats, drastic measures seemed less necessary; in turn, their willingness to suffer side-effects gradually declined.[36]

Naturally, the brightening of electoral prospects that devalued social banditry was good news for Democrats. The broader point, after all, was to reclaim political authority. In spite of their recent gains, though, something still gnawed at John. The culture war he'd first sensed and addressed in "Quantrell" was escalating, and Missouri didn't seem ready or equipped to wage it. This boiled down to John's simple realization that Missouri had a memory problem, one that stemmed from lackluster Confederate credentials and affected how the state's wartime experience would be remembered by other Southerners. Claiborne Jackson's scheming notwithstanding, Missouri never seceded from the Union. And no matter how greatly John admired Jo Shelby, on a Southern stage the leader of the Iron Brigade couldn't hold a candle to the likes of R. E. Lee or Thomas "Stonewall" Jackson, let alone command the spotlight. Neither could Sterling Price, John S. Marmaduke, or Thomas Hindman. In fact, when it came to name recognition, Missouri's marquee generals could scarcely compete with "lesser deities" from the Eastern Theater like A. P. Hill, J. E. B. Stuart, or P. G. T. Beauregard.

Equally as problematic as Missouri's lack of a widely recognized "marble man" was that the early victories claimed by Confederates in the state—at Lexington, for instance—were more or less unknown affairs in the East. If most easterners knew the details of one borderland engagement, it was the Lawrence Massacre. But knowing it and appreciating it were not one and the same. Many Southerners viewed Quantrill's great raid as an embarrassment at best and an atrocity at worst. Owing to these circumstances, John saw Missouri as being at serious risk of being alienated from the Confederate commemoration movements then germinating in places like Richmond and New Orleans.

Ordinance of secession or no ordinance of secession, to be cut off culturally from the rest of the South was unacceptable to John. For him, whether in Missouri or Mexico, the underlying purpose of political power had always been to preserve certain elements of antebellum Southern society and culture. As such, when the political triumphs of 1874 and 1875 signaled that Reconstruction was faltering, John already had the makings of a massive new propaganda campaign on standby. However, before fully devoting himself to the fight for control of Missouri's Civil War legacy, he had a more personal score to settle. It too was a product of contesting how and where the war ought to be remembered. Though on this occasion, it was John, not Quantrill or James or Younger, who would need to be cool, quick, and accurate with his revolver.

Part 2: The Famous Winnebago County Duel

The trouble all started with Jefferson Davis and an invitation to speak at the 1875 Winnebago County Fair. In decades past, the program of a county fair in northern Illinois would hardly have warranted notice from the outside world. If not for the ongoing struggle to ascribe the Civil War with permanent meaning, word of this particular offer might not have raised any eyebrows either. But it did. Because in this context, the invitation was a tinderbox just waiting for ignition.

The people of Rockford, Winnebago County's political seat, asked Davis to talk about agriculture. No one, or at least virtually no one, really cared to hear Davis opine about soil composition or crop rotations. The request was a local publicity stunt, plain and simple—and one likely orchestrated by a newly empowered Democrat riding the Party's midterm success. Then a Unionist newspaperman in St. Louis threw the first spark; he rebuked the fair's organizers for making light of high treason and the death toll wrought by secession. The editor held Davis personally responsible for the latter. Other Unionist editors in nearby Chicago quickly piled on with similar objections. Calls for national reconciliation notwithstanding, it became clear that the ex-Confederacy's one and only president was not a welcomed attraction in the land of Lincoln. Before long, the scheme had backfired so badly that the people of Winnebago were forced to retract their offer. Meanwhile, a mortified Davis claimed that he had never planned to attend in the first place. By then, however, it was too late to extinguish the fire.[37]

Another St. Louis newspaperman, a certain ex-Confederate cavalry officer employed at the *Dispatch*, leaped to Davis's defense—though not because he cared much for the former president. As a matter of fact, he didn't. But taking up for Davis did mean an opportunity to upbraid Republicans in print. Then the editor who'd originally scolded the people of Rockford responded in kind, haranguing Missouri's Democratic Party and its cheerleaders in the press. As tensions escalated, friends of the rival editors attempted to intervene. Requests for public apology and retraction were denied. A huffy correspondence ensued and, eventually, satisfaction was demanded. Thus, it came to be on the first Saturday of September 1875 that John stood at the south end of an open meadow, twenty paces distant from Major Emory S. Foster, editor of the St. Louis *Journal*. In his dominant hand, each man held a loaded .38-caliber Colt Navy revolver.[38]

Born in 1839 in Greene County, Missouri, Emory Stallsworth Foster's early years mirrored John's with remarkable similarity. Foster received a common school education. Then, as a teenager, he ventured into the world of the antebellum newsroom. Foster established a weekly paper with his older brother, Marshall, in Warrensburg, Missouri—but left it abruptly to join the Union army in 1861 after secessionists gunned Marshall down in the street. Foster served with distinction in the Trans-Mississippi theater, including at Lone Jack, where he suffered a serious wound, and at Marshall, where Federals had put an end to Shelby's Raid once and for all. As General E. B. Brown's chief of staff during the October 1863 battle, Foster played a significant role in helping orchestrate the Iron Brigade's defeat. Despite growing up the son of a Methodist minister, he was no stranger to violence. With intense, penetrating eyes, a hawklike nose, and a cigar perpetually clamped in the corner of his mouth, Foster looked every part the formidable pistoleer.[39]

A little less than a week before the duel, John had insisted that Foster retract parts of his Winnebago Fair critique. According to John, the offending segments labeled him a liar. Then the letter took a more dangerous turn. "I must, therefore, construe your letter of this date, and its spirit, as a refusal on your part to do me an act of common justice, and so regarding it, I deem it my duty to ask of you that satisfaction which one gentleman has a right to ask of another." John notified Foster that Col. H. B. Branch, a personal friend, would deliver the request and arrange with a friend of Foster's choosing the "details of further arrangements connected with the subject."[40]

Foster granted John's request the very next day. Before doing so, he made one last effort to sort the situation out with ink before switching to lead. "I have to state," Foster protested, "that I emphatically disclaimed in my note of yesterday any intention of referring to you, or in any way offering to you, a personal offense in the matter in which you have raised the issue." Later coverage of the duel suggested Foster was telling the truth; odds appear good that he was unaware that John, specifically, had penned the pro-Davis editorial because John published it as an op-ed in the *St. Louis Times*, rather than his own paper (the *Dispatch*). That hardly mattered now. Foster could technically decline the challenge, citing a case of mistaken communication, but only at the risk of his personal reputation. That wouldn't do, so he selected W. D. W. Barnard to act as second. Being the challenged party, he was allowed to choose the location. Foster picked Rockford, Illinois. The dispute had begun there and so too would it end.[41]

Both parties agreed to meet in Rockford on September 4, 1875. Affairs of honor were just as illegal in Illinois as in Missouri. Understandably, both parties wanted to proceed out of the public's immediate gaze. For the sake of their manliness, though, they didn't want to give the appearance of hiding, either. Everything about the duel was a performance. They settled on a secluded valley bisected by Turtle Creek five miles north of Rockford along the Beloit Road.[42]

The eight men present—John; his second, H. B. Branch; Dr. Montgomery, John's surgeon; Morry Munford, John's friend; Foster; Foster's second, W. D. W. Barnard; Foster's surgeon, Dr. P. S. O'Reilly; and, John W. Postgate, a Chicago *Tribune* reporter and friend of Foster's— trekked roughly two hundred yards into a sheltered pasture west of the road. Next Barnard and Branch meticulously examined the revolvers to be wielded by each principal for mechanical flaws. Then each revolver was very carefully loaded. As their weapons underwent preparation for battle, the duelists readied themselves for its aftermath. Foster laid down on a bank, collecting himself and puffing away on his signature cigar. His thoughts probably turned to his wife, Jessie.[43]

Just a few feet away, John sat against a tree, conferring with Munford. His departure from the *Kansas City Times* had done nothing to sever their close bond. As proof, John handed Munford a short note that displayed his ultimate trust in their friendship:

> Dear Morry: A little farewell I want to speak to you. I have but three thoughts: my wife, my two children. When you can help

6. Sketch of John sporting his signature mustache. Made in the late 1870s. Mary Virginia Edwards, ed., *John N. Edwards. Biography, Memoirs, Reminiscences and Recollections.* (Kansas City MO. J. Edwards, 1889).

7. Morrison Munford understood John's talents and demons as much as anyone. Pictured here while editor of the *Kansas City Times* in the 1890s. State Historical Society of Missouri, Business Men's Portraits of 1897.

my wife with her pride—help her. It aint much—only it is so much to me. Your friend, J. N. Edwards

The second of those two children, James Shelby Edwards, was less than nine months old—born in February 1875. On one level, John's note is touching. In his own simple way, he saw to the future of his wife and children in the event Foster cut him down. Munford had the financial means to help them, and John knew his closest friend wouldn't refuse the favor. John also might have assumed that Jennie's father, Judge Plattenburg, would support his daughter and grandchildren if required; though given the nature of John's relationship with his in-laws, he likely cringed at the thought of that situation.[44]

On another level, that his request of Munford was necessary at all displayed a remarkable degree of hypocrisy on John's part. Here

8. Major Emory S. Foster dueled and then became close friends with John. State Historical Society of Missouri, Missouri Military Portraits.

was the boy who grew up without a father, who watched his widowed mother struggle for years, now voluntarily risking a repeat performance of the same scenario. At least in the case of John's own father, John Sr. had done nothing to intentionally place his life in jeopardy. Having issued the challenge to duel with his own pen, John could not say the same. On another level still, the inspiration behind the boy's middle name—Jo Shelby—explained why John probably didn't view his presence on the field of honor as voluntary at all. For John, living up to the heroic, cavalier standard of his hero meant risking death before accepting dishonor.

When it was announced that the weapons were ready, it was time to officially count off the distance between the two shooting positions. John won the privilege of choosing between the southern and northern ends of the shooting line. Perhaps as a superstitious throwback to the war, John chose to stand to the south of Foster.[45]

John winning choice of position left Foster in control of the call. This meant that Foster's second, Branch, would issue the verbal commands that commenced the shooting. Very specific directions were outlined concerning the language and cadence of the call: Branch would ask each principal if we were ready and upon receiving two affirmations, he would begin a slow, evenly paced three count. Before either party arrived in Rockford, it had been decided that each man—assuming he planned to shoot—would fire after the word "two." Why the seconds chose this format, as opposed to firing on three, is unknown.[46]

After days of anticipation, John and Foster collected their revolvers and took their respective positions. Each duelist had already emptied his pockets of anything—a watch, diary, bible, tobacco case—that might unfairly stop or deflect a well-placed bullet. Now it was requested, out of an abundance of caution, that the other spectators aside from the seconds relieve themselves of weaponry. Normally, seconds remained armed in the event that a principal broke the rules. In that case, it became the job of the cheated principal's second to gun down the disgraced offender. But the more heavily armed the audience, the greater the risk of an emotional reaction to the shooting's outcome provoking a full-on skirmish. As it happened, only Munford was packing a revolver, and he agreed to discard it. Branch shook John's hand once more. Barnard did the same with Foster. It was time.[47]

At 5:00 p.m. Barnard asked, "Are you ready?" Hearing no reason to delay, he called out "one," then "two." In that instant, both revolvers belched with fire and smoke. Neither John nor Foster fell to the ground. No blood marked the clothing of either man. "A little high," Foster shouted, no doubt pleased with the result. As the challenged party, he didn't have to actually kill John to win the duel. All Foster really needed to do was show up and prove himself willing to receive fire like a man. As such, it is quite likely that Foster intentionally fired over John's head. But whatever relief the associates of both men felt at Foster's pronouncement instantly evaporated. John demanded a second attempt. Foster's party overheard John mutter to Barnard that, "I will go on if it takes a thousand fires."[48]

After giving him time to think things over—and perhaps to locate his better judgment—Barnard asked John to formally state that he wished to shoot again. Despite having a wife, two young children, and a thriving literary career, John affirmed his resolution to continue. While Foster probably fired without intent to wound John, it appeared as though John genuinely sought to harm Foster, which meant that his failure to hit Foster at twenty paces was exactly that—a failure.[49]

Next the question was posed to Foster. He immediately declined. He had no reason to kill John. After all, he'd probably never meant to insult John personally in the first place. As far as Foster was concerned, this was the best possible outcome: his honor intact, his body unmarred by lead, and no killing on his conscience. Barnard informed John of Foster's decision, to which John proclaimed, "I have admitted as much as I can do—[I] have received no satisfaction to take with me." Having made his feelings known, John approached Foster. The two men clasped hands. Not long after sending globs of hot lead whizzing past one another, the duelists opened a bottle of bourbon and explained their respective sides of the Jeff Davis-Winnebago Fair controversy. Before leaving the field, John, Foster, and the rest of the men all drank a cheerful toast to honor fulfilled and to the end, however bloodless, of their editorial feud.[50]

WHILE JOHN AND Foster might have buried the proverbial hatchet—they apparently went on to become good friends despite their opposing political views—the people of Rockford weren't so genial. They didn't appreciate the part of pawns in a partisan feud between hot-headed Missourians. Within weeks of the duel, the Illinois States Attorney had convened a grand jury in Winnebago County for the purpose of indicting Edwards, Foster, their seconds, their surgeons, and even Postgate, who had no official role in the preparations. Only Munford escaped the wrath of the grand jury. He returned to St. Louis on a different train, and his detachment from the other coconspirators somehow confused prosecutors.[51]

Media coverage of the duel back in Missouri depended largely on the duelist being described and the political bent of the paper doing the describing. Despite the lack of blood, the *Kansas City Times,* John's former editorial home, declared him the clear winner. The writeup of September 7, 1875, praised John's "gallant bearing," asserting that he "took all the chances" and "meant business from the start." Foster, the *Times* conceded, also "bore himself very gallantly," but ultimately

John's challenge and the resultant duel would "teach editors that they cannot use publicly abusive language without being held personally responsible for it." That was a lesson—and really, a poorly veiled threat—that the Democratic organs of Missouri appreciated as they geared up for a hotly contested election cycle in 1876.[52]

Elsewhere in the western borderlands, particularly in Kansas, the editors of pro-Republican papers took extreme delight in lampooning John. To them, the entire affair was a farcical performance staged by old Southern honor-culture obsessed buffoons. The *Newton Kansan* sneered that after the pointless shooting, the duelists "returned to their respective quills perfectly satisfied that they are chivalrous, honorable men. Bah!" The next day, the *Emporia Weekly News* dubbed John and Foster "two editorial apes"; the paper was incredulous that men would shoot at each other over something so irrelevant as Jeff Davis giving a speech at the Winnebago fair.[53]

The *Lawrence Daily Journal* took its criticism several steps further— almost daring the *Times* to follow through with the "lesson" it had touted about personal insults and responsibility. In a story headlined "A Pair of Fools," the *Daily Journal* suggested that "such extreme foolishness as theirs [Edwards and Foster] deserves something more of celebrity than the ordinary folly of ordinary folks." Casting John as an unmanly coward, the editorial accused him of abusing the women of Winnebago County in print, of hiding his authorship of the unchivalrous hit piece by publishing it in the *St. Louis Times* (instead of in his own paper), and then of "bushwhacking" an unsuspecting Foster when he responded to the anonymous "writer" of the *Times* article. "Lunatic Foster," the takedown further argued, "made a preposterous and unprecedented donkey of himself by paying attention to the weak-minded Edwards."[54]

The paper ultimately concluded that if Foster *was* crazy enough to duel with Edwards under such idiotic circumstances, he could have at least gone ahead and killed him. Yet neither man, the *Daily Journal* reminded, had been able to hit the other from a distance "at which even a policeman can hit a dog." "There stood Foster with a 'chance' at twenty steps to kill the man who wrote 'Shelby and His

Men,'" the paper lamented, tongue firmly in cheek, "and failed to confer that service on American literature. Great is chivalry. Long live balderdash."[55]

That John's duel with Foster warranted such personalized coverage in Kansas revealed the extent of his recently won notoriety in Republican circles. His propagandizing of the James-Younger Gang's exploits against Reconstruction had made him a powerful voice within the movement of ex-Confederate Democrats vying to regain control of both Missouri and the South more broadly. In turn, John constituted a top-level target for pro-Republican newspapers on both sides of the Missouri-Kansas border—but especially for the Kansans. They bitterly resented his glorification of the same bushwhacker-turned-bandits that had left Lawrence in ruins back in August 1863. In the coming years, John would hit back—rhetorically, that is—against the Kansans. For now, he needed to focus his attention on avoiding extradition to Illinois. In a Winnebago County courtroom, he would face an unfriendly jury and serious time behind bars. That being the case, John and the rest of the men involved in the duel did something curious. As soon as news of the Illinois indictments reached St. Louis, they turned themselves over to the law. *In Missouri.*[56]

Under the terms of Missouri's 1822 antidueling statute, it was illegal to fight a duel within the boundaries of the state, and if one of the parties so engaged died as a result of the duel, everyone involved would face murder charges. This is precisely what John and Foster went to Illinois to avoid, even though Illinois's statute said nearly the same thing. But both men lived in St. Louis. And Section 4 of the statute also made it a penal offence to carry, send, or accept a challenge to duel within the boundaries of Missouri. Virtually all the men had been involved in one way or another with the correspondence that arranged the duel. All, that is, except for Postgate, who as a citizen of Illinois did not require extradition and potentially had bigger problems with the Winnebago grand jury than the Missourians. For their part, the Missourians bet Governor Charles H. Hardin would not extradite them to Illinois while a criminal charge existed in Missouri stemming from the same incident. With that strategy in mind, John and Foster both voluntarily submitted to arrest. They each appeared before the St. Louis Court of Criminal Corrections, posted $500 bail, respectively, and were allowed to leave on their own recognizance.[57]

The plan was relatively simple, but it was very clever. By conceding to the lesser charges under Missouri law, John believed he could shield himself from extradition. No extradition meant no trial in Illinois. And as it turned out, that gamble paid off. Once indictments for conspiring to arrange a duel were issued by the court in St. Louis, Hardin—himself a Democrat but also a Unionist—refused the request of Illinois governor John L. Beveridge to extradite John, Foster, Barnard, Branch, and Drs. Montgomery and O'Reilly, for prosecution. Naturally, when John and Foster submitted to the law in St. Louis, it necessitated that they implicate their seconds, surgeons, and friends. Even Munford, who had escaped charges in Illinois, had to be indicted in Missouri. Yet a quick reading of section 7 of the antidueling code alleviated those concerns. It decreed that "seconds, aiders, abettors, counselors, physicians, and friends" who testified before the grand jury and at trial would themselves become immune from criminal prosecution for aiding, abetting, and counseling. In other words, they only needed to tell the court what John and Foster had already admitted to and they would walk away without punishment.[58]

Of course, all that maneuvering was based on the assumption that prosecutors in St. Louis would, as the statute required, take the indicted men to trial. Surviving court records don't indicate that such proceedings ever took place. Much more likely is that once the Missourians had sufficiently shielded themselves from the reach of prosecutors in Illinois, the matter was quietly dropped by a friendly administration in Jefferson City. Either way, neither John nor Foster ever spent a night in jail related to the duel.

Damning as the criticism from outside Missouri had been, John emerged from the shadow of the "Famous Winnebago County Duel" as a larger-than-life figure among conservatives *within* the state. Some of this newfound celebrity stemmed from the sheer novelty of a pundit proving he wasn't a paper tiger. John authored a work of military history overflowing with headlong charges, hellish artillery fire, and acts of individual dash. He also wrote frequently about gun-toting outlaws and the dashing heists of former bushwhackers. Like so many of his peers in the newspaper business, he issued fiery calls to action and talked boldly—even menacingly—from behind a print set. With the Foster duel, however, John left the relative security of the newsroom and took up the gun himself. When charges came down from Illinois and John became a wanted man there, the favorite editor of the outlaws temporarily became one himself.

That willingness to step forward, gun in hand, struck a genuine chord with the ex-Confederate set of Missourians who truly considered themselves Southerners. For them, John's successful affirmation of his own honor also extended to the version of the war he constructed in *Shelby and His Men* and to the ultra-conservative political positions he'd been espousing since 1867. Put another way, John's successful defense of his honor also extended to things they held dear—and therefore to them directly. In that sense, for many Missouri Democrats, chief among them the ex-Confederates, John became their Preston Brooks. He'd swapped the senate chamber for a creek-side meadow and replaced the hulking Charles Sumner with a cigar-puffing Foster. But the collective sentiment behind the congratulatory notes that poured in for John in the duel's aftermath was clear: as meaningless as Jefferson Davis delivering a speech in Winnebago about agriculture might have been, and as hollow as the duel might have appeared to outsiders, to many ex-Confederate Missourians, it was the moment someone stood up on their behalf and said, no more slander, not without a fight.

IT IS POSSIBLE, though unlikely, that the fallout from the duel played a role in John's abrupt departure from the *St. Louis Dispatch* soon after. Perhaps as a Northerner, Hutchins found the affair unseemly and decided to cut ties with his star editor on principle. His brother *had* been shot down years before over a political disagreement. Then again, if Hutchins had encouraged John's glowing coverage of the James-Younger Gang—as the opening of "A Terrible Quintette" suggested—it seems improbable that a bloodless duel rankled his conscience. Above all else, Hutchins was a businessman. John sold as many papers, if not more, than any other editorialist in Missouri. That fact alone made it much more likely that John decided to leave, probably because Hutchins couldn't, or wouldn't, fulfill the gilded promises used to lure John out of Kansas City.

None of it amazed Morry Munford. He'd seen the ill-fated dynamic between Hutchins and John for what it was back in 1873. As far as Munford was concerned, Hutchins had never planned to deliver on his wild promises, no matter how successful John made the *Dispatch*. Instead, he believed Hutchins was merely using John's voice to help himself become "the dictator of Missouri politics." "The golden promises laid out to John Edwards turned to worse than ashes," Munford wrote years later, even personally blaming Hutchins for derailing John's career as a newspaperman. As it turned out, Munford was right: John would fill a succession of editorial posts, but never again found long-term stability at a well-established paper.[59]

In the moment, neither man knew that the best years of John's editorial career were behind him. Nevertheless, it was clear to those closest him that John's exit from the *Dispatch* had shattered both his confidence and his pride. He refused repeated offers from Munford to reclaim his old job at the *Times*. Then, to what must have been Jennie's utter dismay, John announced his plan to quit journalism entirely—and to take up sheep farming in New Mexico. This was a vocation about which he knew absolutely nothing. New Mexico was a place in which they had zero friends or family. Moving within Missouri for what John had believed was his big break was one thing; the Plattenburgs had no intention of seeing their daughter dragged to the far western territories for a scheme that everyone but John could see was a financial disaster waiting to happen. Judge Plattenburg intervened. It was decided that the entire family, John, Jennie, John Jr., and James—the boys now aged four-and-a-half-years and ten months, respectively—would spend 1876 at the Plattenburg mansion in Dover.[60]

Part 3: An Irregular Lost Cause
John had crossed the threshold of the Plattenburg home on numerous occasions. Sometimes he came as a soldier, others as a civilian;

often he was invited, though in rare instances his presence was less than welcome. Whatever the circumstances, the house served as the backdrop to several pivotal scenes from his adult life. It was there that Shelby began the formation of the Iron Brigade. It was there, after returning from Mexican exile, that John reconnected with Jennie and commenced their courtship. It was there, likely in the front sitting room of the Greek Revival mansion, that Judge Plattenburg refused to bless the couple's marriage. And it was there that visits with one grandson, and then a second, gradually mended family ties. Now in 1876 the house became an asylum for John's midlife crisis and a headquarters for the work that saw him through it.

The elder Plattenburgs must have harbored mixed feelings about the turn of events that brought their daughter home. On one hand, they had to be worried about John's lack of financial prospects and his dogged refusals to take back his old perch at the *Times*. Their original opposition to John and Jennie's marriage had hinged on bloodlines, not money. Even still, it's not difficult to picture Judge Plattenburg wondering "what might have been"—or what might have been avoided—if Jennie had obeyed his wishes back in 1872. On the other hand, Jennie's parents certainly enjoyed having her back in Western Missouri. And of course, where Jennie went, the boys went, making unlimited access to grandchildren another silver-lining of the arrangement. So while one can only imagine the first, awkward encounters between the Judge and John, anything had to seem better to the Plattenburgs than Jennie and their grandsons idling away on a New Mexican sheep ranch.

For better or worse, John was nothing if not a creature of habit. Just as he'd done in moments of crisis past, he threw himself into writing. This wasn't an exercise in poetic self-exploration or emotional healing, either. No matter his professional failings or personal woes or the humiliation that either might have engendered, political machinations drove John's writing. He simply couldn't help himself. And in this case, ironically, that actually proved helpful.

One thing that did change was his medium. Without a paid editorial post for the first time in a decade, John would spend the entire year laboring over his third work of history. The book's subject matter was both the same and different. He wasn't walking away completely from the members of the James-Younger Gang—or from violent young men wreaking havoc from the saddle—but he was no longer interested in weaponizing their bank heists and train robberies against the Republican establishment. As John had first hinted in "A Terrible Quintette," the war years, when the Jameses and Youngers were pro-Confederate bushwhackers, was his primary focus now. How they would be remembered *then*, not as postwar Robin Hoods, was his chief concern.

It's also worth pausing to point out that John's topical jump back in time to the Missouri-Kansas guerrilla war had nothing to do with his outlaw associates going straight. Because that didn't happen. Between the fall of 1873, when John published "A Terrible Quintette," and the summer of 1876, when much of the new book was penned, various incarnations of the gang pulled off burglaries at Hot Springs, Arkansas; Gad's Hill, Missouri; and Otterville, Missouri. Their spree came to a temporary halt in September 1876, when what could have happened on the train in Adair County finally did happen in Northfield, Minnesota.

While attempting to relieve the First National Bank in Northfield of its holdings, the bandits ran into a mob of fed-up locals. A hellish gun battle ensued. The results were catastrophic. Two bandits died in the fighting. Another was killed by a posse hunting the bandits. The Younger brothers—Cole, Jim, and Bob—were captured alive and handed life sentences in Stillwater State Prison. With the Youngers behind bars, the James-Younger Gang ceased to exist in the form that John had promoted. Frank and Jesse James escaped from Northfield with their lives and would rebuild the gang. But without former guerrillas as a nucleus, things would never be the same.[61]

From almost any political angle, Northfield was an ugly spectacle. According to previous justifications for their outlawry, the Jameses and the Youngers wanted to be left alone at war's end. Because vengeful Republicans wouldn't allow that to happen, the bandits would defend their rights and the rights of other downtrodden Missourians with violent force. And for a time, they could at least claim to be doing that within Missouri. However, in that same context, the logic of a bank

9. Confederate bushwhackers Jesse James (standing, right) and
Frank James (seated, middle) circa 1864. State Historical Society
of Missouri, Dr. Richard S. Brownlee Photograph Collection.

JESSE W. JAMES,

I hereby certify that the above is the only late Photograph of my deceased husband, taken before death.

MRS. JESSE W. JAMES.

10. Photograph of Jesse James in 1875, one year before the James-Younger Gang's disaster in Northfield, Minnesota. State Historical Society of Missouri, Photo and View Company Photographs.

robbery in Minnesota, some four hundred miles from their family farms, wasn't easy to explain, even for the gang's remaining cheerleaders. That one of the James brothers murdered a bank clerk in cold blood didn't improve the optics of the situation, either. Therefore, it would be easy—and wrong—to presume that Northfield prompted John to cut professional ties with the Jameses.

In truth, John's working relationship with the outlaw brothers had been dissolving even before the failed raid in Minnesota. His willingness to publish (and edit) letters from Jesse James had always hinged on the outlaws' partisan usefulness—and their usefulness hinged on public support. In 1872 and 1873 the partnership was mutually beneficial. In those political moments it made good sense to throw his editorial weight behind anti-Reconstruction insurgents because enough Missourians believed in what they were doing. Two years later, not so much. By 1876 it made no sense at all.

This was a hard lesson in politics that the Jameses learned the hardest way possible. As Reconstruction ran out of steam—precisely the development John had used them to help bring about—the brothers became expendable. Then two months after the gang foundered at Northfield and gave many former backers an excuse to feign outrage and disgust at the bandits' behavior, the presidential election of 1876 completely remade the political landscape of the United States. Soon the brothers would be hunted by Republicans and Democrats alike.

The contest between Rutherford B. Hayes, a Republican from Ohio, and Samuel Tilden, a Democrat from New York, remains among the closest in American history. After election day, Tilden held a narrow but safe lead in the electoral college of 184 votes to Hayes's 165. He also led in the popular tally by a margin of more than two hundred thousand votes, or roughly 3 percent of all votes cast. For Democrats it appeared Tilden was well on his way to the White House—a miraculous development after more than a decade of Republican rule. But that all changed when reports of disputed votes arrived from South Carolina, Florida, and Louisiana. As former Confederate states, the safe money was on Tilden winning at least one of them. And he only needed a *single vote* from among the disputed twenty to become the nineteenth president of the United States. When all was said and done, he got none of them.[62]

In exchange for all twenty of the votes from South Carolina, Florida, and Louisiana—which secured the presidency for Rutherford B. Hayes—Republicans agreed to evacuate Federal troops from the ex-Confederacy. Without the occupation force to oversee fair elections and hold paramilitaries at bay, the newly won civil rights of Black Southerners came instantly into peril. This was a conscious betrayal of the freedpeople who'd risked life and limb to vote for Grant and then Hayes. Republicans knew it, too. But it was also a pragmatic political move. Reconstruction was ending one way or another, and Republicans figured they might as well get something on the way out. That something was the Oval Office. For their part Democrats saw a prize far more valuable than a single presidential term. The backroom deal guaranteed an outcome congressional Republicans might have refused to allow under a Democratic administration. An understandably bitter Samuel Tilden was swept aside and that was the end of that.[63]

IN THE DECADE following the war, Democrats tried to stymie Reconstruction with the ballot. When those efforts failed to yield adequate results, they threw extralegal violence into the mix. In Missouri, that included the criminal handywork of the Jameses and the Youngers. Yet even amid the surge in paramilitary activity, Reconstruction dragged on. It's easy to see, then, why no Southerners—John included—would have predicted that *letting a Republican win* might be the key to ending Republican rule in the ex-Confederacy. But here it was. And with the issue of Southern political sovereignty finally settled, matters of memory and commemoration took their turn in the spotlight. The timing of this shift worked out almost perfectly for John. He'd spent the past year preparing for the fight. Now, in 1877, from a makeshift office in the Plattenburg house, he would deploy his new book, *Noted Guerrillas, or, The Warfare of the Border* and launch a campaign to decide the fate of Missouri's Civil War legacy as well as its connection to the Lost Cause of the Confederacy.

By the time John committed himself fully to the "memory wars," he was a relative latecomer. Former Confederate general Jubal Early—who also happened to be an acquaintance of John's from Mexico—helped found the Southern Historical Society in 1869. In 1876 the Society began publishing the *Southern Historical Society Papers*, again under Early's watchful eye. As an elite cultural organization, its members worked to craft a legacy of the war that favored the Confederacy in every way possible. For instance, to explain defeat, they asserted that Johnny Reb was actually the superior combatant, but the North's endless population and the willingness of boorish Union commanders to win by attrition eventually turned the conflict.[64]

With some notable exceptions, Confederate commanders were glorified regardless of their wartime records; over time, a hierarchy of military deities took shape. Robert E. Lee stood alone at the top as an icon of chivalry and Christian virtue. Just below him came the martyred generals Thomas "Stonewall" Jackson and J. E. B. Stuart. A slew of well-known generals followed, each occupying a niche in the Confederacy's metaphorical pantheon. True to its gentlemanly portrait of Lee, the society pushed a version of the war in which Southern men fought for home, hearth, and states' rights against a tyrannical government. In this rendering of the Civil War, known generically today as the Lost Cause, white civility and mutual valor on the battlefield were the status quo while slavery and emancipation were of little consequence.[65]

Not by accident, an elite-driven, Virginia-centric memory movement had nothing—and frankly, wanted nothing—to do with the western borderlands or its guerrillas. However late he may have arrived on the scene, in taking up the cause of guerrilla memory, John became a pioneer in the world of Confederate commemoration. As one would expect given his track record, John's take on the Missouri bushwhacker and civil war under the black flag was florid, sensationalized, and as unapologetically partisan as anything he'd previously written about the Iron Brigade or the James-Younger Gang. Indeed, rather than molding the bushwhacker to fit the standards of the mainstream Lost Cause, John intentionally directed light on what distinguished irregulars from their regular war counterparts.

Those unique qualities, he argued, made Missouri's guerrillas the most intransigent of all Confederate warriors.[66]

The premise was classic John—and a culmination of his rhetorical experience. During his years of crusading against Reconstruction, John had become a master of taking seemingly paradoxical ideas and spinning them into effective propaganda. Grant was inept but a grave threat. The South was ruined beyond repair by Republicans but could still be saved in the next election. Jesse James was a quintessential Missouri farm boy but also king of the bandits. In the case of *Noted Guerrillas*, men from a state that never joined the Confederacy were actually the most Confederate *because* their state hadn't seceded. Having to survive as political renegades in a Union state forced men into the guerrilla ranks—and to fight from the bush required an unparalleled dedication to the cause.

This was admittedly a strange position for a former Confederate cavalryman to advance, let alone one that had spent countless hours and hundreds of printed pages lauding Jo Shelby and his Iron Brigade. Did John truly believe that bushwhackers had been more dedicated to the cause than his own unit? Probably not—or at least no more than he really believed the Jameses and Youngers were stealing from the rich and murdering random bystanders to help the poor. But if transforming a handful of bushwhackers turned bandits into Robin Hoods in the early 1870s made good sense in anti-Reconstruction politics, remaking Missouri's best-known guerrillas into Confederate superheroes made even better sense in the context of memory politics. John knew that Missouri was never going to walk hand in hand with the parameters of a Lost Cause designed to suit Virginia's Confederate experience. Missouri had no Robert E. Lee; it had no Fredericksburg or Chancellorsville. To keep Missouri culturally, and thereby socially, anchored to the rest of the South, the state needed its own Lost Cause.

Rather than shying away from the novelty of his approach, John laid out a dramatic case for providing the guerrillas a voice in Confederate commemoration. "He who wore the blue or the gray—if starred, or barred, or epauletted—needed simply the recognition of a monument to become a martyr. But the Guerrilla," John bemoaned, "had no graveyard. What mutilation spared, the potter's field finished." With his audience reminded that guerrillas were human, John proceeded to eulogize them for nearly five hundred pages.[67]

Beginning with how men became pro-Confederate guerrillas in the first place, John explained that Unionists had only themselves to blame. These were not men predisposed to cruelty and slaughter. They had no itch to become hellions on horseback. Atrocities perpetrated by Unionists and abolitionists—fathers and brothers assassinated, women insulted and abused, homes torched, and land stolen—left them with little choice but to band together locally to fight back. The genesis of the bushwhacker, John posited, was a reaction to prolonged trauma, not a premeditated strategy. As such, the average guerrilla "knew nothing of the tiger that was in him until death had been dashed against his eyes in numberless and brutal ways, and until the blood of his own kith and kin had been sprinkled plentifully upon things that his hands touched." In this way, John presented bushwhackers as motivated by revenge but still connected them ideologically to the Confederate cause, because the persecution that drove them was politically inflected.[68]

The guerrilla theater as John painted it was not a pleasant place. Homes, villages, and towns were combat zones. One never knew when or where bushwhackers or Jayhawkers would come calling, and so the threat of domestic violation—and death—loomed always for men, women, and children alike. To operate in this environment, bush-whackers required different tools and abilities than their counterparts on the Napoleonic skirmish line. Without much use for Johnny Reb's signature rifle-musket, guerrillas lived and died by the revolver. As professional pistoleers, John argued they were the absolute best of the best. He backed that claim with myriad anecdotes, including one about Cole Younger practicing with a revolver for weeks before using it to kill a Union militiaman at seventy-one measured yards—a very, *very* long shot with a pistol, then as now.[69]

It was much the same with horses. Guerrillas typically fought in small groups. They engaged when the odds were in their favor; making last stands, especially against regular troops armed with rifles, was not con-sidered a smart play for bushwhackers who wanted to continue living. Instead, they often needed to escape to fight another day. Accordingly, mobility and speed were paramount to guerrilla operations. John assessed their skill with horses as verging on the supernatural and reported that "well authenticated instances are on record" of guerrilla horses actually standing guard at night and warning their masters of impending danger. So strong was this bond between horse and rider that, in John's version of the story, the death of William Quantrill's trusted steed Old Charley prompted the guerrilla chieftain to assume that he would soon be killed.[70]

Mastery over pistol and horse were critical attributes for a bush-whacker because, as John put it, "the warfare of the Guerrilla was the warfare of the fox joined with that of the lion." Guerrillas were supremely talented when it came to detecting an ambush—the fox—and equally adept at lying in wait or stalking a target before striking as a lion on the hunt. Be it on a front porch, in a corn crib, in a muddy field, or along some lonely bend in the road, John's noted guerrillas appear and disappear throughout the book like phantoms, dispensing terror and death wherever they ride. And at the end of the day, whether channeling the fox or the lion, that was the true purpose of the guerrilla war: to kill enemy combatants, wherever and whenever they could be found, regardless of who they happened to be, and irrespective of how uncouth such tactics might appear to outside observers. With that criterion in mind, even the August 1863 massacre at Lawrence and the pair of September 1864 massacres at Centralia are justified in the book as legitimate acts of war.[71]

Making Southerners understand these massacres—and irregular war more broadly—on terms he desired was perhaps John's biggest hurdle in making the Missouri bushwhacker palatable to other ex-Confederates. His stories about extraordinary gun fights and incredible feats of horsemanship, or of daring raids, stoic deaths, and other deeds of heroism, wouldn't matter if guerrillas still came across as murderers. He needed to spin bushwhacking as a more extreme version of soldiering as easterners understood it. To make that point with crystal clarity, he concocted a meeting between William Clarke Quantrill and the Confederate Secretary of War in Richmond.

John claimed that Quantrill had traveled to Richmond to request a colonel's commission under the Partisan Ranger Act. Such a move would have brought Quantrill's guerrillas under the formal umbrella of the Confederate war department which in turn would have signaled that the Confederate War Department approved of the methods employed by Quantrill's men. That meant torture, arson, massacre—all of it. The secretary of war is initially put off by Quantrill's tactics, looking down on the guerrillas and labeling their brand of fighting as barbarism. Quantrill responds with a sharp rebuke and a lesson on the realities of war:

> Barbarism, Mr. Secretary, means war and war means barbarism. . . . For twenty years this cloud has been gathering; for twenty years, inch by inch and little by little those people called the Abolitionists have been on the track of slavery; for twenty years the people of the South have been robbed, here of a negro and there of a negro; for twenty years hates have been engendered and wrathful things laid up against the day of wrath. The cloud has burst. Do not condemn the thunderbolt.

After more lecturing from Quantrill, the cowed secretary finally asks what the guerrilla chieftain would do if given "the power and the opportunity." "Do, Mr. Secretary?" Quantrill replies incredulously. "Why I would wage such a war and have such a war waged by land and sea as to make surrender forever impossible. I would cover the armies of the Confederacy all over with blood. . . . I would win the independence of my people or I would find them graves." According to John, Quantrill left Richmond without the commission but not before getting in one last jab at the secretary. "You have my ideas of war, Mr. Secretary," Quantrill says, "and I am sorry they do not accord with your own, nor the ideas of the government you have the honor to represent so well."[72]

Barbarism means war and war means barbarism. Make surrender forever impossible. I would win the independence of my people or I would find them graves. With this scene set in the Confederate War Department, John was admittedly channeling some of his own wartime frustrations with the higher-ups in Richmond—the same bureaucrats that had left men like Price and Holmes in charge of Shelby. But in the bigger picture, Quantrill's martial sermon was meant to illustrate two things for readers. The first was that the Missouri bushwhacker had fought harder for the cause of Confederate independence than the Confederate government would even allow its own troops to fight. Guerrillas had done the real dirty work required of a successful rebellion only to be thwarted by desk-bound politicians. The second was that the Missouri bushwhacker bore no responsibility for the war's negative outcome. The War Department's refusal to adopt Quantrill, and by extension his means of waging a harder, potentially more effective war, detached guerrillas from Confederate defeat and forced Southerners to wonder "what might have been" if Richmond had found the guts to raise the black flag and win by any means necessary.

It wasn't a coincidence that John employed William Clarke Quantrill to deliver these messages. In the same way the Virginians' pantheon of military heroes orbited Lee, Missouri's irregular Lost Cause revolved around Quantrill. "He was a living, breathing, aggressive, all-powerful reality," John declared. And from him, John further contended, "sprang all the other Guerrilla leaders and bands which belong largely to Missouri and the part Missouri took in the civil war." This was an important element of bushwhacker mythology. It meant that William H. Gregg, George Todd, Cole Younger, George Shepherd, Frank James, and Bill Anderson, all marquee guerrilla leaders in their own rights, were like the young Olympians to Quantrill's Cronos—but with a twist ending. In the Greek myth, not long after Cronos makes them, the Olympians overthrow and overshadow their father. In *Noted Guerrillas* it didn't matter if Quantrill's "offspring" outlived him or, in the cases of Todd and Anderson, eventually turned against him. He created them and his name would always come first and loom largest in the story.[73]

IRONICALLY GIVEN JOHN'S treatment of elite Confederates in the book, when it came down to form and function, *Noted Guerrillas* looked very much like the mainstream Lost Cause material coming out of Richmond. Both narratives included a top-down stable of folk heroes. Each told a story designed to insulate its protagonists from the shame of defeat. And though they presented violence on disparate terms, both accounts involved men fighting to defend their homes, families, and traditions from Yankee invaders—but not explicitly to preserve the Peculiar Institution.

For as much as the Virginia-and Missouri-based memory movements had in common structurally, John also knew his guerrillas would never seem chivalrous, courageous, manly or honorable if readers judged them by the standards of Lee, Jackson, and Stuart. So he abandoned standard cavalier traits. In their place, he focused on what Quantrill and company *physically* did best—killing—and made that the metric for wartime achievement. Thereby in content as well as topic, *Noted Guerrillas* constituted a radical break from mainstream Lost Cause propaganda. John went a step further than just making the case that guerrillas weren't murderers. He pulled the masks off *all* Civil War combatants and exposed the unavoidable truth that *all* war was murder. The opposite of hiding from the ugly necessities of warfighting, his bushwhackers embraced it all.

A reviewer for the *Palmyra Spectator* raved, "the book is written in the author's finest and most picturesque style, and after taking it up no one will feel like laying it down until he has read the last page. There are 490 pages, in addition to the illustration, and there is not an uninteresting one in the entire number." Another for the *St. Louis Globe-Democrat* similarly approved. "Taken altogether," the reviewer declared, "the book is brilliantly written, intensely interesting, and valuable in so far as it thoroughly illustrates a feature of the civil war that has never yet been touched upon or thoroughly understood. The whole inner history of the guerrilla struggle is clearly revealed." Without a doubt, the book had its fair share of critics. Northern papers assailed John's glorification of Missouri's war to the knife as a disgrace to the history of real soldiers and the real war. That said, he did manage to win over Unionists. In a letter to the editor of the *Kansas City Times*, a veteran of the Second Colorado Cavalry—a unit noted for its guerrilla hunting during the war—recognized the harsh criticism from places like New York and Chicago but offered a glowing assessment of the book anyway. "I have just jotted down these thoughts not by way of criticism as to bare testimony to the truth of a narrative which has been assailed by critics who relied more upon partizanship than accurate information to sustain them," the unnamed Coloradan asserted. "As for the book in a literary point of view," he concluded, "I know of no publication made since the war which is more brilliant."[74]

In the simplest terms, *Noted Guerrillas* was John's magnum opus. And for Missourians who'd experienced the Civil War as a guerrilla conflict, it was a godsend. Western Missourians in particular could take heart in the idea that their primary Civil War export, the bushwhacker, was a genuine part of the Confederate Experiment. Their history was now codified and imbued with greater meaning in a book that would stand as the definitive account of Missouri's guerrilla war for almost a century. As architect and narrator, John became a living legend among pro-Confederate Missourians—and they thanked him with their hard-earned cash. "The agent for Major John Edwards' 'Guerrilla Book' is in the city taking subscriptions about as fast as he can write the names," the *Kansas City Times* happily reported on April 6.[75]

Nearly everything in his professional life up to 1877 had prepared John to become the creator of Missouri's irregular Lost Cause. He crafted and published a mythology of the Iron Brigade long before the advent of the Southern Historical Society. Next he spent the 1870s honing his deification skills, temporarily morphing the Jameses and the Youngers into outlaw demigods. As was the case with his coverage of the James-Younger Gang, many Southerners—including ex-Confederates and Democrats—balked at glorifying a man like William Clarke Quantrill or the bloodletting at Lawrence. In due time, the Virginians would push hard to whitewash guerrillas and much of the Far Western Theater from mainstream accounts of the war altogether. In the end, though, how the rest of the South perceived Missouri in the wake of *Noted Guerrillas* mattered less than how the book influenced white Missourians to perceive themselves. If they continued to consider themselves Southern and part of the Confederacy's heritage, they would remain linked to the region's traditions and customs exactly as John envisioned.[76]

The success of *Noted Guerrillas* cemented John's legacy as a builder of other men's legacies—Joseph Shelby, Jesse James, William Clarke Quantrill, the Missouri bushwhacker. This was an interesting turn for a man who left home as a teenager, determined to win glory and obsessed with filling the footsteps of his legendary ancestors. Whether he realized it or not, John had achieved a power over the past that his ancestors lacked. They were the stuff of legend. He was a man who decided what would be legendary.

In the immediate present of 1877 *Noted Guerrillas* signaled that John was back. What he found upon emerging from his midlife crisis disturbed him. Politically, socially, things seemed to be falling apart. With a new editorial post and more clout than ever before, John intended to address those problems—and with increasing frequency, he would do it under his own version of the black flag.

The Ghost and the Monster 𝐓

Late on the morning of April 3, 1882, the borderland version of a Shakespearian tragedy was unfolding at 1318 Lafayette Street. Thomas Howard, who leased the home with his wife and children, balanced precariously on a wooden chair in the parlor. A gun belt and revolvers belonging to Howard were strewn across the nearby sofa. As he tinkered with a picture frame above the mantle, another man—one of Howard's business associates—produced his own revolver, a single action Colt Army. Neither of them uttered a word, but Howard must have heard the multiple "clicks" of the hammer moving past half cock and into firing position. And he must have known what that meant. The man's hand trembled. He aimed as best he could and squeezed off a single round.[1]

The .45-caliber bullet penetrated Howard's skull like a brick through plate glass. At near point-blank range, the impact drove shards of bone deep into his brain. After exiting the opposite side of Howard's head, the largely intact slug had enough energy remaining to burrow into the plaster wall. Howard plunged from the chair, dead before his face hit the floor. Blood, brain fluid, and bits of tissue oozed from his wounds and seeped into the carpet. Startled and fearing the worst, Mrs. Howard ran to the report of the gun. Her fears were more than realized when she stumbled into the gruesome scene. As she cried that her husband had been murdered, the picture that set it all in motion—an embroidery reading "God Bless This House"— hung, still askew, above them both.[2]

St. Joseph, Missouri, was not a provincial backwater in 1882. Just thirty miles from the heart of Kansas City and itself the seat of Buchanan County, "St. Joe" boasted a booming population that had quadrupled since the start of the Civil War. More people meant more opportunities to be recognized; hardly a suitable place for the most wanted bandit in America to hole up. And yet as his neighbors and acquaintances soon learned, Mr. Thomas Howard was none other than Jesse W. James, bandit extraordinaire. In a home overlooking the city's famed Patee House, he'd been hiding in plain sight—and planning a new heist with the Fords, Charley and Robert. Both brothers were in on the assassination plot, but it was Robert Ford who pulled the trigger.[3]

News of the killing swept through the borderlands. Many Missourians were understandably skeptical. They'd heard these rumors many times before. Eventually, Ford's confession and subsequent arrest, combined with an autopsy, verified the unthinkable: Jesse James, invincible leader of the Terrible Quintette, was dead. Questions immediately began to swirl about the government's role in the assassination. Governor Thomas T. Crittenden, though a Democrat, saw Missouri's crime problem as a national embarrassment. He took a hardline stance against banditry in the 1880 election. Two years later, Crittenden denied any prior knowledge of Ford's plan to eliminate James, but his interaction with the brothers after the assassination signaled the opposite. Not only did Crittenden pardon Charley and Robert Ford for murdering a private citizen—he also allowed them to collect a portion of the bounty *his administration* had placed on James.[4]

For John, who'd moved out of the Plattenburg house and returned to the newspaper world as editor of the Sedalia, Missouri, *Democrat*, the arrangement between the Fords and Crittenden smacked of a big government abusing its power. As far as he was concerned, the governor of Missouri had actively sanctioned the murder of one of his own constituents and, in spite of how hard he fought to put a Democrat in office, John had no intention of keeping quiet about it. On April 13, his obituary for Jesse James appeared in print. An editorial rampage, it was unlike any obituary he'd ever penned before or would again. John spared no one, regardless of stature, and made clear to the party establishment that he had the clout to go his own way. While Democratic bosses in Jefferson City breathed a sigh of relief and were privately thrilled to be rid of a prolific criminal menace, John declared that "there was never a more cowardly and unnecessary murder committed in all America than this murder of Jesse James."[5]

Once upon a time, John had argued that the dash and daring of certain criminals could vindicate their illegal activities. The chivalry of crime, he'd called it. Then he abandoned social banditry as a political weapon and appeared to leave the Jameses and Youngers behind. Now he was leaning back into the past and applying his old standards of honor and courageousness to the Fords and Crittenden. In that context, John contended that their plot to murder James, even if he was a murderer himself, was not just cowardly but also dishonorable. Worse still, it undermined Missouri's entire justice system: "If Jesse James had been hunted down as any other criminal, and killed while trying to escape or in resisting arrest, not a word would have been said to the contrary. He had sinned and he had suffered. In his death the majesty of the law would have been vindicated; but here the law itself becomes a murderer."[6]

Readers familiar with John's work knew there was zero possibility of him not saying *anything* to the contrary about James's killing, regardless of the circumstances. That said, for those willing to stop and assess the situation objectively, he did have a point. The governor conspiring with criminals to murder another criminal didn't look all that much better than banditry. It was the sort of corruption John and other Democrats would have associated with Republicans just a few years earlier. At least with bank heists and train robberies, average citizens knew who was on which side. John lamented how the assassination of Jesse James made those lines much, much blurrier.

Frankly, it's difficult to believe that the man who gloried in those bank heists and train robberies—and excused the cold-blooded murders that fueled them—really lost much sleep over a temporary dent in Missouri's reputation for law and order. Nor did he appear to be fuming because the mythical Jesse James, the legendary figure *he'd* created, fell at the hand of an unknown turncoat like Robert Ford. That was just salt in the wound. What really riled John was knowing that he'd played a direct role in setting James up for the fall. The government deemed it necessary to hunt down and neutralize Jesse James by any means necessary because years of propaganda about quick shooting and fast riding had established him as the most dangerous highwayman in American history. John was the architect and driving force behind that propaganda campaign, which made him something like Dr. Frankenstein—the father of a vicious monster that needed destroying. Now on behalf of his slain creation, John spewed rage. "Tear the two bears from the flag of Missouri," he roared in the obituary's conclusion, and "put thereon, in place of them, as more appropriate, a thief blowing out the brains of an unarmed victim, and a brazen harlot, naked to the waste and splashed to the brows in blood."[7]

THE FORD-CRITTENDEN AFFAIR marked the beginning of a dark turn in John. Socially, culturally, politically—he did not like the world he saw developing around him. Entering what would be the final years of his life, John began to realize that halting those changes was increasingly beyond his control. So he receded inward, and slowly but surely became a man fueled more by rage than hope.

Part 1: The *Other* James Brother

By late spring of 1882, Jesse James was dead and buried. John Younger had been below ground for years. The three living Younger brothers—Cole, Jim, and Bob—were still serving life sentences in Minnesota. That left Frank James as the last marquee member of the James-Younger Gang breathing free air. It also made him the most wanted fugitive in America. Yet as much as John had mythologized Frank James into a gunslinging folk hero, in reality he was a rail thin, balding, middle-aged man whom a decade of tough living and habitual paranoia had aged well beyond his forty years. No longer a free-wheeling bachelor, James had both a wife and a four-year-old son. And he was tired of constantly looking over his shoulder for the next sheriff's deputy or the next Pinkerton detective or the next Robert Ford. More than anything, Frank James and his wife, Ann, wanted to settle down and farm—and they wanted to do it *as* Frank and Ann James.[8]

11. The 1882 assassination of Jesse James sent John into a personal rage. His obituary for the slain outlaw excoriated Missouri's state government. State Historical Society of Missouri, George E. Meyer Photograph Collection.

12. A sketch of Frank James made around the time of his surrender and first trial in 1883. State Historical Society of Missouri, Clay County, Missouri, Photograph Collection.

When word of his brother's assassination reached Frank James, it was the final straw. He began to make inquiries about how best, and on what terms, he might surrender himself to the governor of Missouri. After nearly two decades on the run, he would put down his pearl-handled revolver and take his chances with a jury—if allowed. It wasn't nearly that simple. There were likely to be multiple juries considering multiple indictments in a wide range of venues. Some would be friendly, others decidedly not. The governor—the same governor who'd already orchestrated the murder of his brother—would have outsized say in whether James should be extradited to Texas, Alabama, or even Minnesota. Put simply, Frank James needed help.[9]

Interestingly, given James's reputation as a guerrilla, it was a group of veterans from the regular theater that came to the rescue. The

13. Governor Thomas T. Crittenden helped orchestrate the assassination of Jesse James and the peaceful surrender of Frank James. State Historical Society of Missouri, Missouri Governor's Portraits.

14. Group photo of the twelve men that acquitted Frank James at his first trial in Missouri, which turned out to be just the start of his legal odyssey. State Historical Society of Missouri, Frank James Jury Photograph.

THE JURY THAT CLEARED FRANK JAMES.
AT GALLATIN, MO., SEPTEMBER, 1883

clique of Confederates included John, who still anguished over the assassination of Jesse James—and recognized an opportunity for atonement. Elite backers or not, a man with Frank James's reputation couldn't just stroll into the governor's office unannounced and hope for clemency. The first order of business was to settle on terms of surrender with the state. Because he was wanted in so many places, and because Robert Ford had recently blueprinted a path to fame that involved killing a famous outlaw, this was a tricky proposition. James needed a safe way to place himself in government custody and then some sort of assurance that he would receive fair treatment from the courts. For his money, and for John's, that meant staying in Missouri. Or at the very least, it meant keeping the hell out of Northfield, Minnesota. John was no stranger to lobbying power brokers in Jefferson City; since the early 1870s he'd peddled his own influence to help secure numerous political appointments within the Democratic machine. This was good news for Frank James. John not only knew which doors to knock on but also had a trove of favors to call up for return.[10]

Eventually, with the weight of influential friends behind him, John opened a direct line of communication with the governor. Initially, Crittenden had backed pardoning James. It was the easiest way to end Missouri's bandit saga once and for all. That plan fell apart when other states refused to extend James similar treatment. Crittenden had then requested that James surrender forthwith *and* that he testify against any James Gang associates still on the lam. James's wife, Ann, informed the governor what she thought of the latter idea, and it was dropped for good. Next Crittenden suggested that James meet with him, face to face, so they could work out an arrangement for safely surrendering—and possibly even choreograph the postsurrender legal situation. In return, the governor promised fair treatment and no tricks. If James accepted the invitation, he would be taking a major gamble: once he was with the governor, it was very possible that he would not be able to leave again, especially if they failed to agree on terms for a future surrender. To help put James at ease, Crittenden would allow him to bring a friend to the interview while he would only have one government agent in the room for his own protection.[11]

John urged James to take the governor up on his offer. "Both your wife and myself believe that you should have an interview with Crittenden as soon as possible," he advised. "You can rely on his promise." For John to offer this advice represented a stunning about-face. In April he had castigated the government of Missouri, headed by Crittenden, for sanctioning the execution of James's younger brother without trial, judge, or jury. Two months later, he trusted the governor to keep his word. Some of John's confidence stemmed from the belief that he had an inside man. Harrison Trow was a former Confederate bushwhacker who now worked as a government agent; he'd agreed to be Crittenden's bodyguard at the meeting. As such, John assumed that James would gratefully follow his lead and comply.[12]

Frank James knew a thing or two about survival. People had been trying to capture or kill him for more than half of his life. In fairness to Crittenden, the governor was offering real concessions. Most significant was the opportunity to meet somewhere in Western Missouri where James knew the land well and still had a great many friends. Still, something didn't sit right with the old guerrilla. Perhaps he sensed an ambush. Maybe he didn't trust Trow after seeing his brother slain by a onetime friend. Or maybe the offer just seemed too good to be true all the way around. One could hardly fault him for treading cautiously. It wasn't standard operating procedure, after all, for a governor to meet, essentially alone, with the outlaw brother of a man he'd recently had assassinated. Whatever the reason, to John's disappointment, James declined.

For a time, it seemed as though the entire surrender scheme might fall apart; that was, until the afternoon of October 3, 1882, when John boarded a Missouri Pacific train bound for Jefferson City. An incognito Frank James was already aboard and waiting for him. Visibly exhausted and unsure of how he would be received in the state capital, the last of the James-Younger bandits wasn't taking any chances. A shooting iron hung from his hip.[13]

THE LOCOMOTIVE EASED into the depot at Jefferson City, expelled excess steam, and clamped tight the brakes. It was before sunrise on October 5. Immediately after debarking, John led James through a short cut to the McCarty House, where the outlaw registered for his room under the alias "R. F. Winfrey." Their appearance at the McCarty House was anything but a coincidence. For years the hotel had been a personal favorite of John's. Thanks to its location between McCarty Street (so named in 1854 for the hotel's founder, Burr McCarty) and Miller Street, the McCarty House was only a few blocks south of the capitol building and the governor's office; during legislative sessions and elections, it functioned as a de facto headquarters for Democrat politicians and their allies in the press. John and Jennie were also close friends of the McCarty family—so regardless of John's personal woes or legal troubles, he was always welcome.[14]

After checking in, John took "Mr. Winfrey" out into the city. In hindsight, we might view this tour of the area surrounding the capitol as part of a rehearsal for the drama they intended to stage later in the evening. James and John decided to spring an ambush of their own: a formal surrender, to the governor personally, *in his office*, with less than a day's notice. This strategy was as bold as it was risky. By turning himself over to the state without prearranged terms, James was trading his only leverage—the government's inability to physically detain him—for a possible PR coup in the newspapers. Then again, even fleeting control over an otherwise unnerving situation must have been attractive to James. It was certainly more than his brother got. And when the balance of power did start to swing back in the government's favor, as it inevitably would, John had no intention of leaving the outlaw to face Crittenden alone. He would personally accompany James into the executive office, make the necessary introductions, and bear witness to whatever transpired. Peaceful or violent, it was bound to be a historic occasion.[15]

As the pair walked the streets of Jefferson City, it was impossible for John not to attract attention. Virtually everyone in the capital city knew him—or at least knew of him—and more than a few wanted to have a word. That not a single one of them recognized "Mr. Winfrey's" true identity was a testament to the mythology John had created in the 1870s. Very few people had knowingly seen Frank James in the flesh over the course of the last decade. That was by design. Like those of most hunted animals, his was a life lived in the shadows and on the margins. As a result, the portrait of Frank James created by John ruled popular imagination. Larger than life. Forever young. Extremely dangerous. The kind of folk hero you'd know for certain if you saw him. Thus, even if John had introduced his bald, middle-aged companion as Frank James—which was to say, *the* Frank James—people probably would have thought he was joking.[16]

Rehabilitating Missouri's bandit-despoiled reputation had ranked at or near the top of Governor Thomas Crittenden's priority list when he took office in January 1881. Now, nearly two years later, he was about to claim a final, symbolic victory over the James-Younger Gang. Short notice or not, he wanted to make the most of taking Frank James into custody. That meant accepting the surrender in style and having the right people present to see him do it. Crittenden threw together a small soiree for selected members of the government. The state treasurer and auditor were in attendance, as was a justice of the state supreme court, among other dignitaries. Perhaps of greater importance, the governor also made sure to have a squad of reporters on hand to chronicle his moment of triumph.[17]

Not long after 5:00 p.m. two men strode into the office of the governor's secretary, Fine C. Farr. He escorted them into the party, where cocktails and hors d'oeuvres were already in circulation. John marched straight up to Crittenden. "Governor and gentlemen," he announced, "this is Frank James. He is here to give himself up." Despite the *Kansas City Times* calling it "a scene without precedent in the annals of the state," hardly anyone in the room, aside from Crittenden, seemed to understand what was happening. Governor and fugitive faced one another. James's hand, as it had countless times over the last twenty years, darted to his holster. All merriment seemed to pause. For an instant Crittenden and his guests must have wondered if vengeance, not surrender, had brought Frank James to Jefferson City. To their relief, James didn't pull any triggers. Instead, he recited a speech: "Governor, I am Frank James. I surrender my arms to you. I have removed the loads from them. They are not loaded. They have not been out of my possession since 1864. No other man has ever had them since. I now give them to you personally. I deliver myself to you and the law." Crittenden and James spent the next several minutes engaged in a miraculously friendly conservation. Then, just like that, it was all over. Reporters bolted the room. Telegraph wires from Manhattan to San Francisco hummed.[18]

Following their historic encounter, Governor Crittenden allowed James to return with John, essentially under his own recognizance, to spend the night at the McCarty House. In the morning a cadre of state and law enforcement officials would escort James to the jail at Independence, Missouri, from whence his legal odyssey would commence. As Crittenden watched James go, some part of him probably wished the original pardon plan had worked out. Now, politically, the notion was a nonstarter, and Crittenden of all people knew it. However sympathetic James might appear in the present light, he, his brother, and their comrades had made far too great a mockery of law and order in Missouri to walk away scot-free. Across the border in Kansas, to James's old guerrilla war adversaries, it seemed like he was already getting away with it. "Frank James has disclosed the instincts of a shrewd politician," the *Emporia Daily News* reported on October 5, "by placing himself *in the hand of his friends*."[19]

On October 6, 1882, Frank James departed Jefferson City for Independence, proclaiming his innocence and fully intending to avoid a prison sentence. John went too. He'd completed his first task as "fixer," but much work remained. Indeed, getting James safely into state custody was only the beginning. The real fight—the one that would determine if he stayed in custody *forever*—had not yet begun. To have any chance of winning, James would need a significant war chest and a small army of lawyers. Luckily for him, John had been tapping connections and passing the proverbial hat well in advance of the surrender. Now he took up residence at the Merchant Hotel and got down to the business of arranging counsel for what looked more and more like the trial of the century.[20]

FOR ALL THE fireworks that accompanied Frank James's surrender and subsequent transfer to Independence, the lead-up to his actual trial turned out to be long, slow, and tedious. James would remain in the Independence jail for the better part of year while hearings in nearby Kansas City tended to pretrial issues. After connecting James with renowned defense attorneys Charles P. Johnson and John F. Philips, John had to return to Sedalia. He had a job and a family of his own to look after. But he stayed in close contact with James from Sedalia, frequently sending letters meant to buoy the outlaw's spirits.[21]

In March John provided an upbeat assessment of which way the public was leaning. "Up to your surrender," he suggested, "the great mass of mankind regarded you as a human monster, who should be hunted like a wild beast and killed on sight." "Now all this is changed," John announced. "And changed how? By your being in prison, and being permitted to see everybody who called to see you. Your bearing, your good sense, your quiet reserve, and your manly conversation, have made you friends everywhere, and these in turn have made other friends who have never seen you." John let James know that fundraising efforts were progressing well and then, perhaps overcome with his own optimism, made a bold guarantee: "You will never go to Alabama. You will never go to Minnesota."[22]

None of Frank James's letters to John survive, but by late May, James had clearly fallen into a depression and let John know about it. "Why are you so?" John asked, apparently baffled. "No man ever had stauncher and truer friends," he reassured James, adding that "your lawyers are doing some of the best work ever done by men—quietly, effectively, and surely," and money was flowing in for the defense.[23]

While Frank James awaited trial, John used the lull in legal drama to quit his post in Sedalia. He packed up Jennie and the kids, rented an apartment at the Pacific House in St. Joseph, and took over as editor of the *Gazette* in June 1883. Just like his previous stops in St. Louis and Sedalia this was supposed to be *the* job and *the* ideal setup. His new partner, George E. King, would serve as general manager of the paper, much as Morry Munford had at the *Times*, while John handled the editorial end of the house. An early article, perhaps better described as a manifesto, made very clear where John intended to steer the *Gazette's* political commentary. "We register no political decrees save and alone as they emanate from the Democratic Party," he stated flatly. Then with more of a flourish he added, "We have to do with no tickets which have not knelt for endorsement at the feet of some Democratic convention, and arose therefrom, purified by discipline, and made strong before the throne of the caucus." In other words, the *Gazette* was going to be John's artillery piece for shelling all the Republican-backed "isms" and reform movements that he believed were slowly destroying traditional, Southern society.[24]

Three months into the new business arrangement, King abruptly left the *Gazette* and established the St. Joseph *Saturday Democrat*. Along with King's exit, it was announced that John would now serve as both general manager and editor of the *Gazette*. Given his lack of business sense, this must have raised red flags for Jennie and his closest friends. In a farewell statement to readers, King wrote that he was politically "out of harmony" with the tone of the paper but did not cite specific examples. A few months later, King revealed in an interview for the *Ottawa Daily Republic* of Kansas that he'd resigned his position because "the 'James Boy Element' was too conspicuous a feature of the paper." Not content to leave it at that, King described northwest Missouri as having far more in common with Kansas, Nebraska, and Iowa, than with the Little Dixie region, known for pro-Confederate sentiment, guerrillas, and postwar banditry. His new paper, King suggested, "has had a splendid opportunity to represent the real Democracy of the Northwest, and has taken advantage of it to the fullest extent." Then concerning John, who King called "my friend" and labeled "one of the best fellows in the world," he added, "as a political leader he is simply a dismal failure."[25]

For King's money, both figuratively and literally, the brand of Democratic politics John wanted to push wouldn't play in a city like St. Joseph. Nor would it play in Missouri, generally speaking, for much longer. King predicted that "the Democracy of this state is ripe for a revolt, and if St. Louis wants to start the boom it will find enough help to sweep the James Boy element into everlasting oblivion." He warned that the next convention of Missouri Democrats ought not nominate mossbacks like former General John S. Marmaduke and his ilk—out-of-touch old men who condoned the political thuggery of outlaws in their continued waging of a long-lost war. "The people of this state," King iterated, "are ready to rise up against the presumption of this old element, and I, for one, would not object to the issue. It may not be considered orthodox Democracy for me to say so just now, but it suits me."[26]

King's interview with the *Daily Republic* raises the question of why he ever went into business with John in the first place. By 1883 John's whole identity as a writer revolved around traditionalist, pro-Confederate, pro-"Chivalry of Crime" politics. King knew this before becoming general manager of the *Gazette*; frankly, every literate person in Missouri knew where John stood on the partisan spectrum. They also knew he had no intention of changing his stripes. The most probable explanation is that King wanted to sell newspapers— something John excelled at—and thought he could stomach their ideological differences for sake of the business. The rapid breakdown of their partnership indicates that King realized he was mistaken almost immediately. Regardless, with or without King, John hardly had time to worry about backbiting in an interview. Not only did he have a paper to run, but finally, after nine months of hearings and legal maneuvering on both sides, the trial of Frank James was set to begin on August 21, 1883.[27]

Part 2: Trials of All Sorts

For its venue in the Frank James trial, the state chose Gallatin, Missouri. Gallatin had been the site of the 1868 bank robbery that James was accused of committing. It was also the seat of Daviess County, which included Winston, the scene of an 1881 train heist and murder that made up the second and third indictments against James. The courthouse in Gallatin wasn't remotely large enough to accommodate the media circus that would follow Frank James to town, though, so the trial was held in the theater and opera house. John was thrilled when he learned about the trial date and remained optimistic as ever. "When you are as free as other men once more, the past will seem like some impossible and intangible dream," John assured James.[28]

Though it took nearly a year to commence, the trial lasted only a few weeks. John did not attend. At first glance, his absence seems unusual, particularly given how much time and political capital he'd invested in James's defense. However, given John's insider knowledge of the James-Younger Gang's activities and the manner in which he'd glorified those activities in print, it's possible he stayed away to avoid an awkward stint on the witness stand. Certainly, the prosecution could have subpoenaed him anyway—and might have decided it didn't want a master manipulator like John anywhere near the jury.[29]

While John managed to avoid becoming entangled in the trial as a witness, the same could not be said for his friend and hero, General Jo Shelby. On the day he was called to testify on James's behalf, Shelby arrived at the courtroom inebriated; he wasn't falling-down drunk but was clearly not in full possession of his faculties or better judgment. During a particularly heated cross-examination, Shelby challenged the prosecutor in the case, William Wallace, to a duel. These theatrical hiccups aside, John's gauging of public sentiment turned out to be correct. In spite of damning evidence to the contrary, the jury in Gallatin declared Frank James innocent of the first robbery charge. The next two indictments would be addressed in the court's subsequent session.[30]

In the interim period between the trials, John again showed off his skills as a master propagandist. According to the Sedalia *Weekly Bazoo*, John "knew as much about the matter as anybody," and he claimed, for the record—based on face-to-face conversations with the governor—that Crittenden would never grant Minnesota's request to extradite Frank James.[31]

However close he might've grown to the governor, John had more to worry about than planting the seeds of antiextradition sentiment. Even with the lead defense attorney working pro bono, maintaining such a large group of legal specialists through multiple trials was very expensive. With no income of his own, Frank James relied entirely on the charity funds marshaled by John. John frequently updated James on the fundraising situation but never hinted that anything was expected in return for his efforts. He did, however, take exception to James questioning his motives in a letter dated October 17, 1883. A week earlier, John had supplied a statement to Missouri's Richmond *Republican* denying any and all reports that Crittenden promised James a sweetheart deal; to the contrary, it stated definitively that the surrender "was absolutely unconditional." It wasn't entirely clear why James protested, save for him being a very private man by nature. Whatever the reason, he hinted that John was flaunting his role in the surrender proceedings for personal aggrandizement.[32]

Far from apologizing, or even labeling the situation a misunderstanding, John's reply indicated that he would do it again if given the chance. "It had to be done for this reason: Every wolf on your track was lying against Gov. Crittenden in order to poison him against you, and to put him in a false attitude if he ever had your case to come before him." "Hence," John continued, with a discernible touch of annoyance, "it was but simple justice to you and him to make the statement I did." He then closed the subject, matter-of-factly, by stating, "Whatever I do at any time or upon any occasion is done with an eye single to your interests. As for myself, I do not care one tinker's damn what is said, I shall stay to the end."[33]

John might have put out one fire related to the surrender, but Crittenden had others to contend with that fall. In October 1883, his removal of two St. Louis police commissioners exploded into a front-page, partisan row. Various Democratic factions alleged that Crittenden had fired the commissioners in question because they weren't "energetic enough in prosecuting the gamblers" only to turn around and appoint replacements with well-established links to "the gamblers" of the Exchange Market. Naturally, Republicans who made up the legislative minority in Missouri were more than happy to egg on this sort of Democratic cannibalism.

Immediately after the assassination of Jesse James, it would have seemed unthinkable for John to stand the line in Crittenden's defense. Nearly two years later, the legal ordeal of Frank James had turned the governor (a former Union colonel) and John (perhaps the least Reconstructed man in Missouri) into political bedfellows. As he always did when an ally was in trouble, John came out roaring. He blasted the "Democratic dudes"—dubbing them "slobbering, imbecilic creatures"—who he believed were being manipulated by the Radical minority into attacking their own governor. To that end, John concluded one editorial printed on October 26 with the prediction that Crittenden's Democratic critics "will all wheel into line by and by and marvel that they were so easily duped."[34]

With everything else going on, could John really have cared much about who Crittenden appointed to the St. Louis Police Commission? Perhaps, but it was unlikely. Did John think Crittenden's authority as governor or his legal right to appoint commissioners truly was being threatened by a handful of disgruntled Democrats or Republican instigators in the press? Equally unlikely. John appeared to like Crittenden personally after working closely with him on Frank James's behalf, but they were not, and never would be, kindred political spirits. This full-bore counterattack was something else. Governor Crittenden had served as a character witness for Frank James during the first trial, telling the jury about his good behavior since being taken into custody. He also still held the final authority to approve or reject applications for extradition. So while it wouldn't have required much arm-twisting for John to launch an attack against turncoat Democrats, there was undoubtedly an element of quid pro quo at play.

When John backed Crittenden's version of the surrender, he told James he was willing to absorb criticism for the good of the cause. He meant it and was excoriated by opponents in the press as a leader of the nefarious "James Boy Element." Here, with the police commission controversy, he sensed an opportunity to do the governor another favor. Again, he meant it. And again, the criticism rolled in. "Major John N. Edwards is very unfortunate since he took control of the St. Joseph Gazette," a representative attack found in the Cape Girardeau *Courier* declared. "Not a single state question has he attempted to discuss but what he has been on the wrong side. His latest venture is the most unfortunate of all." The occasional duel notwithstanding, John hadn't climbed to the top of the editorial world without learning to absorb hits like these. He would happily take them and fire off all his biggest rhetorical guns—so long as it would be remembered when the time came for Crittenden to make the toughest decision. Put simply, John picking this fight over a local matter in Missouri had everything to do with avoiding Minnesota.[35]

Just as John thrust himself into the police commission spat, the state's lead prosecutor, William Wallace, made a stunning announcement: the remaining two indictments against James were being dismissed owing to problems with the state's star witness. Former James

Gang associate and noted murderer Dick Liddil could no longer testify. Without him the state lacked sufficient evidence to tie James to the train heist or the murder in Winston. Yet James's extradition to Alabama became possible by the sudden lack of charges against him in Missouri.[36]

In February 1884 James was rearrested and taken to Huntsville, Alabama, to face charges for an 1881 heist at Muscle Shoals. John did not blame Crittenden for allowing the extradition; the governor, he realized, was under tremendous national pressure to let the legal process play out without special treatment. If John was going to cash in the political tokens he'd accrued from Crittenden to block an extradition, it would be for Minnesota, not another Confederate state. Even so, James himself was deeply bitter about the Huntsville trial. He complained to his wife that his friends from Missouri had now abandoned him. "I have not heard from one of my MO friends," James carped, adding, "I guess they are waiting until the weather gets warm." Fortunately for James, John's promise to "stay to the end" applied to venues outside of Missouri, and he quickly took the lead in retaining counsel. This time John contracted Leroy Walker, a native of Huntsville and the former Confederate secretary of war, to defend James. For the second trial in a row, Frank James would have a lawyer *almost* as famous as himself.[37]

John had learned his lesson from Wallace's out-of-the-blue dismissal of charges. As the legal process unfolded in Huntsville, he was pulling more strings than ever to get James back to Missouri. That was the best—and really the only—method they had to fully block another extradition and take advantage of John's good standing with the governor. Dating back to October 1882, Crittenden had maintained that if charges existed in Missouri, he would not allow James to be sent elsewhere. The sudden breakdown of the state's case at Gallatin opened the door for Alabama to try James. Now, as soon as the Huntsville trial ended, John planned to have James arrested and brought back to Missouri. This was actually a caveat John knew well from firsthand experience. He and Emory Foster had each used it to avoid an unpleasant return to Illinois in the wake of their illegal duel. In a letter dated March 27, 1884, John informed James of his strategy: "I have used every resource I possess to have a Missouri officer at Huntsville re-arrest you when you are free."[38]

His efforts to shepherd James back to Missouri required even more effort than usual from John. In the same letter he wrote that "my leg is nearly well . . . in a few more days I hope to be up on crutches, but it will be some time before I can walk." As noted by local papers back in February 1884, John took a nasty spill while climbing down from a train coach in Kansas City's Union Depot. The impact of the fall broke his left leg halfway between the ankle and the knee and meant that John was stuck overseeing James's legal saga from a bed hundreds of miles away. Perhaps as a reminder to James to keep his chin up—or perhaps as a reminder to himself that even with a crippled leg, things could be worse—John concluded the letter with a somber update on a mutual friend: "I got a letter from poor Cole Younger this morning. He is still hopeful, brave, and high spirited." However high spirited, Younger and his brothers had been rotting in Minnesota's Stillwater Prison since 1876.[39]

On April 11, having heard nothing from James, John wrote again, saying "[I believe] this is probably the last letter you will receive from me before your trial, and so I need not say in it to face that trial like you have faced ten thousand dangers, and in every shape." John was clearly unsure of how an Alabama jury would react to James and appeared to be laying the initial foundations of a moral victory. In that context, it's difficult to deduce who John was trying to convince, James or himself, when he claimed, "Every point has been made and every single position of the enemy carried to the *last move* was a master stroke and no one yet knows what has been done, or where they [the enemy] have been outflanked." All he could really do now was lay around in his pajamas and wait for a telegram.[40]

When that telegram finally arrived, it revealed that John's hedging had been totally unnecessary. The jury in Huntsville declared Frank James innocent, and according to plan, he was arrested and brought home to Missouri. This time the state planned to charge him for an 1876 robbery in Boonville, but fate again intervened. A key witness died, and Wallace could not proceed to trial, so Frank James was released for the third time. This again opened the door for possible extradition to Minnesota. While James floated in legal limbo, John worked tirelessly behind the scenes to help stonewall Minnesota's demand. "Nothing is lost yet," he told James in a letter from February 1885. "All that you need to do is stand guard. We are moving heaven and earth here, and doing things that are bound to have weight, and to tell with effect in the end." Those "things" John mentioned included a lobbying campaign by elite ex-Confederates, including Shelby, who likely sought to redeem his poor performance in the Gallatin trial. They beseeched Crittenden to quash the application for extradition once and for all.[41]

After beating the odds in Missouri and Alabama, Frank James's handlers weren't taking any chances when it came to possibly facing a hostile, *anti-Confederate* jury in Minnesota. With that in mind, John asked James to compose a letter. He said, "[Write a letter] that I can show to certain parties, who desire to raise some money for you to leave the country on if you have to leave it." "This letter," he directed, "should state your exact condition financially, and say that you surrendered in perfect good faith, meaning to meet any charge in Missouri and to settle down, after your trials were over, into a peaceful and law-abiding citizen." Ever the master propagandist, John further directed James, "Tell why you are not willing to go to Minnesota. Not because you are afraid of justice, but of the prospective passions of the people." "I have an abiding faith. Stand firm," John commanded, before signing the letter "Your friend, as always, J. N. Edwards."[42]

When it came to combating crime, Governor Crittenden was no pushover. Regardless, in the face of pressure from John, Shelby, and a host of other elite ex-Confederate Democrats, Crittenden found reasons to stall Minnesota's extradition request. He was a politician, after all and could feel which way the wind in Missouri was blowing. The average Missourian didn't want to see Frank James hanged in Minnesota. After two acquittals, they wanted to move on and leave the old outlaw in peace.[43]

As it turned out, the gubernatorial election of 1884 provided a break for both Thomas Crittenden and Frank James. Crittenden did not seek reelection and was ultimately replaced by John Sappington Marmaduke, the ex-Confederate general whose nomination George

King had predicted would trigger a Democratic revolt in Missouri. Not only did Marmaduke win the governorship; he rode a major resurgence in pro-Confederate sentiment into office, proving King wrong twice over. John, the "dismal failure," ended up with the last laugh at his former partner's expense. Yet John could have chuckled at himself, too. For all the effort he'd put into grooming the governor to help Frank James when the Minnesota question demanded an answer, it was Marmaduke, not Crittenden, who would make the final call on extradition.[44]

The *Atchison Daily Champion*, the same paper that had once lauded Crittenden for being tough on crime, decried this turn of events. In late February 1885, the *Champion* reported that John and "twenty others, who are described as 'prominent Missouri politicians,'" spent hours lobbying Governor Marmaduke "not to give up the murderer and thief, Frank James, on the requisition of the Governor of Minnesota." Clearly assuming that Marmaduke would side with Missouri's old Confederate set, the editor concluded with a swipe at everyone involved: "The politicians were all Democrats. James, the murderer and thief, is also a Democrat." In the end, Marmaduke did decline Minnesota's request. "I here say to you that under no circumstances in life will Gov. Marmaduke ever surrender you to the Minnesota authorities," John triumphantly wrote to James after a face-to-face meeting with the new governor. Two and a half years after checking into the McCarty House with John, Frank James could finally go home.[45]

IN MAY 1885, once it became clear that no further legal action would be taken, John penned a letter to Frank James. In it he reminisced about all they'd been through since Jesse's assassination. "The more I recall the past," John mused, "the more does it appear like a dream. Never, I reckon, since the world began, did a man, similarly circumstanced, have so many friends as you had. They wanted nothing but to set you free." John clearly considered himself one of those pure-intentioned friends. Usually, whether it was his place in Shelby's wedding party, his actions in battle, or even his experience as a POW, it simply wasn't John's style to spotlight himself in a story. This time, though, he made an exception.[46]

Writing about the final fight against extradition in the first person, John brimmed with pride, exclaiming that "I meant to win that if it took a year." *I* meant to win. James likely didn't give the phrase a second thought. But for John, a victory and literal freedom for James meant a victory and spiritual freedom for himself. In John's mind, even though he had not pulled the trigger in St. Joseph, he owed the James family a life. By doing more than any other supporter to save Frank from prison, or perhaps the hangman, he cleansed his conscience of Jesse's ghost once and for all.[47]

Part 3: The Monster

For the habitually underfed and ill-equipped troops that waged the Civil War, each season brought with it a new misery: the chills of winter meant upticks in deprivation and disease; the rainstorms of spring turned dirt into mud and marching into a nightmare; the intense, inescapable heat of summer carried hordes of bloodsucking, germ-spreading insects; and the changing leaves of fall incited melancholia for bountiful harvests and happier holidays past. With these torments as backdrop, men witnessed unspeakable things: the bloated, splayed open corpses of equine companions and the stench of their charred fur; the intimate, grotesque knowledge of what happens when lead, iron, and steel collide with human flesh and bone; the wholesale slaughter of brigades, those same men rolled into pit graves by the dozen, their bodies contorted and intertwined like rag dolls; and perhaps worst of all, there were the distant, dying wails of comrades, left on the field overnight, condemned to die and rot where they fell. It was truly death and devastation on an unprecedented scale.

Then there were the "lucky ones"—the survivors of battlefield, prison camp, and surgeon's tent, who didn't always seem much better off than the dead. The pain of an old wound or a lost limb, or the emotional trauma of combat, or even the guilt of living when so many others perished, could and often did stay with men indefinitely. Such macabre portraits of the postbellum lives of Johnny Reb and Billy Yank stood in stark contrast to public commemorations of the conflict in the 1870s and 1880s. That was by design. The encampments and reunions, the statues and monuments, and the parading of moss-backed veterans down picturesque main streets were rituals intended to remember a specific version of the war: one that ended in 1865 without lingering mal-effects on the valiant rank and file. Yet behind closed doors, where those men could take honest stock of their minds and bodies, the war went on. It haunted them. And the longer it did, the more consumption of strong drink *literally* became a way of life.[48]

IN SOME WAYS John was a fitting representative for this demographic of silent sufferers. He drank too much, he frequently tried to break his addiction, and just as often relapsed. In at least one way, though, John's alcoholism was unusual compared to other veterans. He had always enjoyed libations, but his drinking did not become debilitating until 1882, nearly two decades after the war's conclusion. It is correct to say that John's dependence on whiskey likely stemmed from the war, but the fits of depression that prompted his postwar binges had less to do with his bad memories or recurring pain. Instead, John's war-related alcohol addiction, and its late onset, had to do with the way the world around him was evolving. His Confederate dreams had failed twice, and now, in the 1880s, the social and political consequences of losing were finally closing in around him.[49]

In booze John found a portal back to his neatly arranged Old World fantasies, though the trips were anything but free. As with any coping mechanism, the greater the problem, the more coping it required. John was not a young man anymore. His body could no longer bear the "self-medication" needed to placate his mind. As a case in point, John collapsed at an August 1885 Confederate reunion at Higginsville, Missouri (soon the site of the state's Confederate Soldiers' Home). One newspaper reported that he "suffered from the effects of over-exertion during the march and exercises." Another suggested that he was "stricken with apoplexy." The benefit of hindsight makes clear what caused John's health emergency.[50]

That acquaintances and even friends around John didn't realize what was going on isn't all that surprising, either. According to Morry Munford, John was able to hide his battle with "the monster of drink" from the public for many years. As Munford put it, "what he [John] did in these last years of his life as it appears on the surface—in his writing—is known to the world, but how much of effort and endeavor, of strife and contention he had to endure, and the fierce contest he waged against his only enemy day and night, no one can know." Ironically, given John's problem and how he hid it behind his pen, some of his sharpest, most forceful political commentaries from this period were diatribes against prohibition. In one such editorial, John took the prohibition faction of Iowa to task for spreading misinformation about Democratic candidates in Missouri. "Any cause is desperate," John hissed, "which turns to falsehood for help or succor. Any cause is doomed which puts its trust in the hallowing wilderness of lies." Furthermore, he concluded, "any cause will be damned which hires a lot of unprincipled mercenaries to perambulate over a State, bearing all sorts of false witness, and concocting and circulating all sorts of malicious stories."[51]

In another article, entitled "A Word to the Democrats," he focused not on the opposition, but on his own party. "A good many of you in Missouri have been ogling Prohibition of late amorously. Quit it." He asserted, "If the recent elections have demonstrated any one thing more clearly than another it is the fact that the Democratic sentiment of the west is absolutely opposed to Prohibition." Nor was it unpopular only among Democrats. In Ohio, Iowa, and Kansas, he reported Republican losses stemming from Prohibition platforms. After struggling for years to regain power in Missouri, John had no interest in seeing Democrats lose ground for the same reason. "The evils of intemperance are fully recognized," he told readers, "but it is not proposed to attempt to cure them with worse evils." In his own way, John was imploring fellow Democrats not to fix something that wasn't broken for the sake of appearing progressive.[52]

John may have claimed to fully recognize the "evils of intemperance" in print—but his private life, and that of the rest of his family, was another matter. Keeping John's addiction secret preserved his career. It also left his wife and their three children—the third, a girl named Laura, had been born in June 1881—to take the brunt of his sudden depressions and debilitating withdrawals without external support. Munford understood this, too, and wanted to help the family.

In late 1886, when John finally agreed to return to the *Times*, part of the deal included getting his drinking under control. "I do not care how hard it is," John declared, "but [I] want to not only paralyze the tiger but also kill him." "You can trust me in all the future about drinking," he promised Munford. "My honor is pledged to our nobleness of character."[53]

In one of his first pieces under the *Times* masthead, John set the political tone of his new editorial tenure with a pseudo-obituary for the Democratic Party. Dating back to the time of Jefferson, he reminisced, "Whatever sprang up in the shape of an ism, a craze, or a local uprising, there was the Democratic Party square in the breach, fighting the one long, eternal fight for the repose and the integrity of the national organization." Now rumors swirled that organized labor would kill the Democratic Party once and for all. John found this hard to believe, so he put the onus on individual laborers with signature hyperbole: "[If] there is a single honest workingman to-day in the country who would vote to destroy the Democratic party, that same workingman would murder his father." To *Times* subscribers, it looked very much like the same John that left in 1873 had come back to them.[54]

But he wasn't the same. After years of addiction, John simply couldn't control his thirst for drink. He relapsed shortly after arriving in Kansas City. Well-intentioned old friends took John out to celebrate a triumphal homecoming, and the resulting bender nearly killed him. It was decided that Jennie and the children would remain in St. Joseph until he could be cured. Munford first sought treatment at the local hospital. Then he attempted to restrain and rehabilitate John in his own home. Both efforts ended in failure, and Munford later recalled that whiskey "seemed to have a spell upon him [John] that no ordinary method could break." With Jennie's permission, Munford wanted to do something drastic. He would take John to the clinic of Dr. Leslie Keeley in Dwight, Illinois. Keeley was a world-famous alcoholism expert known for his patented Gold Cure. If he couldn't help John, it seemed unlikely that anyone could.[55]

While Munford and Jennie plotted an intervention, John wrote when he was sober enough. On February 13, he published a pair of articles. The first honored a member of Frank James's legal team—the one John had admired most of all during the first trial. His obituary for the preacher turned attorney Henry Clay Dean hailed its subject as a "many-sided intellectual giant." Most of all, John respected Dean's way with words: "When the mood was on him he [Dean] put spells upon people through the sheer force of an intellectual necromancy that forced them to listen even as the guest to the marriage feast was forced to listen by the ancient mariner."[56]

In the same issue, John picked up where he'd left off in the *Gazette*, with a heavy fusillade against advocates of prohibition, all of whom he found to be liars, sneaks, and hypocrites. He compared Democrats in the state legislature to the three hundred Spartans at Thermopylae and congratulated them for taking "by the throat the most vicious and disastrous species of legislation ever introduced into a Democratic general assembly, and strangl[ing] it with as little compunction of conscience as if it had been a snake." He then outlined for readers where he—and the *Times*—stood on the matter, which was "utterly opposed to every form and species of prohibition."[57]

For John, even as a man addicted to alcohol, this was a stand made for political principle, not personal access to booze. John contended that "temperance should begin at the fireside; that parents should teach it to their children; that the preachers of the gospel should embody it in their sermons, and insist upon it in all their devout and holy ministrations." In short, drinking was a man's personal choice. If he chose to drink and lost control of himself, it was *his* responsibility to correct the problem.[58]

Of course, disease isn't cut and dry, and certainly not the disease of alcoholism and its effects. Sending John to a rehabilitation clinic, even a private one, risked letting the rest of the world know the family secret. John was a public figure, and a significant part of his job hinged on how strangers perceived him. His railing against prohibition only made the possible fallout worse. Taking all of that into account, in years past Jennie might have bowed to the pressure of protecting John's reputation. Then he nearly drank himself to death, and she had no choice. Jennie agreed to let Munford take John to Illinois in the hope that once he was cured, they could all be together again in

Kansas City—the way things had been before the move to St. Louis. With Jennie's blessing, and with the same hope in mind, Munford and John began the journey almost immediately. That they'd made the right decision to find John professional help couldn't have been more apparent to Munford on the train ride to Illinois. John tried to make the trip sober. Partway through the four-hundred-mile trek, he was overtaken by severe withdrawal symptoms and caused a sensation before being restrained. Upon their arrival in Dwight, on March 21, 1887, they made no extra stops. Munford took John straight to Dr. Keeley.[59]

The Keeley process involved a twenty-one-day stay at the sanitarium in Dwight. At $200 for medical treatment plus an additional $21 per week for room and board, this was private care beyond the means of most Americans. It would have been beyond John, too, were Munford not financing the whole thing. Over the course of the three weeks, patients seeking a cure for alcoholism were given access to gradually diminishing quantities of whiskey. To mitigate withdrawal symptoms, patients took four doses daily of a proprietary medicine that Keeley billed as "Double Chloride of Gold," hence the moniker, the "Gold Cure." No one save Keeley and his most trusted employees knew the full contents of the Gold Cure. Under other circumstances, that might have raised a red flag or two. But the clinic advertised a staggering 95 percent success rate for curing drunkards. Consequently, anyone who could afford treatment at Keeley's tended to accept the mystery concoction without asking too many questions.[60]

It didn't take long for the true sum of the pain he'd inflicted upon Jennie and their children to start dawning on John. When sober, John believed that he was a loving, compassionate husband and father. Yet he understood that his personality had been far more Hyde than Jekyll these past few years. Since John's arrival back in Kansas City, Munford had been trying to guilt him into seeking professional help. Now he finally admitted to Munford, "The picture you draw of the sufferings of my wife and children is as true as God is true." "It is the knowledge of this fact," John lamented, "that has put me in a living hell for the last five years." Since roughly the time of the Huntsville trial and his broken leg, he revealed that his drinking had been "deeper, longer and deadlier than ever before." Given how much John loved Jennie—and how much he didn't want his children to experience a repeat of his fatherless childhood—to concede his failures as a patriarch, and to spell them out on paper, must have been a truly excruciating exercise.[61]

In addition to contemplating the collateral damage wrought by his drinking, John had also been pondering *why* he kept losing control of himself. "Is it not for want of physical courage, for no one has ever doubted that," he explained to Munford. He didn't think his problem stemmed from a want of moral courage, either. "For once at the side of a friend," he declared, "I could defy public opinion with infinite scorn, and go with him into utter darkness." "Omniscience knows," he concluded. This wasn't being dismissive; it was the rhetorical equivalent of throwing up his hands in exasperation. Whatever the true cause of his sickness, it was clearly going to take more than a few days to uncover. In the meantime, John proudly reported to Munford that he was conducting himself as a model patient. It helped that he was receiving more than a little one-on-one time with Dr. Keeley himself. Unbeknownst to John, Munford had written to Keeley and outlined the severity of the situation. But John was also a celebrity, and Keeley clearly enjoyed having a high-profile guest at the clinic.[62]

As far as John was concerned, less than a week into his treatment, the Gold Cure was already working like magic. "I have no more desire to drink than if whiskey were prussic acid," John boasted. He told Munford that he now "abhorred liquor in every shape." Munford had heard just this sort of thing before, though he must have grinned when John promised to send "several bushels of editorials." It seemed that some things, regardless of time or circumstance, never changed. As exuberant as John felt about the rapid progress of his campaign against whiskey, he also knew that repairing his relationship with Jennie was going to require more than a few days. She had stood by him through everything—the business failures, the duel, the midlife crisis, his frequent traveling for work, and the drinking. John understood the one-sidedness of their relationship; that it was the damsel, not the knight, bringing most of the strength and stoicism to their love story. Too ashamed to write her from the clinic, he asked Munford to send word of his progress to Jennie. "There are times," he concluded somberly, "when even I will not commit sacrilege."[63]

Over the next two-and-a-half weeks, John wrote frequently to Munford. With each passing day he expressed a growing confidence that the Gold Cure was remedying him once and for all. "There is a bottle standing upon a table in the room. I hate it," John wrote on March 30, nine days into his treatment. He professed to eating robustly, walking several miles each day, and being "as well as I ever was in my life." Sensing that Munford might not be taking his optimistic reports seriously, John posted a second letter on the thirtieth, intended to reassure his friend. "I was never better physically in all my life," John assured, "and, as I told you this morning, I hate even the smell of liquor. I *feel* and *believe* that I am saved. In fact I *know* it." It remained to be seen whether John was really saved—but one thing was certain: for the first time in a long while he at least thought it was possible.[64]

When it was time for John to return home, he wrote ahead to Munford, "What a glorious thing is freedom. I still hate liquor with an abiding passion." For his part, Dr. Keeley wrote to Munford as well. He verified that John was cured of his addiction to alcohol and confessed that he was sorry to see John go; in his typical fashion, John had made friends with everyone else at the clinic. He arrived back in Kansas City on April 12, ready to begin his new, sober life. Within a month, he'd relapsed and found himself back on a train bound for Dwight, Illinois. The monster, Munford remembered sadly, "had full control again."[65]

After his second round of treatment with Dr. Keeley, John again came home believing himself cured. He wasn't. Later chemical analyses of the Gold Cure probably explain why. The daily doses of medicine prescribed to patients at the Keeley Clinic included cocaine, apomorphine, atropine, and codeine. In effect, these injections masked withdrawal symptoms and temporarily replaced alcohol with powerful narcotics. For an addiction as deeply rooted as John's, after detoxing with the help of narcotics, remaining sober without them was virtually impossible.[66]

Throughout the spring and summer of 1887, John managed to keep up with his editorial duties. He wrote about all manner of current events, from monuments commemorating John C. Calhoun, the death of the Russian journalist Mikhail Katkov, and assassination plots against the Tsar Alexander III to mysterious sightings of British general Charles G. Gordon and the fate of famed explorer Henry M. Stanley in Africa. For the most part, though, the optimism he'd found on that first trip to Illinois was long gone. The bitterness that replaced it frequently seeped into his editorials.[67]

To the dismay of his ex-Confederate subscribers—men who took great pride in the Lost Cause, its monuments and veteran's reunions—John offered a commentary on how the government should handle captured Rebel flags. "As far as the great mass of the Confederate private soldiers are concerned," he asserted, "they do not give two-straws whether these so-called captured flags are to-day in some spread-eagle Federal museum in Washington City, in Nova Scotia, in Booroo-Booroo Ga, or in Afghanistan." After Appomattox, John grumbled, "There was no more cause. No more struggle, no more government, no more armed resistance—no more anything for the South except misery, poverty, graveyards everywhere, *crepe* everywhere, mourning everywhere, and finally the beak of the reconstruction vulture where once had been the musket of the brave invader." This was a peculiarly dismissive take from a man who had, in 1864, accepted a hand-sewn flag from the ladies of Arkansas, then remarking, "Let the affections of your hearts go with this old banner—all tattered and torn though it may be—cling to it, and linger round it, like the dew on a summer hill." A year later John had wept at the river burial of a regimental flag and genuinely believed in the possibility of a second, more prosperous Confederacy in Mexico. This acute sense of loss—and of belonging to a dying breed—became an increasingly prevalent feature of John's writing in the second half of 1887. It remained for the rest of his life.[68]

Once it became clear that terminating John's dependence on liquor was beyond the grasp of the Gold Cure, a desperate Munford starting looking for miracles. In the summer of 1888 he took John to Excelsior Springs, in Clay County, Missouri. He hoped the famed healing waters—a natural remedy—could do for John what Keeley's chemical cocktails had not. Munford left John to convalesce in one of the many spa hotels, which involved a regiment of outdoor recreation and various mineral tonics. Whatever belief he had in the healing powers of the water quickly dissipated; increasingly, he viewed his stay at Excelsior Springs as a waste of time. "Every hour here is purgatory," he complained to Munford, "with no priest in a thousand miles to help pray me out." "Still," he conceded, perhaps remembering that his friend had already paid for two stays at the Keeley Clinic and now for this latest treatment, "I will stay for [as] long as you desire."[69]

A few days later, likely going through severe withdrawal and finding no relief from spring water, John took all his frustrations out on Munford. First, he threw a tantrum over his recent editorial assignments. "I have gone over the entire political field from Washington City to Jefferson City. And yet you would put me to writing 'literary articles'," he sneered. "No, no Morry. I can not dance attendance upon 'Sweet Miss Fanny, of Trafalgar Square,' while outside the bugles are singing, 'All the Blue Bonnets are over the border.'" The real issue—which both understood but John would not admit—was that he wasn't capable of truly covering the political circuit from distant sick beds. In reality, Munford was doing a John a favor even letting him write about literature given his current instability. Next, John lashed out at Munford for pointing out that John had hardly given his treatment at Excelsior Springs a full try. "You also say: 'This is a sad ending to all our hopes and expectations.' Say, rather, their resurrection, Morry." "There comes a time to every one of my disposition," John snapped, "when he regains his second youth, or rather, second manhood. That period was very near to me." John planned to return to Kansas City in a week, vowing, "The fight from this on I must make myself, and, God willing, I intend to make it."[70]

After nearly two years of sparing no expense to help John find a cure for alcoholism, Munford started to accept that his friend was just going to be this way until the end. He had heard all the promises and pronouncements before, which is not to say that he stopped caring but that he no longer put any stock in John's will to resist drinking. Thus, when John wrote a few days later, professing "Morry, I will be a sober man. Our last days shall be our best," or again the day before departing Excelsior Springs, "Having fully resolved to change my whole life as far as whisky drinking is concerned, I only ask an opportunity to show you what is in me," Munford could do nothing but shrug and await the inevitable news of a crash. In fact, there were several crashes throughout the summer of 1888. By late August John claimed to be "at home working like a gopher, and taking gold cure within an inch of [his] life." He declared, "This time I will anchor the old ship or wreck her."[71]

In fact, John didn't do either; he continued to bail water just fast enough to keep the crippled ship afloat. Summer turned to fall and fall gave way to winter. In January 1889 he celebrated his fifty-first birthday. In a letter to Munford announcing the occasion, John revealed that he had recently experienced a religious awakening. John believed in God, but for most of his adult life, newsrooms and writing desks had been his churches. Therefore, when he wrote, "I went to my priest, laid my hands upon the crucifix, and swore to God who made us all never to touch liquor again," it presumably grabbed Munford's attention. Assuming that Munford wouldn't take his birthday covenant seriously, John claimed this bout with the monster would be different. After years of broken vows and premature declarations of victory from John, if Munford didn't accept this latest promise at face value, it's hard to blame him. Even John realized his credibility was worn paper thin. "You laugh," he wrote, admitting, "very well—you have good cause." But "watch and Wait," John told his friend. "Watch and wait."[72]

Several weeks later, on February 26, John published a commentary on the state of the Democratic Party entitled "A Very Plain Remedy." In the most recent election, Democrats had retained a majority in the state legislature, but barely. "The results of the late election showed all too plainly that the Democratic Party in Missouri was sick—sick enough to call in a doctor," John assessed. "Its malady," he continued, "came from a tampering with too many poisons. It had wandered far afield from the spot where stood many of its ancient landmarks." At this point in his life, with his broader dreams of building a new, traditional society in the South extinguished, political success in Missouri was John's last rampart. He had warned for years against accepting the "poisons"—liberal reform movements—into the party and now claimed the damage was done.[73]

Readers anticipating an explosion of blame and bombast were disappointed that morning. "We name no names and we make neither a crimination nor a recrimination," John stated with unexpected calm. "We have simply pointed out the wounds upon the body of the Democratic party—yet all unhealed and bleeding—and cry aloud for that blessed balm we know to be still somewhere abiding in this our political Gilead." And in this hour of crisis, John ignored his instinct to go on the attack himself, instead becoming an advisor to the Party. Put another way, and in terms he certainly would have understood, John laid down his sword and armor, stepped back from the Round-table, and slipped into the robes of Merlin.[74]

In this new capacity, John prophesied that the general assembly could win back the confidence of the people if "it will teach by example that the Democratic party of Missouri is what it once was—the protector of the poor man, the friend of the laboring man, a fore to proscription in all its Protean shapes, a zealous guard over the people's money, free from all manner of envies, jealousies, and spites, a true lover of the Constitution, a stalwart champion of home rule and States' rights." In short, the man whose verbosity had made him a household name throughout the western borderlands was warning that the people didn't want more words. They were tired of speeches and pronouncements. They wanted action. Better still, as John diagnosed it, they wanted the Democratic Party to "reform its ranks, and go forward into the next fight with all of its old-time resolution and audacity." He clearly believed that resurgence was possible. Whether John believed that he would be around to witness the battle was another matter.[75]

A few days before "A Very Plain Remedy" went to print, John penned Munford the sort of note that must have worried him. It was a mix of guilt, resignation, and fatalism. "You have done for me what but few brothers would have done," he wrote with appreciation to Munford. "I recognize the situation as fully as a I recognize the overthrow of the Confederacy." The situation was that John had relapsed.

Again. And the effects of the vicious cycle—binge, quit, withdrawals, hope, disappointment, binge—were impeding his ability to work. "I shall make one more effort," John informed Munford, and "if I fail I will come to you—loyally, frankly, and honestly, and say: 'It is finished. Choose some one else to do what you had a right to expect me to do.'" It's difficult to discern what exactly John intended with the letter. It's possible this was a final plea for help—a subtle invitation for Munford to swoop in one last time and attempt a rescue. It's also possible, and more likely, that John knew Munford would never fire him; feeling utterly ashamed of himself for taking advantage of their relationship, John knew he owed it to the long-suffering Munford to release him from his charge as caretaker.[76]

Part 4: Laura, Always Remember

On April 15, 1889, John dashed off a very different kind of letter. Word had reached him in Jefferson City that Morry Munford was seriously ill. Perhaps fearing the worst, John took a moment to remind Munford again just what their friendship had meant to him over the years. "There are but few men in this world for whose sake I would be willing to die, if nothing else but death would avail," John confessed. "You are one, Jo Shelby is another." Coming from John, a place alongside Shelby was the highest praise a man could earn. But it didn't shield Munford from admonition. "For God's sake take care of yourself," John ordered. "You think that you do, but there are times when you forget yourself and undergo ruinous exposure. That infernal steam heat in your room at the office would kill a Ganges crocodile."[77]

As their correspondence always did, the letter next turned to politics. "I think the fight here is won," John reported. That was a positive development, though his longer-term prognosis for Democrats in Missouri was decidedly gloomy. He apparently believed his "Plain Remedy" had fallen on deaf ears—that Democrats would not "come back to first principles" as he'd prescribed. With radicals and reformists still pushing in from all sides, he complained, "Everything is being attacked—beef, hogs, liquor, telegraphs, telephones, express companies, stock yards, school text books—everything." He predicted, "In about two more years, good-bye, Democracy!" He then launched into the sort of hyperbolic—and premature—eulogy for the Democratic Party that only John could produce:

> For a blessing it knelt at the feet of patriotism, and where it arose a long line of statesmen had been created. When the Civil War came it made all the lists of it jubilant with the clanking of its armor. And now what? Wolf scalps, imbecility, cowardice, demagogy, the chattering of monkeys, and the want of daily washing.

John was exhausted in Jefferson City. He looked forward to coming home to Kansas City "just as soon as we can force the fight here to a final vote." Then, forgetting his own troubles for a moment, concluded the letter on a decidedly cheerful note. "This is a glorious April day," he exclaimed. "Such days as these will soon make you as of old." And indeed, they did. Munford made a full recovery from his illness.[78]

John never made it home.

LATE ON THE morning of Saturday, May 4, John had just finished reading the paper. All was quiet in the Edwards family apartment. Jennie was laying down in the next room over. Their sons, sixteen-year-old John Jr. and fourteen-year-old James, were in Kansas. Both boys attended Saint Mary's College, just north of Topeka. Jennie felt just as strongly about schooling as John's mother had, and though Topeka was just a day trip away, the distance helped screen the boys from John's frequent relapses. Laura, just two months shy of her eighth birthday, was playing quietly next to her father's chair with a bubble pipe. Amid this tranquil scene, something suddenly felt wrong. He'd been unwell for the past few days—but he was almost always unwell these days. This was different. John asked Charles, the family's African American servant, to fetch his wife. Not wanting to disturb Jennie's nap, Charles said, "No let Mrs. Edwards rest." John asked for Jennie twice more. Each time, Charles demurred.[79]

John turned his attention to Laura. Because her birth coincided so closely with the eruption of his drinking problem, she had suffered in a way unlike her older brothers. John had been chronically absent—either debilitated or away seeking treatment—for long stretches of

KANSAS CITY, MO.

15. Perhaps the only truly verified photograph of John Newman Edwards, likely taken in the 1880s. His face shows the toll of war, politics, and addiction. State Historical Society of Missouri, Nancy Ehrlich Collection.

16. The virtually forgotten headstone of John Newman Edwards in Dover Cemetery. The headstone reflects the discrepancy over John's year of birth. Author's private collection.

EDWARDS

JOHN NEWMAN EDWARDS
BORN
in Warren Co. Va.
Jan. 4. 1839
DIED
in Jefferson City Mo.
May 4. 1889.

her most formative years. Gazing at his daughter now, regretting that time apart, and somehow understanding that the absence was soon to be permanent, he gently took the pipe. After playfully blowing a bubble in her direction, he said, "Laura, always remember that papa bought you that pipe." He laid down. Not understanding what was happening, Laura played nurse, wiping beads of sweat from her father's forehead. John closed his eyes.[80]

It is impossible to know what went through John's mind in this moment. He had survived so many near meetings with the afterlife, from the battlefield to the surgeon's table. He had survived disease-infested Union prisons, the escape from Texas and the crossing of the Rio Grande, Juaristas laying waste to Carlota, and the duel with Colonel Foster, not to mention the countless times he all but drank himself to death. Confronted with these and the other episodes of violence and addiction that defined so much of John's adult life, any skilled gambler would have bet against a tranquil ending. Here he was though, dying quietly, in a sober moment, in his own home, with his oft-neglected daughter at his side. John was just fifty-one years old when death overtook him that Saturday morning. Yet somehow, because of everything he'd survived, even making it to fifty-one seemed as though he had cheated death.

Epilogue

Fallen Prince

Word of John's death spread through Jefferson City like chain lightning. Various causes of death were reported—mainly to do with his heart—but John's closest friends and family knew the truth: that after years of constant struggle the monster had finally claimed him. When news reached the capitol building, shock swept over legislators from both parties. As a sign of respect, both chambers of the general assembly passed resolutions to adjourn for the rest of the day.[1]

For Democrats, John Newman Edwards was an irreplaceable voice and an icon of conservativism in the western borderlands. So too was he the shrewd political operator who used Confederate bushwhackers to crusade against Reconstruction in the 1870s and who then, in spite of his own "ultra-southern" tendencies, castigated the Party for electing ex-Confederates to high-profile positions in Congress in the 1880s. "He wanted the Democrats to elect the President next year," reported the Brown County *World* in December 1883, "and he knew that this could not be done if the Speaker and Clerk were taken from the Confederate ranks, as they have been." It didn't matter that Grover Cleveland proved John wrong by winning the 1884 presidential election. "The Democracy," as he typically referred to the Party, had to be smarter to survive long-term.[2]

For Republicans, John was the adversary they most loved to hate; an opponent to be reckoned with on all issues. It was hardly a coincidence that when students at the University of Kansas chose to lampoon a political editor in an 1875 stage production called "Quantrell the Queer," they chose him. In the play, the title character, "William

257

Clarke Quantrell," is a cuckold, played by an actor in a red wig, spectacles, and a fat suit. He berates Mr. Scoville, who was a caricature of John, calling him a "pencil pusher of the meanest class . . . Who'd steal the nails from a pauper's coffin . . . and to spite the children, [would] squash their mudpies!" Outraged, Scoville demands satisfaction. The two men exchange gunfire right there in the newsroom. Quantrell kills Scoville, and as the scene ends, a witness to the duel stands comically over Scoville's corpse and declares, "Now, like all true editors, he lies!"[3]

For *every* Missourian, regardless of partisan affiliation, John's writing had been a fixture of daily life for two decades. Subscribers didn't necessarily know the man whose list of "The Best One Hundred Books"—published just a month before his death—ran the gamut from Shakespeare, *The Bible, The Koran, The Pilgrim's Progress,* and "Tennyson's poems as a whole" to Voltaire, *The Iliad, Ivanhoe, The Wealth of Nations,* Gibbon's *Decline and Fall of the Roman Empire,* Carlyle's *The French Revolution,* and Dr. Francois Antommarchi's medical records of Napoleon. Indeed, even a close friend once described John enigmatically as "a stranger wherever he goes . . . one of the oddest and best of men . . . equally at home in the battle and the flowery fields of the imagination . . . noble, generous, childlike in simplicity, but great in mind." But they loved his eccentricities, his candor, his loyalty, and his fallibility.[4]

Across town, in the office of the Jefferson City *Tribune,* a dozen or so newsmen huddled over a copy sheet. They were gathered to honor the loss of one of their own—and to compose a statement on behalf of their guild that would be circulated throughout Missouri, Kansas, and Arkansas. Following a brief rundown of John's life and career, the assemblage of bereaved editors and correspondents declared that "his death has left a vacancy in Missouri journalism that can never be filled . . . [it] is a calamity to the press of the State." Later that evening, in another nod to John's editorial eminence, his body was laid out for public viewing at the McCarty House. Mourners, including numerous state legislators and government officials, offered their condolences to Jennie and paid final respects to "the Chevalier Bayard of Missouri."[5]

Such outward displays of affection would have mortified John. He was never comfortable with being singled out for celebration; it was why he always avoided the spotlight in his written work. On more than one occasion, Morry Munford interrogated John about this habit of dodging accolades. "His unvarying answer," Munford recalled, "was that he had almost the horror of seeing his name in print as he would have of facing hydrophobia." That was in life. In death it was a different story. John had always hoped to achieve lasting glory in the afterlife. This was the quest that had animated him from boyhood to grave—to join his heroic forebears in everlasting memory. So far, everything seemed to be going according to plan.[6]

At 12:30 p.m. the next day, a grand procession departed from the McCarty House. Led by recently elected governor David R. Francis, it walked slowly and somberly toward the Jefferson City train depot. Behind the governor strode a cavalcade of state senators, house reps, and other officials all dressed in black. A hearse, flanked by pallbearers, followed after the politicians. Jennie and Laura, along with several of John's closest friends, were brought to the depot by carriage. There a special train furnished by the Missouri Pacific Railroad Company waited to transport the casket and the funeral party to Dover in Lafayette County. The boys, John Jr. and James, made their own train journey home from Kansas. They met their mother and sister in Dover. Rather than the vast Confederate Cemetery at Higginsville—where John had attended reunions of the Iron Brigade—Jennie, in keeping with John's own wishes, chose to inter her husband at the Plattenburg family burial ground. John would rest just a stone's throw from the old Plattenburg Mansion where he and Jennie first met and where so much of their story together had unfolded.[7]

At 8:30 on the morning of Monday, May 6, Jennie's mother, Laura Plattenburg, hosted a public viewing in the family home. (Judge Plattenburg had died in 1886 and was buried a few paces from John's plot.) According to a correspondent from the Kansas City *Times*, "The casket was opened, and the citizens of Dover and the people from the country for miles around, filed in to take a last look at the face which was loved throughout the length and breadth of Lafayette

County, where he passed his early life, and from which he went to make a name that was honored and loved wherever it went." As many as six hundred mourners turned out. Hundreds more had planned to attend but misunderstood the time of the service. The *Lexington Intelligencer* observed that virtually everyone who viewed the corpse "was astonished and delighted to find their friend undisfigured by death, but looking as natural as though he had just fallen into a pleasant sleep." The peaceful sight touched even the most grizzled of borderland veterans. "Moist eyes of strong men gave evidence of the sincere affection with which the dead soldier and journalist had been regarded," the *Times* reported.[8]

At 10:00 a.m. the casket was closed and loaded into the hearse. Once a caretaker and now a pallbearer, Morry Munford wept as he walked next to his fallen friend. Other men tasked with accompanying the hearse included Alexander A. Lesueur, Missouri's sitting secretary of state; J. F. Merryman, one of the state's most prominent attorneys; and Major John L. Bittinger, one of John's closest friends despite his being an ardent Republican. Two days earlier, he'd arrived at the Edwards apartment for a visit just in time to enter the room with Jennie and discover John's body.[9]

The Reverend George Plattenburg was Jennie's second cousin and had known John since before the war. He oversaw the graveside services, which the *Times* noted "were simple, as Major Edwards had wished them to be." Plattenburg's eulogy covered John's service in the Iron Brigade, his intellect, his literary gifts, his generosity to friends, and his unique spiritualism—as fitting a tribute as could be presented in the moment to such a complicated figure as John. In addition to the on-site coverage provided by the *Times*, in the weeks and months following the funeral, dozens—if not hundreds—of obituaries and personal tributes poured in from all over the country. Some were sent to Jennie, others to Munford; still more were published in local newspapers. These memorials came from the pens of judges, congressmen, old friends, Confederate comrades, literary admirers, longtime subscribers, history buffs, and even Union veterans.[10]

Jo Shelby, who himself knew something about the "monster of drink," said "God never created a more noble, magnanimous, and truer man than John N. Edwards." Former speaker of the House of Representatives Samuel J. Randall wrote to Munford, "[John's] excellent judgement and splendid mental accomplishments are a loss which, in common with the good people of Missouri, I deeply deplore." George W. Terrell wrote in the Boonville *Advertiser* that one could easily imagine John as "this knight-errant of the nineteenth century riding down from the Arthurian days right into the heart of this grand State of ours, and into the very midst of the time in which we move and rejoice." And the Jefferson City *Tribune*, owned by the Republican John Bittinger, lamented that "John N. Edwards, the brilliant writer and prince of journalists, is dead."[11]

This commemorative torrent notwithstanding, Morry Munford captured the sentiment of nearly everyone who'd attended the funeral when he later confessed: "I have felt that no pen but his own could do full justice to such a character as that of John N. Edwards. To us who were for so many years his daily companions; who have experienced the loyalty of his friendship, the ineffable charm of his personality, and the masterful force of his genius, the loss is a bitter one, and words die upon the lips as we look into his open grave." It was the highest compliment any writer can be paid.[12]

For all that John observed and wrote about in his own time, it's fascinating—and more than a little entertaining—to imagine what he might have done with just a little more. Had John lived another month, he could have covered the Johnstown Flood. Had he somehow overcome his addiction and lived another decade, it isn't a stretch to foresee him editorializing the 1890s as only he could. The opportunities to wield his signature bombast and purple prose would have been endless: from the Wounded Knee Massacre, the Homestead Strike at Carnegie Steel, and the Spanish-American War to the meteoric political rise of William Jennings Bryan and the literary debuts of Count Dracula, Dorian Gray, and Sherlock Holmes. A bitter loss indeed.

IN THE COURSE of living out his fifty-one-year saga, John strung together a supporting cast of loved ones, friends, rivals, and enemies that was as extensive as it was eclectic. Some had already beat him to the grave. Henry W. Allen died of illness in 1866. Emperor Maximilian was shot to death in 1867. General Sterling Price succumbed to choleric diarrhea in 1867. In 1868, political assassins gunned down General Thomas C. Hindman. A heart attack killed Benito Juarez in 1872. Theophilus Holmes died quietly from old age in 1880. Halfway through his first term as governor, John Sappington Marmaduke died of pneumonia, in 1887. That same year, the former Confederate governor of Missouri, Thomas C. Reynolds—John's and Shelby's great ally in 1863 and '64—began to suspect he was losing his mind and "committed suicide by plunging headlong down the elevator shaft at the customs house."[13]

Here are the stories of the many more who *survived* John:

Charlotte, Empress of Mexico. Following her husband's execution by a Juarista firing squad in 1867, it was widely reported that Charlotte's mental health failed. Her exact disorder has never been definitively established. Either way, her brother, King Leopold II of Belgium, kept her locked away for decades. She died in January 1927 at the age of 86, outlasting John by thirty-seven years.[14]

Thomas T. Crittenden. Crittenden remained a Democrat for the rest of his life, but he left public office in 1884 after a single term as governor of Missouri. He practiced law in Kansas City for several years and in May 1909 suffered a stroke and died while attending a baseball game. He was seventy-seven. Though he denied to his dying day any direct knowledge of the Ford brothers' plot to murder Jesse James, popular culture has typically depicted Crittenden as a willing coconspirator.[15]

Susan "Edmonia" Edwards. In 1894, at the age of fifty-three, Edmonia married a school teacher named James F. Brawner. She remained in Virginia—near her sister Fannie—for the rest of her life, dying in 1909 at the age of sixty-seven.[16]

James Shelby Edwards. The younger of John's two sons, James did not follow his father into journalistic or literary pursuits. Instead, he owned and operated a factory stack painting business in rapidly industrializing St. Louis. Likely as a result of his constant exposure to smoke and chemical byproducts, he died of tuberculosis in 1915 at the age of thirty-nine. He left behind a wife and two children.[17]

John Newman Edwards Jr. Much like his namesake, John Jr. became a newspaperman. He made his bones as a night editor for the St. Louis *Republic* and by 1910 was a foreign correspondent for the *New York Herald.* Also like his father, John Jr. spent extensive time in Mexico, though he had no intention of building an Old-World Eden. His life ended suddenly while on assignment in Mexico City in 1912. The official cause of death was acute rheumatism. Like his brother James, he was thirty-nine years old.[18]

Laura Virginia Edwards. Laura attended Maryville College in St. Louis until she met Irwin Donovan, a recent graduate of Cornell Law School. They married in 1903. Irwin suffered a mild heart attack on the morning of their wedding, but the ceremony went on that evening. By 1910, the couple had moved to Muskogee, Oklahoma, where Irwin went into private practice. In spite of her education, census records from then on listed Laura as a housewife. What became of the bubble pipe is lost to history, but even without it, she always remembered. Upon her death in 1955, Laura's body was brought back to the Plattenburg family plot in Dover and interred near her father's grave.[19]

Mary Catherine Francis "Fannie" Edwards. Fannie was the youngest of the four Edwards siblings and carried the odd distinction of being born *after* the death of her father. She never married or had children but did keep an unfortunate tradition of the Newman women alive; like her grandmother and mother before her, Fannie fell victim to cancer. After her passing in 1918, Fannie was buried near Edmonia in Loudoun County's Union Cemetery.[20]

Thomas S. Edwards. Thomas abruptly disappears from the records of the Iron Brigade after being sent on special assignment in August 1863. Following the war, he settled in Arkansas, married, and fathered several children. Although he was John's only brother and the pair had been quite close as children, they did not appear to remain close after John's attempt to bring Thomas to Mexico and the subsequent collapse of the colony. Thomas did not attend John's funeral (neither did Edmonia or Fannie), likely because it was over before word reached him. He died in 1910 in Oklahoma aged seventy-five.[21]

Mary Virginia "Jennie" Plattenburg Edwards. Though John's work travel, his dueling, and later his addiction had greatly stressed her as both a wife and mother, Jennie still loved him dearly. She never remarried. And she never forgave Charles, the family servant in 1889, for neglecting to fetch her when John requested. Though initially devastated, Jennie rallied and published a collection of essays, articles, poems, and reminiscences in honor of John. It was in this volume that Morry Munford finally revealed to the public John's protracted struggle with whiskey. In 1892 Jennie was appointed secretary of the Ladies' World's Fair Board. Four years later, after a lengthy selection process, the Missouri Supreme Court appointed her to the post of state librarian for a term of six years and at a salary of $900 annually. The Sedalia *Weekly Democrat* welcomed the decision and labeled Jennie a "thoroughly competent lady." Around the turn of the twentieth century, she was the state-wide president of the United Daughters of the Confederacy in Missouri. Though she refused to allow the organization to reinter John's body at Higginsville, her lobbying efforts played a significant role in the construction of the Confederate memorial to Sterling Price and his troops in Springfield. All the while Jennie worked as a freelance writer for various newspapers and periodicals. Unfortunately, as she put her own intellect and literary talents to use, tragedy continued to stalk her—even after relocating to Oklahoma with Laura around 1910. She grieved the losses of John Jr. in 1912 and James in 1915. Not long after James's death, his widow passed as well, leaving two teenaged children behind. Jennie took guardianship and the children came to live with their grandmother and aunt in Oklahoma. When she died aged sixty-nine three years later, in July 1918, she had outlived John by nearly thirty years. Laura transported her mother's body home to Dover for burial next to John. For the first time in a very, very long time, they were together *and* at peace.[22]

Major Emory S. Foster. John's dueling foe turned friend, Emory Foster, suffered from Civil War wounds for the rest of his life. He eventually moved to Oakland, California, where he died in 1902 of mitral insufficiency, a common form of heart disease in which valves cease to function properly. Before his death, however, Foster lobbied for the release of Cole Younger from Stillwater Prison in Minnesota.

Though Foster was a Unionist who disapproved of banditry, Younger had saved his life during the war, and he intended to return the favor.[23]

Alexander Franklin "Frank" James. Upon the conclusion of his legal odyssey, James returned to Western Missouri with his wife and son. He worked various jobs—from shoe salesmen to lecturer—and occasionally attended reunions of the Quantrill Men Survivor's Association. In 1903 he and Cole Younger founded a touring show modeled off Buffalo Bill Cody's famed Wild West Circus. The venture was mired in controversy, and the former guerrillas did not enjoy much financial success. By the time James died in 1915, he'd already left strict instructions for his nephew Jesse James Jr. His corpse was to be secreted away in a special vault until it could be cremated. Weary of ambush even in death, James worried that scientists seeking to explain criminal behavior would steal and conduct experiments on his brain.[24]

Dr. Morrison "Morry" Munford. Since around the time of John's death, Morry had been suffering from pleurisy, a very painful condition in which lung lining deteriorates and inhibits breathing. His condition chronically worsened over the years, which made his catching pneumonia in February 1892 a virtual death sentence. The man who had done more than anyone else to rescue John from himself died, surrounded by family and friends, on March 27, 1892. He's become an obscure figure today, yet at the time, his obituary noted, "His career as the exponent of the West and as the founder and editor of the Kansas City Times, and the great part he played in the political, journalistic and business world are too well known and of too recent date to need lengthy recapitulation here." Though he was actually four years younger than John, Morry became the father, in many ways, that John had lacked as a boy.[25]

General Joseph Orville Shelby. In 1893 Jo Shelby came full circle: the Confederate general who once led a daring raid into Missouri was appointed a United States Marshal for its Western District by President Grover Cleveland. As Missouri's most celebrated Confederate officer, Shelby remained a prominent figure in and around Kansas City until pneumonia killed him in 1897. In 1908 a historian named William Elsey Connelley—known for his pro-Kansas, antibushwhacker interpretation of the war—made a number of controversial claims involving Shelby. Connelley alleged Shelby had confided to him that, among other things: slavery had driven Missourians to madness; John Brown had been right; and the Jameses and Youngers were "common thieves and robbers." It is impossible to know what Shelby actually told Connelley. Shelby's stance on race did soften later in life. He angrily defended his decision to employ an African American man in the marshal's office. Then again, Shelby's efforts on behalf of Frank James and his love for all things Lost Cause contradicted significant parts of Connelley's statement. Betty Shelby, who nearly survived long enough to see the stock market crash in 1929, hinted at no such regrets concerning her husband and the Confederacy. Not long before her death, she told a newspaper that she enjoyed "living in the world of yesterday with the sweet memory of her husband's achievements."[26]

TODAY THE PLATTENBURG-EDWARDS burial ground in Dover Cemetery is all but forgotten. For the most part, so is John Newman Edwards. His oversized marble headstone bares no epitaph. Sitting as it does in the middle of a large, open field, not a single thing about the rural cemetery hints at the political influence or the literary stature John once enjoyed. We do, however, remember the names and the deeds of the men he transformed into legends: Jesse and Frank James, William Clarke Quantrill, "Bloody Bill" Anderson, Joseph Orville Shelby, the Iron Brigade. This commemorative arrangement underscores the great irony of John's personal, lifelong quest for glory. He ran headlong into the Civil War, fully intending to win a place alongside his famous ancestors with saber and musket. But it was as a writer—as a chronicler of dash and daring—that John produced immortality for *other men.* This initially won him great fame as well. With the passage of time, though, his maker's mark faded from popular memory, and the creations lived on without him.

The visions of grandeur that drove John were part and parcel of his broader mission to "restore" Southern society. He dreamed of a traditional, hierarchical state modeled after the Old World of his imagination—one replete with emperors, knights, damsels, courtly love, and the unquestioned authority of a superior class of cavalier gentleman. Once established, either in the Confederacy or in Imperial Mexico or in the postbellum borderlands, it would remain frozen in time, immune from the "progress" of reformers, immigrants, atheists, anarchists, and all the political "isms" he loathed. Spanning from Virginia to Missouri to Mexico and then back again, John's travels in search of this mythical place—and his knack for showing up as a supporting character in so many pivotal historical dramas along the way—made him a once-in-a-generation thread. In that capacity, he stitched together the simultaneously unfolding plots of European royals, Civil War generals, Confederados, Mexican revolutionaries, noted guerrillas, infamous outlaws, pioneering journalists, famous writers, quack doctors, and western Americans of all persuasions.

To narrate the life of John Newman Edwards, then, is to do so much more than refresh his trademark on the legends of Shelby, James, and Quantrill. This is an accounting of the true size and scope of the American Civil War and its aftermath. It's the chronicle of a man who conceptualized and experienced the Civil War on international terms and then refused to accept Confederate defeat west of the Mississippi River *or* south of the Rio Grande. It's a story of Indians, Mexicans, Frenchmen, Belgians, and Americans brought together by conquest and the erosion, real or imagined, of Old World power. It's a tale about the meaning of the West to the American project. It's an epic about the nature of reactionism and modernity, revealed by a little boy who never grew up and a man who fantasized about returning to a boyhood that never was.

Taken together, John's story is a grand collage of nineteenth-century America—and of the American Experience—more meaningful than any of its individual components. This collage is the world that made and destroyed John Newman Edwards as he attempted to reshape it. The more we come to understand that world, and the better our grasp of the source of John's never-ending Civil War, the more we will appreciate how it made *us* too. And how it could destroy us yet.

Acknowledgments

Over the years, Joseph Beilein, Matthew Stanley, Patrick Lewis, Eric Burke, and Andrew Fialka have become something like a Civil War borderlands Rat Pack. They each read parts of the manuscript. So too did Trae Welborn, Katherine Mellen-Charron, and Megan Kate Nelson. All their collective generosity and thoughtfulness undoubtedly made this a better book. Later in the process, peer-reviewers Todd Wahlstrom and Christopher Phillips provided immensely helpful feedback. Chris—who it's worth noting is the historical dean of the Missouri-Kansas borderlands—continued to assist even as the manuscript moved toward final production. I'm also greatly indebted to Andrew Fialka, though he'll never admit it, for being so magnanimous with his digital cartography skills.

My editor at UNP, Bridget Barry, is as good as they come. If you're a fan of classic American West literature—like I am—the Bison imprint really means something special. From my opening pitch about this being a Bison title, Bridget saw why the saga of John Newman Edwards demanded a feature-length treatment. Better still, we were immediately on the same page about avoiding a monograph in disguise; she fully supported the idea of a biography researched and vetted to academic standards but genuinely narrated for nonacademic readers. The book was supposed to be finished in two years and ended up taking five. Bridget never blinked. I can't thank her enough.

If thirty-six-year-old me could send a message back in time to twenty-four-year-old me, it would read: "John is right. If you want to tell this story, wait until you can really tell it. You're gonna owe him big." As an incoming doctoral student, I thought this biography would make a great dissertation. Needless to say, I was utterly oblivious to how much I didn't know about the craft of writing. I was equally unaware of the fact that biographies are just damned hard things to finish, even for the people who write them for a living. (How T. J. Stiles does it, I will never comprehend.) So now knowing a little bit of what I didn't know then, bless John Inscoe—my advisor and dear friend—for counseling me to wait. I really *do* owe him big, and I truly hope he knows how much I appreciate all his guidance.

I BEGAN RESEARCHING John Newman Edwards about two years before my future wife and I met; I then started writing this book a few years after we got married. Most relationships don't come with the specter of an alcoholic, duel-fighting politico for a third wheel. Kylie has handled it with immeasurable grace. She's been a wellspring of encouragement and support and an astute historical consigliere, and she has never once complained about my obsession with the life of an obscure man who has been dead for more than thirteen decades. She miraculously helped me find the time to write multiple chapters while both of us were teaching virtually and trying to keep two toddlers entertained amid the chaos of COVID-19 lockdowns. I couldn't do any of this without her, and more to the point, I never want to try.

I would be remiss not to thank my parents, Jerry and Becky, and Kylie's parents, Jack and Peggy. They've been wonderfully supportive from start to finish. (Understanding that obsession with the dead guy, again.) In their own special ways, so have our three children, Eleanor, Grant, and Beatrice. Each arrived while this manuscript was in progress, and though they have no idea what daddy has been writing about after bedtime for the last five years, watching them grow up has been a constant source of inspiration and happiness. My goodness are they funny—and smart—and the antithesis of what so much of this book is about. Fittingly then, if not a little ironically, it is for them.

Notes

Abbreviations

(This list of abbreviations is not a complete account of sources cited in the notes.)

APC	Copy of image in author's private collection
ATQ	"A Terrible Quintette," November 22, 1873
CSR-NARA	*Compiled Service Records of Confederate Soldiers Who Served in Organizations from the State of Missouri*, National Archives and Records Administration, Washington DC
EL-SHSMC	John Newman Edwards Letters, State Historical Society of Missouri, Columbia
FCCC	Frederick County Circuit Court, Winchester, Virginia
GR-MSR	Governors Records, Missouri State Archives
JIC-OHC	Johnson's Island Collection, Ohio History Center, Columbus OH
JIOL-OHC	Johnson's Island, Ohio Letters, 1863–65, Ohio History Center, Columbus OH
JNE	*John N. Edwards: Biography, Memoirs, Reminiscences and Recollections.* Edited by Mary Virginia Edwards. Kansas City MO: J. Edwards, 1889.
KCT	*Kansas City Times*
MT	*Mexican Times*
NHGIS	*National Historical Geographic Information System*, University of Minnesota
NG	*Noted Guerrillas.* John N. Edwards. Bryan, Brand, 1877.
OR	*The War of the Rebellion: A Compilation of the Official Records of the Union and Confederate Armies.* Washington DC: Government Printing Office, 1880–1901.
PB-SHC	Preston S. Brooks Papers, Southern Historical Collection
PB-SCL	Preston Smith Brooks Papers, South Caroliniana Library

RGGC	Rebecca Good Genealogy Collection, Laura Virginia Hale Archive
SEM	*Shelby's Expedition to Mexico.* John N. Edwards. Austin TX: Steck, 1964.
SHM	*Shelby and His Men.* John N. Edwards. Cincinnati OH: Miami Printing, 1867.
SHSMC	State Historical Society of Missouri, Columbia
SJBJ	Stewart J. Bell Archives, Handley Library, Winchester VA
WHL	*Watts-Hays Letters*
WCCC	Warren County Circuit Court, Front Royal VA

Preface

1. Sutherland, "Long, Hard Winter," 11, 14; Chad Evans, "Reconstructing January 1855–56 . . . ," Weather Blog, 44News Evansville; "Coldest Day of the Age," *Western Reserve Chronicle,* January 23, 1856; "Cool," *Belmont Chronicle,* January 10, 1856; "Cold Weather," *Anti-Slavery Bugle,* January 12, 1856; "River Closed," *Spirit of Democracy,* December 31, 1856; "The Slave Exodus—Its Results," *Western Reserve Chronicle,* March 12, 1856; "The Weather," *Louisville Daily Courier,* February 13, 1856.

2. Coffin, *Reminiscences,* 557–58; Reinhardt, *Who Speaks,* 4.

3. Coffin, *Reminiscences,* 558–59. For the full text of the Fugitive Slave Law of 1850, see *Public Acts of the Thirty-First Congress of the United States,* September 18, 1850, vol. 9, Pub.—59, 462–66.

4. Reinhardt, *Who Speaks,* 4; "Arrest of Fugitive Slaves," *Buffalo Commercial,* February 1, 1856. "The Late Negro Murder in Cincinnati," *Weekly Indiana State Sentinel,* February 7, 1856; "The Cincinnati Tragedy," *Indiana Herald,* February 20, 1856; "Another Stampede," *Pittsburgh Gazette,* February 5, 1856; "The Fugitive Slaves," *Fremont Weekly Journal,* February 8, 1856.

5. Coffin, *Reminiscences,* 558; "Stampede of Slaves, A Tale of Horror," *Eaton Democrat,* February 7, 1856.

6. Coffin, *Reminiscences,* 559; "The Fugitive Slave Case," *Cincinnati Enquirer,* January 31, 1856; "Dreadful Slave Tragedy," *The Liberator,* February 8, 1856.

7. Coffin, *Reminiscences,* 559–60; Reinhardt, *Who Speaks,* 5; "The Slave Case," *Anti-Slavery Bugle,* February 9, 1856.

8. Walther, *The Shattering,* 34–36; Monaghan, *Civil War,* 34–44.

9. Cordley, *A History,* 1–6, 79, 87, 104; Castel, *William Clarke Quantrill,* 1–2.

10. Cordley, *A History,* 28–32, 41–43; Castel, *William Clarke Quantrill,* 2–8.

11. Cordley, *A History,* 92–94; "The 'Free State Hotel' Finished," *Squatter Sovereign,* May 27, 1856.

12. Cordley, *A History,* 99; "Lawrence Taken!" *New-York Tribune,* May 31, 1856; "The Destruction of Lawrence," *Buffalo Daily Republic,* May 28, 1856.

13. Cordley, 100.
14. Cordley, *A History*, 99–100; Monaghan, *Civil War*, 56–57; Castel, *William Clarke Quantrill*, 9.
15. Cordley, *A History*, 100–101; Monaghan, *Civil War*, 58; Castel, *William Clarke Quantrill*, 10.
16. Cordley, *A History*, 101–3; Monaghan, *Civil War*, 56–58; Castel, *William Clarke Quantrill*, 10; Walther, *The Shattering*, 91; "The Fate of Lawrence," *Squatter Sovereign*, May 27, 1856; "The Sacking of Lawrence," *New-York Tribune*, June 9, 1856.
17. Berry and Welborn, "Cane," 6; Sinha, "The Caning," 243–44.
18. Berry and Welborn, "Cane," 13; Butler, "On the Difficulty of Messrs. Brooks and Sumner"; Sumner, "The Crime," 3.
19. Walther, *The Shattering*, 98–99; "Statement of Preston Brooks, May 28, 1856," PB-SCL; "Preston Brooks to J. H. Brooks, May 23, 1856," PB-SHC. Thanks to Steve Berry for generously providing copies of Preston Brooks correspondence and statements.
20. "Mr. Sumner's Statement Before the Investigating Committee," *The Liberator*, May 30, 1856; Campbell, "Alleged Assault Upon Senator Sumner," 1–5; "Statement of Preston Brooks, May 28, 1856," PB-SCL; "Preston Brooks to J. H. Brooks, May 23, 1856," PB-SCL.
21. "Preston Brooks to J. H. Brooks, May 23, 1856," PB-SHC; "Attempt to Murder Hon. Charles Sumner," *The Liberator*, May 30, 1856; Walther, 99; Berry and Welborn, "Cane," 15; Sinha, "The Caning," 233–34.
22. "Preston Brooks to Hampton Brooks, June 21, 1856," PB-SCL; "J. Swanson to Preston Brooks, May 30, 1856," PB-SCL; "J. R. Adams to Preston Brooks, May 26, 1856," PB-SCL; Berry and Welborn, 16; *The Sumner Outrage*; Bingham, "The Assault," 1–8; Giddings, "Privilege of the Representative."
23. Walther, *The Shattering*, 101–2.

Introduction

1. Frederick County Virginia Marriage Register #1, July 14, 1782, to October 6, 1853, FCCC, 20-A, 48; Hackett and Good, *Frederick County Virginia Marriage Bonds*; Virginia, Select Marriages, 1785–1940, Ancestry.com; "Edwards Surname Files," RGGC; Warren County Virginia Register of Deaths, 1853–1874, WCCC, 12. "June 29, 1857, Deed of John W. Newman to Mary Ann Edwards," RGGC.
2. Frederick County Virginia Index to Wills #1, 1743–1917, FCCC, 34.
3. "Francis C. Brown's Appraisiment [sic]," Frederick County Virginia Will Book #15, SJBJ, 370–73, 375, 380–87; "Francis C. Brown's Estate," Frederick County Virginia Will Book #15, SJBJ, 418–20; "Francis C. Brown Estate A/C," Frederick County Virginia Will Book #19, SJBJ, 159.

4. 1850 United States Federal Census; "Inventory and Appraisement of the Personal Estate of John Edwards," Warren County Virginia General Index to Wills, 1835–1845, Book A, WCCC, 223–24; "A Beloved Resident Goes to Her Final Rest," *Loudoun Times-Mirror*, March 27, 1918.

5. "Departed this life . . . ," *Genius of Liberty* (Leesburg, Virginia) February 11, 1843.

6. "Inventory and Appraisement," Warren County Virginia General Index to Wills, 1835–1845, WICK, 223–24.

7. 1850 United States Federal Census; 1860 United States Federal Census; 1870 United States Federal Census; 1880 United States Federal Census; 1900 United States Federal Census; 1910 United States Federal Census; "A Beloved Resident," *Loudoun Times-Mirror*, March 27, 1918.

8. Conard, *Encyclopedia*, 354.

9. Conard, *Encyclopedia*, 354. In his study of Jo Shelby, Anthony Arthur goes out of his way to claim that Edwards was both poorly educated ("largely self-taught") and a "friendless" child. These claims, which have been echoed by other writers, appear to be based on George Plattenburg's retrospective biography in *JNE* (1889)—but given the underlying sentiment of Plattenburg's piece, he was almost certainly guilty of overstating the qualities that he believed made Edwards an enigmatic and romantic figure in death. Arthur, *Shelby's March*, 18; *JNE*, 9; Saults, "Don Quixote," 20–23.

10. *JNE*, 9.

11. *JNE*, 9–10; Conard, *Encyclopedia*, 355.

12. Hollister and Norman, *Five Famous Missourians*, 336, 339, 340; O'Flaherty, *Undefeated Rebel*, 24–25.

13. Castel, *William Clarke Quantrill*, 4–5; Hollister and Norman, *Five Famous Missourians*, 341–42.

14. Connelley, *Quantrill*, 207. It's worth noting that Connelley was equally prone to political bias and exaggeration in his historical writing. For instances of Connelley critiquing Edwards the historian, see 162–65, 204, 207, 243, 246, 312; Stiles, *Last Rebel*, 226, 289, 355; Arthur, *Shelby's March*, 18, 32–33, 173.

15. On the "New Civil War in the West" and an expanded chronology of the American Civil War, see Nelson, *Three-Cornered War*; Waite, *West of Slavery*; Downs, *After Appomattox*; also see essays in Scharff, *Empire and Liberty*; and Arenson and Graybill, *Civil War Wests*.

16. For standout examples of internationally oriented scholarship see Pani, "Law, Allegiance, and Sovereignty"; Karp, *This Vast Southern Empire*; Wahlstrom, *The Southern Exodus*; Hahn, *A Nation Without Borders*; and essays by Gregory Downs and Nicholas Guyatt in Arenson and Graybill, *Civil War Wests*.

1. Into the Forge

1. Chesnut, *Diary*, 35–36.
2. Population, crop yield, slave population, and acreage data for Lafayette County from NHGIS; *History of Lafayette County*, 205–310.
3. City of Lexington, 1860 Manufacturing figures, NHGIS; 1860 United States Federal Census. *History of Lafayette County*, 431–63, 642; Shelby House Registration Form.
4. Beasley, *Shelby's Expedition*, xiii—xv; Saults, "Don Quixote," 21; Evans, "John Newman Edwards," 282–83; Lavery, "The Man," 3.
5. Sadie Claude Curtis, "Tiny Woman, Once General Shelby's Bride, Tells of Great Adventure and Romance When Mexico Had an Emperor," n.d., from Joseph Orville Shelby, Scrapbook, 1865–1932, SHSMC; O'Flaherty, *Undefeated Rebel*, 48–50.
6. Owing to the visit of Kansas Red Legs to the offices of the *Expositor* in 1862, John's original descriptions of the Shelby wedding were lost to posterity. However, witnesses recalled both the wedding and John's ornate coverage of it. For firsthand accounts of John's account, see O'Flaherty, *Undefeated Rebel*, 49–50.
7. *History of Lafayette County*, 272; Young, *Young's History*, 260; "Oliver Anderson to his Wife," February 4, 1865, in Byars, *Memoirs*, 86–87; "Oliver Anderson Biography," Missouri State Parks.
8. "Insurrection at Harper's Ferry: Old John Brown Mortally Wounded," *Topeka Tribune*, October 22, 1859.
9. Thoreau, "A Plea."
10. "John Brown's Speech," *New York Times*, November 3, 1859.
11. Warren County Register of Deaths, 1853–1874, 12, WCCC; U.S. Federal Census Mortality Schedules, 1850–1885.
12. Monaghan, *Civil War*, 119, 129–31; Phillips, *Missouri's Confederate*, 238–39, 242–44, 246–51; Gerteis, *The Civil War*, 9–10; Castel, *William Clarke Quantrill*, 47–49.
13. Phillips, *Missouri's Confederate*, 238–39, 241, 245, 248; Castel, *General Sterling Price*, 30–32.
14. Phillips, *The Rivers*, 138; Phillips, *Missouri's Confederate*, 251–52; SHM, 21–24, 28–30; Monaghan, 140–42; Gerteis, *The Civil War*, 34; Rorvig, "The Significant Skirmish," 129–30, 137, 140–45; "J. D. McKown to Mother," October 19, 1863, Pearce Civil War Collection, Navarro College.
15. *History of Lafayette County*, 374; "Southern Forces at the Battle of Lexington," Battle of Lexington State Historic Site, Missouri Department of Natural Resources, Division of State Parks.
16. McGhee, *Guide to Missouri*, 72–73; *History of Lafayette County*, 374; "Southern Forces at the Battle of Lexington," Lexington State Historic Site. Examples

of histories that do not have John enlisting until 1862 include Webb, *Battles and Biographies*, 327; Beasley, *Shelby's Expedition*, xvi; Lavery, "The Man," 4; Evans, "John Newman Edwards," 282.

17. O'Flaherty, *Undefeated Rebel*, 66; *SHM*, 30.

18. "No. 2, Report of Colonel Franz Sigel, Third Missouri Infantry (Union)," July 11, 1861, *OR*, series 1, vol. 3, part 1, 17.

19. "Report of Franz Sigel," *OR*, 17; "No. 3, Report of Brig. Gen. James S. Rains, Missouri State Guard (Confederate)," July 20, 1861, *OR*, series 1, vol. 3, part 1, 20–21; Hinze and Farnham, *The Battle of Carthage*, 101, 115; *SHM*, 30–31.

20. "Report of James S. Rains," *OR*, 20; "No. 4, Report of Col. Richard H. Weightman, commanding First Brigade, Second Division, Missouri State Guard," July 17, 1861, *OR*, series 1, vol. 3, part 1, 22–23; Hinze and Farnham, *The Battle of Carthage*, 115–18; *SHM*, 30–31; O'Flaherty, *Undefeated Rebel*, 68; Gerteis, *The Civil War*, 45.

21. "No. 1, Report of Capt. Thomas Sweeny, Second U. S. Infantry," July 12, 1861, *OR*, series 1, vol. 3, part 1, 15; "Report of Franz Sigel," *OR*, 17; Monaghan, *Civil War*, 153–54; Hinze and Farnham, *The Battle of Carthage*, 127–28; O'Flaherty, *Undefeated Rebel*, 68–69; "Report of James S. Rains," *OR*, 20–21.

22. "Report of Franz Sigel," *OR*, 17–18; *SHM*, 31; Hinze and Farnham, *The Battle of Carthage*, 91–93 129–30; Monaghan, *Civil War*, 151; Gerteis, *The Civil War*, 46–47.

23. *SHM*, 31; "Report of Franz Sigel," *OR*, 18–19; Hinze and Farnham, *The Battle of Carthage*, 132–33, 140–42; Monaghan, *Civil War*, 154.

24. "Report of Thomas Sweeny," *OR*, 15; "Report of Franz Sigel," *OR*, 18–19; "Report of James S. Rains," *OR*, 21; "No. 5, Report of Col. James McCown," *OR*, series 1, vol. 3, part 1, 26; "No. 6, Report of Col. R. L. Y. Peyton," July 19, 1861, *OR*, series 1, vol. 3, part 1, 28; "No. 8, Report of Brig. Gen. John B. Clark," July 19, 1861, *OR*, series 1, vol. 3, part 1, 31; Monaghan, *Civil War*, 154; Gerteis, *The Civil War*, 47.

25. "Report of Richard H. Weightman," *OR*, 23–24; "Report of James S. Rains," *OR*, 21–22; Monaghan, *Civil War*, 151, 154–56; Gerteis, *The Civil War*, 47–48; Hinze and Farnham, *The Battle of Carthage*, 172–75, 178–79; "Battle of Carthage, July 5," Civil War Trust.

26. H. L. Boon, "The Battle of Carthage," *Glasgow Weekly Times*, July 18, 1861; "Report of James S. Rains," July 20, 1861, *OR*, 21–22.

27. "Glorious Victory!," *Weekly Atchison Champion*, July 13, 1861; "Another Battle in Missouri," *Evening Star* (Washington DC), July 11, 1861; "The Battle of Carthage, Near Missouri," *New York Times*, July 13, 1861; "Report of Franz Sigel," July 25, 1861, *OR*, 19.

28. *SHM*, 31–32.

29. *SHM*, 32–33.

30. Monaghan, *Civil War*, 170–71; Gerteis, *The Civil War*, 65–67; Patrick, *Campaign*, 135; *SHM*, 34; Knapp, *Staff Ride*, 15–17; O'Flaherty, *Undefeated Rebel*, 37.

31. "No. 3, Report of Major John M. Schofield," August 20, 1861, *OR*, series 1, vol. 3, part 1, 60; "No. 4, Report of Major Samuel D. Sturgis," August 20, 1861, *OR*, series 1, vol. 3, part 1, 71; "No. 13, Report of Col. Franz Sigel," August 12, 1861, *OR*, series 1, vol. 3, part 1, 87–88; Patrick, *Campaign*, 158–59, 161, 162–63; Gerteis, *The Civil War*, 69–70; Monaghan, *Civil War*, 177–78; Knapp, *Staff Ride*, 12.

32. "No. 6, Report of Capt. James Totten," August 19, 1861, *OR*, series 1, vol. 3, part 1, 74; "No. 19, Report of Maj. Gen. Sterling Price," August 12, 1861, *OR*, series 1, vol. 3, part 1, 99–101; Patrick, *Campaign*, 136–38; Knapp, *Staff Ride*, 12, 34–38, 42–43, 59–60, 61–62; Gerteis, *The Civil War*, 71–72; *SHM*, 34–35; O'Flaherty, *Undefeated Rebel*, 84–85; Monaghan, *Civil War*, 174–75.

33. "Report of John M. Schofield," *OR*, 61–63; "Report of Sterling M. Price," *OR*, 99; Monaghan, *Civil War*, 179–80; O'Flaherty, *Undefeated Rebel*, 77, 87; Gerteis, *The Civil War*, 72.

34. "Report of Samuel D. Sturgis," *OR*, 67–69; "No. 21, Reports of Brig. Gen. Ben McCulloch," August 13, 1861, *OR*, series 1, vol. 3, part 1, 107; Patrick, *Campaign*, 184–85, 192.

35. Knapp, *Staff Ride*, 69; "Report of Sterling M. Price," *OR*, 100; "No. 40, Congratulatory Letter from Confederate Secretary of War," August 28, 1861, *OR*, series 1, vol. 3, part 1, 130.

36. "No. 16, Congratulatory Orders from General Fremont," August 25, 1861, *OR*, series 1, vol. 3, part 1, 92–93.

37. *SHM*, 36, 36–37.

38. *SHM*, 34, 35.

39. *SHM*, 36.

40. *SHM*, 34–35, 35.

41. *SHM*, 35.

42. "Report of Capt. James Totten," *OR*, 74.

43. "Reports of Brig. Gen. Ben McCulloch," *OR*, 109.

44. "No. 1, Miscellaneous reports, correspondence, and orders of the several Union commanders, September 12–23," *OR*, series 1, vol. 3, part 1, 171–72, 173, 174, 175, 176; *SHM*, 43; *The Battle of Lexington*, 29.

45. Webb, *Battles and Biographies*, 28–29, 33; "Miscellaneous reports," *OR*, 184; "No. 2, Report of Maj. Gen. Sterling Price," September 21, 1861, *OR*, series 1, vol. 3, part 1, 186; Monaghan, *Civil War*, 187–88, 189, 191; Gerteis, *The Civil War*, 107; "Battle field of Lexington, Mo.," Library of Congress.

46. "Report of Sterling Price," *OR*, 187; *SHM*, 45; Monaghan, *Civil War*, 191; *The Battle of Lexington*, 30–31, 32; Gerteis, *The Civil War*, 106–8; Webb, *Battles and Biographies*, 98–99.

47. "Report of Sterling Price," *OR*, 187; "No. 4, Report of Brig. Gen. Thomas A. Harris," September 23, 1861, *OR*, series 1, vol. 3, part 1, 191–92; *SHM*, 44; *The Battle of Lexington*, 32–33; Monaghan, *Civil War*, 192–94; Gerteis, *The Civil War*, 109; Webb, *Battles and Biographies*, 100–101.

48. "Report of Sterling Price," *OR*, 187–88; *The Battle of Lexington*, 33, 48, 52–53, 57–58.

49. Bansik, *Missouri in 1861*, 187; "Report of Sterling Price," *OR*, 188; Castel, *General Sterling Price*, 55–56; Gerteis, *The Civil War*, 109; Monaghan, *Civil War*, 193–94; Webb, *Battles and Biographies*, 102–3.

50. "Miscellaneous reports," *OR*, 184–85.

51. "Report of Sterling Price," *OR*, 188.

52. *SHM*, 43–45; Webb, 97.

53. *SHM*, 45.

54. *SHM*, 43–45

55. *SHM*, 37, 43–44.

56. *SHM*, 44.

57. *SHM*, 46–47; Monaghan, *Civil War*, 198–200, 204–6; O'Flaherty, *Undefeated Rebel*, 96–98; Castel, *General Sterling Price*, 64.

58. *SHM*, 46; Phillips, *The Rivers*, 143–44; Castel, *General Sterling Price*, 58–59.

59. *SHM*, 48–49; Hess et al., *Wilson's Creek*, 81.

60. "Battle of Pea Ridge," Civil War Trust; Josephy Jr., *The Civil War*, 336–37, 338; Monaghan, *Civil War*, 239.

61. "No. 2, Report of Brig. Gen. Samuel R. Curtis," March 6, 1862, *OR*, series 1, vol. 3, part 1, 191.

62. Josephy, *The Civil War*, 335–36; "Earl Van Dorn (1820–1863)," *The Encyclopedia of Arkansas History & Culture*.

63. Josephy, *The Civil War*, 340–42; *SHM*, 49; Monaghan, *Civil War*, 239; Hess et al., *Wilson's Creek*, 82.

64. *SHM*, 49; "No. 42, Report of Maj. Gen. Sterling Price," March 22, 1862, *OR*, 305–6; Josephy, 344–45; Monaghan, 243–45; Hess et al., 84; "Battle of Pea Ridge, March 7," Civil War Trust.

65. "No. 2, Report of Brig. Gen. Samuel R. Curtis," March 9, 1862, *OR*, 192; "No. 3, Report of Brig. Gen. Franz Sigel," March 15, 1862, *OR*, 215; "Report of Sterling Price," *OR*, 306; Josephy, *The Civil War*, 346; Monaghan, *Civil War*, 246, 247–49; "Battle of Pea Ridge, March 8," Civil War Trust.

66. "No. 54, Report of Brig. Gen. James S Rains," March 20, 1862, *OR*, 327–28; *SHM*, 50; Josephy, *The Civil War*, 346.

67. "Report of Brig. Gen. James S. Rains," *OR*, 328.

68. *SHM*, 49–50.

69. *SHM*, 50.

70. *SHM*, 50, 50–51.

71. *SHM*, 50–51.

72. *SHM*, 50–51.

2. A Brigade of Iron

1. *SHM*, 72; "Antebellum Resources of Northern Lafayette County," Show-Me Regional Planning Commission, Warrensburg, Missouri (November 1991), 11, 30–31; "Architectural/Historic Inventory Survey Form for Dover Township," Missouri Office of Historic Preservation (August 1988), I-no. 100; 1850 United States Federal Census; 1860 United States Federal Census.

2. *SHM*, 72; 1850 United States Federal Census; 1860 United States Federal Census; James S. Plattenburg, U.S., Appointments of U.S. Postmasters, 1832–1971, Ancestry.com.

3. *SHM*, 72.

4. *SHM*, 72; "Henry W. Plattenburg," *CSR*-NARA; "Harvey Plattenburg," *CSR*-NARA.

5. *SHM*, 56; McGhee, *Guide to Missouri*, 73; "Joseph O. Shelby," *CSR*-NARA.

6. *SHM*, 72; "James S. Plattenburg," *CSR*-NARA.

7. *SHM*, 72, 73; "Joseph O. Shelby," *CSR*-NARA; "John N. Edwards," *CSR*-NARA.

8. *SHM*, 73; McGhee, *Guide to Missouri*, 73.

9. "General Orders No. 19," July 22, 1862, *OR*, series 1, vol. 13, part 1, 506–7; Sellmeyer, *Iron Brigade*, 38.

10. *SHM*, 74–76; "Lone Jack: The Celebrated Battle Between the Guerrilla Bands of Missouri," *St. Louis Post-Dispatch*, April 14, 1882. For the best account of the Battle of Lone Jack, see Matthews and Lindberg, "Shot All to Pieces."

11. *SHM*, 56, 75–76, 77; Hulston and Goodrich, "John Trousdale Coffee," 274.

12. *SHM*, 77–78.

13. *SHM*, 79–83.

14. *SHM*, 73, 84; Monaghan, *Civil War*, 255; Hale and Eakins, *Branded as Rebels*, 198; "Elizabeth Watts Hays to Her Parents," February 23, 1857, *WHL*; "Gen. Frederick Salomon (1826–1897)," Wisconsin Historical Society.

15. *SHM*, 83–85; "Elizabeth Watts Hays to Her Mother," October 31, 1862, *WHL*; "Elizabeth Watts Hays to Her Mother," November 24, 1862, *WHL*.

16. *SHM*, 84–86; Sellmeyer, *Iron Brigade*, 36, 41; O'Flaherty, *Undefeated Rebel*, 124.

17. *SHM*, 85–86.

18. "No. 8, Report of Col. Douglas H. Cooper," October 2, 1862, *OR*, series 1, vol. 13, part 1, 297; "No. 1, Report of Brig. Gen. Frederick Salomon," October 1, 1862, *OR*, series 1, vol. 13, part 1, 287; "No. 3, Report of Col.

George H. Hall," October 1, 1862, *OR*, series 1, vol. 13, part 1, 289; *SHM*, 86, 87; O'Flaherty, *Undefeated Rebel*, 125.

19. *SHM*, 87–88; Gerteis, *The Civil War*, 148.

20. *SHM*, 87–88; "Report of Frederick Salomon," *OR*, 287; Sellmeyer, *Iron Brigade*, 42–43.

21. Various official Confederate records—including some penned by John— referred to Shelby's 5th Missouri Cavalry as the "1st." In the Department of the Trans-Mississippi, Shelby's regiment was also known by that unit number, though the First was never its official designation. See McGhee, *Guide to Missouri*, 72.

22. *SHM*, 87–88; "No. 7, Report of Capt. Job B. Stockton," October 1, 1862, *OR*, series 1, vol. 13, part 1, 296; "Report of Douglas Cooper," *OR*, 297–98; "No. 9, Report of Maj. J. M. Bryan," October 13, 1862, *OR*, series 1, vol. 13, part 1, 301.

23. *SHM*, 88–89; "Report of Frederick Salomon," *OR*, 287.

24. "Report of Douglas Cooper," *OR*, 299–300; *SHM*, 88–90; "No. 14, Report of Col. A. M. Alexander," *OR*, October 13, 1862, series 1, vol. 13, part 1, 306–7; O'Flaherty, *Undefeated Rebel*, 126–27.

25. "No. 1, Report of Maj. Gen. Samuel R. Curtis," October 6, 1862, *OR*, series 1, vol. 13, part 1, 311; "No. 2, Report of Brig. Gen. John M. Schofield," October 4, 1862, *OR*, series 1, vol. 13, part 1, 311.

26. Woodworth, *Jefferson Davis*, 122–23, 185, 314–15.

27. *SHM*, 105–6, 106–10.

28. *SHM*, 94; "Maj Gen. T. H. Holmes to Gen. S. Cooper," November 3, 1862, *OR*, series 1, vol. 13, part 1, 908; "Maj. Gen. T. H. Holmes to Secretary of War," November 15, 1862, *OR*, series 1, vol. 13, part 1, 918; Sellmeyer, 47–48; O'Flaherty, 131; McGhee, *Guide to Missouri*, 94. On Marmaduke's background, see "John Sappington Marmaduke (1833–1887)," *Encyclopedia of Arkansas*; and Perkins, "Marmaduke, John S," *Civil War on the Western Border: The Missouri-Kansas Conflict, 1854–1865*.

29. *SHM*, 94–95; "No. 2, Reports of Brig. Gen. James G. Blunt," November 29, 1862, *OR*, series 1, vol. 22, part 1, 42; Sellmeyer, *Iron Brigade*, 51, 53.

30. "No. 9, Report of Col. Joseph O. Shelby," December 1, 1862, *OR*, series 1, vol. 22, part 1, 55–56; *SHM*, 96–98.

31. *SHM*, 100; "Report of Joseph O. Shelby," *OR*, 57; "Reports of James G. Blunt," *OR*, 42, 45; O'Flaherty, *Undefeated Rebel*, 142–43.

32. "Reports of James G. Blunt," November 29, 1862 and December 3, 1862, *OR*, 42, 46; *SHM*, 103; "Report of Joseph O. Shelby," *OR*, 58.

33. "Reports of James G. Blunt," 46; "No. 1, Report of Maj. Gen. Samuel R. Curtis," November 29, 1862, *OR*, series 1, vol. 22, part 1, 41.

34. "Report of Joseph O. Shelby," *OR*, 57–58; *SHM*, 103.

35. *SHM*, 113–15; "No. 1, Reports of Maj. Gen. Samuel R. Curtis," December 9, 1862 [3 p.m.], *OR*, series 1, vol. 22, part 1, 68–69; "No. 2, Reports of Brig. Gen. James G. Blunt," December 8, 1862 and December 20, 1862, *OR*, series 1, vol. 22, part 1, 70, 71; "No. 36, Reports of Maj. Gen. Thomas C. Hindman," December 9, 1862, *OR*, series 1, vol. 22, part 1, 138; Monaghan, *Civil War*, 260–64.

36. *SHM*, 115–16; "No. 37, Report of Brig. Gen. John S. Marmaduke," December 16,1862, *OR*, series 1, vol. 22, part 1, 147–48; "No. 38, Report of Col. Joseph O. Shelby," December 11, 1862, *OR*, series 1, vol. 22, part 1, 149–50.

37. *SHM*, 118–19, 124–26, 126–27; "Reports of James G. Blunt," December 8, 1862, *OR*, 70; "Reports of Thomas C. Hindman," *OR*, 138–39, 141, 145; Monaghan, 268–69. "Report of Joseph O. Shelby," *OR*, 151–53; "No. 14, Reports of Brig. Gen. Francis J. Herron," December 9,1862, *OR*, series 1, vol. 22, part 1, 101; Monaghan, *Civil War*, 265, 267–70.

38. *SHM*, 126, 127; "Reports of Brig. Gen. James G. Blunt," December 8, 1862, *OR*, 70, 76; Monaghan, *Civil War*, 270.

39. "Reports of James G. Blunt," *OR*, December 9, 1862 and December 10, 1862, 78, 80. (Inclosure No. 3 consists of Hindman's note to Blunt).

40. "Reports of James G. Blunt," *OR*, 80–81.

41. "Report of Joseph O. Shelby," *OR*, 151–52, 153.

42. *SHM*, 125–26, 131.

43. *SHM*, 127–28.

44. *SHM*, 116–18.

45. *SHM*, 128.

46. *SHM*, 130–31; "Thomas Edwards," *CSR-NARA*; Bartels and McGhee, *Gallant Breed*, 28.

47. *SHM*, 131–33.

48. *SHM*, 131–33; *Monaghan, Civil War*, 272–73; Gerteis, *The Civil War*, 150, Sellmeyer, *Iron Brigade*, 76–78.

49. "No. 8, Report of Brig. Gen. John S. Marmaduke," January 18, 1863 and February 1, 1863, *OR*, series 1, vol. 22, part 1, 194–95, 196; *SHM*, 134.

50. *SHM*, 134–36; Sellmeyer, *Iron Brigade*, 79–80; Gerteis, *The Civil War*, 150–51.

51. "No. 2, Report of Brig. Gen. Egbert R. Brown,"January 8, 1863 [10 a.m.], *OR*, series 1, vol. 22, part 1, 179–80.

52. "Report of John S. Marmaduke," February 1, 1863, *OR*, 196–97; "No. 10, Report of Col. Joseph O. Shelby," January, 31 1863, *OR*, series 1, vol. 22, part 1, 201; *SHM*, 136, 138; Sellmeyer, 80–81; "Report of Egbert R. Brown," January 8, 1863 [3 p.m.], *OR*, 180; "No. 4, Report of Col. Benjamin Crabb," January 10, 1863, *OR*, series 1, vol. 22, part 1, 186.

53. "Report of John S. Marmaduke," January 18, 1863 and February 1, 1863, *OR*, 195, 196–97.

54. "Report of Egbert R. Brown," January 8, 1863 [11:50 p.m.], *OR*, 180–81; "No. 1, Reports of Major Gen. Samuel R. Curtis," January 12, 1863, *OR*, series 1, vol. 22, part 1, 179.

55. "Report of Joseph O. Shelby," *OR*, 201–2, 203.

56. See "No. 8, Report of Brig. Gen. John S. Marmaduke," January 18, 1863, *OR*, series 1, volume 22, part 1, 198.

57. *SHM*, 146–47, 149–50; Sellmeyer, *Iron Brigade*, 86–88.

3. The Costs of Valor

1. *SHM*, 147–48; "No. 13, Report of Brig. Gen. J. S. Marmaduke," May 20, 1863, *OR*, series 1, vol. 22, part 1, 285; O'Flaherty, *Undefeated Rebel*, 160–61; Sellmeyer, *Iron Brigade*, 88–89.

2. *SHM*, 149–50.

3. *SHM*, 151; "No. 13, Report of Brig. Gen. J. S. Marmaduke," May 20, 1863, *OR*, series 1, vol. 22, part 1, 285–86; Gerteis, *The Civil War*, 154.

4. *SHM*, 152–55, 398–99, 401; "No. 14, Report of Col. G. W. Thompson," *OR*, series 1, vol. 22, part 1, 289; "No. 13, Report of Brig. Gen. J. S. Marmaduke," May 20, 1863, *OR*, series 1, vol. 22, part 1, 286–87; "No. 16, Report of Col. John Q. Burbridge," May 11, 1863, *OR*, series 1, vol. 22 part 1, 297; O'Flaherty, *Undefeated Rebel*, 172–73.

5. *SHM*, 156.

6. *SHM*, 156–57; "No. 14, Report of Col. G. W. Thompson," May 15, 1863, *OR*, series 1, vol. 22, part 1, 290–92; Gerteis, *The Civil War*, 155–56.

7. "No. 14, Report of Col. G. W. Thompson," May 15, 1863, *OR*, series 1, vol. 22, part 1, 290–91; "John Newman Edwards," May 22, 1863, *CSR*-NARA.

8. *SHM*, 157.

9. "John Newman Edwards," Roll of Prisoners of War received at Myrtle Street Prison, *CSR*-NARA; "John Newman Edwards," U.S.A. Post Hospital, Cape Girardeau, Admission Form, April 26, 1863, *CSR*-NARA.

10. "John Newman Edwards," Roll of Prisoners at Myrtle Street Prison, *CSR*-NARA.

11. Eakin, *Missouri Prisoners*, viii–x; "Military Prisons," *The Civil War in Missouri*; *Library of Congress Civil War Desk Reference*, 590, 593, 607, 609.

12. Eakin, *Missouri Prisoners*, viii–x; "Military Prisons," *The Civil War in Missouri*; *Library of Congress Civil War Desk Reference*, 590, 593, 607, 609.

13. "John Newman Edwards," Cape Girardeau Hospital Parole, 5 May 1863, *CSR*-NARA; "John Newman Edwards," Adjutant Interview, June 18, 1863, *CSR*-NARA.

14. *Library of Congress Civil War Desk Reference*, 583–84, 600–604.

15. "John Newman Edwards," Adjutant Interview, June 18, 1863, *CSR*-NARA; "John Newman Edwards," Discharge from Myrtle Street Prison, *CSR*-NARA;

"John Newman Edwards," Roll of Prisoners forwarded from St. Louis to Johnson's Island, Ohio, CSR-NARA.

16. Frohman, *Rebels*, 1–3, 4–5, 7, 15–17, 26–28 (also see diagrams of prison layout, no page numbers provided); *Library of Congress Civil War Desk Reference*, 591, 607; Britten, "'Cooped Up and Powerless,'" 55, 63; Zombek, *Penitentiaries*, 96–101.

17. "Letter from Henry Massie Bullitt to My Dear Sister Helen," September 9, 1862, Helen Bullitt Papers, Ohio History Center; "Reminiscences of M. Jeff Thompson," 252, Meriwether Jeff Thompson Papers, Southern Historical Collection; "W. Marshall Rives to Mr. H. A. Rives," June 16, 1863, JIC-OHC. "Reminiscences of M. Jeff Thompson," 250–51; "Letter from Samuel Alutihuus to Cousin Sophie," November 24, 1864, JIOL-OHC.

18. Hathaway, "The Recollections of Leeland Hathaway," 67, Leeland Hathaway Recollections, Southern Historical Collection; "William Starr Basinger Reminiscences," 175–79, Hargrett Library, University of Georgia; "Love E. Gilbert to S. M. Pettingill," December 2, 1864, Correspondence, 1864–1865, Ohio History Center.

19. "J. J. Mitchell to My Dear Cousin," December 15, 1864, JIOL-OHC; "Henry Massie Bullitt to My Dear Sister Helen," September 14, 1862, Helen Bullitt Papers; "Reminiscences of M. Jeff Thompson," 251; Frohman, 36.

20. *Library of Congress Civil War Desk Reference*, 585; Varon, *Armies of Deliverance*, 326–28; "W. Marshall Rives to Mr. H. A. Rives," June 16, 1863, JIC-OCH.

21. "John Newman Edwards," Roll of Prisoners of War at Depot Prisoners of War, near Sandusky, Ohio, CSR-NARA; "John Newman Edwards," Roster of Field and Staff Officers of Shelby's Brigade, December 1863, CSR-NARA.

22. *SHM*, 164–68, 182–85; "No. 1, Report of Maj. Gen. Stephen A. Hurlbut," July 5, 1863, *OR*, series 1, vol. 22, part 1, 384; "No. 2, Report of Maj. Gen. B. M. Prentiss," July 5, 1863, *OR*, series 1, vol. 22, part 1, 386–87; "No. 14, Reports of Lieut. Gen. Theophilus J. Holmes," August 14, 1863, *OR*, series 1, vol. 22, part 1, 408–9, 411; "No. 26, Report of Maj. Gen. J. S. Marmaduke," July 25, 1863, *OR*, series 1, vol. 22, part 1, 437; O'Flaherty, *Undefeated Rebel*, 177–79, 181, 184, 187; "No. 1, Report of Major General John M. Schofield," September 27, 1863, *OR*, series 1, vol. 22, part 1, 469–70; "No. 2, Reports of Maj. Gen. Frederick K. Steele," September 22, 1863, *OR*, series 1, vol. 22, part 1, 480, 482; "No. 22, Report of Maj. Gen. Sterling Price," November 20, 1863, *OR*, series 1, vol. 22, part 1, 522; Sellmeyer, *Iron Brigade*, 104–10, 121–23.

23. *SHM*, 193–96, 196–97.

24. *SHM*, 218. On the Lawrence Massacre see Hulbert, "Larkin Skaggs and the Massacre(s) at Lawrence"; and, Hulbert, "How to Remember."

25. *SHM*, 217; Phillips, *The Rivers*, 314; Brownlee, *Gray Ghosts*, 125–27. On the concept of "household war," see Beilein, *Bushwhackers*, specifically chapter 1, "Household War."

26. *SHM*, 196–98; Sellmeyer, *Iron Brigade*, 125; O'Flaherty, *Undefeated Rebel*, 188, 190–91.

27. *SHM*, 198, 199, 201; "No. 24, Reports of Col. Joseph O. Shelby," November 16, 1863, *OR*, series 1, vol. 22, part 1, 671; O'Flaherty, *Undefeated Rebel*, 195; Sellmeyer, *Iron Brigade*, 126–27.

28. *SHM*, 202–3; "No. 24, Reports of Col. Joseph O. Shelby," November 16, 1863, *OR*, series 1, vol. 22, part 1, 671–72; O'Flaherty, *Undefeated Rebel*, 195.

29. *SHM*, 203–4; "No. 24, Reports of Col. Joseph O. Shelby," November 16, 1863, *OR*, series 1, vol. 22, part 1, 671–72; Gerteis,, 157–58; O'Flaherty, *Undefeated Rebel*, 195; Sellmeyer, *Iron Brigade*, 127–28.

30. *SHM*, 204; "No. 24, Reports of Col. Joseph O. Shelby," November 16, 1863, *OR*, series 1, vol. 22, part 1, 672; Sellmeyer, *Iron Brigade*, 128.

31. *SHM*, 204–5; "No. 24, Reports of Col. Joseph O. Shelby," November 16, 1863, *OR*, series 1, vol. 22, part 1, 672–73; O'Flaherty, *Undefeated Rebel*, 196–97; Sellmeyer, *Iron Brigade*, 128–29.

32. *SHM*, 205; "No. 24, Reports of Col. Joseph O. Shelby," November 16, 1863, *OR*, series 1, vol. 22, part 1, 672–73; Sellmeyer, *Iron Brigade*, 129–30.

33. *SHM*, 205–10, 213–17; "No. 24, Reports of Col. Joseph O. Shelby," November 16, 1863, *OR*, series 1, vol. 22, part 1, 673; O'Flaherty, *Undefeated Rebel*, 196–98; Sellmeyer, *Iron Brigade*, 131–34.

34. *SHM*, 216–17; "No. 24, Reports of Col. Joseph O. Shelby," November 16, 1863, *OR*, series 1, vol. 22, part 1, 674–75; Gerteis, *The Civil War*, 159; Sellmeyer, *Iron Brigade*, 135.

35. *SHM*, 218–20; "No. 24, Reports of Col. Joseph O. Shelby," November 16, 1863, *OR*, series 1, vol. 22, part 1, 675; Gerteis, *The Civil War*, 159–60; O'Flaherty, *Undefeated Rebel*, 202–4; Sellmeyer, *Iron Brigade*, 134–35.

36. *SHM*, 220–21; "No. 24, Reports of Col. Joseph O. Shelby," November 16, 1863, *OR*, series 1, vol. 22, part 1, 675–6=76; Sellmeyer, *Iron Brigade*, 135–37.

37. *SHM*, 221–22, 231–32; "No. 24, Reports of Col. Joseph O. Shelby," November 16, 1863, *OR*, series 1, vol. 22, part 1, 676–77; Sellmeyer, *Iron Brigade*, 137–39, 141–42.

38. *SHM*, 237–38; "No. 24, Reports of Col. Joseph O. Shelby," November 16, 1863, *OR*, series 1, vol. 22, part 1, 678–79. O'Flaherty labeled the closing of Shelby's report as "almost sarcastic"—see *Undefeated Rebel*, 207—but given the context of Shelby's relationship to Price and John's previous track record in writing about it, the tone is unmistakable.

39. "Shelby's Raid," November 18, 1863, *Washington Telegraph*.

40. *SHM*, 237–39.

41. *SHM*, 238–39.

42. "From St. Louis," October 14, 1863, *Chicago Tribune.*

43. *SHM*, 239–40.

44. *SHM*, 251–52; McGhee, *Guide to Missouri*, 72.

45. *SHM*, 378; Castel, *General Sterling Price*, 3–7, 223–24; Shalhope, *Sterling Price*, 5–8, 41–44, 47–49, 54–55, 66–67, 71–75, 75–77, 137–38; Sellmeyer, *Iron Brigade*, 208.

46. Castel, *General Sterling Price*, 3; *SHM*, 382, 392, 395–96, 430, 433, 435, 437, 465, 470. On the expedition's failures related to Smith's orders, see O'Flaherty, *Undefeated Rebel*, 216.

47. *SHM*, 381–83; "No. 88, Reports of Maj. Gen. Sterling Price," September 6, 1864, *OR*, series 1, vol. 41, part 1, 622–23; "No. 88, Reports of Maj. Gen. Sterling Price," September 19, 1864, *OR*, series 1, vol. 41, part 1, 623; "No. 88, Reports of Maj. Gen. Sterling Price," December 28, 1864, *OR*, series 1, vol. 41, part 1, 626–27; "No. 92, Reports of Brig. General Joseph O. Shelby," December 1864, *OR*, series 1, vol. 41, part 1, 652; O'Flaherty, *Undefeated Rebel*, 217; Sellmeyer, *Iron Brigade*, 208–9; Castel, *General Sterling Price*, 204–5.

48. *SHM*, 385–89; "No. 88, Reports of Maj. Gen. Sterling Price," December 28, 1864, *OR*, series 1, vol. 41, part 1, 627–30; "No. 92, Reports of Brig. General Joseph O. Shelby," December 1864, *OR*, series 1, vol. 41, part 1, 652–53; Gerteis, *The Civil War*, 182–87; O'Flaherty, *Undefeated Rebel*, 218; Sellmeyer, *Iron Brigade*, 209–13; Castel, *General Sterling Price*, 210–16, 218, 221.

49. *SHM*, 386, 392; "No. 88, Reports of Maj. Gen. Sterling Price," December 28,1864, *OR*, series 1, vol. 41, part 1, 630; "No. 92, Reports of Brig. General Joseph O. Shelby," December 1864, *OR*, series 1, vol. 41, part 1, 652; O'Flaherty, *Undefeated Rebel*, 218–20.

50. *SHM*, 392–96; "No. 88, Reports of Maj. Gen. Sterling Price," December 28, 1864, *OR*, series 1, vol. 41, part 1, 630–31; "No. 92, Reports of Brig. General Joseph O. Shelby," December 1864, *OR*, series 1, vol. 41, part 1, 654–55; Sellmeyer, *Iron Brigade*, 218, 220–21; Castel, *General Sterling Price*, 224.

51. *SHM*, 397–98, 403–8; "No. 88, Reports of Maj. Gen. Sterling Price," December 28, 1864, *OR*, series 1, vol. 41, part 1, 631–32, 633; "No. 92, Reports of Brig. General Joseph O. Shelby," December 1864, *OR*, series 1, vol. 41, part 1, 655–57; Gerteis, *The Civil War*, 192–94; Sellmeyer, *Iron Brigade*, 221–22, 228–29; Castel, *General Sterling Price*, 225–27.

52. *SHM*, 418–28; "No. 88, Reports of Maj. Gen. Sterling Price," December 28, 1864, *OR*, series 1, vol. 41, part 1, 633–34; "No. 92, Reports of Brig. General Joseph O. Shelby," December 1864, *OR*, series 1, vol. 41, part 1, 657–58; O'Flaherty, *Undefeated Rebel*, 221; Sellmeyer, *Iron Brigade*, 230–36; Castel, *General Sterling Price*, 229–31.

53. *SHM*, 429; "No. 88, Reports of Maj. Gen. Sterling Price," December 28, 1864, *OR*, series 1, vol. 41, part 1, 634–35; "No. 92, Reports of Brig. General Joseph O. Shelby," December 1864, *OR*, series 1, vol. 41, part 1, 658; "No. 13, Reports of Maj. Gen. Alfred Pleasanton," November 1, 1864, *OR*, series 1, vol. 41, part 1, 336–38; Gerteis, *The Civil War*, 197–98.

54. *SHM*, 429–32; "No. 88, Reports of Maj. Gen. Sterling Price," December 28, 1864, *OR*, series 1, vol. 41, part 1, 635; "No. 92, Reports of Brig. General Joseph O. Shelby," December 1864, *OR*, series 1, vol. 41, part 1, 658–59; "No. 93, Reports of Brig. Gen. M. Jeff Thompson," November 24, 1864, *OR*, series 1, vol. 41, part 1, 667; "No. 94, Report of Colonel Sidney D. Jackman," November 30, 1864, *OR*, series 1, vol. 41, part 1, 676; "No. 80, Report of Major General James G. Blunt," December 24, 1864, *OR*, series 1, vol. 41, part 1, 575–76; "No. 81, Report of Col. Charles R. Jennison," November 23, 1864, *OR*, series 1, vol. 41, part 1, 585–86; Gerteis, *The Civil War*, 198; O'Flaherty, *Undefeated Rebel*, 222; Sellmeyer, *Iron Brigade*, 241–42.

55. *SHM*, 431–36; "No. 88, Reports of Maj. Gen. Sterling Price," December 28, 1864, *OR*, series 1, vol. 41, part 1, 636; "No. 92, Reports of Brig. General Joseph O. Shelby," December 1864, *OR*, series 1, vol. 41, part 1, 659–61; Gerteis, *The Civil War*, 198–99; O'Flaherty, *Undefeated Rebel*, 222–24; Sellmeyer, *Iron Brigade*, 244–49.

56. *SHM*, 442–43, 456–59, 471–72; "No. 88, Reports of Maj. General Sterling Price," December 28, 1864, *OR*, series 1, Vol. 41, part 1, 636–38, 646; "No. 92, Reports of Brig. General Joseph O. Shelby," December 1864, *OR*, series 1, vol. 41, part 1, 660–61; "No. 13, Reports of Maj. Gen. Alfred Pleasanton," November 30 1864, *OR*, series 1, vol. 41, part 1, 341–42; "No. 80, Report of Major General James G. Blunt," December 24, 1864, *OR*, series 1, vol. 41, part 1, 577–78; Sellmeyer, *Iron Brigade*, 241–42, 253, 258–61; O'Flaherty, *Undefeated Rebel*, 222–24; Arthur, *Shelby's March*, 223.

57. "No. 92, Reports of Brig. General Joseph O. Shelby," December 1864, *OR*, series 1, vol. 41, part 1, 661; "No. 93, Reports of Brig. Gen. M. Jeff Thompson," November 24, 1864, *OR*, series 1, vol. 41, part 1, 669–70; "No. 94, Report of Colonel Sidney D. Jackman," November 30, 1864, *OR*, series 1, vol. 41, part 1, 677.

58. "No. 88, Reports of Maj. General Sterling Price," December 28, 1864, *OR*, series 1, vol. 41, part 1, 640, 648; O'Flaherty, *Undefeated Rebel*, 226–27.

59. "No. 88, Reports of Maj. General Sterling Price," December 28, 1864, *OR*, series 1, vol. 41, part 1, 639.

60. "No. 92, Reports of Brig. General Joseph O. Shelby," December 1864, *OR*, series 1, vol. 41, part 1, 662; Reynolds's report as reprinted (facsimile) in *SHM*, 467, 470, 472.

61. *SHM*, 475–76.
62. *SHM*, 395–96.
63. *SHM*, 430, 435, 437.
64. *SHM*, 501–2.
65. *SHM*, 499.
66. *SHM*, 448–49, 499.
67. *SHM*, 448–49
68. *SHM*, 450.
69. *SHM*, 450–51.
70. *SHM*, 507, 515–16.
71. *SHM*, 520, 523, 524–25, 533–34; Sellmeyer, *Iron Brigade*, 279–80; Arthur, *Shelby's March*, 59–60.
72. *SHM*, 538.
73. *SHM*, 538–41.
74. *SHM*, 533–34.
75. *SHM*, 540.
76. *SHM*, 535, 541–42.

4. In Quest of Camelot

1. *SEM*, 8–9, 22–23.
2. *SEM*, 11, 12–13, 13–14
3. *SEM*, 16–20.
4. *SEM*, 22–23, 86–90.
5. *SEM*, 87–89
6. *SEM*, 98–99; "Empress Charlotte to Maria Amalia," December 23, 1865, Jay I. Kislak Collection, Library of Congress; "Emperor Maximilian to Degollado," October 19, 1865, Mexico Documents Collection, Special Collections, University of Houston.
7. "Phillip H. Sheridan to Ulysses S. Grant," May 7, 1866, Phillip H. Sheridan Letter, Abraham Lincoln Presidential Library; Rister, "Carlota," 34–35.
8. *SEM*, 532.
9. *SEM*, 24.
10. *SEM*, 24–25.
11. After his offer of military service was rejected by Maximilian, Shelby confessed to his men that he was also an imperialist at heart and that he knew the men would rebuff Viesca's offer back in Piedra Negras. See *SEM*, 94.
12. *SEM*, 25–26.
13. *SEM*, 547–49; "Thomas Westlake Memoir," Watson-Westlake Papers, 1813–1949, 136, SHSMC; "End of War-Exiles in Mexico," *Confederate Veteran* 11 (1903), 121–22; "Confederate Flag in the Rio Grande," *Confederate Veteran* 14 (1906), 64.

14. *SEM*, 28–30; *SHM*, 547.

15. "Thomas Westlake Memoir," 137–38, SHSMC.

16. *SEM*, 32–34, 36–39, 49–51,52–53, 54–56; Rister, 37–38.

17. *SEM*, 90–91; Rister, 36–37.

18. *SEM*, 91–93.

19. *SEM*, 93–94.

20. *SEM*, 78–79, 95–97.

21. Rister, "Carlota," 41–43.

22. *SEM*, 96; "John Newman Edwards to Sisters," September 1865, EL-SHSMC.

23. On Confederados more generally see Dawsey and Dawsey, *The Confederados*; Harter, *The Lost Colony*; Rolle, *The Lost Cause*; Wahlstrom, *The Southern Exodus*.

24. *SEM*, 97–98; Rister, "Carlota," 45.

25. *SEM*, 96–97; 100, 119–20; Rister, "Carlota," 40, 45; Hanna, "A Confederate Newspaper," 67–68.

26. *SEM*, 105, 113–14; Sheridan, *Personal Memoirs*, 218–19.

27. *SEM*, 99–100.

28. "John Newman Edwards to Sisters," September 1865, EL-SHSMC.

29. "John Newman Edwards to Sisters," April 6, 1866, EL-SHSMC.

30. "John Newman Edwards to Sisters," April 6, 1866, EL-SHSMC; "John S. Tisdale," CSR-NARA.

31. "John Newman Edwards to Sisters," April 6, 1866, EL-SHSMC; Hanna, "A Confederate Newspaper," 69.

32. "National Mass Seating Chart," September 1865, Maximilian, Emperor of Mexico Collection, University of Arizona. (Translated from Spanish by Clemente Gomez)

33. *SEM*, 98–99.

34. *SEM*, 85–86.

35. "Maximilian to Dr. Jilek," February 10, 1865, Maximilian, Emperor of Mexico Collection. (Translated from German by Norman Saliba); "Dispatch on New Alcohol Regulations," December 23, 1863, Charlotte and Maximilian Collection, Rice University. (Translated from Spanish by Clemente Gomez)

36. *SEM*, 113–14, 123; Rister, "Carlota," 48.

37. *SEM*, 110–11.

38. "John Newman Edwards to Sisters," April 6, 1866, EL-SHSMC.

39. "John Newman Edwards to Sisters," April 6, 1866, EL-SHSMC.

40. "The United States and Mexico," May 12, 1866, MT.

41. "The United States and Mexico," May 12, 1866, MT.

42. "The French Evacuation of Mexico," May 19, 1866, MT.

43. *SEM*, 106–7; "John Newman Edwards to sister Fanny," September 18, 1866, EL-SHSMC. While virtually everyone, including Mary Catherine Edwards herself, spelled her nickname "Fannie," John habitually wrote "Fanny." As such, I have used "Fannie" in the text but in the notes have cited John's letters to her from Mexico as he addressed them.

44. "John Newman Edwards to sister Fanny," September 18, 1866, EL-SHSMC; *SEM*, 119–20; Hanna, "A Confederate Newspaper," 76–77.

45. "Cordova and Colonization," June 16, 1866, *MT*.

46. "John Newman Edwards to sister Fanny," September 18, 1866, EL-SHSMC.

47. "John Newman Edwards to brother Thomas," September 18, 1866, EL-SHSMC.

48. "John Newman Edwards to brother Thomas," September 18, 1866, EL-SHSMC.

49. "American Extremity is Mexican Opportunity," October 8, 1866, *MT*.

50. "All That Glitters is Not Gold," November 19, 1866, *MT*; Hanna, "A Confederate Newspaper," 77.

51. "Shelby's Tuxpan Colony," November 19, 1866, *MT*; Rister, "Carlota," 50; Hanna, "A Confederate Newspaper," 79.

52. "John Newman Edwards to Sisters," n.d. (post-9/18/66), EL-SHSMC.

53. *SEM*, 120–21; Rister, "Carlota," 49.

54. *SEM*, 120–21.

55. *SEM*, 114, 115–16, 121, 123–24, 129–31, 132; "Circular No. 19 from Military Headquarters of Nuevo Leon," March 27, 1867, Charlotte and Maximilian Collection, Rice University. (Translated from Spanish by Clemente Gomez)

56. O'Flaherty, *Undefeated Rebel*, 310–13.

57. O'Flaherty, *Undefeated Rebel*, 311–12.

58. *SEM*, 122, 131–35.

59. *SEM*, 136–37; "Fitzhugh Lee to Kimmel," October 1, 1867, Fitzhugh Lee Papers, College of William and Mary.

60. Allen, *Recollections*, 309, 329, 331, 342, 344–45.

61. Allen, *Recollections*, 309, 323, 328, 329, 331, 341.

5. War by Other Means

1. *JNE*, 18; Conard, *Encyclopedia*, 355.

2. Ads for the book ran in numerous papers in and outside of Missouri, including the *Daily Missouri Republican*, the *Daily Arkansas Gazette*, the *Missouri Telegraph*, the *Canton Press*, the *St. Joseph Herald*, the *Louisville Daily Courier*, and even the *New Orleans Times-Picayune*.

3. "Shelby and His Men," September 15, 1867, *Memphis Daily Appeal*.

4. *SHM*, preface.

5. Stevens, *Centennial History*, 373–74.

6. Stevens, *Centennial History*, 373–74; *JNE*, 18.

7. Stevens, *Centennial History*, 373–74; *JNE*, 18, 37.

8. Foner, *Reconstruction*, 339–42.

9. "1868 General Election Statistics," *U.S. Election Atlas*; Switzler, *Illustrated History*, 464; *Congressional Directory for the Third Session of the Fortieth Congress*, 25, 25–26.

10. On guerrilla warfare in Missouri see Hulbert, *The Ghosts of Guerrilla Memory*; Beilein, *Bushwhackers*; Fellman, *Inside War*.

11. On bushwhackers attempting to return to "normalcy," see Hulbert, "The Trials of Frank James."

12. Yeatman, *Frank and Jesse James*, 85–86, 93–95.

13. "From the Kansas City Times. More of the Shooting at Gallatin," *Liberty Tribune*, June 24, 1870. The *Tribune* reprinted the letter originally run by John at *KCT*. Photocopy from William A. Settle Jr. Papers, SHSMC.

14. "From the Kansas City Times. More of the Shooting at Gallatin," *Liberty Tribune*, June 24, 1870.

15. Phillips, "'The Chrysalis State,'" 150, 157.

16. Switzler, *Illustrated History*, 465, 469–72; Foner, *Reconstruction*, 416–17.

17. Stiles, *Last Rebel*, 213–14; Triplett, *Life and Times*, 56–60.

18. "Poor Carlotta," May 29, 1870, *KCT*.

19. "Poor Carlotta," May 29, 1870, *KCT*.

20. 1850 United States Federal Census; 1870 United States Federal Census.

21. *JNE*, 18.

22. *JNE*, 18.

23. Wedding notice,, *Atchison Daily Champion*, April 4, 1871; *JNE*, 18.

24. "Business Notice," August 20, 1871, *KCT*; *National Cyclopedia*, 272–73; *JNE*, 38.

25. *JNE*, 37–38

26. *JNE*, 38.

27. "Is He of the 'New Departure'?" *Daily Kansas Tribune*, July 23, 1871.

28. "State Printer," December 10, 1871, *Fort Scott Daily Monitor*.

29. "Shelby's Expedition to Mexico," May 26, 1872, *KCT*.

30. "Mexico. Death of Juarez," July 26, 1872, *KCT*.

31. "William H. Seward," October 12, 1872, *KCT*.

32. "William H. Seward," October 12, 1872, *KCT*.

33. "William H. Seward," October 12, 1872, *KCT*.

34. On New Departure and Liberal Republicans, see Foner, *Reconstruction*, 412–18.

35. "Here and There," September 19, 1871, *KCT*; "Minor Topics," September 22, 1871, *KCT*; "Wisconsin," September 23, 1871, *KCT*; "A Chat with Governor Magoffin, of Kentucky," October 1, 1871, *KCT*.

36. "What They Depend Upon," September 22, 1871, *KCT*; "Wanted—Somebody to Blame," September 19, 1871, *KCT*.

37. "War to the Knife," November 15, 1871, *KCT*; Foner, 501–3.

38. "Here and There," November 26, 1871, *KCT*.

39. "Here and There," November 26, 1871, *KCT*.

40. "For President: Horace Greeley. For Vice-President: B. Gratz-Brown," May 12, 1872, *KCT*; "Political," May 4, 1872, *KCT*; "The Campaign Times," July 20, 1872, *KCT*; "Greeley Surprised at His Nomination," May 9, 1872, *St. Joseph Weekly Gazette*; "Mr. Greeley in Cincinnati," September 22, 1872, *KCT*; untitled commentary on Greeley, September 19, 1872, *KCT*; "Bourbonism," September 5, 1872, *Missouri Republican*; 1880 United States Federal Census.

41. "Exposition. Opening Scenes of the Great Fair," September 24, 1872, *KCT*.

42. "High Handed," September 27, 1872, *KCT*; Stiles, *Last Rebel*, 222–23; Triplett, *Life and Times*, 69–71; Yeatman, *Frank and Jesse James*, 103.

43. "High Handed," September 27, 1872, *KCT*.

44. "The Chivalry of Crime," September 29, 1872, *KCT*.

45. "The Chivalry of Crime," September 29, 1872, *KCT*.

46. "The Chivalry of Crime," September 29, 1872, *KCT*.

47. "The Fair Robbery," October 15, 1872, *KCT*. T. J. Stiles, the undisputed authority on the criminal and political career of Jesse James, agrees that while no smoking gun exists to prove James wrote the October 15 letter, all circumstantial evidence points to him. See Stiles, *Last Rebel*, 225–26.

48. "The Importance of Registration," September 24, 1872, *KCT*.

49. "A Card From Jesse W. James," October 20, 1872, *KCT*.

50. "A Card From Jesse W. James," October 20, 1872, *KCT*.

51. "Some Few Words More," November 3, 1872, *KCT*; untitled comments, November 5, 1872, *KCT*.

52. "Forward, Along the Whole Line," November 5, 1872, *KCT*.

53. 1872 Statistics, *The American Presidency Project*; 1872 General Election Results—Missouri, *U.S. Election Atlas*; "The Result," November 6, 1872, *KCT*.

54. "The Result," November 6, 1872, *KCT*.

55. "Obituary. Honors to the Memory of the Dead Journalist," December 1, 1872, *KCT*.

6. Architect

1. *US Biographical Dictionary*, 222–23.

2. *US Biographical Dictionary*, 223–24.

3. *US Biographical Dictionary*, 224–25; untitled commentary, December 6, 1884, *Brown County World* (Hiawatha, Kansas).

4. *JNE*, 38.

5. Untitled commentary, September 20, 1873, *Weekly Caucasian*.

6. "Crimes and Casualties," August 2, 1873, *Ironton County Register* (MO); "Fiendish Crime in Iowa," July 31, 1873, *California Democrat* (MO); "The Railway Robbers," July 28, 1873, *Harrisburg Telegraph* (PA); "Crime," July 23, 1873, *KCT*; Yeatman, *Frank and Jesse James*, 106–8; Stiles, *Last Rebel*, 233–36.

7. "Atrocious Crime," July 25, 1873, *Muscatine Weekly Journal* (IA); "Proclamation," July 24, 1873, *Des Moines Register*; "John Rafferty," *Des Moines Register*, August 9, 1873; "The Railroad Bandits," *St. Joseph Gazette*, July 25, 1873; "Crimes and Casualties," *Ironton County Register* (MO) August 2, 1873; "Fiendish Crime in Iowa," *California Democrat* (MO) July 31, 1873; "The Railway Robbers," *Harrisburg Telegraph* (PA) July 28, 1873; "Crime," July 23, 1873, *KCT*; Stiles, *Last Rebel*, 233–36; Yeatman, *Frank and Jesse James*, 106–8.

8. "Crimes and Casualties," *Ironton County Register* (MO) August 2, 1873; "Fiendish Crime in Iowa," *California Democrat* (MO) July 31, 1873; "The Railway Robbers," *Harrisburg Telegraph* (PA) July 28, 1873; "Crime," July 23, 1873, *KCT*; Stiles, *Last Rebel*, 233–36; Yeatman, *Frank and Jesse James*, 106–8.

9. "Crimes and Casualties," *Ironton County Register* (MO) August 2, 1873; "Fiendish Crime in Iowa," *California Democrat* (MO) July 31, 1873; "The Railway Robbers," *Harrisburg Telegraph* (PA) July 28, 1873; "Crime," July 23, 1873, *KCT*; Stiles, *Last Rebel*, 233–36; Yeatman, *Frank and Jesse James*, 106–8.

10. "An Incident of the Train Robbery," *Kingston Daily Freeman* (NY) August 4, 1873; "The Railroad Robbers," *Leavenworth Times*, July 29, 1873; "Iowa," *Daily Journal* (NC), July 23, 1873.

11. "A New Peril of the Rail," *New York Times*, July 24, 1873.

12. "A New Peril of the Rail."

13. "A New Peril of the Rail."

14. "Crime," July 23, 1873, *KCT*; "Iowa KuKlux Described," July 25, 1873, *KCT*.

15. "The Train Band," *Memphis Daily Appeal*, September 8, 1873; "The Train Robbers," *Boston Globe* (MA) September 13, 1873; "The Train Robbers," *Rutland Daily Globe* (Vermont), September 18, 1873.

16. "The Train Robbers," *Rutland Daily Globe* (Vermont), September 18, 1873.

17. "The Train Robbers."

18. ATQ, 3.

19. ATQ, 4.

20. ATQ, 4.

21. ATQ, 4–5.

22. ATQ, 5–6.

23. ATQ, 6.

24. ATQ, 6–12.

25. ATQ, 19–23.

26. ATQ, 25.

27. ATQ, 26.

28. T. J. Stiles pioneered the argument that Jesse James and his early James-Younger Gang associates (also former bushwhackers) took to crime as a deadly form of political terrorism against social and political changes in the postbellum South and Border West. This was a major shift away from previous interpretations that represented the outlaws as apolitical brigands and sociopaths. On "A Terrible Quintette" see Stiles, *Last Rebel*, 241–42. Also see Yeatman, *Frank and Jesse James*, 109.

29. ATQ, 3.

30. "Jesse James to the *St. Louis Dispatch*," December 20, 1873, reprinted in the *Gallatin North Missourian* on January 8, 1874, William A. Settle Jr. Papers, SHSMC.

31. "Jesse James to the *St. Louis Dispatch*," SHSMC; Yeatman, 109–10, 126–27, 156–58. For a handy timeline of James-Younger Gang robberies, also see "Robberies" *Civil War St. Louis* (online).

32. ATQ, 12–19, 21.

33. "Quantrell" May 12, 1872, KCT.

34. "The Elections," *St. Louis Republican* November 4, 1874; Switzler, *Illustrated History*, 466.

35. "The Missouri Banditti," *Chicago Tribune*, December 10, 1874.

36. "The Missouri Banditti."

37. JNE, 18–19.

38. JNE, 18–19; "Illinois," *Lawrence Daily Journal*, September 5, 1875; untitled commentary, September 16 1875, *Union Recorder* (MO).

39. Grover, "Major Emory Foster," 425–30.

40. JNE, 20.

41. JNE, 20–21. Considering his employer, Stilson Hutchins, owned both papers, it was an odd thing to do—though the *St. Louis Times* was purchased as a reclamation project, so perhaps Hutchins was using John's feud to orchestrate sales. On the legal history of dueling in America, see Wells, "The End of the Affair?"

42. JNE, 21; "Twenty Paces!" *St. Louis Republican*, September 7, 1875.

43. JNE, 21–22; "Twenty Paces!" *St. Louis Republican*, September 7, 1875.

44. JNE, 23; "Twenty Paces!" September 7, 1875, *St. Louis Republican*; 1880 United States Federal Census

45. JNE, 22; "Twenty Paces!" *St. Louis Republican*, September 7, 1875.

46. *JNE*, 22; "Twenty Paces!" *St. Louis Republican*, September 7, 1875.

47. *JNE*, 22.

48. *JNE*; "Twenty Paces!" September 7, 1875, *St. Louis Republican*; "Illinois," *Lawrence Daily Journal*, September 5, 1875.

49. *JNE*, 22–23; "Twenty Paces!" *St. Louis Republican*, September 7, 1875.

50. *JNE*, 23.

51. "The Winnebago County Duel to be Investigated," *St. Louis Globe-Democrat*, October 6, 1875; "The Winnebago Duel," , *St. Louis Republican*, October 17, 187.

52. "Pistols and Coffee," September 7, 1875, *KCT*.

53. Untitled commentary, *Newton Kansan*, September 9, 1875; "Saturday, Sept. 4," *Emporia Weekly News*, September 10, 1875.

54. "A Pair of Fools," *The Lawrence Daily Journal*, September 21, 1875.

55. "A Pair of Fools."

56. "Missouri," *Atchison Daily Patriot*, October 18, 1875; "On the War Path," October 17, 1875, *KCT*; "Missouri," *Lawrence Daily Journal*, October 17, 1875; untitled commentary, October 28, 1875, *Wichita Eagle*.

57. *Laws of the State of Missouri*, 340–42; untitled commentary, *The Lexington Intelligencer*, October 23, 1875; "Winnebago," *Missouri Granger*, October 26, 1875; "George W. Gilson to Charles Henry Hardin," October 22, 1875, GR-MSR; "Affidavit from the St. Louis Court of Criminal Correction," October 22, 1875, Governors Records, Missouri State Archives; "Indictment of P. S. O'Reilly," October 1875, GR-MSR.

58. "The Winnebago Warriors," *St. Louis Globe-Democrat*, November 19, 1875; "The Winnebago Duel," *St. Louis Globe-Democrat*, October 19, 1875; *Laws of the State of Missouri*, 340–42.

59. *JNE*, 38.

60. *JNE*, 24.

61. Stiles, *Last Rebel*, 327–35; Yeatman, *Frank and Jesse James*, 172–75, 182–84.

62. "1876 General Results," *U.S. Election Atlas*; Foner, *Reconstruction*, 575–76.

63. Foner, *Reconstruction*, 580–82.

64. For what is still the seminal organizational history of the early Lost Cause Movement, see Foster, *Ghosts of the Confederacy*.

65. On how white cooperation and mutual valor (at the expense of slavery and emancipation) became the dominant commemorative narratives of the Civil War, see Blight, *Race and Reunion*.

66. For my previous work on Edwards as the architect of Missouri's "irregular Lost Cause," see Hulbert, "Constructing Guerrilla Memory" and *The Ghosts of Guerrilla Memory*, specifically chapter 2, "An Irregular Lost Cause."

67. *NG*, 13.

68. *NG*, 19.

69. *NG*, 14–15, 39–41, 47–48, 54–56, 66–67, 299, 438–39.

70. *NG*, 15–16, 165–66, 300, 390.

71. *NG*, 14, 188–91, 243–44, 292–302.

72. *NG*, 156–58.

73. *NG*, 31.

74. "Noted Guerrillas," *St. Louis Globe-Democrat*, April 27, 1877; "Noted Guerrillas, or, The Warfare of the Border," *Palmyra Spectator*, March 23, 1877; "Noted Guerrillas," May 1, 1877, *KCT*.

75. Untitled commentary, April 6, 1877, *KCT*.

76. On the whitewashing of irregular combatants from the mainstream Lost Cause, see Hulbert, *The Ghosts of Guerrilla Memory*, chapters 7 and 8.

7. The Ghost and the Monster

1. Yeatman, *Frank and Jesse James*, 269; Petrone, *Judgement at Gallatin*, 17.

2. Stiles, *Last Rebel*, 375; Yeatman, *Frank and Jesse James*, 269.

3. 1860 Census, Decennial Census Data, United States Census Bureau; 1880 Census, Decennial Census Data, United States Census Bureau.

4. "Jesse James," *St. Louis Post-Dispatch*, April 6, 1882; "Plain English," *St. Louis Post-Dispatch*, April 6, 1882; "The James Tragedy," *St. Louis Post-Dispatch*, April 6, 1882; "Assassination Made to Order," *St. Louis Post-Dispatch*, April 7, 1882; "Crittenden's Offense," *St. Louis Post-Dispatch*, April 7, 1882; "The Bold Brigands," *St. Joseph Weekly Herald*, April 13, 1882; Stiles, 376–78; Yeatman, *Frank and Jesse James*, 271, 275; Muehlberger, *The Lost Cause*, 127, 131–32.

5. *JNE*, 24; "Sedalia Democrat," *Sedalia Democrat*, January 11, 1880; Conard, *Encyclopedia*, 355; "The Killing of Jesse James," *Sedalia Democrat*, April 13, 1882.

6. "The Killing of Jesse James."

7. "The Killing of Jesse James."

8. Petrone, 20, 22–23, 39, 46–48. Pinkerton detectives had hunted the James brothers for years. In 1875 Pinkerton men bombed the home of Frank's mother, Zerelda James Samuel. She survived the explosion minus her right arm. Frank's half-brother, Archie Samuel, was killed in the blast. See Yeatman, 134–38.

9. Petrone, *Judgement at Gallatin*, 22, 24; Yeatman, *Frank and Jesse James*, 270, 277–78.

10. John was an old hand when it came to lobbying governors for favors, particularly in the form of political appointments, ranging from coal oil inspector to adjutant general. See "John Newman Edwards to Charles H.

Hardin," November 14, 1874, GR-MSR; "John Newman Edwards to Charles H. Hardin," November 24, 1874, GR-MSR.

11. "John Newman Edwards to Frank James," June 22, 1882, APC; Petrone, *Judgement at Gallatin*, 25–26.

12. "John Newman Edwards to Frank James," June 22, 1882, APC.

13. Petrone, *Judgement at Gallatin*, 33, 47; Yeatman, *Frank and Jesse James*, 279.

14. Petrone, *Judgement at Gallatin*, 33, 47; Yeatman, *Frank and Jesse James*, 279; Michelle Brooks, "Cole County History: McCarty House greeted Jefferson City visitors for 70 years," Jefferson City *News Tribune*, May 15, 2021, https://www.newstribune.com/news/local/story/2021/may/15/cole-county-history-mccarty-house-greeted-jefferson-city-visitors-for-70-years/871226/.

15. Petrone, *Judgement at Gallatin*, 33; Yeatman, *Frank and Jesse James*, 279. Though Crittenden had once been willing to issue James a pardon, owing to political backlash, that was no longer possible. Crittenden informed John and James prior to their trip to Jefferson City that no pardon could or would be forthcoming. See Petrone, *Judgement at Gallatin*, 32.

16. Petrone, *Judgement at Gallatin*, 33; Yeatman, *Frank and Jesse James*, 279; Muehlberger, *The Lost Cause*, 133.

17. Stiles, *Last Rebel*, 378–79; Petrone, *Judgement at Gallatin*, 33–34; Muehlberger, *The Lost Cause*, 133–34.

18. "The James Boys. Frank Surrenders,", *Lawrence Daily Journal*, October 6, 1882; "Frank James," *Atchison Daily Patriot*, October 6, 1882; "Frank James Surrenders Himself," *Kansas City Star*, October 6, 1882; "Frank James," *St.Louis Globe-Democrat*, October 6, 1882; Petrone, *Judgement at Gallatin*, 34–37; Muehlberger, *The Lost Cause*, 134–35.

19. Untitled commentary, *Emporia Daily News*, October 5, 1882.

20. "Facts About Frank," October 7, 1882, KCT; "Frank James Meets His Mother, Wife and Child," *St. Louis Post-Dispatch*, October 6, 1882; Petrone, *Judgement at Gallatin*, 37–41.

21. Stiles, *Last Rebel*, 379; Petrone, *Judgement at Gallatin*, 27, 54, 58, 69; Muehlberger, *The Lost Cause*, 136.

22. "John Newman Edwards to Frank James," March 27, 1883, APC.

23. "John Newman Edwards to Frank James," May 29, 1883, APC.

24. "The St. Joseph Gazette," *Brown County World* (Hiawatha KS), June 28, 1883; "Gazettlings," *St. Joseph Herald*, May 2, 1883; "The Gazette Sale," *St. Joseph Herald*, June 12, 1883; "Notes About People," *St. Joseph Herald*, June 19, 1883.

25. "Personal," *St. Joseph Gazette*, September 11, 1883; "The James Boy Element," *Ottawa Daily Republic* (Ottawa KS), January 21, 1884.

26. "The James Boy Element," *Ottawa Daily Republic* (Ottawa KS), January 21, 1884.

27. Petrone, *Judgement at Gallatin*, 54; Miller, *The Trial of Frank James*, 6–7.

28. "John Newman Edwards to Frank James," January 24, 1883, APC.

29. "John Newman Edwards to Frank James"; Petrone, *Judgement at Gallatin*, 71–75.

30. Miller, *The Trial of Frank James*, 102–10; Petrone, *Judgement at Gallatin*, 112, 127–28, 168.

31. "Major Edwards Speaks," *Sedalia Weekly Bazoo*, September 11, 1883.

32. "John Newman Edwards to Frank James," October 17, 1883, APC.

33. "John Newman Edwards to Frank James."

34. "Who Are After Crittenden?," *St. Joseph Gazette*, October 19, 1883; untitled commentary, *St. Joseph Gazette*, October 26, 1883.

35. "Bound to be Wrong," November 3, 1883, reprinted in the *St. Louis Post-Dispatch*.

36. "Frank James to Wife," February 14, 1884, APC; Petrone, *Judgement at Gallatin*, 189–91.

37. "Frank James to Wife," February 14, 1884, APC; "Frank James to Wife & Son," February 24, 1884, APC; Petrone, *Judgement at Gallatin*, 191–92; Muehlberger, *The Lost Cause*, 190–91.

38. "John Newman Edwards to Frank James," March 27, 1884, APC; "John Newman Edwards to Frank James," April 3, 1884, APC.

39. "John Newman Edwards to Frank James," March 27, 1884, APC

40. "John Newman Edwards to Frank James," April 11, 1884, APC.

41. Petrone, 193; "John Newman Edwards to Frank James," February 24, 1885, APC.

42. "John Newman Edwards to Frank James," February 24, 1885, APC.

43. "Awake at Last," *Atchison Daily Champion*, September 17, 1881; Petrone, *Judgement at Gallatin*, 14–16, 196.

44. Stiles, *Last Rebel*, 380; Hulbert, "Constructing Guerrilla Memory," 74–77.

45. Untitled commentary, *Atchison Daily Champion*, February 21, 1885; Stiles, *Last Rebel*, 380; Yeatman, *Frank and Jesse James*, 289; Petrone, *Judgement at Gallatin*, 195–96.

46. "John Newman Edwards to Frank James," May 10, 1885, APC.

47. "John Newman Edwards to Frank James."

48. On Civil War veterans and alcohol, see Achenabum, "Patterns of alcohol use and abuse among aging Civil War veterans, 1865–1920," 69–85; Frueh and Smith, "Suicide, Alcoholism, and Psychiatric Illness Among Union Forces," 769–75; Lender and Martin, *Drinking in America*; Sommerville, *Aberration of Mind*; Jordan, *Marching Home*.

49. *JNE*, 41.

50. "Major Edwards All Right," *Topeka Daily Capital*, August 27, 1885; "Major John N. Edwards," *Leavenworth Times*, August 26, 1885.

51. *JNE*, 38–39; "Prohibition Tactics," *St. Joseph Gazette*, October 2, 1883.

52. "A Word to the Democrats," *St. Joseph Gazette*, October 13, 1883.

53. *JNE*, 39.

54. *JNE*, 88–89.

55. *JNE*, 39.

56. *JNE*, 77–78.

57. *JNE*, 85.

58. *JNE*, 85–86.

59. *JNE*, 40–41.

60. White, *Slaying the Dragon*, 73–75, 79.

61. *JNE*, 41.

62. *JNE*, 40, 41.

63. *JNE*, 40–41.

64. *JNE*, 42–43.

65. *JNE*, 44, 45–46, 48.

66. White, *Slaying the Dragon*, 74, 80–82.

67. *JNE*, 82–85, 97–98, 100–102, 104–5.

68. *JNE*, 88, 99–100, 167.

69. *JNE*, 49.

70. *JNE*, 49–50.

71. *JNE*, 49–50.

72. *JNE*, 51.

73. *JNE*, 93–94.

74. *JNE*, 94.

75. *JNE*, 95.

76. *JNE*, 52.

77. *JNE*, 58.

78. *JNE*, 58–59.

79. *JNE*, 26–27; "Major Edwards Dead," *Independence Daily Reporter* (Kansas), May 7, 1889.

80. *JNE*, 26.

Epilogue

1. *JNE*, 27.

2. "The Confederacy in the Saddle," *Brown County World* (Hiawatha KS), December 6, 1886.

3. "Quantrell the Queer, or, The Busted Bonanza," 1875, State Historical Society of Missouri, Kansas City, 1, 2–7, 27.

4. *JNE*, 180; "Major John N. Edwards," *State Journal* (Jefferson City MO), April 30, 1875.

5. *JNE*, 27–29; "Suddenly Stricken," *Topeka Daily Capital*, May 5, 1889.

6. *JNE*, 62.

7. *JNE*, 30–31.

8. *JNE*, 32–33; "Shorts," *Lexington Intelligencer*, May 11, 1889.

9. *JNE*, 31, 32, 33; *National Cyclopedia*, vol. 1, 187–88.

10. *JNE*, 33–36; "The Funeral of Major Edwards," *Lexington Intelligencer*, May 11, 1889.

11. *JNE*, 187–88, 188–89, 204–5, 206–7.

12. *JNE*, 63.

13. Allen, *Recollections*, 364–65; Shalhope, *Sterling Price*, 289–90; Castel, *General Sterling Price*, 278–79; "The Governor Dead," December 29, 1887, *KCT*; "A Leap to Death," *Bloomfield Vindicator* (Bloomfield MO), April 9, 1887; "Mad With Pain," March 31, 1887, *KCT*; "Victor Hugo Dead," *Democrat and Chronicle* (Rochester NY), May 23, 1885.

14. Hochschild, *King Leopold's Ghost*, 40–41; "Charlotte, Tragic Former Empress of Mexico, Is Dead," *Brooklyn Daily Eagle*, January 19, 1927.

15. "T. T. Crittenden Dead," *Kansas City Star*, May 29, 1909; "T. T. Crittenden is Dead," *St. Louis Globe-Democrat*; *Dictionary of Missouri Biography*, May 30, 1909, 217–18.

16. 1900 United States Federal Census; "S Edmonia Edwards," Virginia, U.S., Select Marriages, 1785–1940; "Loudoun Notes," *Alexandria Gazette*, December 21, 1894.

17. James Shelby Edwards, Certificate of Death, Missouri State Board of Health, September 10, 1915; "Edwards," *St. Louis Post-Dispatch*, September 12, 1915.

18. "Dies in Mexico City," *Moberly Weekly Monitor* (Moberly MO), April 16, 1912; untitled death notice, *Lexington Intelligencer*, April 19, 1912; "John N. Edwards is Dead," *Evening Missourian* (Columbia MO), April 16, 1912; "Hardship in Mexico Kills News Writer," *St. Louis Star and Times*, April 15, 1912.

19. 1900 United States Federal Census; 1920 United States Federal Census; 1930 United States Federal Census; 1940 United States Federal Census; Wedding announcement, January 8, 1903, *St. Louis Globe-Democrat*; "Wedding Delayed," January 9, 1903, Sedalia *Democrat*; "Mrs. Laura E. Donovan," March 20, 1955, *Kansas City Star*; Application for Guardianship of James Edwards, Jr., Oklahoma Wills and Probate Records, 1801–2008.

20. Fannie Edwards, Certificate of Death, Commonwealth of Virginia, March 24, 1918; "A Beloved Leesburg Resident Goes to Her Final Rest," *Loudoun Times-Mirror*, March 27, 1918.

21. 1900 United States Federal Census; Bartels and McGhee, *The Gallant Breed*, 28.

22. "Death of Mrs. Jennie Edwards," *Lexington Intelligencer*, July 19, 1918; "Mrs. Edwards Dead," *St. Joseph Observer*, July 27, 1918; Application for Guardianship of James Edwards, Jr., Oklahoma Wills and Probate Records, 1801–2008; "A State Reunion," Sedalia *Weekly Democrat*, October 5, 1905; "New State Librarian," Sedalia *Weekly Democrat*, November 20, 1896; "The Late John N. Edwards," *Weekly Democrat* (Natchez, MS), October 16, 1889; Conard, *Encyclopedia*, 356.
23. Grover, "Major Emory Foster," 428, 431; Younger, *The Story of Cole Younger*, 29–31; Matthews and Lindberg, "'Shot All to Pieces,'" 66–67.
24. "Frank James' Body to Be Cremated Here," *St. Louis Post-Dispatch*, February 19, 1915; Hulbert, *The Ghosts of Guerrilla Memory*, 206–9, 250; "Cole Younger and Frank James Here with Their Show Today," *Lexington Morning Herald*, August 15, 1903; "Own a Wild West Show," *Kansas City Star*, February 18, 1903.
25. *National Cyclopedia*, vol. 6 (New York: James T. White, 1896), 272–73.
26. O'Flaherty, *Undefeated Rebel*, 394–95; Hollister and Norman, 382–83; "Jo Shelby," William Elsey Connelley Papers, 1878–1931, Kansas State Historical Society, 1–3; "Good For Shelby," *Henry County Republican* (Clinton MO), April 19, 1894; "Bettie Shelby Interview," Shelby Scrapbooks, 1865–1932 (c3558), SHSMC.

Works Cited

Archive and Manuscript Materials

Abraham Lincoln Presidential Library, Springfield, Illinois
    Phillip H. Sheridan Letter
Authors Private Collection, Moseley, Virginia
    Letters of Frank James
Frederick County Circuit Court, Frederick County, Virginia
    Frederick County Virginia Marriage Register #1
    Frederick County Virginia Index to Wills #1, 1743–1917
Hargrett Library, University of Georgia
    William Starr Basinger Collection
Kansas State Historical Society, Topeka, Kansas
    William Elsey Connelley Papers, 1878–1931
Kentucky Historical Society, Frankfort, Kentucky
    The Gratz Papers, vol. 1
Laura Virginia Hale Archive, Front Royal, Virginia
    Rebecca Good Genealogy Collection
Minnesota Population Center, University of Minnesota
    National Historical Geographic Information System
Missouri State Archives, Jefferson City, Missouri
    Governors Records (Charles Henry Hardin, 1875–77)
National Archives and Records Administration
    Compiled Service Records of Confederate Soldiers Who Served in Orga-
        nizations from the State of Missouri, National Archives and Records
        Administration, Washington DC
Ohio History Connection, Columbus, Ohio
    Correspondence, 1864–65
    Helen Bullitt Papers
    Johnson's Island Collection
    Johnson's Island, Ohio Letters, 1863–65

Pearce Collections Museum, Navarro College
  Pearce Civil War Collection
Southern Historical Collection, University of North Carolina
  Leeland Hathaway Recollections
  Meriwether Jeff Thompson Papers, 1860–1940
  Preston S. Brooks Papers
South Caroliniana Library, University of South Carolina
  Preston Smith Brooks Papers
Special Collections, College of William and Mary
  Fitzhugh Lee Papers, 1866–87
Special Collections, Library of Congress, Washington DC
  Jay I. Kislak Collection
Special Collections, Rice University
  Charlotte and Maximilian Collection
Special Collections, University of Arizona
  Maximilian, Emperor of Mexico Collection
Special Collections, University of Houston
  Mexico Documents Collection
State Historical Society of Missouri, Columbia
  John Newman Edwards Letters
  Joseph Orville Shelby, Scrapbook, 1865–1932
  Watson-Westlake Family Papers, 1813–1949
  William A. Settle Jr. Papers, c. 1920–87
State Historical Society of Missouri, Kansas City
  "Quantrell the Queer, or, The Busted Bonanza," 1875
Stewary J. Bell Archives, Handley Library, Winchester, Virginia
  Frederick County Virginia Will Book No. 15
  Frederick County Virginia Will Book No. 19
Warren County Circuit Court, Front Royal, Virginia
  Warren County Virginia General Index to Wills, 1835–45
  Warren County Register of Deaths, 1853–74
The Watts-Hays Letters, http://www.wattshaysletters.com/letters/
  Watts-Hays Letters (1861–65: The Civil War)

Published Works

"1868 General Election Statistics." *U.S. Election Atlas.* https://uselectionatlas
  .org.
"1872 General Election Statistics—Missouri." *U.S. Election Atlas.* https://us
  electionatlas.org.

"1872 Statistics." *The American Presidency Project.* UC-Santa Barbara. https://www
.presidency.ucsb.edu/statistics/elections/1872.

"1876 General Results." *U.S. Election Atlas.* https://uselectionatlas.org/results.

"A Terrible Quintette." Reprinted by Hurstwood Enterprises Limited, 2002.
Originally printed in the *St. Louis Dispatch,* November 22, 1873.

Achenabum, W. A. "Patterns of Alcohol Use and Abuse Among Aging Civil
War Veterans, 1865–1920," *Bulletin of the New York Academy of Medicine* 69,
no. 1 (January—February 1993).

Allen, Henry Watkins. *Recollections of Henry Watkins Allen.* Edited by Sarah A.
Dorsey. New York: M. Doolady, 1866.

"Antebellum Resources of Northern Lafayette County." Show-Me Regional
Planning Commission, Warrensburg, Missouri, November 1991.

"Architectural/Historic Inventory Survey Form for Dover Township." Missouri
Office of Historic Preservation, I-no. 100, August 1988.

Arenson, Adam, and Andrew Graybill, eds. *Civil War Wests: Testing the Limits of
the United States.* Berkeley: University of California Press, 2015.

Arthur, Anthony. *General Jo Shelby's March.* New York: Random House, 2010.

Bansik, Michael E., ed., *Missouri in 1861: The Civil War Letters of Frank B. Wilkie,
Newspaper Correspondent.* Iowa City IA: Camp Pope Book Shop, 2001.

Bartels, Carolyn M., and James E. McGhee, eds., *The Gallant Breed the 5th Missouri Cavalry: A Roster of the Men Who Rode under the Flag of Shelby's Iron Brigade.*
Independence MO: Two Trails Publishing, 2009.

"Battle field of Lexington, Mo., showing plan of earthwork defended by Federal and State troops under command of Col. James A. Mulligan, U.S.A.
during the 18th, 19th and 20th Sept. 1861. Surrendered to Genl. Sterling
Price, C.S.A., Sept. 20th 1861." Library of Congress Geography and Map
Division. Washington DC. https://lccn.loc.gov/99447444.

"Battle of Carthage, July 5." Civil War Trust. https://www.battlefields.org/learn
/maps/battle-carthage-july-5-1861.

The Battle of Lexington. Lexington MO: Lexington Historical Society, 1903.

"Battle of Pea Ridge." Civil War Trust. https://www.battlefields.org/learn/civil
-war/battles/pea-ridge.

Beasley, Conger Jr, ed., *Shelby's Expedition to Mexico: An Unwritten Leaf of the
War.* By John Newman Edwards. Fayetteville: University of Arkansas Press,
2002.

Beilein, Joseph M. *Bushwhackers: Guerrilla Warfare, Manhood, and the Household
in Civil War Missouri.* Akron OH: Kent State University Press, 2016.

Berry, Stephen, and James Hill Welborn III. "The Cane of His Existence:
Depression, Damage, and the Brooks-Sumner Affair." *Southern Cultures*
(Winter 2014).

Bingham, John A. "The Assault Upon Senator Sumner, A Crime Against the People." Washington DC: Buell & Blanchard, Printers, 1856.

Blight, David. *Race and Reunion: The Civil War in American Memory*. Cambridge: Harvard University Press, 2001.

Britten, Christopher. "'Cooped Up and Powerless When My Home is Invaded': Southern Prisoners at Johnson's Island in their Own Words," *Ohio Valley History* (Spring 2010).

Brownlee, Richard S. *Gray Ghosts of the Confederacy: Guerrilla Warfare in the West, 1861–1865*. Baton Rouge: Louisiana State University Press, 1958.

Butler, Andrew P. "On the Difficulty of Messrs. Brooks and Sumner, And the Causes Thereof." Washington DC: Congressional Globe Office, 1856.

Byars, William Vincent. *Memoirs of a Scottish Whig Family*. St. Louis MO: W. V. Byars, 1919.

Campbell, L. D. "Alleged Assault Upon Senator Sumner." *Journal of the House of Representatives*, Thirty-Fourth Congress, First Session. Washington DC: Cornelius Wendell, Printer.

Castel, Albert. *General Sterling Price and the Civil War in the West*. Baton Rouge: Louisiana State University Press, 1968.

———. *William Clarke Quantrill: His Life and Times*. New York: F. Fell, 1962.

Chesnut, Mary B. *A Diary from Dixie*. New York: D. Appleton & Company, 1905.

Christensen, Lawrence O., William E. Foley, Gary R. Kremer, and Kenneth H. Winn, eds. *Dictionary of Missouri Biography*. Vol. 1. Columbia MO: University of Missouri Press, 1999.

Coffin, Levi. *Reminiscences of Levi Coffin: The Reputed President of the Underground Railroad*. Cincinnati: Western Tract Society, 1876.

Conard, Howard Louis. *Encyclopedia of the History of Missouri*. Vol. 2. New York: Southern History Company, 1901.

Congressional Directory for the Third Session of the Fortieth Congress. Washington DC: Government Printing Office, 1869.

Connelley, William Elsey. *Quantrill and the Border Wars*. New York: Smithmark, 1909.

Cordley, Richard. *A History of Lawrence, Kansas*. Lawrence KS: Lawrence Journal Press, 1895.

Dawsey, Cyrus B., and James M. Dawsey. *The Confederados: Old South Immigrants in Brazil*. Tuscaloosa: University of Alabama Press, 1995.

Downs, Gregory. *After Appomattox: Military Occupation and the Ends of War*. Cambridge: Harvard University Press, 2015.

Eakin, Joanne Chiles. *Missouri Prisoners of War*. Independence MO: J. C. Eakins, 1995.

"Earl Van Dorn (1820–1863)." *The Encyclopedia of Arkansas History & Culture.* http://www.encyclopediaofarkansas.net/encyclopedia/entry-detail.aspx ?entryid=2367.

Edwards, Mary Virginia., ed. *John N. Edwards: Biography, Memoirs, Reminiscences and Recollections.* Kansas City MO: J. Edwards, 1889.

Edwards, John Newman. *Noted Guerrillas, or, The Warfare of the Border.* St. Louis MO: Bryan, Brand & Company, 1877.

———. *Shelby and His Men: Or, The War in the West.* Cincinnati OH: Miami Printing and Publishing Company, 1867.

———. *Shelby's Expedition to Mexico: An Unwritten Leaf of the War.* 1872. Reprint, Austin TX: Steck Company, 1964.

Evans, Clement, A. "John Newman Edwards." *Confederate Military History,* vol. 9. Atlanta: Confederate Publishing Company, 1899.

Fellman, Michael. *Inside War: The Guerrilla Conflict in Missouri During the American Civil War.* Oxford: Oxford University Press, 1989.

Foner, Eric J. *Reconstruction: America's Unfinished Revolution, 1863–1877.* New York: Harper, 2002.

Foster, Gaines M. *Ghosts of the Confederacy: Defeat, the Lost Cause, and the Emergence of the New South, 1865–1913.* New York: Oxford University Press, 1987.

Frohman, Charles. *Rebels on Lake Erie.* Columbus OH: Ohio Historical Society, 1965.

Frueh, Christopher, and Jeffrey A. Smith. "Suicide, Alcoholism, and Psychiatric Illness Among Union Forces during the U.S. Civil War." *Journal of Anxiety Disorders* 26 (2012) 769–75.

"Gen. Frederick Salomon (1826–1897)." Wisconsin Historical Society. https://www.wisconsinhistory.org/Records/Article/cs3280.

Gerteis, Louis. *The Civil War in Missouri: A Military History.* Columbia: University of Missouri Press, 2012.

Giddings, Joshua R. "Privilege of the Representative—Privilege of the People." Washington DC: Buell & Blanchard, Printers, 1856.

Grover, George S. "Major Emory Foster." *Missouri Historical Review* 14 (October 1919–July 1920): 425–32.

Hackett, Joan D., and Rebecca H. Good, eds., *Frederick County Virginia Marriage Bonds.* Bowie MD: Heritage Books, 1992.

Hahn, Stephen. *A Nation Without Borders: The United States and Its World in an Age of Civil Wars, 1830–1910.* New York: Viking Press, 2016.

Hale, Donald R., and Joanne C. Eakin, eds. *Branded as Rebels: A List of Bushwhackers, Guerrillas, Partisan Rangers, Confederates and Southern Sympathizers from Missouri during the War Years.* Lee's Summit MO: J. C. Eakin & D. R. Hale, 1993.

Hanna, Alfred J. "A Confederate Newspaper in Mexico." *Journal of Southern History* 12, no. 1 (February 1946): 67–83.

Harter, Eugene C. *The Lost Colony of the Confederacy.* Jackson: University Press of Mississippi, 1985.

Hess, Earl J., Richard W. Hatcher III, William G. Piston, and William L. Shea. *Wilson's Creek, Pea Ridge & Prairie Grove.* Lincoln: University of Nebraska Press, 2006.

Hinze, David C., and Karen Farnham. *The Battle of Carthage: Border War in Southwest Missouri, July 5, 1861.* Gretna LA: Pelican Publishing Company, 2004.

History of Lafayette County, Mo. St. Louis: Missouri Historical Company, 1881.

Hochschild, Adam. *King Leopold's Ghost.* Boston: Mariner Books, 1998.

Hollister, Wilfed R., and Harry Norman. *Five Famous Missourians.* Kansas City MO: Hudson-Kimberly, 1900.

Hulbert, Matthew C. "Constructing Guerrilla Memory: John Newman Edwards and Missouri's Irregular Lost Cause." *Journal of the Civil War Era* 2, no. 1 (March 2012): 58–81.

———. *The Ghosts of Guerrilla Memory: How Civil War Guerrillas Became Gunslingers in the American West.* Athens GA: University of Georgia Press, 2016.

———. "How to Remember 'This Damnable Guerrilla Warfare': Four Vignettes from Civil War Missouri." *Civil War History* 59, no. 2 (June 2013): 142–67.

———. "Larkin Skaggs and the Massacre(s) at Lawrence." In *The Guerrilla Hunters: Exploring the Civil War's Irregular Conflicts,* edited by Barton A. Myers and Brian D. McKnight, 260–81. Baton Rouge LA: Louisiana State University Press, 2017.

———. "The Trials of Frank James: Guerrilla Veteranhood and the Double-Edge of Wartime Notoriety." In *The War Went On: Reconsidering the Lives of Civil War Veterans,* edited by Brian Matthew Jordan and Evan C. Rothera, 81–100. Baton Rouge LA: Louisiana State University Press, 2020.

Hulston, James K., and James W. Goodrich. "John Trousdale Coffee: Lawyer, Politician, Confederate." *Missouri Historical Review* 77, no. 3 (April 1983): 272–95.

"John Sappington Marmaduke" (1833–87). *Encyclopedia of Arkansas.* https://encyclopediaofarkansas.net/entries/john-sappington-marmaduke-6489/.

Jordan, Brian Matthew. *Marching Home: Union Veterans and Their Unending Civil War.* New York: Liveright, 2016.

Josephy, Alvin M. Jr. *The Civil War in the American West.* New York: Alfred A. Knopf, 1991.

Karp, Matthew. *This Vast Southern Empire: Slaveholders at the Helm of American Foreign Policy.* Cambridge MA: Harvard University Press, 2016.

Knapp, George E. *The Wilson's Creek Staff Ride and Battlefield Tour.* Fort Leavenworth KS: Combat Studies Institute, 1993.

Lavery, Ray. "The Man Who Made a Folk-God Out of Jo Shelby and Created a Legend for Jesse James." *Trail Guide* 6, no. 4 (December 1961): 1–15.

Laws of the State of Missouri: Revised and Digested by Authority of the General Assembly. Volume 1. St. Louis: E. Charless, 1825.

Lender, Mark E., and James Kirby Martin. *Drinking in America: A History.* New York: Free Press, 1987.

Matthews, Matt, and Kip Lindberg. "'Shot All to Pieces': The Battle of Lone Jack, Missouri, August 16, 1862." *North & South* 7, no. 1 (January 2004): 56–72.

McGhee, James E. *Guide to Missouri Confederate Units, 1861–1865.* Fayetteville: University of Arkansas Press, 2008.

"Military Prisons." *The Civil War in Missouri.* http://www.civilwarmo.org /educators/resources/info-sheets/military-prisons.

Miller, George. *The Trial of Frank James for Murder with Confessions of Dick Liddil and Clarence Hite and History of the "James Gang."* Columbia MO: E. W. Stephens, 1898.

Monaghan, Jay. *Civil War on the Western Border: 1854–1865.* Boston: Little, Brown, 1955.

Muehlberger, James P. *The Lost Cause: The Trials of Frank and Jesse James.* Yardley PA: Westholme, 2013.

The National Cyclopedia of American Biography. Vol. 1. New York: James T. White, 1898.

The National Cyclopedia of American Biography. Vol. 6. New York: James T. White, 1896.

Nelson, Megan Kate. *The Three-Cornered War: The Union, the Confederacy, and Native Peoples in the Fight for the West.* New York: Scribner, 2021.

O'Flaherty, Daniel. *General Jo Shelby: Undefeated Rebel.* Chapel Hill: University of North Carolina Press, 2000.

"Oliver Anderson Biography." Missouri State Parks, Battle of Lexington. https://mostateparks.com/page/55021/oliver-anderson-biography.

Pani, Erika. "Law, Allegiance, and Sovereignty in Civil War Mexico, 1857–1867," *Journal of the Civil War Era* 7, no. 4 (December 2017): 570–96.

Patrick, Jeffrey L. *Campaign for Wilson's Creek: The Fight for Missouri Begins.* Buffalo Gap TX: McWhiney Foundation, 2011.

Perkins, Russell. "Marmaduke, John S." *Civil War on the Western Border: The Missouri-Kansas Conflict, 1854–1865.* Kansas City MO: The Kansas City Public Library, n.d. https://civilwaronthewesternborder.org/encyclopedia /marmaduke-john-s.

Petrone, Gerard S. *Judgment at Gallatin: The Trial of Frank James.* Lubbock: Texas Tech University Press, 1998.

Phillips, Christopher. "'The Chrysalis State': Slavery, Confederate Identity, and the Creation of the Border South." In *Inside the Confederate Nation: Essays in*

Honor of Emory M. Thomas, edited by Lesley J. Gordon and John C. Inscoe, 147–64. Baton Rouge: Louisiana State University Press, 2005.

———. *Missouri's Confederate: Claiborne Fox Jackson and the Creation of Southern Identity in the Border West*. Columbia: University of Missouri Press, 2000.

———. *The Rivers Ran Backward: The Civil War and the Remaking of the American Middle Border*. Oxford: Oxford University Press, 2016.

Public Acts of the Thirty-First Congress of the United States. September 18, 1850. Vol. 9, Pub.—59.

Reinhardt, Mark. *Who Speaks for Margaret Garner?: The True Story That Inspired Toni Morrison's Beloved*. Minneapolis: University of Minnesota Press, 2010.

Rister, Carl C. "Carlota, A Confederate Colony in Mexico." *Journal of Southern History* 11, no 1 (February 1945): 33–50.

"Robberies." Civil War St. Louis (website). Accessed August 1, 2022. http://www.civilwarstlouis.com/History/jamesgangrobberies.

Rolle, Andrew F. *The Lost Cause: The Confederate Exodus to Mexico*. Norman: University of Oklahoma Press, 1965.

Rorvig, Paul. "The Significant Skirmish: The Battle of Boonville, June 17, 1861." *Missouri Historical Review* 86, no. 2 (January 1992): 127–48.

Saults, Dan. "Missouri's Forgotten Don Quixote." *Focus/Midwest* 1, no. 5 (October 1962): 20–23.

Scharff, Virginia, ed. *Empire and Liberty: Civil War and the West*. Oakland: University of California Press, 2015.

Sellmeyer, Deryl P. *Jo Shelby's Iron Brigade*. New Orleans: Pelican, 2007.

Shalhope, Robert E. *Sterling Price: Portrait of a Southerner*. Columbia: University of Missouri Press, 1971.

Sheridan, Phillip H. *Personal Memoirs of P. H. Sheridan*. Vol 2. New York: Charles L. Webster, 1888.

Sinha, Manisha. "The Caning of Charles Sumner: Race, Slavery, and Ideology in the Age of the Civil War." *Journal of the Early Republic* 23, no. 2 (Winter 2003): 233–62.

Sommerville, Diane. *Aberration of Mind: Suicide and Suffering in the Civil War-Era South*. Chapel Hill: University of North Carolina Press, 2018.

Stevens, W. B. *Centennial History of Missouri*. St. Louis: S. J. Clarke, 1921.

Stiles, T. J. *Jesse James: Last Rebel of the Civil War*. New York: Knopf, 2002.

Sumner, Charles. "The Crime Against Kansas." Boston: John P. Jewett, 1856.

The Sumner Outrage: A Full Report of the Speeches at the Meeting of Citizens in Cambridge, June 2, 1856. Cambridge MA: John Ford, Printer, 1856.

Sutherland, Donald. "The Long, Hard Winter of 1855–1856." No publisher information available.

Switzler, William F. *Switzler's Illustrated History of Missouri*. St. Louis: C. R. Barnes, 1879.

"Thomas Shelby House." National Register of Historic Places Registration Form. Washington DC: United States Department of the Interior, National Park Service, October 1990.

Thoreau, Henry David. "A Plea for Captain John Brown." October 30, 1859.

Triplett, Frank. *The Life and Times of Jesse James.* Old Saybrook CT: Konecky & Konecky, 2016.

The United States Biographical Dictionary & Portrait Gallery, Missouri Edition. New York: United States Biographical Publishing Company, 1878.

Varon, Elizabeth. *Armies of Deliverance: A New History of the Civil War.* New York: Oxford, 2019.

Wagner, Margaret E., Gary W. Gallagher, Paul Finkelman, eds. *The Library of Congress Civil War Desk Reference.* New York: Simon & Schuster, 2002.

Wahlstrom, Todd. *The Southern Exodus to Mexico: Migration across the Borderlands after the American Civil War.* Lincoln: University of Nebraska Press, 2015.

Waite, Kevin. *West of Slavery: The Southern Dream of a Transcontinental Empire.* Chapel Hill: University of North Carolina Press, 2021.

Walther, Eric H. *The Shattering of the Union: America in the 1850s.* Lanham MD: SR Books, 2004.

The War of the Rebellion: A Compilation of the Official Records of the Union and Confederate Armies. Washington DC: Government Printing Office, 1880–1901.

Webb, W. L. *Battles and Biographies of Missourians.* Kansas City MO: Hudson-Kimberly, 1900.

Wells, C. A. Harwell. "The End of the Affair?: Anti-Dueling Laws and Social Norms in Antebellum America," *Vanderbilt Law Review* 54, no. 4 (May 2001): 1805–47.

White, William L. *Slaying the Dragon: The History of Addiction Treatment and Recovery in America.* Bloomington IL: Chestnut Health Systems, 2014.

Woodworth, Steven E. *Jefferson Davis and His Generals: The Failure of the Confederate Command in the West.* Lawrence: University Press of Kansas, 1990.

Yeatman, Theodore P. *Frank and Jesse James: The Story behind the Legend.* Naperville IL: Cumberland House, 2000.

Young, William. *Young's History of Lafayette County Missouri.* Vol. 1. Indianapolis: B. F. Bowen & Company, 1910.

Younger, Cole. *The Story of Cole Younger, by Himself.* Chicago: Henneberry, 1903.

Zombek, Angela. *Penitentiaries, Prisons, and Military Punishment.* Akron: Kent State University Press, 2018.

Index

Charlotte I, xxi, xxviii, xxxi, 117, 122, 129; ancestry, 105; colony name, 113; Confederados, 133, 134; death, 262; John's description of, 121; leaving Mexico, 126, 132; "Poor Carlota" (Edwards), 148–51

Chesnut, Mary Boykin, 1–2

"The Chivalry of Crime" (1872), 161–63, 178, 186. *See also* Edwards, John Newman; James, Jesse Woodson

Clement, Archie, 183

Coffee, John Trousdale, 40, 48, 77

Coffin, Levi, xii

Cooper, Douglas, 44–46

Crittenden, Thomas T., xxviii, 224, 262; assassination of Jesse James, 220–21, 222; governor of Missouri, 234–35; surrender of Frank James, 225–29, 296n15; trial of Frank James, 233–35, 236, 238–39

Curtis, Samuel, 31; Battle of Pea Ridge, 31–34, 47; Battle of Westport, 89–91; departmental commander, 50, 59, 61, 62, 63

Davis, Jefferson, xxviii, xxxiv, 73, 98, 159; cause of Winnebago duel, 192, 194, 198, 199, 202; management of Trans-MS, 47–48, 56, 76; Missouri secession, 9

Davis, Jefferson C., 33

Dean, Henry Clay, 244. *See also* James, Alexander Franklin "Frank"

Dix-Hill Cartel, 73

Douglas, Stephen, xiv

Eagle Pass TX, 101–5

Early, Jubal, xxviii, 210

Edwards, James Shelby, 195, 253, 262

Edwards, John, xxii, xxiii–xxiv, xxv, 120, 151, 196

Edwards, John Newman, xix, 195, 254; adjutant of Iron Brigade, 85; adjutant of regiment, 39, 54–55; alcoholism, 241–52; anti-Indian views, 35–36, 44–45; architect of irregular Lost Cause, 188–91, 204–5, 209–18; author, 138, 154, 209, 289n2; battle experiences, 16, 21–24, 28–30, 32–35, 67–68; childhood, xxv–xxvi; "The Chivalry of Crime" (Edwards), 161–63, 178, 186; criticism of Confederate leaders, 47–48, 82–84, 93–96, 98–99, 284n38; death, 253–55; duel with Foster, 192–202, 293n41; early newspaper days, 3–5, 7, 10; editorial positions, 138, 140–41, 172–74, 202–3, 230–31, 243; education, xxiv–xxv, 274n9; enlistment, 11, 275–76n11; family, 7, 58, 160, 195, 203, 246, 253, 259; friendship with Munford, 152–53, 194–95, 243, 248–50, 251–53, 261; friendship with Shelby, xxvii, 151, 153; funeral, 259–60; genealogy, xxi–xxii; historical coverage of, xxviii–xxix; marriage, 151, 203–4; Mexican exile, 106–7, 118–31, 134–35; military promotion, 39, 74; naming Iron Brigade, 42; parodied, 256–57; "Poor Carlota" (Edwards), 148–50; POW, 67–74; reaction to his death, 257–59; relationship with Frank James, 182–84, 205–8, 225–29, 230–38, 239–40, 295n10, 296n15; relationship with Jennie, 37–38, 150–51; relationship with Jesse James, 145–48, 149–50, 164–65, 182–84, 205–8, 220–22; "A Terrible Quintette" (Edwards), 180–89, 293n28; worldview, xxx–xxxiii, xxxv, 57–58. See also *Noted Guerrillas* (Edwards); *Shelby and His Men* (Edwards); *Shelby's Expedition to Mexico* (Edwards)

Price, Sterling (*cont.*)
command at Wilson's Creek, 17–21; death, 262; feud with Thomas Reynolds, 76, 93–94; John's criticism of, 29–30, 82, 94–96, 214, 284n38; Mexican exile, 104, 114–15; Missouri Raid, 86–92; secession crisis in Missouri, 8–12, 30–31. *See also* Edwards, John Newman

"Quantrell" (1872), 189–90
"Quantrell the Queer" (1875), 257–58
Quantrill, William C., 52, 143, 183–84, 266, 267; as irregular Lost Cause icon, 189–91, 213–18; Lawrence Massacre, 75, 118; parodied, 257–58. See also *Noted Guerrillas* (Edwards); "Quantrell" (1872); "Quantrell the Queer" (1875)

Rains, James, 46, 48; command at Carthage, 12–15; command at Pea Ridge, 34; command at Wilson's Creek, 20
Randall, Samuel J., 261
Reynolds, Thomas C., 9, 262; championing Shelby, 76, 84–85; feud with Sterling Price, 93–94; Mexican exile, 104, 111, 112
Robinson, Charles, xiv, xvi,

Salomon, Frederick, 42–43, 45–46
Schofield, James M., 40, 46, 48, 79
Scott, Winfield, 27, 85
Seward, William, 112, 155–56
Seymour, Horatio G., 141–42
Shanks, David, 67, 80–82, 88, 94
Shelby, Elizabeth N. "Betty," 4–5, 132
Shelby, Joseph O., 5, 75, 154, 185, 191, 265–66; command at Cape Girardeau, 66–68; expedition commander, 75–85, 86; Frank

James trial, 233, 238; friendship with John, xxvii, 151, 153, 196, 252, 260–61; Iron Brigade, 42–43, 45–47, 48–51, 52, 54–58, 65; John's deification of, xxxi, 16, 35, 95–96, 217; Lafayette County Mounted Rifles, 10–11, 13–14, 17, 20, 28–30, 34; Marmaduke's Expedition, 59, 61–63; marriage, 3–4, 151, 275n6; Mexican exile, 111–12, 114, 123, 129, 131–32, 287n11; military promotions, 41–42, 84–85; plot to continue war in the West, 97–99; postwar Texas, 101–4, 105–11; Price's Expedition, 87–94; recruiting Fifth Cavalry, 36–40, 280n21. *See also* Battle of Cape Girardeau; Edwards, John Newman; Iron Brigade; Kirby Smith, Edmund; Lafayette County Mounted Rifles; Maximilian I; Shelby, Elizabeth N. "Betty"; *Shelby and His Men* (Edwards); Shelby's Expedition; *Shelby's Expedition to Mexico* (Edwards)
Shelby and His Men (Edwards), 66, 138–40, 153–54, 202; Cane Hill, 48–51; Cape Girardeau, 66–67, 68; Carthage, 16; criticism of Kirby Smith, 98–99; Prairie Grove, 56–58; Price's Expedition, 94–96; Shelby's Expedition, 78, 80, 83, 84; Springfield, 62–63; Wilson's Creek, 21–24. *See also* Edwards, John Newman; Iron Brigade; Price, Sterling; Shelby, Joseph O.; Shelby's Expedition
Shelby's Expedition, 81; Bower's Mill, 78; Cole Camp, 79; Marshall, 80–82; Neosho, 77–78; organization, 76–77; reception of, 82–85; Sarcoxie, 78; Stockton, 79; Warsaw, 79. *See also* Iron Brigade; Shelby, Joseph O.; *Shelby and His Men* (Edwards)